Lecture Notes in Economics and Mathematical Systems

Managing Editors: M. Beckmann and W. Krelle

337

A. Lewandowski I. Stanchev (Eds.)

Methodology and Software for Interactive Decision Support

Proceedings of the International Workshop
Held in Albena, Bulgaria, October 19–23, 1987

Springer-Verlag
Berlin Heidelberg New York London Paris Tokyo Hong Kong

Editors

Dr. Andrzej Lewandowski
Project Leader
Methodology of Decision Analysis Project
System and Decision Sciences Program
International Institute for Applied Systems Analysis (IIASA)
Schloßplatz 1, A-2361 Laxenburg, Austria

Prof. Dr. Ivan Stanchev
Institute for Systems Analysis & Management
Economic University "Karl Marx"
Georgy Dimitrov 53
Sofia, Bulgaria

ISBN 3-540-51572-0 Springer-Verlag Berlin Heidelberg New York
ISBN 0-387-51572-0 Springer-Verlag New York Berlin Heidelberg

Printed in Germany

Printing and binding: Druckhaus Beltz, Hemsbach/Bergstr.
2142/3140-543210

Preface

These Proceedings report the scientific results of an International Workshop on *Methodology and Software for Interactive Decision Support* organized jointly by the System and Decision Sciences Program of the International Institute for Applied Systems Analysis (IIASA, located in Laxenburg, Austria) and The National Committee for Applied Systems Analysis and Management in Bulgaria. Several other Bulgarian institutions sponsored the Workshop — The Committee for Science to the Council of Ministers, The State Committee for Research and Technology and The Bulgarian Industrial Association. The workshop was held in Albena, on the Black Sea coast.

More than 80 scientists from 15 countries attended the workshop; 50 lectures were presented and 17 computer demonstration sessions took place. This Workshop is one of a series of meetings organized by IIASA with the collaboration of scientific institutions from the National Member Organization countries. The previous meetings took place in Austria (1983), Hungary (1984) and the German Democratic Republic (1985). All proceedings of these meetings have been published by Springer Verlag in the series Lecture Notes in Economics and Mathematical Systems.

The research on decision support systems has long tradition at IIASA. The Institute, being the forum for common research of scientists from East and West, with different cultural backgrounds and different experiences with real life applications of their results, operates the international network of scientific institutions involved in research related to the methodology of decision analysis and decision support systems. The approach to this research assumes high level of synergy between three main components: methodological and theoretical backgrounds, computer implementation of decision support systems and real life applications. This synergy is reflected in the subject of papers presented during the workshop as well as in the structure of the Proceedings which is divided in three main sections.

In the first section, *Theory and Algorithms for Multiple Criteria Optimization*, new theoretical developments in multiple criteria optimization are presented. *Tanino* presents new approach for application of multiple objective optimization in hierarchical systems, *Wierzbicki* discusses the relation between simulation and gaming for conflict resolution as well as proposes the interactive framework for supporting this kind of decision problems. The other group of papers addresses purely theoretical questions — *Nakayama* presents recent developments in sensitivity and trade–offs analysis in multiobjective programming, *Ramesh* and others discuss the degeneracy problem. Finally, several papers are more algorithmic oriented — like paper by *Katoh* with presentation of new algorithms for bicriteria combinatorial optimization or the paper presenting the reachable set approach by *Lotov.* Finally, *Steuer* presents the current state–of–the art in the interactive multiple criteria optimization.

In the second section, *Theory, Methodology and Software for Decision Support Systems*, the principles of building decision support systems are presented as well as software tools constituting the building components of such systems. Moreover, several papers are devoted to the general methodology of building such systems or present experimental design of systems supporting certain class of decision problems. For example, paper by *Makowski* presents the HYBRID system for solving dynamic linear multiple criteria problems using the aspiration level paradigm. This system has been used as component of several practical implementations of DSS. Similar nature has the paper by *Ogryczak*, presenting a software system for solving multiple criteria problems for network analysis. In a more general paper, *Nitchev* discusses the relationships between DSS and knowledge based systems. Some other papers present the analysis of specific decision situations and discuss problems of development decision support systems supporting this specific classes of decision situations. Paper by *Bronisz* describing an experimental system for supporting multiple objective bargaining problems belongs to this category; the other is presented by *Serafini* and presents a decision support system for manufacturing management. Finally, some papers address more general problems, like software engineering principles in building the decision support systems — the issue discussed by *Stanchev*.

The third section addresses issues of *Applications of Decision Support Systems and Computer Implementations of Decision Support Systems.* The most substantial series of applications is presented in the paper by *Danev*, who describes the experience of using multiple criteria optimization and decision support system technology for supporting management problems in Bulgarian industry. Other papers address such problems like bank management (*Langen*), management of research and development problems (*Petrovsky*) or water systems management (*Rathke*).

Another part of this section has a special character. Beside theoretical and methodological papers, several practical implementations of software for decision support have been presented during the workshop. These software packages varied from very experimental and illustrative implementations of some theoretical concept to well developed and documented systems being currently commercially distributed and used for solving practical problems.

The editors of this proceedings would like to thank IIASA for financing the Workshop and continuous support and encouragement for research in the field of Decision Support Systems. This support and encouragement came especially for Academician Alexander Kurzhanski, Chairman of the System and Decision Sciences Program at IIASA. It would not be possible to organize the workshop without strong support from the Bulgarian Academy of Sciences and its Vice President, Academician Blagovest Sendow, as well as without support from several scientific and industrial institutions in Bulgaria. Finally, we would like to thank the authors for their participation in the Workshop and permission to publish their contributions in this volume.

A. Lewandowski, I. Stanchev

Table of Contents

Part 1

Theory and Algorithms for Multiple Criteria Optimization

Part 3b

Computer Implementation of Decision Support Systems

Part 1

Theory and Algorithms for Multiple Criteria Optimization

Approximational Approach to Multicriteria Problems

V. Borzenko
Institute for Control Sciences
Moscow, USSR

In this paper we consider some methodological aspects of multicriteria programming, i.e. theory and methods of solving multicriteria problems with the help of computer. Special attention is paid to the problem of adequacy of real DM preference systems modelling. After a short introduction I am going to formulate certain conception and methodological principles that form the approximational approach to DM preferences modelling, then some relevant theoretical results and approximational models will be presented. Afterwards, a number of applications and experiments will be described, which have enabled the estimation of the efficiency of these methods and the approach itself.

1 Introduction

It is typical of decision making practice that DM cannot choose by himself the best solution from a given presentation (i.e. set of alternatives, feasible solutions, etc.). Such difficulties may stem from the size of presentation, which may be a domain in some decision space, as well as from complexity of the DM preference system, involving several conflicting criteria, characterizing quality of decisions. Moreover, in many multicriteria problems a purely automatic choice is required. These are problems, in which no interaction is possible from the moment when the presentation is determined till the moment when the decision is to be made. Problems of data processing organization may be taken for example.

In all such cases some formal choice mechanism (including utility functions, binary relations, choice functions, etc.) is to be used as a model of real DM preference system for supporting the decision process. This choice mechanism is often parametric, the parameters value being determined with the help of DM. It is clear that such a mechanism is to reflect (model) the real preferences of DM in a given problem. So we can see that the problem of adequate modelling of preferences is a central one for multicriteria programming — the accuracy of modelling determines to a great extent the quality of the resulting decision. This is why the importance of many multicriteria problems necessitates the development of models allowing any required accuracy of real preferences modelling.

Demands of practice have led to appearance of several hundreds works on various methods, but still, to my mind,

1. they lack a general theoretical base in the area of preferences modelling,
2. the adequacy problem is hardly being paid proper attention to, and as a result,
3. means of choosing an adequate model and method for a given problem are really scarce.

Priority of setting the adequacy problem belongs to the choice theory, see for example (Arrow, 1959; Plott, 1976; Sen, 1977; Iserman et al., 1981). Thus, prof. Iserman and his colleagues (1981) have clearly demonstrated, that many popular mechanisms do not possess some properties which seem to be quite natural for human preferences. So far, however, theoretical research in this area has been mostly focused on various set–theoretical aspects of choice and on finite problems, paying little attention to rich geometrical structures of criteria space and to specific demands of applications. To bridge the gap between theory and practice of preferences modelling was the basic aim of my research. Some of the results, mentioned in this paper, can be found in (Berezovsky et al., 1981).

2 Some drawbacks of preferences modelling

Now consider some obvious examples illustrating the previous remarks. First of all, assumptions about the nature of a DM preference system are often dubious or not formulated at all. For example, the traditional assumption that DM preferences correspond to some utility function is hardly realistic, for it does not allow for the existence of incomparable points in criteria space. In other words, this assumption implies, that the incomparability relation is transitive, which hardly holds in practice. Moreover, even in the framework of accepted assumptions, accuracy of modelling is strictly limited by the model itself — no matter how accurate the DM can be and how much time and other resources are granted. Thus, any attempt to model DM preferences by means of linear utility functions is inaccurate — as it is in the case of approximating a curve by a straight line. One more drawback is that questions to DM are being stated in terms of the model and therefore messages are being interpreted rather arbitrarily. Thus, one and the same message from DM about the comparative criteria importance can be sometimes interpreted in terms of coefficients of a linear utility function and sometimes in lexicographical sense, which evidently leads to absolutely different solutions. Besides, a cooperative DM is interested in answering even when he is not sure — lest his competence is questioned.

All these examples are typical, though trivial. It can be shown, that many of more advanced methods are not free from similar drawbacks either. As a rule,

1. these methods consist of a more or less arbitrary combination of certain heuristical steps,
2. the interpretation of DM messages in terms of the chosen model is often poorly grounded,

3. the question about the ability of the chosen model to accurately reflect the real preferences is not being discussed at all.

3 Conception and principles of approximational modelling

The analysis of multicriteria problems and methods has led me to the following conception of preferences modelling. As the formal object associated with the notion of DM preference system we accept choice function (as a set–theoretic operator) in a given criteria space R^n i.e. a triple (A, P, C), where $A \subseteq R^n$ is a universal set, $P \subseteq 2^A$ is a family of presentations, $C : P \to 2^A : X \mapsto C(X) \subseteq X$ is a choice operator. We often refer to this operator as choice function — as it is accepted in the case of mappings. This operator C is generally unknown, but some of its properties may be clear from the general sense of the given problem. Besides, its values $C(X)$ for some presentations $X \in P$ can be indicated by the DM — such presentations are referred to as simple. To solve a given problem is to extrapolate operator C from a certain set of simple presentations to the presentations required by the problem in question. It is done by means of a model of DM preferences, which is a parametric family of choice functions C_α, defined on the same universal set A. This interpretation allows the use of criteria–space topology for formalizing the notion of approximation accuracy.

Now we can formulate the following principles of preferences modelling:

- all the assumptions about general properties of the DM preference system C must be explicitly stated and properly justified;
- in the framework of these assumptions the model must allow approximating of the DM preference system with any required accuracy ($C_\alpha \to C$);
- any question to DM may be stated in terms of his preferences only — and never in terms of the model;
- DM may answer "I don't know", whenever he really does not.

Having this conception in mind, a theoretical research has been undertaken concerning some practically important properties of choice functions and (binary) relations in criteria space.

4 Geometry of choice and relations

First of all, notions of *induced choice* and *induced relation* were introduced, allowing establishment of a correspondence between choice functions and relations, defined on different universal sets.

Def. Let (A, P, C) be a choice function on A, $f : B \to A$. Then for all $Y \subseteq B$ s.t. $f(Y) \in P$

$$f^*(C)(Y) \stackrel{\text{def}}{=} f^{-1} \circ C \circ f(Y) \cap Y$$

Def. Let $R \subseteq A \times A$ be a (binary) relation on A, $f : B \to A$. Then

$$f^*(R) \stackrel{\text{def}}{=} \{ (x,y) \in B \times B : f(x)Rf(y) \}$$

These notions are in mutual agreement, as the following shows.

Prop. $f^*\mathrm{Max}_R = \mathrm{Max}_{f^*R}$

It was demonstrated, that these notion possess certain general properties allowing further considerations in a fairly wide context. To put it more accurately, these are properties of contravariant functor, acting (in the case of choice functions) from the category of sets into the category of choice functions spaces, built by the author. On the base of this, the notions of *invariant* and *semiinvariant* choice functions and relations were introduced.

Def. Choice function C (relation R) is f–invariant iff

$$f^*(C) = C \quad (f^*(R) = R).$$

Then a general classification of choice functions and relations invariant w.r.t. various groups of space transformations (symmetries) was built. Here are the groups: *translations (shifts)(T)*, *dilatations(D)*, *monotone mappings(M)*, etc. This may be viewed as a development of the idea of preferences invariance w.r.t. scales transformations. Representatives of the introduced classes were used for description of preferences in some problems with the corresponding scale types, as well as for approximation in the general case. The form of upper sections of relations ($R_x = \{y \in A : xRy\}$) of these classes was studied.

Prop. If relation R is T–invariant, then $R_x - x = const = S(R)$, called as the (upper) section of relation R; if R is D–invariant, then $S(R)$ is a cone; if R is M–invariant, then $S(R)$ consists of orthants.

In the framework of this classification certain connections were established between some geometric and set–theoretic properties of relations, such as transitivity and existence of cycles of a given length (k–cyclicity), interpreted as the degree of preferences consistency.

Theorem. Let relation R be D–invariant. Then R is transitive iff its section $S(R)$ is convex; R has k–cycles iff $k < \min \dim L(S)$, $S \subseteq S(R)$, S is obtuse; ($L(S)$ is the linear span of S, S is referred to as obtuse if it has no plane of support in $L(S)$).

These results allowed us to propose some algorithms for determination of such characteristics of M–invariant relations. For example, if M–invariant relation is "in strict scales" (which implies that its section $S(R)$ consists of only n–dimensional orthants), then the following holds:

Theorem. Let R be M–invariant. Then R is transitive iff it is Pareto relation; R has k–cycles iff k is less or equal to the minimal number of orthants from $S(R)$, s.t. the convex hull of their union is the whole space.

A number of useful results were obtained concerning *homomorphisms* of acyclic relations.

Def. Let R be a relation on a set A, R' — relation on B and $f : B \to A$. Then f is a homomorphism (isomorphism) of R' to R iff $f^*R \supseteq R'$ ($f^*R = R'$). If A is real axis and $R =$'$<$', such f is referred to as homomorphic (isomorphic) function.

Theorem. Let R' be acyclic relation. Then (a classical result of Spielrein) it is a part of some complete ordering;

- if R' is a relation on R^n, then the measure of lower section of transitive closure of R' ($\mathrm{Mes}(\mathrm{Tr}R')^x$) is a homomorphic function for R';
- if R' is D–invariant, then there is a linear homomorphism to L (lexicographic relation);
- if R' is M–invariant, then it is a part of L–relation;
- if R' is M–invariant "in strict scales", then one of the criteria is homomorphic function for R';
- if R' is smooth (see def. below), then the field of its indifference planes is integrable, the integral being an ordinal function, homomorphic for R' and isomorphic for its transitive closure $\mathrm{Tr}R'$.

These results proved to be a useful instrument for determining maximal points and for studying the convergence of some interactive methods.

Furthermore, a new notion of *smooth relation* was introduced for spaces and manifolds.

Def. Relation R is smooth if its boundary(frontier) in $A \times A$ is a smooth surface(submanifold).

Prop. If R is smooth, then its section R_x is also bounded by a smooth surface (in A)

- for almost every point x;
- for every point x, if $R \supseteq$ Pareto.

Tangent planes at x of upper and lower sections coincide.

To this case such notions were extended as indifference plane, substitution coefficients, etc., considered before only in connection with smooth utility functions.

Def. The tangent plane of upper section of R at x ($T_x\, R_x$) is referred to as indifference plane of R at x.

Note that in contrast with utility function, the assumption of smooth relation allows for incomparable points and seems in general much more realistic. Nevertheless, it was demonstrated that for a smooth relation the integral of indifference planes field exists and is isomorphic for TrR (see above). Quasiconcavity of this function can be interpreted in terms of criteria saturability.

The obtained results allow to substantially extend the application area that have been as far restricted to somewhat dubious assumption of utility function.

All these theoretical results allowed the development and justification of a number of procedures and methods.

5 Some approximational procedures and methods

We consider two types of problems: problems with fixed presentation (when there is a possibility of interaction after presentation is determined) and problems with variable presentation (for such problems a model of the whole DM preference system must be constructed in advance). Of the first type of problems the use of various iterative procedures is characteristic. So iterative procedures of three different types were considered:

- contraction of presentation
- transition to a better point
- transition to an equivalent point.

For presentation contraction procedure some correctness conditions were established.

Theorem. Let a choice function C satisfy H–condition (Iserman et al., 1982)
[for any presentations X, X' $X' \subseteq X \Rightarrow \bar{C}(X') \subseteq \bar{C}(X)$, where $\bar{C}(Y) = Y \setminus C(Y)$]
and M–condition for a given presentation X_0
[for any presentation X $C(X_0) \subseteq X \subseteq X_0 \Rightarrow |C(X)| \leq |C(X_0)|$]
Then for any $C' \supseteq C$ and any family of presentations $P' \subseteq P \subseteq 2^{X_0}$ all the C'–rejected points may be ignored:

$$C(X_0 \setminus \bigcup_{Y \in P'} \bar{C}'(Y)) = C(X_0).$$

Theorem. Let $R_i \uparrow R$. Then $\mathrm{Max}_{R_i} \downarrow \mathrm{Max}_R$. (Here the topology is pointwise, the condition $R_i \subseteq R$ is essential for convergence.)

These results justify the use of binary relations in many situations when the choice differs from just obtaining maximum with respect to some relation. Some convergence problems were considered as well.

For transition to a better point and to an equivalent point certain approximational procedures were developed and studied. On this base approximational versions of some well–known methods were proposed as well as two new methods — of comparison and of sorting frames (Borzenko et al., 1986, 1987). The idea of comparing of two points consists in drawing a polygonal approximation of the integral curve of indifference lying in a certain two–dimensional plane. The method of sorting frames was designed for problems with variable presentation and is based upon stratification of small pieces of the criteria values area along the corresponding indifference planes and the aggregation of the strata with the help of the proposed method of comparison.

6 Experiments and applications

Now about experiments. This aspect of multicriteria research seems to be of particular interest, for it is rather difficult to find a practical multicriteria problem with feedback. Indeed, in real–life projecting and evaluation planning problems means of objective estimation of a multicriteria method effectiveness as well as of a DM reliability are really scarce.

I was lucky to find such problems in the area of OS programming. In particular, we have experimented with the problem of scheduling queues in batch processing mode and obtained simultaneous 10 to 20 per cent improvement of all the main characteristics as compared with other disciplines. Besides, we have tried the described methods in some other problems of computer science, such as distributed storage organization, distribution of branches in multiprocessor computers, etc. The presence of feedback in these problems allows not only to compare methods and decision makers, but even to utilize means of automatic adaptation. More details about these applications can be found in (Borzenko et al., 1985, 1986, 1987, 1988).

In these papers we tried to demonstrate that the approximational methods can provide fairly convenient, flexible and accurate means for solving various multicriteria problems.

References

Arrow, K. J. (1959). Rational choice functions and orderings. *Econometrica*, 26(102), pp. 121–127.

Berezovsky, B. A., Borzenko, V. I., and Kempner, L. M. (1981). Binary relations in multicriteria optimization. Nauka, Moscow(in Russian).

Borzenko, V. I., Trakhtengerts, E. A., and Shershakov, V. M. (1985). Approximational multicriteria scheduling in computer systems. IFIP Conf. on Syst. Modelling and Optimization, 12th, Budapest, September 1985, Abstr. 1, pp. 59–60.

Borzenko, V. I., Trakhtengerts, E. A., and Shershakov, V. M. (1986). Approximational multicriteria scheduling in computer systems. *Avtomatika i telemekhanika*, No 9, pp. 152–162.

Borzenko, V. I., Guft, M. G., and Sergeev, V. I. (1987). An interactive method for multicriteria evaluation of the technical level of industrial production. Doklady Akad. Nauk, 295(3), pp. 549–553.

Borzenko, V. I., Golubenkov, A. A., Trakhtengerts, E. A., and Shershakov V. M. (1988). A multicriteria approach to the problem of distributed data storage. *Avtom. i telem.*, No 2.

Borzenko, V. I., and Ioshpa, A. Z. (1988). Multicriteria control over branches in multiprocessor systems. *Avtom. i telem.*, No 3.

Iserman, M. A. and Malishevsky A. V. (1982). General choice theory: some aspects. *Avtom. i telem.*, No 2.

Plott, C. R. (1976). Axiomatic social choice theory: an overview and interpretations. *American Journal of Political Science*, vol. 20.

Sen, A. K. (1977). Social Choice Theory: A Re-Examination. *Econometrica*, 45(1), pp. 53–90.

About Some Applications of a Special Fuzzy–Concept of Efficiency in Multicriteria Decision–Making

J. Ester
Technische Universitaet Karl-Marx-Stadt
Sektion Automatisierungstechnik
PSF 964
Karl-Marx-Stadt, GDR 9010

1 Introduction

It is understood that there is no generally applicable and accepted concept for the (more or less automated) choice of best elements from the Pareto set of a Multicriteria Decision Making Problem. I am sure that this situation will also obtain in future. For computer-aided decision making systems, this means that they must make available a lot of different methods, based on different theoretical concepts. In this way, it is possible to choose the suitable method for the decision maker and his problem. The choice of the method must be made in collaboration with the decision maker, while basic ideas of the methods and the basic information, which is needed, are being explained. Recently, an increasing number of papers, topic of which is the introduction of FUZZY THEORY into MCDM, have been published. A good analysis of desirable properties of mathematical operations, used in FUZZY MULTICRITERIA DECISION MAKING (FMCDM), is presented by Werners (1984). In this paper it is pointed out that there is no aggregation rule for fuzzy sets, which incorporate all these properties. In (Ester, 1986) an aggregation rule, based on the equation of the weighted L_p-norm, is given. In (Ester, 1987) it is shown that this rule has all these desirable properties.

In MCDM-problems fuzziness (or uncertainty, perturbations etc.) can be located in three places ($z(\cdot)$ — membership function):

a) The set X of all feasible decisions is a fuzzy set:

$$X = \{\, x \mid z_X(x)\, \}, \quad x \in R^n$$

b) The mapping from the decision space into the criteria space is a fuzzy set:

$$\{(x,q)\} = \{\, (x,q) \mid z_{XQ}(x,q)\, \}, \quad (x,q) \in R^n \times R^m$$

c) The rule for the choice of the final decision from the set of the best solutions (e.g. the Pareto set) is fuzzy.

In this paper we consider only the problem c). Let us start with the following considerations:

The "goodness" of a decision is a fuzzy notion, which can be characterized by a set of concrete attributes. The fuzzy set G of good decisions is an aggregation of fuzzy sets G_i of good decisions with respect to the single attributes $i = 1(1)m$. The membership functions of these sets depend on the performance degrees of the single attributes, which can be measured by the values of the single criteria. By normalization of these values to the interval $[0,1]$, where "1" means the "best" performance index and "0" means the "worst". We can use the criteria q_i in the sense of membership functions of the fuzzy sets G_i. We get

$$G = \{\, q \mid z_G(q)\,\}, \quad q \in Q \subseteq R^m \,. \tag{01}$$

Now we choose the following equation as an aggregation rule (cf. Ester, 1986)

$$\begin{gathered} z_G = \Big\{ \sum_{i=1}^{m} g_i(q_i)^p \Big\}^{(1/p)}, \\ 0 \le g_i \le 1, \quad i = 1(1)m, \quad (1_m)^T g = 1, \quad -\infty < p < +\infty \,. \end{gathered} \tag{02}$$

This aggregation rule of fuzzy sets has the following properties, which are regarded as very advantageous for decision problems:

a) commutative,

b) associative,

c) inductive,

d) strongly monotonically increasing (for finite p),

e) idempotent,

f) continuously controllable between intersection ($p \to -\infty$) and union ($p \to +\infty$),

g) compensatory,

h) stable,

i) continuous with respect to each component,

j) continuously differentiable.

For the proof of some of these properties it is necessary to take into consideration that, in case of adding a new criterion, the weighting factors g_i must be modified by a recursive equation

$$g_i := (1 - g_{\text{new}})g_i . \tag{03}$$

It is possible to vary (03). In this way, we can take into consideration possible dynamics of the notion "goodness" or "quality". This leads, of course, to the loss of such properties like associativity, for instance. It is easy to prove that well-known aggregation rules are special cases of (02):

a) $p \to -\infty$: minimum operator,

b) $p = 0$: product operator,

c) $p = 1$: sum operator,

d) $p \to +\infty$: maximum operator.

Moreover, some other properties of (02) are proved in (Ester and Troeltzsch, 1986). These properties apply to the optimal fuzzy decision (Werners, 1984), which is usually given, due to maximization of the membership function z_G.

$$z_G(q(x)) = \max_x! \qquad \text{or} \qquad z_G(q) = \max_q! \tag{04}$$

Completing (02) with (04), a special nonlinear parametric substitute optimization problem for multicriteria decision making arises. We denote the solution set of these problems (g varying, p fixed) by $E(p)$. The additional properties are shown in (Ester and Troeltzsch, 1986):

A. It holds

$$E(p_2) \subseteq E(p_1) \quad \text{for} \quad -\infty < p_1 \leq p_2 < +\infty. \tag{05}$$

B.

$$E(p) \subseteq PM \quad \text{for} \quad -\infty < p < +\infty, \tag{06}$$

where PM denotes the Pareto set of the multicriteria optimization problem.

C. Suppose $p \to E(p)$ is continuous for $p < p'$. Then for a given arbitrary positive ε, we find a $p < p'$, satisfying the following condition:

$$\forall\, q \in PM : \exists q' \in E(p) : |q - q'| < \varepsilon. \tag{07}$$

If g and p are fixed, we get a solution $E(p, g)$. Now, if p is increasing (increasing disjunctive property of (02)), then $E(p)$ is moving in the direction of the individual optima of the single criteria, which are reached at $p \to +\infty$ for any $g > 0$. In contrast to this, decreasing p leads to solutions, which have an increasing character of compromise. Simultaneously, we can obtain decreasing compensatority. Therefore, all these properties permit us to state that in (02) an aggregation rule for decision making is found, which reflects human's decision behaviour reasonably well.

Indeed, the unknown parameters p (p controls the logical property of (02)) and g (g controls the relative importance of the criteria) must be found. To do this, a questionnaire procedure with the decision maker is necessary. There are a lot of possibilities. One of them is described in the following.

2 Decision analysis

Some — real or hypothetical — alternatives, given in the criteria space, are proposed to the decision maker. Let k_0 be the number of these samples (sample size). For all these alternatives (points in R^m) the marginal rates of substitutions have been inquired from the decision maker. These rates are estimates for the local direction of the level surfaces of z_G in these points and therefore also estimates for the local gradient directions of z_G. After the definition of a suitable estimation error, we can compute the values of p and g, which minimize the estimation error (divergence between the gradient directions of z_G and their estimates by the marginal rates of substitution). Here a problem arises. The problem is the definition of the error. At a first glimpse, we would measure the error by the angle between the directions. But, unfortunately, this leads to a nonlinear parametric definition of the error, which is not useful for further computation. Instead of g_i, we use new variables $v_i = g_i/g_m$, $i = 1(1)(m-1)$, and linearize the single error with respect to these new variables. We obtain the following definition of the single estimation error

$$e_{jk} = \left[1 + (m_{jk})^2\right]^{-1}\left[v_j(q_{jk}/q_{mk})^{(p-1)} - m_{jk}\right], \tag{08}$$

where the symbols mean:

e_{jk} : angular deviation by the projection in the (j,m)-plane at the point k.

m_{jk} : marginal rate of substitution $-(\Delta q_m/\Delta q_j)$ at the point k.

q_{jk} : value of the criterion j at the point k.

$j = 1(1)(m-1), \quad k = 1(1)k_0$

This expression has an error of linearization less than 5% in the interval $0 \leq m_{jk} \leq 1$, if the difference between the substitution rate and the quotient of the partial derivations is not greater than 40%. For $m_{jk} > 1$ the error of linearization increases like the *tg*-function.

For this reason, the definition of the estimation error must be modified:

$0 \leq m_{jk} \leq 1$: then (08) is valid,

$1 < m_{jk} < \infty$: $m_{jk} := 1/m_{jk}$, $v_j := 1/v_j$, $q_{jk} := q_{mk}$, $q_{mk} := q_{jk}$: then (08) is also valid.

Therefore, in case of large values of m_{jk}, we use the difference between the reciprocals, and the error of linearization is in each case less than 5% (if the difference between the substitution rate and the quotient of the partial derivations or their reciprocals, respectively, is less than 40%). With $v = (v_1, \ldots, v_{m-1})^T$ the following estimation algorithm arises

$$\sum_{k=1}^{k_0}\sum_{j=1}^{m-1}(e_{jk})^2 = \min_{v,p}! \tag{09}$$

The necessary conditions for a minimum of the error function lead, owing to the nonlinear parametric error, to the following decoupled equations for optimal v_j

$$A_j(p) * (v_j)^4 + B_j(p) * (v_j)^3 + C_j(p) * v_j + D_j(p) = 0, \quad j = 1(1)(m-1) \tag{10}$$

From the partial derivation to p follows an equation, which cannot be exploited for computation. But for (10) it can be proved that the largest positive real zero is the solution for the minimum of (09) and, in consequence, (09) can be solved by a onedimensional search along the p-axis.

With the aim of developing computer-aided decision methods, a new software module (ZUG) for the interactive decision support system POLYP.BC was implemented and tested. With ZUG, decision analysis can be carried out in the way described and for discrete MADM problems the alternatives can be ordered by the values of z_G.

3 Test results

First, we show the results of the estimation algorithm by two simple, constructed examples. The first example is an exact problem. This means the problem setting corresponds exactly to equation (02).

EXAMPLE 1: $m = 3,\ k_0 = 7$

k	1	2	3	4	5	6	7
m1k	.2	.1	.2	.4	.1	.2	.4
m2k	.8	.8	.4	1.6	.4	1.6	.8
q1	.33	.5	.25	.25	.4	.4	.2
q2	.33	.25	.5	.25	.4	.2	.4
q3	.33	.25	.25	.5	.2	.4	.4

Supported by ZUG, we get the following values:

$$g1 = .100000, \quad g2 = .400000, \quad g3 = .500000, \quad p = 0.000000.$$

This corresponds exactly to the given problem. The values of the error function $EPS_{min}(p)$ and the values of a corresponding weighting coefficient, maybe g_2, are given in the next table:

p	-10	-9	-8	-7	-6	-5	-4
EPS	.770885	.769416	.766483	.760631	.748983	.725920	.6807
g2	.444340	.444236	.444027	.443608	.442768	.441079	.4376
p	-3	-2	-1	0	1	2	3
EPS	.594154	.437058	.192951	.000000	.695048	5.78858	30.62
g2	.430877	.418225	.403044	.400000	.414267	.444683	.4641
p	4	5	6	7	8	9	10
EPS	139.667	595.760	2460.12	9997.59	40307.6	161868.	6E+05
g2	.471955	.474964	.476234	.476811	.477085	.477218	.4772

Now we give a next example, where the error cannot be zero, because the substitution rates do not correspond to an exact problem.

EXAMPLE 2: $m = 2,\ k_0 = 10$

k	1	2	3	4	5	6	7	8	9	10
m1k	8.00	2.33	.867	2.50	1.25	1.33	.600	.428	.333	.111
q1	.2	.3	.4	.5	.5	.6	.7	.7	.8	.9
q2	.9	.7	.3	.8	.6	.7	.5	.3	.4	.1

With ZUG we get the results:

$$p = -0.3, \quad g1 = 0.514138, \quad g2 = 0.485862.$$

We can compute the membership values $z_G(k)$ of the alternatives and the angular error $phi(k)$ for each alternative (measured in degree).

k	1	2	3	4	5	6	7	8	9	10
zG	.38	.44	.34	.62	.54	.64	.59	.45	.56	.26
phi	.5	6.0	5.0	5.0	2.0	1.0	3.0	4.0	5.0	3.0

Even in this example the values of $\mathrm{EPS}_{\min}(p)$ and of any weighting coefficient — for instance g_1 — are very interesting.

p	-10	-9	-8	-7	-6	-5	-4
EPS	.954	.944	.929	.906	.871	.815	.727
g1	.956	.941	.921	.895	.860	.814	.746
p	-3	-2	-1	0	1	2	3
EPS	.566	.367	.138	.082	2.74	86.8	3E+3
g1	.456	.528	.523	.511	.495	.424	.336
p	4	5	6	7	8	9	10
EPS	1E+5	5E+6	2E+8	9E+9	3E11	1E13	6E14
g1	.262	.200	.150	.111	.081	.059	.042

In all investigated examples (about 100) we found, that $\mathrm{EPS}_{\min}(p)$ was a quasiconvex function of p. The steepness of the ascent was very different from example to example. Almost symmetric curves occur and so do totally asymmetric curves. It seems that it is possible to apply onedimensional, local search algorithms to fast computation.

4 Applications

With the method described above, we have investigated practical problems in the field of designing textile articles. The results are very interesting. In this paper we shall present the problem of choosing a concrete technology of refining cotton fabric. With respect to 25 criteria we must find out the best variant from 16 different ways of refining cotton fabric.

By consulting 14 engineers, economists and managers, who are concerned with the decision making process, the marginal rates of substitution have been determined for each alternative. The basic criterion was "total cost".

criterion	unit of measurement	symb.	max/min
washfastness	mark 1–5	q1	max!
washfastness, modified	mark 1–5	q2	max!
handle	mark 1–0	q3	min!
crease recovery	mark 1–5	q4	max!
tensile strength, longit.	N	q5	max!
tensile strength, horiz.	N	q6	max!
fastness to rubbing	mark 1-5	q7	max!
washfastness (pigment dyes)	mark 1–5	q8	max!
pilling resistance	mark 1–5	q9	max!
angular crease recovery 1	degree	q10	max!
angular crease recovery 2	degree	q11	max!
modification of dimensional stability, longit.	%	q12	min!
modification of dimensional stability, horiz.	%	q13	min!
resistance to roughening	mark 1–5	q14	max!
fastness to perspiration	mark 1–5	q15	max!
fastness to ironing	mark 1–5	q16	max!
water vapor permeability	$mg/cm^2 24h$	q17	min!
power to tear glide seam, longit.	N	q18	max!
power to tear glide seam, horiz.	N	q19	max!
power to tear out seam, longit.	N	q20	max!
power to tear out seam, horiz.	N	q21	max!
breaking elongation, longit.	%	q22	max!
breaking elongation, horiz.	%	q23	max!
resistance (el.)	Teraohm	q24	max!
total cost	$TM/10^6 m^2$	q25	min!

The values of the criteria differ in the following intervals:

criterion	best value	worst value
q1	5.	4.
q2	4.7	1.
q3	0.	.9
q4	4.7	3.2
q5	599.	488.
q6	439.	318.
q7	5.	5.
q8	4.	1.
q9	5.	4.
q10	155.	132.
q11	165.	140.
q12	.9	2.4
q13	1.7	3.7
q14	4.	3.
q15	5.	4.
q16	5.	5.
q17	1.	2.2
q18	97.	76.
q19	119.	64.
q20	243.	161.
q21	268.	159.
q22	13.4	8.5
q23	18.2	14.5
q24	.90	9.30
q25	188.6	387.2

All alternatives were Pareto optimal. Differences in some of the criteria were very large and in others were not measurable. After normalization of the criteria to the interval [.1, 1.] and application of ZUG we get the results shown in Tab. 1. Average value of the angular error: 10.6537 degree, p = .69,

The values of the membership function differ rather strongly. The computed order of alternatives was stable, even if the normalization interval was changed ([.25, 1.], [.5, 1.], [.1, .75], [.1, .5], [.4, .8]), and the average value of the angular error changed in the first digit after the decimal point only. The order of the alternatives was been accepted. This applies especially to the alternative 13, which dominates due to the good values in the most important criteria: washfastness, handle, crease recovery, fastness to rubbing, pilling resistance, modification of dimensional stability, fastness to ironing, total cost. In this practical decision making problem the parameter p, which controls the logical property of the aggregation rule, was computed with the value $p = .69$, which means "weak conjunctive aggregation".

Weighting coefficients	
g1	.0215923
g2	.2568180
g3	.0333461
g4	.2094010
g5	.0015245
g6	.0035447
g7	.0168755
g8	.0995977
g9	.0037298
g10	.0057991
g11	.0066219
g12	.0175869
g13	.2348320
g14	.0087173
g15	.0022823
g16	.0270121
g17	.0058949
g18	.0028019
g19	.0068365
g20	.0072689
g21	.0068123
g22	.0067682
g23	.0018330
g24	.0077332
g25	.0107700

$\mathrm{EPS}_{\min}(p)$	p
1.1E+22	-10
1.4E+20	-9
8.1E+09	-8
3.8E+16	-7
4.8E+08	-6
2.9E+07	-5
1.8E+06	-4
1.2E+05	-3
8068.52	-2
594.28	-1
46.66	0
19.78	1
1256.71	2
1.2E+04	3
5.5E+05	4
2.9E+07	5
1.6E+09	6
9.3E+10	7
5.4E+12	8
3.1E+14	9
1.5E+24	10

z_G of 16 alternatives
.712
.665
.611
.740
.693
.359
.247
.724
.682
.648
.679
.299
.945
.583
.765
.700

Order of alternatives
13. altern.
15. altern.
4. altern.
8. altern.
1. altern.
16. altern.
5. altern.
9. altern.
11. altern.
2. altern.
10. altern.
3. altern.
14. altern.
6. altern.
12. altern.
7. altern.

Tab. 1

5 Open problems

In (Ester, 1986) the idea was developed that a multilevel hierarchy of attributes characterizes the quality of decisions. For instance, a two-level hierarchy can be described in the following way:

$$\begin{aligned} G &= \mathrm{aggr}_1(G_{11}, \ldots, G_{1m}), \\ G_{1j} &= \mathrm{aggr}_{1j}(G_{21}, \ldots, G_{2mj}) \end{aligned}$$

The goodness G is an aggregation of partial "qualities" G_{1j}, which are aggregations of basic attributes G_{2j}. It is possible that a concrete basic attribute is basic for more than one partial quality.

With the normalized criteria as membership functions of the basic attributes, the aggregation rule (02) and the decision rule (04), the following equations hold:

$$z_G = \left\{\sum_{i=1}^{m} g_i (z_i)^p\right\}^{1/p}, \qquad g > 0_m, \quad -\infty < p < +\infty,$$

$$z_i = \left\{\sum_{j=1}^{mi} gi_j (qi_j)^{pi}\right\}^{1/pi}, \qquad gi > 0_{mi}, \quad -\infty < pi < +\infty, \quad i = 1(1)m, \quad z_G = \max_q !$$

In case of a known structure of the hierarchy (e.g. if the decision maker can give corresponding information), it is necessary to determine the unknown parameters p and g for each element of the hierarchy. The solution of a corresponding estimation problem (analogously (09)) will be more difficult than in the problems described above. On the other hand, the detection of an unknown structure of the hierarchy is very hard and there is no creative idea for solving this structure-building problem. Because the assumption that a hierarchic structure can better reflect the human's decision behaviour, it is reasonable to think about appropriate methods and algorithms.

References

Bellman, R.E. and Zadeh, L.A. (1970). Decision-making in a fuzzy environment, *Management Science* 17:141–164.

Ester, J. (1986). Concepts of efficiency and fuzzy aggregation rules. In G. Fandel, M. Grauer, A. Kurzhanski, A. Wierzbicki (eds.): Large-Scale Modelling and Interactive Decision Analysis, Springer.

Ester, J. (1987). Einbeziehung der Theorie der unscharfen Mengen in die Methoden der mehrkriteriellen Entscheidung, WZ der TH Ilmenau, 33: Heft 6.

Ester, J. and Troeltzsch, F. (1986). On generalized notions of efficiency in MCDM. *Syst. Anal. Model. Simul.* 3: Heft 2.

Slowinski, R. (1986). A multicriteria fuzzy linear programming method for water supply system development planning. *Fuzzy Sets and Systems* 19: 217–237.

Werners, B. (1984). Interaktive Entscheidungsunterstuetzung durch ein flexibles math. Programmierungssystem, Minerva Publikation Muenchen.

Zadeh, L.A. (1965). Fuzzy sets. *Inform. and Control* 8: 338–353.

Safety Principle in Multiobjective Decision Support in the Decision Space Defined by Availability of Resources

H. Gorecki, A.M. Skulimowski
Institute of Automatics
St. Staszic University of Mining and Metallurgy
Al. Mickiewicza 30
30–059 Krakow, Poland

1 Introduction

The choice of a compromise solution fulfilling additional conditions with regard to its location in the criteria space is essential in numerous real-life multiple criteria optimization problems. For instance, the choice of a technological process from many variants proposed by experts, taking into account the total cost of investment and the minimal necessary time to start the production, is often based on the analysis of upper and lower bounds for values of the above criteria (Gorecki, 1981). Such bounds are usually not strict; they are called aspirations levels and are assumed to be imposed independently by experts or the decision-maker after the formulation of the problem, therefore serving as an additional information for selecting the compromise solution.

The nature of aspiration levels is often uncertain and the arising set of demanded values of criteria may be represented as random or fuzzy set. When selecting a compromise solution, the decision-maker is obliged to take into account the possibility of unexpected change of aspiration levels using an uncertainty handling technique. For the case where the demanded set is defined by two aspiration levels such a method has been proposed by Gorecki (1981). In this approach, the search for a non-dominated solution has been executed on a line which joins the aspiration levels, and lies inside of so-called skeleton of the demanded set. An outline of the skeleton method may be found in Gorecki (1981) and Wiecek (1984). The numerical implementation of this method has been developed by Gorecki et al. (1982, 1985). Here, we will present some of its theoretical foundations.

Throughout this paper we will assume that the set defined by the lower and upper aspiration levels, called demanded set, and the attainable set of the criteria values have a non-empty intersection. Then we will analyse the problem of selecting a non-dominated compromise solution from this intersection which is — in some sense — most reliable to the changes of the demanded set. Namely, we look for a problem solution on a specific class of lines called the ordinal skeleton curves of the demanded set. The solution thus obtained will possess the property that the expected value of the distance form the boundary of the demanded set is maximal, or equivalently, that the probability of remaining within the demanded set — which boundary changes according to some random rules — is maximal.

In this paper we will concentrate our attention on the particular case of the criteria space constraints, namely on the sets defined by aspiration levels of the form:

$$Q := (q_1 + \Theta) \cap (q_2 - \Theta) \tag{1}$$

where: q_1 and q_2 are the aspiration levels for criteria, denoting the maximal admissible, and the most desired values of the criteria, respectively, and Θ is the positive cone of the partial order in the criteria space. Usually $\Theta = R^N_+$, and

$$Q = \bigcap_{i=1}^{N} [q_{1i}; q_{2i}] \tag{2}$$

where $q_1 = (q_{11}, \ldots, q_{1N})$ and $q_2 = (q_{21}, \ldots, q_{2N})$, $q_{1i} \leq q_{2i}$ for $1 \leq i \leq N$ and the product of intervals is understood in the Cartesian sense.

2 Problem formulation

Definition 1. The *interval demanded set* for the problem

$$\left(F : U \to R^N\right) \to \min(\Theta) \tag{3}$$

is given by the formula (1) where

$$q_1 \leq_\Theta q_2, \qquad q_1 \notin F(U), \qquad q_2 \in F(U)$$

Interval demanded set in the case $\Theta := R^N_+$ may be represented as

$$Q_1 = \bigcap_{i=1}^{N} [q_1^i; q_2^i]$$

where q_1^i, q_2^i are lower and upper estimates of the i-th criterion demanded values respectively.

Definition 2. The subset S_1 of the interval demanded set Q_1 defined by the formula:

$$S_1 := \Big\{ x \in Q_I : \exists G_i, G_j,\ i \neq j - \text{facets of Q, such that} \\ d(x, \partial Q_I) = d(z, G_i) = d(z, G_j) \Big\}$$

where ∂Q_I — the boundary of Q_I — will be called the *skeleton* of Q_I.

Now, let $C(Q_I)$ be the subset of Q_I consisting of points maximally distant form the boundary of Q_I, i.e.

$$C(Q_I) := \Big\{ x \in Q_I : \forall y \in Q_I,\ d(y, \partial Q_I) \leq d(x, \partial Q_I) \Big\} \tag{4}$$

and let q_1 and q_2 be two distinct elements of ∂Q_I such that $q_1 \leq_\Theta q_2$. If Q_I is convex then for each element q of the boundary of Q_I there exists a unique half-line $v(q)$ starting in q and such that the function $d(\cdot, \partial Q_I)$ grows fastest on $v(q)$ in a neighborhood of each point belonging to $v(q)$. It is easy to see that $v(q)$ links q and $C(Q_I)$ and it is linearly ordered. Thus we may formulate the following:

Definition 3. The *ordinal skeleton* of Q_I is the set

$$S_0 := v(q_1) \cup v(q_2) \cup C(Q) \tag{5}$$

It is evident that if $Q = Q_I$ then $S_0 \subset S_1$.

Lemma 1. (a maximal safety principle). Let $L(q_1, q_2)$ be the set of all curves joining q_1 and q_2 inside Q_I and being linearly ordered. Then for every $g \in L(q_1, q_2)$ and every c such that $c^* \subset S_0$

$$\int_g d(x, \partial Q_I)\, dP \leq \int_c d(x, \partial Q_I)\, dP \tag{6}$$

where P is a uniform probability distribution on g or c, and d is the l_1 or l_∞ distance in the criteria space. In particular, (6) holds for the skeleton curve S.

Corollary 1. In the situation where there is no information about the location of the Pareto set, the search along the skeleton curve S results in finding a non-dominated solution maximally distant to the boundaries of Q_I.

Theorem 1. Let X be an arbitrary subset of Q_I. The probability distribution η defining the changes of ∂Q is assumed uniform. Then the maximally safe element of X with respect to the changes of Q belongs to S whenever $S \cap X \neq \emptyset$.

3 An application to a design problem

Let us consider the problem of designing a construction lift taking into account the set of parameters which decide about the commercial success of the product. These criteria include the time of evaluation of the project, the lifting capacity, the maximal range of the arm — F_1, F_2, F_3 respectively. We assume that may exist other criteria such as reliability coefficient, or the production price per unit (F_4, F_5 — respectively) which should be simply optimized, without paying attention to the constraints in the criteria space. Such criteria are not included in the model of preferences here presented. The total cost of design and investment may be regarded as a constraint, together with the employment, materials and technology limitations. We assume that all constraints for a set U of admissible design strategies. The annual net income anticipated I may serve as an aggregated utility function which, however, depends on the above listed criteria in an unknown way. We can only assume that I is monotonically depending on the measure of fulfillment of the market's expectations which are expressed by the set Q.

According to the preference model presented in the preceding subsections U is defined by upper and lower limitations for the values of criteria. These parameters can have the following practical interpretation:

F_{11} – the minimal time necessary to distribute an announcement about the new product to the potential customers, also — if all or a prevailing part of lifts is to be sold to one company — the minimal supply time required by this company;

F_{1u} – estimated upper limit of period warranting a sufficient market's demand, or the maximal supply time required by the commissioning company, or the estimated time a similar lift will be designed and offered be other producers;

F_{21} – minimal lifting capacity admissible for lifts of this type;

F_{2u} – maximal reasonable lifting capacity estimated basing on the knowledge of potential scope of application of lifts;

F_{31}, F_{3u} – similarly as above — the minimal admissible, and maximal reasonable values of the range of arm.

Each criterion should be optimized inside of the bounds F_{i1}, F_{iu}, $1 \leq i \leq 3$, whereas F_1 should be minimized, the other criteria — maximized. To treat the functions F_i in an uniform way, we will instead minimize the function $(-F_1)$ and (F_3), replacing simultaneously lower bounds be upper ones with opposite signs and vice versa.

The demanded set Q can be expressed in the form

$$Q = \bigcap_{i=1}^{3} [F_{i1}, F_{iu}]$$

The bounds of Q are uncertain as the values of F_{i1} and F_{iu}, $1 \leq i \leq 3$ are only estimates of the real user's needs. By Theorem 1 the strategy chosen on the skeleton set S ensures that the probability of remaining within a perturbed set Q_η is minimal, η being a random perturbation coefficient of Q. Roughly speaking, the better the solution chosen fits into the set Q_η, the higher is the income I, on the other hand I should be monotonic with respect to the criteria F_1, F_2, ..., F_N. Thus we can conclude that I should be monotonically proportional to the utility function defined by the formula

$$G(u) = d\big(\tilde{F}(u), \partial Q\big) I_1\big(\tilde{F}(u)\big) + I_2\big(\tilde{F}(u)\big) \tag{7}$$

where $d(\cdot, \partial Q)$ is the distance to the boundary of Q, $\tilde{F} = (F_1, F_2, F_3)$, $\hat{F} = (F_4, F_5)$, and I_1 and I_2 are certain order representing functions defined so that the maximum of G were non-dominated and situated within $Q \times R^2$ (cf. also formula (9) in the final subsection). Let us denote that the values of I_1 and I_2 are entirely independent if the values of $\tilde{F}$ and $\hat{F}$ are not depending on each other.

Hence it follows that the maximal safety with respect to $\tilde{F}$ of a compromise solution chosen is not conflicting with the goal of optimizing F in $Q \times R^2$. According to the results of the preceding subsection, such a compromise value of F should be found on the skeleton curve S.

Since we do not impose any decision choice rule for the remaining criteria F_4 and F_5, we might consider two subcases:

1. $\tilde{F}$ and $\hat{F}$ are independent — then we get a family of solutions of form

$$\left(\tilde{F}_c, \hat{f}\right)_{f \in FP(U,\Theta)}$$

where $\tilde{F}_c$ is the compromise value of $\tilde{F}$ found on the skeleton curve S.

2. the values of $\hat{F}$ are uniquely determined by $\tilde{F}$ — then we get a unique solution

$$\left(\tilde{F}_c, \hat{F}(\tilde{F}_c)\right).$$

A simple example is presented below.

3.1 A simple numerical example

In the above model suppose that

$$\begin{aligned} F_{11} &= 2 \text{ months}, \\ F_{1u} &= 12 \text{ months}, \\ F_{21} &= 5000 \text{ kilograms}, \\ F_{2u} &= 25000 \text{ kilograms}, \\ F_{31} &= 10 \text{ meters}, \\ F_{3u} &= 50 \text{ meters}. \end{aligned}$$

Then we get

$$Q = \bigcap_{i=1}^{3} [F_{i1}, F_{iu}], \qquad q_1 := (2; 5000; 10), \qquad q_2 := (12; 25000; 50).$$

The decision space is defined as the intersection of Q and

$$\tilde{F}(u) := \Big\{ (x_1, x_2, x_3) \in R^3_+ : x_1 - 0.002x_2 + 3x_3 \le 100, \\ x_1^2 + 3(0.001x_2)^2 + 0.5x_3^2 \le 1600 \Big\},$$

where U is the set of available design strategies connected with the employment, investment of financial strategies which are not considered here.

The distance in R^3 which serves to define the safety coefficients inside Q is given by

$$d(x,y) = |x_1 - y_1| + \frac{|x_2 - y_2|}{1000} + |x_3 - y_3|.$$

Since F_1 is only minimized objective function, the criteria F_2 and F_3 can be equivalently taken into account in the minimization problem:

$$(F_1', F_2', F_3') \to \min \tag{8}$$

after the following transformation:

$$F_1' := -F_i, \qquad F_{i1}' := -F_{iu}, \qquad F_{iu} := -F_{i1}, \qquad i = 2,3 \tag{9}$$

Simultaneously,

$$F_1' := F_1; \qquad Q' := \bigcap_{i=1}^{3} [F_{i1}', F_{iu}'],$$

and

$$q_1' := (2; -25000; -50), \qquad q_2' := (12; -5000; -10).$$

After finding the skeleton curve S and the compromise solution f_c for the transformed problem (8)–(9), one should perform the transformation reverse to (9) to obtain the numerical values interpretable for the decision-maker.

There exist 4 breaking points in the skeleton curve S which can be found according to the construction algorithm given in (Gorecki et al., 1982; Gorecki and Skulimowski, 1987) and amount to

$$q_1 = (7, 10, 15); \qquad q_2 = (7, 15, 20); \qquad q_3 = (7, 15, 40); \qquad q_4 = (7, 20, 45);$$

The core $C(Q)$ is the rectangle

$$C(Q) := \left\{ (f_1, f_2, f_3) \in R^3 : f_1 = 7, \ 10 \le f_2 \le 20, \ 15 \le f_3 \le 45 \right\}.$$

The ordinal skeleton S_Q consists of $C(Q)$ and the intervals $[\tilde{F}_1, q_1]$ and $[q_4, \tilde{F}]$.

The compromise solution $\tilde{f}_c$ can be found on the interval $[q_3, q_4]$ and amounts to $(7; 15.58; 40.58)$. One can observe that in the above case $\bar{f}_c \in C(Q)$.

4 Final remarks

Another possibility of investigating the theoretical fundamentals of the method consists in interpreting the search for a non-domain solution on S as maximizing certain utility function φ which admits its local maxima on S. In this approach φ can be taken as the membership function of certain fuzzy set which describes the uncertainty of the demanded set Q. This function can have the form

$$\varphi_Q(x) := \frac{d(x, q_1) \cdot d(x, \partial Q)}{d(q_1, q_2) \max\{ d(y, \partial Q) : y \le_\Theta x \}}$$

It follows immediately from the above formula that φ_Q has the desired property mentioned above i.e.

$$0 \le \varphi_Q(x) \le 1; \qquad \varphi_Q(x) = 1 \Leftrightarrow x_2 = q; \qquad \arg\max\{ \varphi_Q(x) : x \le_\Theta q_1 \} \subset S;$$

and, moreover, φ_Q is order representing (Wierzbicki, 1980).

These properties could provide for a combination of fuzzy set theory and the skeleton method.

References

Gorecki, H. (1981). Problem of choice of an optimal solution in a multicriteria space. Proceedings of the 8th IFAC World Congress. Kyoto 1981; Pergamon Press, London, Vol. 10, pp. 106–110.

Gorecki, H., Dobrowolski, G., Kopytowski, J., Zebrowski, M. (1982). The Quest for a Concordance between Technologies and Resources as a Multiobjective Decision Process. In: M. Grauer, A. Lewandowski, and A.P. Wierzbicki, eds., Multiobjective and Stochastic Optimization, IIASA Collaborative Proc., Ser. CP-82-S12, Laxenburg, Austria, pp. 463–476.

Gorecki, H., Dobrowolski, G., Rys, T., Wiecek, M., Zebrowski, M. (1985). Decision Support System Based on the Skeleton Method — the HG Package. Interactive Decision Making, Proc. Sopron 1984, pp. 269–280.

Gorecki, H. and Skulimowski, A.M. (1986). A joint consideration of multiple reference points in multicriteria decision-making. *Found. Contr. Engrg.* 11; No. 2, pp. 81–94.

Gorecki, H. and Skulimowski, A.M. (1987). A decision support system based on reference points and its applications to design problems. Methodology and Software for Interactive Decision Support, Oct. 19–23, 1987, Albena, Bulgaria, IIASA, Laxenburg, Austria.

Skulimowski, A.M. (1985a). Solving vector optimization problems via multilevel analysis of foreseen consequences. *Found. Contr. Engrg.* 10; No. 1, pp. 25–38.

Skulimowski, A.M. (1985b). Generalized distance scalarization in Banach spaces. *Belgian J. Operations Research* 25; No. 1, pp. 3–16.

Wierzbicki, A.P. (1980). On the Use of Reference Objectives in Multicriteria Optimization. In: G. Fandel, T. Gal, eds., Multiple Criteria Decision Making — Theory and Application, Springer, Berlin–Heidelberg–New York, pp. 360–391.

Wiecek, M. (1984). The Skeleton Method in Multicriteria Problems. *Found. Contr. Engrg.* 9; No. 4, pp. 193–200.

Multicriteria Game Models and Negotiation Processes

V.A. Gorelik
Computing Center of the USSR Academy of Sciences
Moscow, USSR

1 Introduction

Recently questions connected with the analysis of conflict situations and negotiation processes have excited the common interest and become the subject of scientific investigations for economists, historians, politologists, sociologists, ecologists. Taking into consideration certain limitations of mathematical models and difficulty of checking its adequacy of reality in this field we want to consider these problems from the point of view of mathematics.

Generally there is a special area of mathematics, i.e. the game theory, for analysis of conflict situations. So it's natural to use game models in investigations of real conflicts and negotiation processes in different fields (for example, international trade agreements). However, to our regret, the game-theory approach is not widely used in practical researches. This is caused by a number of reasons, but the most important that there is no the common principle of optimal behaviour in the game theory. This means that the rational agreement from the point of view of one principle of optimality is not the same from the point of view of the other. As a result there is an element of subjectivity in the investigation of real conflicts connected with the choice of the conception of solution for corresponding game models.

There are at least two ways out of this situation: 1) to find such classes of game models which have just the same solutions for different principles of optimality; 2) to construct basing on an initial game which is a model of real conflict another dynamic game which describes a negotiation process of choosing acceptable agreement among those solutions which are connected with different principles of optimality.

2 Games with stable and Pareto optimal solutions

Our investigations show that conflicts and their game models have good structure which is characterized by the existence of stable and mutually profitable agreements if each participant has several criteria connected with different spheres of interests among which there are private, common and antagonistic goals. For example, let's consider two-person game in which each player has two efficiency criteria. One criterion describes personal achievements of the player in his own sphere of activity (let's name it internal sphere). We'll denote this criterion $F_i(u_i)$, $i = 1,2$. The second criterion describes achievements of the player in a competition with the other player in some common sphere of activity (let's name it external sphere). We'll denote this criterion $G_i(u_1, u_2)$, $i = 1,2$. Strategies (controls) of players u_1, u_2 are the proportions of distributions of resources or products between the internal and external spheres of activity. Thus the value of the first criterion of each player depends only on an amount of his own resources invested in internal sphere. The value of the second criterion of each player depends on strategies of both players because this criterion evaluates the relative achievements or influence in external (common) sphere.

The definition of these criteria is insufficient for describing exactly individual principles of behaviour. It's necessary to introduce one general criterion or to determine a concept of vector optimum. It's well known that there is a general criterion which is connected with one of the most used concepts of vector optimum — Pareto optimality. This criterion can be formed from several criteria by the operation of taking minimum ("estimation by worse result"). In our case it looks like

$$H_i(u_1, u_2) = \min\{\, F_i(u_i),\ \lambda_i G_i(u_1, u_2)\,\}, \qquad i = 1,2\ , \tag{1}$$

where λ_i is weighting coefficient. Each point of Pareto set in the space of two criteria (for one player knowing a strategy of the other player) can be obtained as a solution of maximization problem for criterion (1) with accordingly determined λ_i.

We'll suppose that individual preferences of players can be described by the criteria (1) with fixed λ_i, $i = 1,2$. Such transformation leads us to non-differential optimization which is connected with difficult mathematical problems. We'll not discuss these problems in detail because in the case considered here these difficulties can be easily overcome. It can be mentioned that for more general problems of such type rather convenient conditions of optimality and some interesting qualitive results are obtained.

Game models with criteria (1) are investigated in static and dynamic cases. In dynamic cases all criteria are determined in virtue of systems of multistep or differential equations. As an example we'll consider the economic system which can be described by linear differential equations

$$\left\{ \begin{array}{lcll} \dot{x}_i & = & (a_i u_i - \mu_i) x_i, & x_i(0) = x_i^0, \\ \dot{y}_i & = & a_i(1 - u_i) x_i - \delta_i y_i, & y_i(0) = y_i^0, \end{array} \right. \tag{2}$$

where phase variables x_i and y_i describe processes states in internal and external spheres correspondingly and the control $u_i \in [0,1]$. Real data for big economic systems show that the control of such type (for example a share of unproductive expenses) changes in time slowly, so we'll suppose in this paper that player's controls are constants as functions of time on fixed plan period $[O,T]$ (for program controls results are interesting but rather complicate and must be discussed separately).

Criteria $F_i(u_i)$, $G_i(u_1, u_2)$, $i = 1,2$, are supposed to be unimodal functions. More exactly $F_i(u_i)$ are unimodal functions with maximum points $u_i^+ \in (0,1]$, $G_i(u_1, u_2)$ as functions of u_i are unimodal with maximum points $u_i^- \in [0,1)$ and as functions of u_j increase for $u_j \geq u_j^-$, where $u_i^+ > u_i^-$, $i,j = 1,2$, $i \neq j$. These suppositions are in accordance with the meaning of criteria because the value u_i determines the share of resources in internal sphere and the value $1 - u_i$ determines the share of resources in external sphere. For dynamic variant of the model, for example, terminal criteria

$$\begin{aligned} F_i(u_i) &= x_i(T) - \hat{x}_i, \\ G_i(u_1, u_2) &= \lambda_i^i y_i(T) - \lambda_j^i y_j(T), \end{aligned} \tag{3}$$

which are determined in virtue of system (2), answer these suppositions. In (3) λ_i^i, λ_j^i are coefficients comparing achievements of participants in external sphere, $\hat{x}_i$ are standards in internal spheres.

Let us remind some concepts which we'll use further. The point (u_1^*, u_2^*) is (Nash) equilibrium point (situation), if

$$\begin{aligned} H_1(u_1^*, u_2^*) &\geq H_1(u_1, u_2^*) \qquad \forall u_1 \in [0,1], \\ H_2(u_1^*, u_2^*) &\geq H_2(u_1^*, u_2) \qquad \forall u_2 \in [0,1]. \end{aligned} \tag{4}$$

If inequalities (4) are strict under $u_1 \neq u_1^*$, $u_2 \neq u_2^*$, than the situation of equilibrium is called strict.

The point (u_1, u_2) is called Pareto optimal if there is no point (u_1', u_2'), for which

$$H_i(u_1', u_2') \geq H_i(u_1, u_2), \qquad i = 1, 2, \tag{5}$$

and at least one of inequalities (5) is strict.

The point (u_1, u_2) belong to γ-core C_γ if it is Pareto optimal and $H_i(u_1, u_2) \geq \gamma_i$, $i = 1, 2$, where

$$\begin{aligned} \gamma_1 &= \max_{u_1^- \leq u_1 \leq u_1^+} H_1(u_1, u_2^0(u_1)) = H_1(u_1^*, u_2^0(u_1^*)), \\ \gamma_2 &= \max_{u_2^- \leq u_2 \leq u_2^+} H_2(u_1^0(u_2), u_2) = H_2(u_1^0(u_2^*), u_2^*) \end{aligned} \tag{6}$$

and functions $u_i^0(u_j) = \operatorname{Arg\,max}_{u_i^- \leq u_i \leq u_i^+} H_i(u_1, u_2)$, $i, j = 1, 2$, are single value. Here γ_i is a result of player i when he is a leader, that is he plays first and communicates his choice to the other player (such game was introduced by Stackelberg in the case of single value functions $u_i^0(u_j)$ and was named a game with hierarchical structure and studied in general case by Gorelik and Kononenko (1982)).

For the game with criteria (1), where $F_i(u_i)$, $G_i(u_1, u_2)$ are unimodal functions, in particular, have form (3) and are determined by system (2), such results are valid:

1. there exists at least one situation of (Nash) equilibrium, all situations of equilibrium are strict and can be found with the aid of necessary and sufficient conditions

$$[F_i(u_i) - G_i(u_1, u_2)](u_i - u_i^-)(u_i - u_i^+), \qquad i = 1, 2; \tag{7}$$

2. if there are several equilibrium situations, then among them there is the best one for both participants, in which they gain more than in any other equilibrium situation;

3. if the function
$$G(u_1, u_2) = G_1(u_1, u_2) + G_2(u_1, u_2) \tag{8}$$
does not increase by u_1, u_2, in particular, $G(u_1, u_2) \equiv const$, then (u_1^*, u_2^*) is the unique situation of equilibrium, Pareto optimal and is a point of γ-core C_γ;

4. if additionally the function $G(u_1, u_2)$ decreases monotonously by one argument u_1 or u_2, then $C_\gamma = \{(u_1^*, u_2^*)\}$;

5. if equilibrium situation is unique then it is stable, that is any tatonnement process converges to it.

As examples show (Gorelik, 1986), conditions of monotonity for function $G(u_1, u_2)$, determined by (8), are essential (without these conditions properties 3 and 4 may be not valid). These conditions can be easily interpreted: thought achievements of each participant in external sphere decrease, when his opponent augments a share of resources here, summary achievements of both players don't change (closed system) or increase (maybe at the expense of third party). For dynamic variant of the model these conditions are equivalent $\lambda_i^i \geq \lambda_i^j$ $(\lambda_i^i > \lambda_i^j)$.

Results obtained can be generalized in the case of n-person game. We'll not discuss this case in detail here, only note that there also exists an equilibrium point under analogical suppositions and it is strong, that is even coalitions of players can not break it (Gorelik, 1986).

These results show that in the game of type considered different principles of optimal behaviour (equilibrium and Pareto optimality) give just the same solution. There is also no sense to struggle for leadership because in games with an arbitrary sequence of moves (with a hierarchical structure) equilibrium strategies (controls) are optimal for both players. Thus, in conflicts of such type there are stable and mutually profitable agreements. Moreover even individual actions of players which don't know or don't take into account interests of the other party lead to the same stable and Pareto optimal situation. It means that in such conflicts there is no a reason for negotiations, in spite of the fact that they are not antagonistic.

3 Negotiation processes

A subject for negotiations appears when equilibrium point isn't Pareto optimal, or there are several equilibrium situations among which players prefer different points, or there are no equilibrium points at all. Let's consider a case when there is unique and even stable equilibrium situation but it's not Pareto optimal. In this case players can achieve equilibrium point by means of individual actions trying to maximize their own gains. Here tatonnement process stops and players can't improve their positions acting individually. But there are situations which are more preferable for both players simultaneously than equilibrium situation. Now it's profitable for players to achieve some reasonable agreement. So in such situation individual behaviour is not efficient and group (collective) behaviour is preferable.

There are several principles of collective behaviour in the game theory connected with different axioms of choice (arbitration schemes, Shaply vector and so on). But there is one demerit inherent to these concepts of solutions, that is statical approach (one-step choice). This circumstance combined with instability of solutions reduces their practical significance. But real conflicts of such type can be usually resolved by means of negotiations, which are dynamic multistep process with intermediate suggestions and agreements. We'll try to describe this process using the game-theory approach.

So players have achieved an equilibrium situation by means of individual actions. It seems real conflicts often develop without resultive collective actions of participants till a definite moment. Then a process becomes stationary and players come little by little to an idea that they can't achieve better results, which are possible in principle, without collective actions. At this moment really resultive negotiations may begin. As negotiations are also a collision of interests we may describe them by a game which is a kind of superstructure on an initial game describing a real conflict (economic, trade, ecologic and so on). This new game is dynamic with the initial point (u_1^0, u_2^0), which is equilibrium point for the first game. At each step K one player by turns suggests a new point (agreement) $(\tilde{u}_1^K, \tilde{u}_2^K)$ and the other player accepts it or declines, that can be described by boolean variable δ^K. Thus we have dynamic process

$$u_i^K = \begin{cases} \tilde{u}_i^K, & \delta^K = 1, \\ u_i^{K-1}, & \delta^K = 0, \quad i = 1, 2, \quad K = 1, 2, \ldots, \end{cases} \tag{9}$$

which terminates in Pareto set, because further any suggestion more profitable for one player is less profitable for the other. Strategies of players are sequences

$$\left\{ (\tilde{u}_1^{2K-1}, \tilde{u}_2^{2K-1}),\, \delta^{2K},\, K = 1, 2, \ldots \right\}, \qquad \left\{ \delta^{2K-1},\, (\tilde{u}_1^{2K}, \tilde{u}_2^{2K}),\, K = 1, 2, \ldots \right\}, \tag{10}$$

where variables at each step are functions of preceding choice (a game with full information). New criteria of players in the dynamic multistep game must be determined on these strategies and trajectories of the process (9), for example, it may be the discounted sum

$$W_i = \sum_{K=0}^{\infty} \alpha_i^K H_i(u_1^K, u_2^K), \qquad i = 1, 2. \tag{11}$$

This multistep game may be investigated in traditional game-theoretical manner (for example, we can put a question of an equilibrium situation existence), but it seems more realistic approach is to estimate and to compare some heuristic strategies of type (10) basing on an imitation of the process (9). Such gaming can be used in a negotiation decision support system.

References

Gorelik, V.A. and Kononenko, A.F. (1982). Game-theoretical decision models in ecological-economical systems. Radio and Communication, Moscow (Russian).

Gorelik, V.A. (1986). About one class of games with stable and Pareto optimal solutions. *Problems of Control and Information Theory*, 15(4):309–318.

On the Class of Dynamic Multicriteria Problems in the Design of Experiments

M. I. Gusev
Institute of Mathematics and Mechanics
Ural Branch of the Academy of Science
Sverdlovsk, USSR

1 Introduction

The optimal design of experiments constitutes an important part in data processing. In the theory of the inverse problems in control system dynamics two basic procedures of the design of experiments are usually considered: the measurement allocation for estimation of the state of the system and the design of optimal inputs for systems parameters identification. Both these problems were studied carefully in control literature (Aoki and Staley, 1970; Athans, 1972; Herring and Melsa, 1974; Mehra, 1974 and others) for the systems with statistical description of unknowns. At the same time there exist applied problems concerned with the design of experiments for dynamic systems where either statistical description of disturbances is not available or disturbances are not probabilistic in their character. The models with setmembership description of unknowns, considered in the theory of control and observation under uncertainty conditions (Krasovski, 1968; Kurzhanski, 1977) appear to be more suitable in the last case.

The problem of choice of the optimality criterion for experiments arises within this models, because of it is impossible to use the standard statistical criteria, such as the trace of the error covariance matrix, or the trace of the Fisher information matrix, etc. Usually a maximal possible error of estimation is considered as a criterion instead of statistical characteristics.

Both problems of measurement allocation and of optimal inputs design can be considered within united general scheme. Further we describe this scheme and its detailing for each of the problems under consideration.

2 The design of experiments under uncertainty conditions (general statement)

A wide range of problems of estimations for dynamic systems, when the measurements are performed on a fixed interval of time, admit the following statement.

Let X, Y, Z be real Banach spaces, let operators $A : X \to Y$, $F : X \to Z$, a point $y \in Y$ and a set $W \subseteq X$ be given. It is necessary to find $z = Fw$ under the conditions $Aw = y$, $w \in W$. Here w may be treated as unknown input of the system, W gives an apriori information on w, y is the result of measurements of the output.

Let us assume, that $Z = R^N$, $z = (z_1, \ldots, z_N)^T$, $Fw = (\langle f_1, w\rangle, \ldots, \langle f_N, w\rangle)^T$, where f_i are linear continuous functionals. Let operator $A = A(u)$ depend on the control parameter $u \in U$, where U is a given set.

The experiments design procedure may be treated as follows. Consider two decision makers involved in the procedure. The first one (DM1) tries to get the best (in a certain sense) possible estimate of vector z from the results of measurement of y, while the second (DM2) controls the process of measurements, choosing control $u \in U$.

The aims of DM1 and DM2 do not coincide in general. The last circumstance leads to the game theoretic statement of the problem analogous to the one considered by Kurzhanski and Gusev (1978).

Here we assume that DM1 and DM2 have the same aim, this gives a possibility to suppose that choice of $u \in U$ and estimation of parameters z_i, $i = 1, \ldots, N$, are carried out by the unique DM.

Let A be linear continuous operator, $W = X$. Let DM obtain $y + \varsigma$ as the result of measurements instead of y, and all available information on error ς is given by the inequality $\|\varsigma\| \leq \delta$, where δ is known positive number. Consider an apriori estimate $\hat{z}_k = \langle b^k, y\rangle$, $b^k \in Y^*$ (Y^* denotes the space adjoin to Y) (Krasovski, 1968). Under the condition $\varsigma = 0$ the following equality should be fulfilled

$$\hat{z}_k = \langle b^k, y\rangle = \langle b^k, A^*(u)w\rangle = \langle A^*(u)b^k, w\rangle = \langle f^k, w\rangle,$$

hence $A^*(u)b^k = f^k$ ($A^*(u)$ denotes the operator adjoin to A). Maximal possible value of an error of estimation is given as follows ($\|\cdot\|_*$ is a norm in the space Y^*)

$$\max\{\, |\hat{z}_k - z| : \|\varsigma\| \leq \delta \,\} = \delta\|b^k\|.$$

Hence the best guaranteed value of an estimation error — $J_k(u)$ may be obtained as the solution to the following extremal problem

$$J_k(u) = \min\{\, \|b^k\|_* : A^*(u)b^k = f^k \,\} \tag{1}$$

The problem of the experiments design consists in the choice of $u \in U$, minimizing vector functional $J(u) = \big(J_1(u), \ldots, J_N(u)\big)$

It may be shown, under some assumptions, that $J_k(u)$ may be determined from the solution of the following "dual" problem (see, for example, Krasovski, 1968; Kurzhanski, 1977; Kurzhanski, 1983):

$$J_k(u) = \Big(\min\{\, \|A(u)w\| : \langle f^k, w\rangle = 1\}\Big)^{-1}.$$

So minimization of $J(u)$ is equivalent to maximization of $I(u) = (I_1(u), \ldots, I_N(u))$, where

$$I_k(u) = \min\{\, \|A(u)w\| : \langle f, w\rangle = 1\} \tag{2}$$

3 The measurement allocation problem

3.1 Geometrical restrictions

Consider the linear system on interval $T = [t_0, t_1]$

$$dx/dt = A(t)x, \qquad x(t_0) = x^0, \qquad t \in T, \tag{3}$$

and the equation of measurements

$$y(t) = G(t)x(t) + \varsigma(t), \tag{4}$$

where $x \in R^n$, $y \in R^m$, $\varsigma(t)$ is an error of measurements (initial vector x^0 is assumed to be unknown).

Let us assume that the measurable matrix function $G(t)$ takes its values in the given finite set of matrices $\{ G_1, \ldots, G_r \}$ and $\varsigma(t)$ is restricted to the inclusion

$$\varsigma(t) \in \Xi(G(t)), \qquad t \in T, \tag{5}$$

where $\Xi(G_i) = \Xi_i$, $i = 1, \ldots, r$ are convex compact sets.

It is necessary to specify function $G(t)$ which determines the allocation of measurements, so that to ensure the best estimate of scalar parameter $z = f^T x^0$ (vector $f \in R^n$ is assumed to be given). This problem constitute a special case of the one considered in the previous section, with $u = G(\cdot)$, $w = x^0$, $y = y(\cdot)$, $N = 1$, and input-output operator $A : x^0 \to y(\cdot)$ determined by the equations (3), (4).

Using the results on duality in observation theory (Krasovski, 1968; Kurzhanski, 1977; Kurzhanski, 1983) we can reduce calculation of the estimation error value to the solution of the following problem

$$I_p = \max_{G(\cdot)} \inf_{f^T l = 1} \max_{t \in T} \rho\Big(G(t)x(t,l) \mid \Xi^0(G(t))\Big)$$

Here $\rho(\cdot|\Xi)$ is a support function of Ξ, Ξ^0 denotes a set polar to Ξ, and $x(t, l)$ is a solution of the system (3) corresponding to the initial vector l.

Let us denote

$$\psi_q(x) = \rho(G_q x \mid \Xi_q^0), \qquad q = 1, \ldots, r,$$
$$\phi(l) = \max_{t \in T} \max_q \psi_q(x(t,l)).$$

It is not difficult to show that function $\phi(l)$ is convex.

Consider the following convex programming (dual) problem

$$I_d = \min\{ \phi(l) : l^T f = 1 \}.$$

Theorem 1 (duality theorem). Let there exists $k \in \{1, \ldots, r\}$, such that the pair $A(t)$, G_k is completely observable on T, and $0 \in \operatorname{int} \Xi(G_k)$. Then $I_p = I_d$.

The theorem states that the values of the primal and the dual problems coincide.

Theorem 2. Let l^* be the solution to the dual problem. Then the optimal measurement allocation function $G^*(t)$ may be specified as follows: $G^*(t) = G_{k(t)}$, $t \in T$ where

$$\psi_{k(t)}(x(t, l^*)) = \max_q \{ \psi_q(x(t, l^*)) : \quad q = 1, \ldots, r \}.$$

3.2 Integral restrictions

Consider the problem of measurement allocation for the system (3), (4), assuming that all available information on the errors is restricted to the integral inequality

$$\int_{t_0}^{t_1} \varsigma^T(t) R\big(G(t)\big) \varsigma(t)\, dt \le \mu^2 \tag{6}$$

instead of the inclusion (5). Here $R(G)$ is positive definite matrix for every $G \in \{G_1, \ldots, G_r\}$.

The solution of the problem with integral constraints may be obtained as follows. Consider the matrix differential equation

$$dP/dt = -PA - A^T P - G^T R^{-1}(G) G, \qquad t \in T, \tag{7}$$

with boundary condition $P(t_1) = 0$.

If the pair $A(t), G(t)$ is completely observable on T, then $P(t_0)$ is the positive definite matrix.

Consider the optimal control problem for the system (7): determine measurable function (control) $G(t)$ which takes values in the set $\{G_1, \ldots, G_r\}$ and minimizes functional

$$J(G(\cdot)) = f^T P^{-1}(t_0) f \to \min \tag{8}$$

Theorem 3. Every solution $G^*(\cdot)$ of the measurement allocation problem is the solution to the optimal control problem (7), (8) and vice versa.

Function $\Phi(P) = f^T P^{-1} f$ is convex on the cone of positive definite matrices. The optimal measurement allocation function $G(t)$ can be specified from the following maximum principle conditions.

Theorem 4. In order that $G^*(t)$ be the solution of the measurement allocation problem it is necessary and sufficient that

$$\langle S(t),\ G^{*T}(t) R^{-1}(G^*(t)) G^*(t) \rangle = \max\{\, \langle S(t),\ Q \rangle : Q \in \Theta \,\},$$

where $S(t)$ is the solution to the equation

$$dS/dt = -AS - S^T A, \qquad S(t) = (P^{-1}(t_0) f)(P^{-1}(t_0) f)^T,$$

$\Theta = \{G_1^T R^{-1}(G_1) G_1, \ldots, G_r^T R^{-1}(G_r) G_r\}$, $\langle A, B \rangle = \mathrm{tr} A^T B$ (tr denotes the trace of matrix).

The optimal guaranteed estimate of z is given as follows

$$\hat{z} = \int_T w^{*T}(t) (G^*(t) x(t) + \varsigma(t)) dt.$$

$$w^*(t) = P^{-1}(t_0) R(G^*(t)) X(t, t_0) f,$$

where $X(t, \tau)$ is the fundamental matrix of the system $dx/dt = A(t)x$.

The solution to the problem of measurements allocation with vector-valued functional and disturbances in the right hand side of the systems (3) is described by Gusev (1985).

4 Optimal inputs for system identification

Let us consider the problem of identification of the parameters of stationary control system

$$dx/dt = Ax + bu, \qquad x(0) = 0, \tag{9}$$

on the interval $[0,1]$ ($x \in R^n$, $u \in R$ is control parameter). Let us assume that vector $x(t)$ is accessible for measurements. It is necessary to reconstruct the matrix A and the vector b from the results of measurements of $x(t)$. It may be shown, that if $u \neq 0$ (as an element of L_2) then the necessary and sufficient condition of identifiability of A, b from the results of exact measurements of $x(t)$ is the complete controllability of the system (9). Denoting by w the vector $(a_{i1}, \ldots, a_{in}, b_i)$, $i = 1, \ldots, n$ we get the following infinite system of equations

$$x(t) = \sum_{j=1}^{n+1} w_j y_j(t), \qquad 0 \leq t \leq 1,$$

where

$$dy_j/dt = x_j(t), \quad j = 1, \ldots, n, \quad dy_{n+1}/dt = u(t), \quad y_j(0) = 0, \quad j = 1, \ldots, n+1.$$

Let us define operator $A : R^{n+1} \to C$ as follows

$$(Aw)(t) = \sum_{j=1}^{n+1} w_j y_j(t), \qquad 0 \leq y \leq 1,$$

Consider the problem of estimation of (f^k, w), $k = 1, \ldots, n+1$, ($f^k \in R^n$ are assumed to be given) under condition $(Aw)(t) = x_i(t)$, $0 \leq t \leq 1$.

Let $x_i(t)$ be given with an error non exceeding δ in the norm of the space C. Then the maximal value of estimation error can be obtained as the solution to the problem (1) (we neglect the influence of measurement errors on the operator A).

Let us consider the problem of the design of the input (control) $u(t)$ (selected from the given set $U = \{u(\cdot) \in L_2 : |u(t)| \leq 1\}$) which minimizes the value of estimation error. This problem may be reduced to the following optimal control problem:

- specify control $u(\cdot)$ which maximizes vector-valued functional

$$I(u(\cdot)) = (I_1, \ldots, I_n)(u(\cdot)),$$

$$I_k(u(\cdot)) = \min_{(f,w)=I} \max_{t \in [0,1]} \left| \sum_{j=1}^{n+1} w_j y_j(t) \right|,$$

on the trajectories of the linear control system

$$d/dt \begin{pmatrix} x \\ y \end{pmatrix} = \begin{pmatrix} A & 0 & 0 \\ 0 & I & 0 \\ 0 & 0 & 0 \end{pmatrix} \begin{pmatrix} x \\ y \end{pmatrix} + \begin{pmatrix} b \\ 0 \\ 1 \end{pmatrix} u, \qquad x(0) = 0, \qquad y(0) = 0 \tag{10}$$

We shall consider the special case of the last problem, arising when f^k, $k = 1, \ldots, n+1$, are coordinate vectors and linear functionals b^k from (1) are sought for in the form of

$\langle b^k, x(\cdot)\rangle = x(\tau_k)$. Here $\tau_k \in [0,1]$, $k = 1,\dots,n+1$, are given instants of time such, that $\tau_i \neq \tau_j$ if $i \neq j$.

In this case functionals $I_k(u(\cdot))$ from the "dual" problem (2) are determined by the equalities $I_k(u(\cdot)) = |y_k(\tau_k)|$ if

$$y_i(\tau_j) = 0 \qquad i \neq j, \qquad i,j = 1,\dots,n+1, \tag{11}$$

and $I_k\big(u(\cdot)\big) = -\infty$ otherwise.

So multicriteria control problem, arising from the problem of input design, takes the following form:

- specify control $u(\cdot) \in U$, that maximize vector functional

  $$I(u(\cdot)) = (|y_1(\tau_1)|,\dots,|y_{n+1}(\tau_{n+1})|)$$

  under the restrictions (10), (11).

Let us define function $\phi(l)$ as follows

$$\phi(l) = \inf_{p^i_j, i\neq j} \int_0^1 \Big|\sum_{j=1}^{n+1}(s(\tau,\tau_j,p^j)b + p^j_{n+1}\chi(\tau-\tau_j))\Big| d\tau \tag{12}$$

Here $p^i = (p^i_1,\dots,p^i_n)^T \in R^n$, $p^i_{n+1} \in R$, $l_i = p^i_i$, $i = 1,\dots,n+1$, $s(\tau,\tau_j,p)$ is the solution to the second order differential equation $d^2s/d\tau^2 = -ds/d\tau A^T$, with initial conditions $ds/d\tau(\tau_j) = p$, $s(\tau_j) = 0$, $\chi(\tau) = 1$ if $\tau \geq 0$ and $\chi(\tau) = 0$ if $\tau < 0$.

Theorem 5 (duality theorem). Let $\nu = (\nu_1,\dots,\nu_{n+1})^T$. There exists $u(\cdot) \in U$, such that conditions (10), (11) and equalities $y_i(\tau_i) = \nu_i$, $i = 1,\dots,n+1$, are fulfilled if and only if $\nu \in \partial\phi(0)$.
Here $\partial\phi(l)$ is the subdifferential of convex function ϕ at the point l.

The set $\partial\phi(0)$ is symmetric with respect to the origin, if rank $(b, Ab,\dots,A^{n-1}b) = n$ then $0 \in \text{int}\ \partial\phi(0)$.

Theorem 6. Let the system (9) be completely controllable, $u^*(\cdot)$ be Pareto optimal control in the problem (10), (11) and $y_i(\tau_i, u^*(\cdot)) = \nu_i$. Then

1. $\nu \in \text{fr}(\partial\phi(0))$;

2. there exist the solution l^* to the problem

   $$\phi(l) - \nu^T l \to \min$$

   and solution p^{i*}_j of the problem (12) with $p^i_j = l^*_i$;

3. the equality

   $$u^*(\tau) = \text{sign}\Big[\sum_{j=1}^{n+1} s(\tau,\tau_j,p^{j*})b + p^{j*}_{n+1}\chi(\tau-\tau_j)\Big]$$

   holds true.

Theorems 5, 6 permit to reduce the design of optimal input to the description of the boundary of subdifferential of convex function.

The solution of the problem of input design for the system (9) with energy constraints

$$\int u^2(\tau)d\tau \leq 1$$

can be obtained by the analogous way. The corresponding function $\phi(l)$ takes the following form: $\phi(l) = (l^T Q l)^{1/2}$, where Q is positive definite matrix. Matrix Q can be determined directly from the coefficients of the system (9), we omit the details here. The Pareto set (in the criteria space) constitute in this case the part of the boundary of the ellipsoid

$$\partial\phi(0) = \{\nu : \nu^T Q^{-1} \nu \leq 1\}$$

References

Aoki, M. and Staley, R. M. (1970). On input signal synthesis in parameter identification. *Automatica*, 6.

Athans, M. (1972). On the determination of optimal cost measurement strategies for linear stochastic systems. *Automatica*, 18, pp. 397–412.

Gusev, M. I. (1985). Multiple criteria problems of optimization of measurements for dynamic systems under uncertainty conditions. Proc. of the Institute of Math. and Mech. Evolution systems in the problems of estimation. Sverdlovsk.

Herring, K. D. and Melsa, J. L. (1974). Optimum measurements for estimation. *IEEE Trans. on Automatic Control*, AC-19(3), pp. 264–266.

Krasovski, N. N. (1968). Theory of control of motion. Nauka, Moscow.

Kurzhanski, A. B. (1977). Control and observation under conditions of uncertainty. Nauka, Moscow.

Kurzhanski, A. B. (1983). Evolution equations for problems of control and estimation of uncertain systems. Proc. of the Int. Congress of Mathematicians, August 16-24, 1983, Warsaw.

Kurzhanski, A. B. and Gusev, M. I. (1978). Multiple criteria game theoretic problems of control for systems with incomplete information. Proc. of the 7-th IFAC congress, Helsinki, 2, pp. 94–96.

Mehra, K. (1974). Optimal inputs for linear system identification. *IEEE Trans. on Automatic Control*, AC-19 (3), pp. 192–201.

Methodology of Hierarchical Multiobjective Optimization and its Use in the Planning of Agricultural Development

Zs. Harnos
University of Horticulture and Food Industry
Department of Mathematics and Computer Sciences
Budapest, Hungary

1 Introduction

From among the mathematical models applied for development of the various branches of the national economic planning, the multilevel (hierarchical) models represent a big model-family.

The characteristics of the hierarchical models derive from the organizational structure of the economy known from the planning practice:

- there is a central planning organization which — on the basis of information for the whole of the economy — makes decisions regarding the distribution of resources,
- there are the various sectors of the economy which, being aware of their own resource possibilities, make decisions about the proportions of production and use,
- there is some information relationship between the center and the sectors, this plays an important role in their decision-making.

The aim of the multi-level decision-making is the elaboration of such a plan that meets both central and sectoral conditions and central and sectoral optimum requirements. (The first type of the two-level decision-making models was elaborated in 1963 by Kornai and Lipták.)

It is also a characteristic feature of the multi-level decision-making that the goals of the center and the sectors do not always coincide by any means. The handling of the contradicting interests leads up to the use of the methodology of multiobjective optimization.

This paper presents a special multicriterial hierarchical model and its use in the planning of agriculture.

2 Background of the modelling work

The problem arose from the planning of agricultural development. In the past few years a research project was carried out on the developmental problems of Hungarian food and agriculture.

In this project the investigation of the following problems was stressed:

- short and long term possibilities of biomass utilization,
- the economic and environmental consequences of the more complete and rational utilization of the biomass produced year by year.

In the selection of the mathematical model the following viewpoint was paramount:

- Changing the behaviour of the system is possible over a longer period only. For this it is necessary to study the system in its dynamics.
- The operation of the system is determined basically by plant production, the productivity of the soil and the level of nutrient supply.

These factors are controlled by the allocation of financial resources. For this the system was described by a control problem, with the allocation of resources playing the role of control.

The model system is divided into three elements:

- plant production model,
- model of animal husbandry,
- the block of biomass utilization.

The first two models can be directly linked via feeding and product output respectively. The models of plant production and animal husbandry are connected by biomass utilization and the controlling conditions. The models presented here have been elaborated on two levels of aggregation. Relationships are described on the macro level by the more aggregated version, while the more detailed version are used to describe the production within regions or sectors. This solution was necessitated by two causes:

- the detailed model describing the production and utilization of biomass in the whole country is practically unsolvable because of its large size,
- real decision processes are better represented by a hierarchical structure.

Central planners make their decisions on the basis of macro-level relationships concerning the allocation of central resources, and formulate at the same time productions targets. The production structure is then set up by the sectors according to their preference system — which is not necessarily identical with central goals. We tried to represent these by a hierarchical model system as follows:

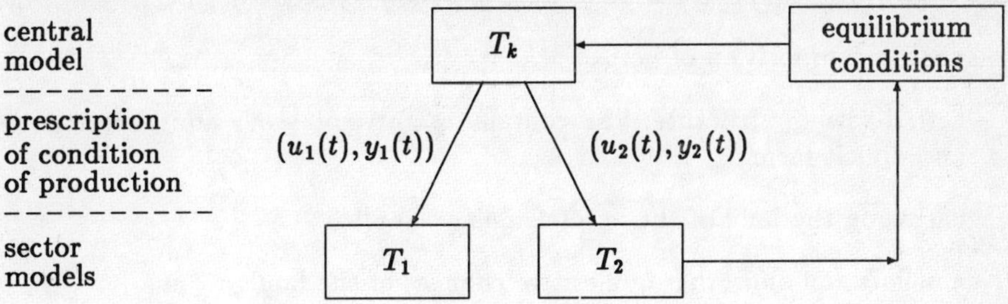

Figure 1

3 Mathematical model

The blocks of the model system — central model, plant production model and model of animal husbandry are developed by similar ways, therefore we give only the mathematical description of the plant production model (Csáki, Harnos and Láng, 1984).

Control conditions

$$\begin{aligned} B\underline{u}_N(t) &\le \underline{u}_N^0(t) \\ \underline{u}_N(t) &\ge \underline{0} \end{aligned}$$

State equation

$$\begin{aligned} \underline{x}_N(t+1) &= D\underline{x}_N(t) + E\underline{z}_N(t) + C\underline{u}_N(t) \\ \underline{x}_N(t_0) &= \underline{x}_N^0 \end{aligned}$$

Equations describing the functioning of the system

$$\begin{aligned} \underline{x}_N(t) &= F\underline{z}_N(t) \\ A\underline{z}_N(t) &= \underline{b}(t) \\ H_N(\underline{z}_N(t), \underline{y}_N(t), \underline{u}_N(t)) &\le 0 \end{aligned}$$

The output of the system (the product mix) is described by

$$\underline{y}_N(t) = \underline{G}(t)\underline{z}_N(t)$$

together with the constraints

$$\underline{y}_N^0(t) \le \underline{y}_N(t) \le \underline{y}_N^1(t)$$

The meaning of the different groups of conditions is as follows:

The characteristics of the production site in plant production — i.e. area of land available and its composition according to fertility classes — are represented by the state variables of the system.

The individual groups of variables have the following meanings:

$\underline{x}(t)$ – quality composition of lands

$\underline{z}(t)$ – actual sowing structure, also containing nutrient levels and agrotechnology in an implicit form

E – effects on the land of the agrotechnology applied

C – amelioration and other qualitative changes of the land.

The equality

$$\underline{x}_N(t) = F\underline{z}_N(t)$$

in the equations describing the functioning of the system refers to the utilization of available area, while the condition

$$A\underline{z}_N(t) \leq \underline{C}(t)$$

to the relationships of sowing structure, and the condition

$$H\left(\underline{z}_N(t), \underline{y}_N(t), \underline{u}_N(t), S(t)\right) \leq 0$$

to the connections between nutrient supply and product mix. Representing the product mix, $\underline{y}_N(t)$ is the output of the system, to be computed from sowing structure and average yields on the basis of the equality

$$\underline{y}_N(t) = \underline{G}(t)\underline{z}_N(t)$$

The matrix $\underline{G}(t)$ is for describing the development of yields, with the elements determined by using a prognoses.

The product mix, $\underline{y}_N$ is controlled by

- domestic consumption,
- fodder needs of animal husbandry,
- processing capacity of the food industry,
- raw material needs of different industrial sectors, and
- export-import possibilities.

We chose two types of objective function. One of them characterized the productivity of the arable land (Harnos, 1986), i.e. it served to regulate the change of productivity, the second described the economic targets.

4 The model structure

As is shown in Figure 1, the model system has a hierarchical feature, but it can be represented as one single system of inequalities.

In this case the matrix of coefficients has the following structure:

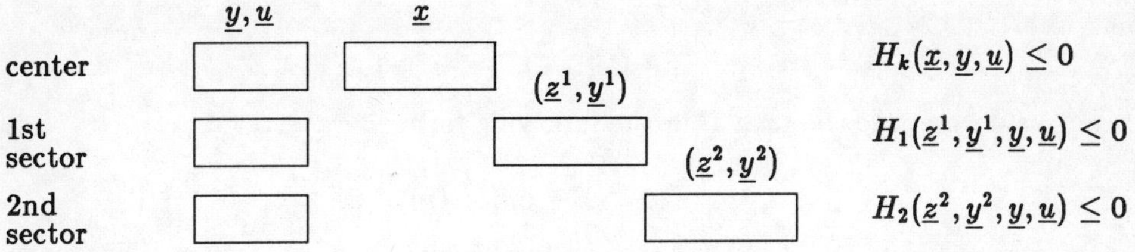

Figure 2

The conflicting interest of the center and the sectors can be expressed by the objective functions. Let f_k and f_i, $i = 1,2$ denote the objective functions belonging to the central and sector problems respectively, and let $\underline{f} = (f_k, f_1, f_2)$ be the common objective function of the problem. The basic task is to find the Pareto optimal solutions of the task T, i.e. we have to solve the following problems:

$$T: \quad \begin{array}{ll} P - \text{opt } f(\underline{x}, \underline{y}_1, \underline{y}_2) & \\ (\underline{x}, \underline{y}, \underline{u}) \in \Omega_k & \\ (\underline{z}^j, \underline{y}^j) \in \Omega_j(\underline{y}, \underline{u}) & j = 1,2. \end{array}$$

Here we used the following notion system:
The set of

$$\Omega_k = \left\{ (\underline{x}, \underline{y}, \underline{u}) \in R^{m+n+k};\ H_k(\underline{x}, \underline{y}, \underline{u}) \le 0 \right\}$$

denotes the feasible solutions of the central model, where $\underline{u} \in R^k$, $\underline{y} \in R^n$, $\underline{x} \in R^m$ denotes the control, decision and state variables respectively. The projection of the feasible solutions on the R^{n+k} represent the plans of centre:

$$P_k = \left\{ (\underline{y}, \underline{u}) \in R^{n+k};\ (R^m \times (y, u)) \cap \Omega_k \ne \emptyset \right\}$$

Every $(\hat{y}, \hat{u})$ central plan determines the set of feasible sector plans. The set

$$\Omega_j(\hat{y}, \hat{u}) = \left\{ (\underline{z}^j, \underline{y}^j) \in R^{m_j+n_j};\ H_j(\underline{z}^j, \underline{y}^j, \hat{y}, \hat{u}) \le 0 \right\}$$

represents the feasible solutions of the j-th sector belongs to the central plan

$$(\hat{y}, \hat{u}) \in P_k.$$

An $(\hat{y}, \hat{u})$ element of P_k is called consistent plan if

$$\Omega_j(\hat{y}, \hat{u}) \ne \emptyset \qquad j = 1,2.$$

The common solutions of the whole system are represented by the vector

$$(\underline{x}, \hat{y}, \hat{u}, \underline{z}^1, \underline{z}^2, \underline{y}^2)$$

where

$$(\underline{x}, \hat{y}, \hat{u}) \in \Omega_k, \qquad \text{and} \ \ (\hat{y}, \hat{u}) \ \ \text{is a consistent plan}$$

and

$$(\underline{z}^j, \underline{y}^j) \in \Omega_j(\hat{y}, \hat{u}), \qquad j = 1, 2.$$

Let us decompose the task T in the following form

$$T_k \ : \qquad \begin{array}{l} P - \text{opt } f_k(\underline{y}) \\ (\underline{x}, \underline{y}, \underline{u}) \in \Omega_k \end{array}$$

and

$$T_j(\underline{y}, \underline{u}) \ : \qquad \begin{array}{ll} P - \text{opt } f_j(\underline{y}^j), & j = 1, 2 \\ (\underline{z}^j, \underline{y}^j) \in \Omega_j(\underline{y}, \underline{u}) & \end{array}$$

It can easily be controlled if $(\underline{x}, \underline{y}, \underline{u})$ is an optimal solution of T_k i.e. (y, u) is a consistent plan and $(\underline{z}^j, \underline{y}^j)$ is an optimal solution of T_j, $j = 1, 2$, then $(\underline{x}, \underline{y}, \underline{u}, \underline{z}^1, \underline{z}^2, \underline{y}^2)$ is an optimal solution of T.

This observation means: the determination of some solution of T can be reduced on determination of smaller size, decomposed mathematical programming problems. The main problems connected with the shown hierarchical model are:

- how can a consistent plan be determined ?
- among the consistent plans how can an optimal solution be selected ?

We are unable to give a positive answer to the first question in general. However, if there is a special interrelationship between T_k and T_j, $j = 1, 2$, then the solutions of T_k formulate consistent plans.

Before formulating the theorem in exact terms, we introduce some notions. Supposing that T_k is linear and can be divided into three parts

$$H_k(x, y) = \begin{cases} H_k^1(\underline{x}, \underline{y}, \underline{u}) \leq 0 \\ H^2(\underline{x}, \underline{y}, \underline{u}) \leq 0 \\ H_0(\underline{x}, \underline{y}, \underline{u}) \leq 0 \end{cases}$$

where H_k^j $(j = 1, 2)$ represent the more aggregated version of the sector models.

The aggregation are connected with the coefficients of the system which express the efficiency of the investments and the productivity of land and animals on the central and sectoral levels.

As the detailed model is yet to be expounded, it is unnecessary to give the exact aggregation formula here. It can be found in (Harnos, 1985).

Theorem: Let us suppose the system T_k and T_j, $j = 1,2$ are linear, and T_k satisfies the conditions regarding the aggregation. If $(\underline{x}, \underline{y}, \underline{u})$ is a feasible solution of T_k, then $T_j(y, u) \neq 0$, i.e. $(\underline{y}, \underline{u})$ is a consistent plan.

From this theorem follows: The problem T is solvable independent of the objective function, i.e. (x, y, u) is a Pareto optimal solution of T_k and $(\underline{z}^j, \underline{y}^j)$, $j = 1,2$ are Pareto optimal solutions of T_j, $j = 1,2$ respectively, then $(\underline{x}, \underline{y}, \underline{u}, \underline{z}^1, \underline{y}^1, \underline{z}^2, \underline{y}^2)$ is a Pareto optimal solution of T.

The next simple example proves that the previous theorem is not valid in the general case.

Let us consider the following problem:

$$T_k : \quad \begin{aligned} & u_1 + u_2 \leq 1 \\ & y_k^1 + y_k^2 \leq 1 \\ & u_i \geq 0, \quad y_k^i \geq 0 \\ & 2y_k^1 + y_k^2 \to \max \end{aligned}$$

$$T_j : \quad \begin{aligned} & y_j \geq y_k^j \\ & \frac{1}{2} u_1 \geq y_j \\ & y_j \to \max \end{aligned}$$

It is easy to check

$$y_k^j = y_j = u_j = 0.5, \qquad j = 1,2$$

is an unique Pareto solution of T, but it cannot be derived from optimal solutions of T_k and T_j, $j = 1,2$, because the $(1, 0, u_1, u_2)$ form vectors construct the set of optimal solutions of T_k, and $\Omega_j(1, 0, u_1, u_2) = \emptyset$.

In many cases the T_k is not derived from T_j, $j = 1,2$, and so the determination of consistent plan causes a computation problem.

In this case the problem may be solved iteratively. In the first step we solve T_k. Let (y^*, u^*) denote the corresponding plan. There may be two cases if

$$\Omega_j(y^*, u^*) \neq \emptyset, \qquad j = 1,2,$$

then (y^*, u^*) is a consistent plan, and to solve T_j, $j = 1,2$ problems we obtain a solution T,

$$\text{if} \quad \Omega_j(y^*, u^*) = \emptyset, \qquad j = 1 \text{ or/and } 2,$$

then we modify the whole system. First we determine a solution of the T_j system by a modified goal function using y^* as a reference point.

Let y_j^{opt}, $j = 1,2$ denote the optimal solutions of T_j, $j = 1,2$. In the knowledge of y^*, y_1^{opt}, y_2^{opt} we formulate a new equilibrium condition $H(y^*, y_1^{\text{opt}}, y_2^{\text{opt}}) = 0$ and modify T_k. The set of feasible solutions of the new T_k system is

$$\Omega_k^1 = \Omega_k \cap \left\{ (x, y, u);\ H(y^*, y_1^{\text{opt}}, y_2^{\text{opt}}) \leq 0 \right\}.$$

We solve T_k again and continue this process. It can be seen from the construction that we successively receive better and better solutions.

We are not able to prove the convergence by this iteration process, but if in some iteration step the set Ω_j is not empty, then we obtain a consistent plan.

By using the tools of game theory the existence of consistent plan under some further condition can be proved (Sivák, 1983).

References

Csáki, Cs., Harnos, Zs. and Láng, I. (1984). Agricultural Development and Ecological Potential: The Case of Hungary. Kieler Wissenschaftsverlag Vauk.

Harnos, Zs. (1985). Mathematical modelling of agroecological system (in Hungarian), Budapest (dissertation).

Harnos, Zs. (1986). Perspectives for Developing the Land Component of the Biosphere Program. CP-86-22. IIASA, Laxenburg.

Harnos, Zs., Pór, A. and Sivák, J. (1983). A Hierarchical Multiobjective Planning Model. XII Hungarian Conference on Operations Research, Balatonfűred.

Kornai, J. and Lipták, I. (1963). Two level planning: game theoretical model and interactive computing process for solution of long term macro level planning problems (in Hungarian). MTA Matematikai Kutatóintézet Közleményei VII. évf., B sorozat, 4. füzet.

Sivák, J. (1983). The multilevel decision making and the model building (in Hungarian), Budapest (manuscript).

Algorithms for Bicriteria Combinatorial Optimization Problems

Naoki Katoh*
SDS Program
International Institute for Applied Systems Analysis
Laxenburg, Austria

1 Introduction

In recent years, many types of interactive optimization methods have been developed in order to support multicriteria decision makings (see the book by Sawaragi, Nakayama and Tanino, 1985 and Wierzbicki and Lewandowski, 1987). Given a ***feasible decision set*** $X \subseteq R^n$, and p objective functions, $f_1, f_2, \ldots, f_p$ (all are assumed to be minimization for convenience), the following problem has been used in various situations of interactive multicriteria decision makings:

$$\underset{x \in X}{\text{minimize}} \max_{1 \leq i \leq p} \{\alpha_i f_i(x) + \beta_i\}, \tag{1}$$

where α_i and β_i are positive and real constants respectively, which are computed based on the information supplied by the decision maker and/or the decision support system. For example, α_i and β_i are determined from aspiration and reservation levels in the reference point method which is one of the well known methods used in interactive multicriteria decision support systems (see Wierzbicki and Lewandowski, 1987, for the survey of reference point methods).

In view of this, it is of great significance to study the computational complexity required for solving the problem (1).

We concentrate on the case where $p = 2$ and each single objective problem P_i, $i = 1, 2$ defined below

$$P_i : \quad \underset{x \in X}{\text{minimize}} \ f_i(x) \tag{2}$$

is a minimum cost circulation problem (SMCP). Both problems are assumed to have optimal solutions. We shall study problem (1) with such restrictions, which we call a *bicriteria minimum-cost circulation problem* (BMCP). Given a directed graph $G = (V, E)$, where V and E denote the sets of vertices and edges respectively, a single objective

*On leave from Department of Management Science, Kobe University of Commerce, Japan

minimum-cost circulation problem (SMCP) can be written as follows.

$$\text{SMCP}: \quad \text{minimize} \sum_{e\in E} c(e)x(e) \tag{3}$$

subject to

$$\left\{ \sum x(e) \mid e = (u,v) \in E \right\} = \left\{ \sum x(e') \mid e' = (v,w) \in E \right\} \text{ for } v \in V \tag{4}$$

$$a(e) \leq x(e) \leq b(e) \text{ for } e \in E. \tag{5}$$

Here $a(e)$, $b(e)$ and $c(e)$ are given integer numbers. $a(e) = -\infty$ and $b(e) = +\infty$ are allowed. Hence the feasible set X of SMCP and BMCP is the set of vectors $\{ x(e) \mid e \in E \}$ satisfying (4) and (5).

Let the objective functions f_1 and f_2 for Problem BMCP be

$$f_1(x) = \sum_{e\in E} c_1(e)x(e) \quad \text{and} \quad f_2(x) = \sum_{e\in E} c_2(e)x(e), \tag{6}$$

and define

$$g_i(x) = \alpha_i f_i(x) + \beta_i, \qquad i = 1,2, \tag{7}$$

where $c_1(e)$ and $c_2(e)$ are integers.

Recently Tardos (1985) discovered a strongly polynomial algorithm for SMCP. Roughly speaking, an algorithm is called *strongly polynomial* if the running time is polynomially bounded only in the number of input data but not in the input size (see Tardos, 1986, for the precise definition of "strongly polynomial"). The best known strongly polynomial algorithm for SMCP is due to Galil and Tardos (1986), which runs in $0(n^2(m + n\log n)\log n)$ time, where $n = |V|$ and $m = |E|$. See (Fujishige, 1986) and (Orlin, 1984) for other versions of strongly polynomial algorithms for SMCP.

The major goal of this paper is to propose a strongly polynomial algorithm for solving Problem BMCP.

Notice that BMCP can be equivalently transformed to the following form:

$$\begin{aligned} \text{BMCP'}: \quad & \text{minimize } z \\ & \text{subject to } x \in X \text{ and} \\ & \qquad g_i(x) \leq z, \quad i = 1,2 \,. \end{aligned}$$

Such formulation has been used in the more general setting in order to solve problem (1) (see Chapter 7 of the book by Sawaragi, Nakayama and Tanino, 1985). This approach may not be recommended in case the set X has a good structure, since the new constraints $g_i(x) \leq z$, $i = 1,2$ added to the original feasible decision set X may destroy the good structure of X. In our problem, we cannot guarantee any more the total unimodularity of the constraint matrix associated with the constraints for the above problem BMCP'.

The algorithm proposed here, on the other hand, does not use the above formulation, but takes full advantage of the good structure of the constraints (4) and (5). It employs as a subroutine the strongly polynomial algorithm for solving Problem SMCP by Galil and Tardos (1986) and finds an optimal solution of Problem BMCP in

$O(\min\{n^6 \log^3 n, n^4(m + n \log n) \log^5 n\})$ time. The techniques we use are related to Megiddo (1979, 1983), though our problem is different form those treated in Megiddo (1979, 1983). We shall also show that the idea developed to solve BMCP can be applied to solve two other variants of BMCP.

2 Basic concepts and properties

The following auxiliary problem with nonnegative parameter λ plays a central role in our algorithm.

$$P(\lambda) : v(\lambda) \equiv \text{minimize}\{\, f_1(x) + \lambda f_2(x) \mid x \in X \,\} \tag{8}$$

It is well known (see Gal, 1984, for example) that the function $v(\lambda)$ is piecewise linear and concave in λ, as illustrated in Figure 1, with a finite number of joint points $\lambda_{(1)}, \lambda_{(2)}, \ldots, \lambda_{(N)}$ with $0 < \lambda_{(1)} < \lambda_{(2)} < \ldots < \lambda_{(N)}$. Here N denotes the number of total joint points, and let $\lambda_{(0)} = 0$ and $\lambda_{(N+1)} = \infty$ for convenience. Define for each $\lambda \in [0, \infty)$

$$X^*(\lambda) \equiv \{\, x \in X \mid x \text{ is optimal to } P(\lambda) \,\} \tag{9}$$

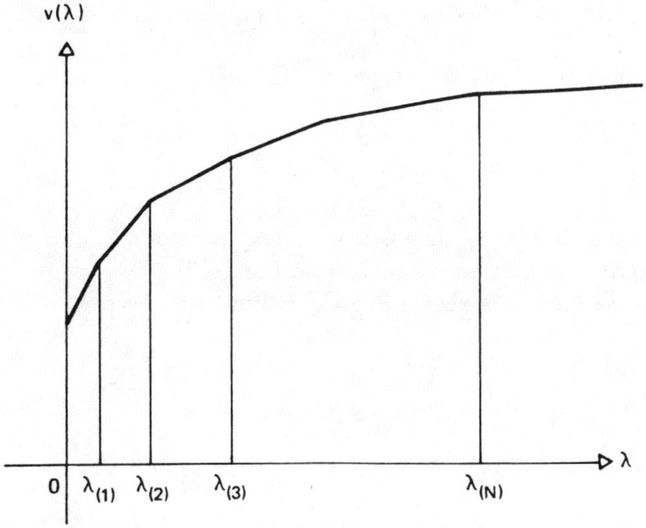

Figure 1: Illustration of $v(\lambda)$.

The following lemma is well known in the theory of linear parametric programs (see Gal, 1984, for the survey of this topic).

Lemma 1. For any $\lambda \in (\lambda_{(k-1)}, \lambda_{(k)})$, $k = 1, \ldots, N+1$, and any $x \in X^*(\lambda)$, $x \in X^*(\lambda')$ holds for all $\lambda' \in [\lambda_{(k-1)}, \lambda_{(k)}]$.

□

By Lemma 1, $X_k^* = X^*(\lambda)$ holds for any $\lambda \in (\lambda_{(k-1)}, \lambda_{(k)})$. We use the notation $f(x)$ to stand for a vector $(f_1(x), f_2(x))$. Let

$$Y = \{\, (f_1(x), f_2(x)) \mid x \in X \}.$$

The set Y is illustrated in Figure 2. The thick piecewise linear curve in the figure is the efficient set.

Lemma 2.

(i) For any two $x, x' \in X_k^*$ with $1 \le k \le N+1$, $f_1(x) = f_1(x')$ and $f_2(x) = f_2(x')$ hold.

(ii) For any $x \in X_{k-1}^*$ and any $x' \in X_k^*$ with $2 \le k \le N+1$, $f_1(x) < f_1(x')$ and $f_2(x) > f_2(x')$ hold.

□

Therefore, we use the notation x^k to stand for any x that is optimal to $P(\lambda)$ for all $\lambda \in [\lambda_{(k-1)}, \lambda_{(k)}]$.

Lemma 3.

(i) For any $\lambda \ge 0$ and any $x \in X^*(\lambda)$, $f(x)$ is weakly efficient.

(ii) For any $\lambda > 0$ and any $x \in X^*(\lambda)$, $f(x)$ is efficient.

(iii) For any x^k, $k = 1, 2, \ldots, N+1$, $f(x^k)$ is a vertex of set Y.

□

As k increases from 1 to $N+1$, the efficient vertex corresponding to x^k moves from top-left to bottom-right in the objective place (see Figure 2).
The following lemma gives a basis for our algorithm.

Lemma 4.

(i) If $g_1(x^1) > g_2(x^1)$, then x^1 is optimal to Problem BMCP.

(ii) If $g_1(x^{N+1}) < g_2(x^{N+1})$, then x^{N+1} is optimal to Problem BMCP.

(iii) If neither (i) nor (ii) holds, there exists k^* with $1 \le k^* \le N$ such that

$$g_1(x^{k^*}) \le g_2(x^{k^*}) \quad \text{and} \quad g_1(x^{k^*+1}) \ge g_2(x^{k^*+1}) \tag{10}$$

hold. Letting μ be the solution of the following linear equation

$$\mu g_1(x^{k^*}) + (1-\mu) g_1(x^{k^*+1}) = \mu g_2(x^{k^*}) + (1-\mu) g_2(x^{k^*+1}), \tag{11}$$

then

$$x^* = \mu x^{k^*} + (1-\mu) x^{k^*+1} \tag{12}$$

is an optimal solution of BMCP. □

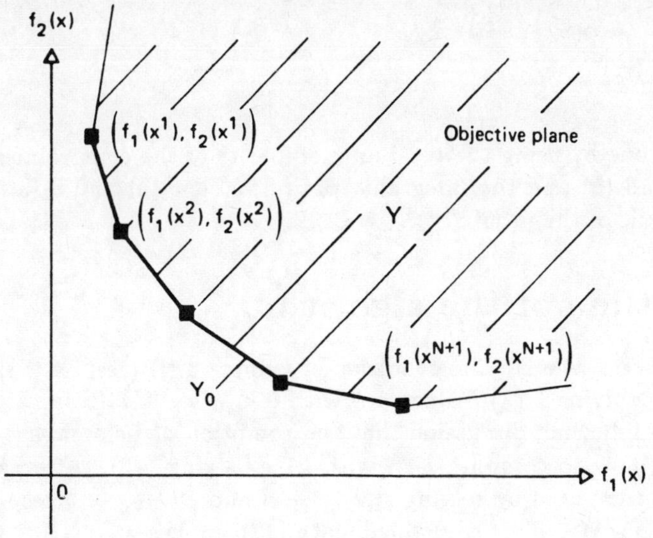

Figure 2: Illustration of the set Y and efficient vertices.

Proof. (i) If x^1 is not optimal to BMCP, there exists $\hat{x} \in X$ such that $f_1(\hat{x}) < f_1(x^1)$ and $f_2(\hat{x}) < f_1(x^1)$ hold. $f_1(\hat{x}) < f_1(x^1)$ implies that x^1 is not optimal to $P(0)$, but x^1 is optimal to $P(0)$ by Lemma 1. This is a contradiction. (ii) is proved in a manner similar to (i). (iii) First note that by Lemma 2 (ii) and by definition of $g_i(x)$, there exists k^* such that x^{k^*} and x^{k^*+1} satisfy (10). In addition, by Lemma 2 (ii), the linear equation of (11) in μ has a unique solution satisfying $0 \leq \mu \leq 1$. x^* defined by (12) is then optimal to $X^*(\lambda_{(k^*)})$ by Lemma 1, and $f(x^*)$ is efficient by Lemma 3 (ii). It follows from (11) and (12) that

$$g_1(x^*) = g_2(x^*)$$

holds. Since $f(x^*)$ is efficient, there is no $x \in X$ such that $f_1(x) < f_1(x^*)$ and $f_2(x) < f_2(x^*)$ hold. Thus there is no $x \in X$ such that $g_1(x) < g_1(x^*)$ and $g_2(x) < g_2(x^*)$ by (7) and $\alpha_1, \alpha_2 > 0$, implying that there is no $x \in X$ such that $\max\{g_1(x), g_2(x)\} < \max\{g_1(x^*), g_2(x^*)\}$ holds.

□

Lemma 5. Let

$$\begin{aligned} a_1 &= \max\Big\{ \max\{\,|a(e)| \mid e \in E,\ a(e) \text{ is finite}\,\}, \\ &\qquad \max\{\,|b(e)| \mid e \in E,\ b(e) \text{ is finite}\,\}\Big\}, \quad (13) \\ a_2 &= \max\{\,|c_i(e)| \mid i = 1, 2,\ e \in E\,\}, \quad (14) \end{aligned}$$

and

$$M = (n + 2m)ma_1a_2. \quad (15)$$

Then

$$\lambda_{(1)} \geq M^{-1}, \qquad \lambda_{(N)} \leq M \quad (16)$$

and

$$\lambda_{(k+1)} - \lambda_{(k)} \geq 1/M^2, \qquad k = 1, \ldots, N-1 \tag{17}$$

hold.

□

The proof is done by using the total unimodularity of the constrained matrix associated with (4) and (5) and the integrality of $a(e)$, $b(e)$, $c_1(e)$ and $c_2(e)$. See (Katoh, 1987) for the details of the proof.

3 The outline of the algorithm

By Lemma 5, the test whether the condition of Lemma 4 (i) (resp. 4 (ii)) holds or not is simply done by solving $P(\lambda)$ for some λ with $0 < \lambda < 1/M$ (resp. $\lambda > M$). Thus, we assume in the following discussion that the condition of Lemma 4 (iii) holds, and we shall focus on how to compute $\lambda_{(k^*)}$ with k^* satisfying (10). After $\lambda_{(k^*)}$ is found, x^{k^*} and x^{k^*+1} are computed by solving $P(\lambda_{(k^*)} - \epsilon)$ and $P(\lambda_{(k^*)} + \epsilon)$ respectively. Here ϵ satisfies $0 < \epsilon < 1/M^2$. This is justified since (17) implies $\lambda_{(k^*)} - \epsilon \in (\lambda_{(k^*-1)}, \lambda_{(k^*)})$ and $\lambda_{(k^*)} + \epsilon \in (\lambda_{(k^*)}, \lambda_{(k^*+1)})$. Then x^* can be computed by (11) and (12).

The idea of finding $\lambda_{(k^*)}$ is similar to the one given by Megiddo (1979). It tries to solve $P(\lambda_{(k^*)})$ by applying the algorithm of Galil and Tardos (the *GT-algorithm*) without knowing the exact value of $\lambda_{(k^*)}$. The computation path of the GT-algorithm may contain conditional jump operations, each of which selects proper computation path depending upon the outcome of comparing two numbers. Notice that the GT-algorithm contains arithmetic operations of only additions, subtractions, multiplications and divisions, and comparisons of the numbers generated from the given problem data, and that when applying the GT-algorithm to solve $P(\lambda)$ with λ treated as unknown parameter, the numbers generated in the algorithm are all linear functions of λ or constants not containing λ. Note that comparisons are necessary at conditional jumps. If a comparison for a conditional jump operation is made between two linear functions of $\lambda_{(k^*)}$, the condition can be written in the form of

$$\lambda_{(k^*)} > \hat{\lambda}, \qquad \lambda_{(k^*)} = \hat{\lambda} \quad \text{or} \quad \lambda_{(k^*)} < \hat{\lambda} \tag{18}$$

for an appropriate critical constant $\hat{\lambda}$, which can be determined by solving the linear equation in $\lambda_{(k^*)}$ constructed from the compared two linear functions. Here λ is assumed to be positive since otherwise $\hat{\lambda} < \lambda_{(k^*)}$ is clearly concluded.

An important observation here is that condition (18) can be tested without knowing the value $\lambda_{(k^*)}$. For this, solve $P(\hat{\lambda} - \epsilon)$, $P(\hat{\lambda})$ and $P(\hat{\lambda} + \epsilon)$ by the GT-algorithm, where $\hat{\lambda}$ is now a known constant, and ϵ is a positive constant satisfying $\epsilon < 1/2M^2$. Let x, x', x'' be the obtained solutions of $P(\hat{\lambda} - \epsilon)$, $P(\hat{\lambda})$ and $P(\hat{\lambda} + \epsilon)$ respectively. First we test whether $\hat{\lambda}$ is a joint point or not, based on the following lemma.

Lemma 6. (Katoh, 1987). Let x, x' and x'' be those defined above. Then $\hat{\lambda}$ is a joint point if and only if the following linear equation in λ has the unique solution λ' equal to $\hat{\lambda}$.

$$f_1(x) + \lambda f_2(x) = f_1(x'') + \lambda f_2(x''). \qquad \square$$

After computing x, x' and x'' defined above, the algorithm proceeds as follows. If one of x, x' and x'' (say, $\hat{x}$) satisfies

$$\alpha_1 f_1(\hat{x}) + \beta_1 = \alpha_2 f_2(\hat{x}) + \beta_2, \tag{19}$$

$\hat{x}$ is an optimal solution of BMCP by Lemma 3 (i). So, assume in what follows that none of x, x', x'' satisfies (19). Depending upon whether $\hat{\lambda}$ is a joint point or not, consider the following two cases.

Case 1. $\hat{\lambda}$ is not a joint point. We then compare the two values $g_1(x')$ and $g_2(x')$. Two subcases are possible.

Subcase 1A. $g_1(x') < g_2(x')$. Then $\lambda^* > \hat{\lambda}$ is concluded, and the algorithm chooses the computation path corresponding to $\lambda^* > \hat{\lambda}$.

Subcase 1B. $g_1(x') > g_2(x')$. Then $\lambda^* < \hat{\lambda}$ is concluded, and the algorithm chooses the computation path corresponding to $\lambda^* < \hat{\lambda}$.

Case 2. $\hat{\lambda}$ is a joint point. Then we consider the following three subcases.

Subcase 2A. $g_1(x'') < g_2(x'')$. Then $g_1(x) < g_2(x)$ follows and $\lambda^* > \hat{\lambda} + \epsilon$ holds. The algorithm chooses the computation path corresponding to $\lambda^* > \hat{\lambda}$.

Subcase 2B. $g_1(x) > g_2(x)$. Similarly to Subcase 2A, $g_1(x'') > g_2(x'')$ follows. This implies $\lambda^* < \hat{\lambda} - \epsilon$ and the algorithm chooses the computation path corresponding to $\lambda^* < \hat{\lambda}$.

Subcase 2C. $g_1(x) < g_2(x)$ and $g_1(x'') > g_2(x'')$. Then $\hat{\lambda}$ is the desired joint point $\lambda_{(k^*)}$ by Lemma 4 (iii). By Lemma 5 and $0 < \epsilon < 1/M^2$, $x \in X^*_{k^*}$, and $x'' \in X^*_{k^*+1}$ follow. Therefore, by Lemma 4 (iii), an optimal solution x^* of BMCP is found by (11) and (12) after letting $x^{k^*} = x$ and $x^{k^*+1} = x''$.

With this observation the algorithm starts with the initial interval $(\underline{\lambda}, \overline{\lambda}$, where $\underline{\lambda}$ and $\overline{\lambda}$ are typically determined by $\underline{\lambda} = 1/(M+1)$, $\overline{\lambda} = M+1$, and every time it performs the conditional jump operation, the critical value $\hat{\lambda}$ is computed, and $P(\hat{\lambda}-\epsilon)$, $P(\hat{\lambda})$ and $P(\hat{\lambda}+\epsilon)$ are solved. Depending upon the cases explained above, the length of the interval may be reduced in such a way that the desired joint point $\lambda_{(k^*)}$ exists in the reduced interval. It can be easily shown that Subcase 2C always occurs during the course of the algorithm, which proves the correctness of our algorithm. Since the GT-algorithm requires $O(n^2(n \log n + m) \log n)$ jump operations, and at each jump operation at most three minimum cost circulation problems, i.e., $P(\hat{\lambda} - \epsilon)$, $P(\hat{\lambda})$ and $P(\hat{\lambda} + \epsilon)$, are solved by calling the GT-algorithm, the entire algorithm requires $O(n^4(n \log n + m)^2 \log^2 n)$ time in total.

Theorem 1. BMCP can be solved in $O(n^4(n \log n + m)^2 \log^2 n)$ time.

□

The algorithm is in fact strongly polynomial, since the running time depends only on the numbers of vertices and edges in a graph.

The running time $O(n^4(n \log n + m)^2 \log^2 n)$ can be further reduced to $O(\min\{n^4(n \log n+m) \log^5 n, n^6 \log^3 n\})$ by applying the idea of Megiddo (1983). Instead of using $O(n \log n + m)$ shortest path algorithm when applying the GT-algorithm, a parallel shortest path algorithm such as (Dekel, Nassimi and Sahni, 1981) and (Kucěra, 1982) is simulated in a serial manner. We omit the details here. See (Katoh, 1987) for the details of the time reduction.

4 Extensions

We mention two other variants of BMCP for which we can develop a strongly polynomial time algorithm with the same running time as the one explained in the previous section.

The first problem is the minimum-cost circulation problem with one additional linear constraint (MCPLC), which is described as follows.

$$\begin{aligned} \text{MCPLC:} \quad & \text{minimize } f_1(x) \\ & \text{subject to } x \in X \text{ and } f_2(x) \le d. \end{aligned} \tag{20}$$

Here f_1 and f_2 are those defined in (6), and d is a given constant. This problem was studied by Brucker (1983), but he did not give a strongly polynomial time algorithm.

The above problem is solved as follows. It is easy to see that there exists an optimal solution x^* of MCPLC such that $f(x^*)$ is efficient. Define x^k, $k = 1, \ldots, N+1$, as before. If $f_2(x^1) \le d$, x^1 is optimal to MCPLC. If $f_2(x^{N+1}) > d$, there is no feasible solution to MCPLC. So assume $f_2(x^{N+1}) \le d < f_2(x^1)$. Let

$$\lambda_{(k_1)} = \min\{\, \lambda_{(k)} \mid 1 \le k \le N,\ f_2(x^{k+1}) \le d \}, \tag{21}$$

$$\lambda_{(k_2)} = \max\{\, \lambda_{(k)} \mid 1 \le k \le N,\ f_2(x^{k+1}) > d \}. \tag{22}$$

Lemma 7. Let μ satisfy

$$\mu f_2(x^{k_1+1}) + (1-\mu) f_2(x^{k_2+1}) = d. \tag{23}$$

Then

$$x^* = \mu x^{k_1+1} + (1-\mu) x^{k_2+1} \tag{24}$$

is optimal to MCPLC.

Proof. By (6), x^* satisfies $f_2(x^*) = d$ and $f(x^*)$ is efficient since $f(x^{k_1+1})$ and $f(x^{k_2+1})$ are adjacent efficient vertices by (21), (22) and Lemma 3. Thus, there is no $x \in X$ such that $f_1(x) < f_1(x^*)$ and $f_2(x) \le f_2(x^*)$ hold. This proves the lemma. □

By the lemma, all what we do is to compute $\lambda_{(k_1)}$ and $\lambda_{(k_2)}$. Once $\lambda_{(k_1)}$ and $\lambda_{(k_2)}$ are obtained, x^{k_1+1} (resp. x^{k_2+1}) are computed by solving $P(\lambda_{(k_1)} + \epsilon)$ (resp. $P(\lambda_{(k_2)} + \epsilon)$), where ϵ satisfies $0 < \epsilon < 1/M^2$. Computation of $\lambda_{(k_1)}$ and $\lambda_{(k_2)}$ is done in a manner similar to the way of finding $\lambda_{(k^*)}$ given in Section 3 by following the GT-algorithm to solve $P(\lambda_{(k_1)})$ (or $P(\lambda_{(k_2)})$) without knowing the exact value of $\lambda_{(k_1)}$ (or $\lambda_{(k_2)}$). In addition, we can also apply the idea of the time reduction given in Section 3 and Problem MCPLC can be solved in $O(\min\{n^6 \log^3 n, n^4(n \log n + m) \log^5 n\})$ time.

The second problem is described as follows:

$$\underset{x \in X}{\text{minimize}} \left\{ \sum_{i=1}^{2} (\alpha_i |f_i(x) - q_i|^p) \right\}^{\frac{1}{p}},$$

where p is a positive integer constant, q_i are real constants and α_i are positive constants. This problem arises in the following situation of interactive multicriteria decision making. Consider the situation in which only aspiration level $q = (q_1, q_2)$ is specified by the decision maker and q is unattainable. In this case, the distance between $f(x)$ and q can be considered to represent a measure of regret resulting from unattainability of $f(x)$ to q. If we measure the distance by the weighted l_p-norm, we have the above problem.

Because of the space constraint of the paper, we do not give the details of the algorithm (see Katoh, 1987). However, we notice that this problem can be solved in the same running time as the above two problems.

References

Brucker, P. (1983). Parametric programming and circulation problems with one additional linear constraint. *Osnabrücker Schriften zur Mathematik*, Reihe P, Heft 56, Fachbereich Mathematik, Universität Osnabrück.

Dekel, E., Nassimi D. and Sahni S. (1981). Parallel matrix and graph algorithms. *SIAM J. Comput.*, 10, pp. 657–675.

Fujishige, S. (1986). A capacity-rounding algorithm for the minimum-cost circulation problem: a dual framework of the Tardos algorithm. *Mathematical Programming*, 35, pp. 298–308.

Gal, T. (1984). Linear parametric programming — a brief survey. *Mathematical Programming Study*, 21, pp. 43–68.

Galil, Z. and Tardos E. (1986). An $0(n^2(m + n \log n) \log n)$ min-cost flow algorithm. Proceedings of 27th Annual IEEE Symposium on Foundations of Computer Science, pp. 1–9.

Katoh, N. (1987). An efficient algorithm for bicriteria minimum-cost circulation problem. Working paper WP-87-98, IIASA, Laxenburg, Austria.

Kučera, L. (1982). Parallel computation and conflicts in memory access. *Information Processing Letters*, 14, pp. 93–96.

Megiddo, N. (1979). Combinatorial optimization with rational objective functions. *Math. Oper. Res.*, 4, pp. 414–424.

Megiddo, N. (1983). Applying parallel computation algorithm in the design of serial algorithms. *J. ACM*, 30, pp. 852–865.

Orlin, J.B. (1984). Genuinely polynomial simplex and non-simplex algorithm for the minimum cost flow problem. Working Paper No. 1615-84, A.P. Sloan School of Management, MIT, December.

Sawaragi, Y., Nakayama, H. and Tanino, T. (1985). Theory of multiobjective optimization. Academic Press, New York.

Steuer, R.E. and Choo, E.V. (1983). An interactive weighted Chebyshev procedure for multiple objective programming. *Mathematical Programming*, 26, pp. 326–344.

Tardos, E. (1985). A strongly polynomial minimum cost circulation algorithm. *Combinatorica*, 5, pp. 247–255.

Tardos, E. (1986). A strongly polynomial algorithm to solve combinatorial linear programs. *Operations Research*, 34(2), pp. 250–256.

Wierzbicki, A.P. and Lewandowski, A. (1987). Dynamic interactive decision analysis and support. Working paper, IIASA, Laxenburg, Austria.

Dynamic Control Problems with Many Decision Makers

A.F. Kleimenov
Institute of Mathematics and Mechanics
Ural Branch of the Academy of Science
Sverdlovsk, USSR

1 Introduction

In the present paper the following dynamic models of decision making are considered. Dynamics of the process is described by a vector differential equation with right-hand side depending on vector controls of many decision makers. Each decision maker has some personal control resource and tends to extremize his own scalar cost functional. The following two elements are of importance for the statement of the problem:

(I) description of the information available for each decision maker while choosing his control

(Naturally, decision makers form their controls (admissible strategies) as functions depending on the available information. Having the personal control resource every decision maker is able to guarantee himself some value of his cost functional for any current position. This property is not valid for multicriteria control problems because of the fact that total control resource is not distributed among decision makers a priori.)

(II) description of the rules which regulate the decision making procedure; without loss of generality it is assumed that these rules do not influence on the informational structure given in (I)

(For instance rules of this type are assumed in dynamic Stackelberg game (see Sec. 2); dialogue decision making procedures give one more example of these rules.)

Such models can be formalized within the framework of the theory of nonantagonistic differential games. If the accessible to all players information (I) contains the complete information about the current phase state then the game is a positional one.

The author is of the opinion that any sensible notion of a solution to the game must satisfy the Nash equilibrium condition. For a solution of the dynamic game this condition means that for every player it is unprofitable to deviate individually from this solution at any moment of time. A deviation from the solution is profitable for some player or not depending on the change of his guaranteed result. The rules (II) usually select some subset of the set of Nash equilibrium strategies and this subset is taken as a set of solutions of the game.

Contents of this paper are as follows. Sec. 2 deals with a positional nonantagonistic two-person differential game. Three variants of rules (II) are considered. In Variant (a) rules (II) state the simultaneity of strategy choice by all players. In Variant (b) rules (II) make the game the Stackelberg one. In Variant (c) we have a modified Stackelberg game. In Sec. 3 an m-person game is considered. It is assumed that if one of the players deviates from the solution of the game it becomes known to all the players immediately.

2 A positional dynamic two-person game

Consider a control system described by the equation

$$\dot{x} = f(t, x, u, v), \qquad u \in P, \quad v \in Q, \quad x[t_0] = x_0, \quad t \in [t_0, \vartheta] \tag{1}$$

where $x \in R^n$ is a phase vector, $u \in P \subset R^p$ and $v \in Q \subset R^q$ are vector controls handled by Player 1 (P1) and Player 2 (P2), respectively, the sets P and Q are compacts, ϑ is the fixed final time. The function f is continuous with respect to all arguments, satisfies the Lipschitz condition in x and a condition of extendability for solutions of the equation (1) on the interval $[t_0, \vartheta]$.

P1 and P2 choosing controls u and v tend to minimize the cost functionals

$$I_i = \sigma_i(x[\vartheta]), \qquad i = 1, 2 \tag{2}$$

where σ_i are given continuous functions.

(I.1) P1 and P2 have the complete information of the current phase state $x[t]$ at time t

Under the condition (I.1) both players can use pure positional strategies or — under additional informational assumptions — mixed positional strategies and positional counterstrategies. Further we use the formalization of strategies and motions which was introduced for antagonistic differential games (Krasovski and Subbotin, 1974; Krasovski, 1978, 1985). For nonantagonistic differential games this formalization is described in (Kleimenov, 1987b). Now we single out its basic elements.

A pure positional strategy (or strategy for short) of P1 is identified with a pair $U = \{u(t, x, \varepsilon), \beta_1(\varepsilon)\}$ where $u(\cdot, \cdot, \cdot)$ is any function depending on the position (t, x) and on a positive precision parameter ε and having values in the set P. The function $\beta_1 : (0, \infty) \to (0, \infty)$ is continuous monotonous one and satisfies a condition $\beta_1(\varepsilon) \to 0$ if $\varepsilon \to 0$. The usage of precision parameter as an argument of the strategy allowed to prove the existence of universal saddle points for antagonistic differential games in sufficiently general form (Krasovski, 1978). The function $\beta_1(\cdot)$ has the following sense. For a fixed ε the value $\beta_1(\varepsilon)$ is the upper bound for the step of a subdivision of the interval $[t_0, \vartheta]$ which P1 uses when forming approximate motions.

Motions of two types: approximate ones (Euler splines) and ideal (limit) ones are considered as motions generated by strategies of players. Approximated motion

$x[\cdot, t_0, x_0, U, \varepsilon_1, \Delta_1, V, \varepsilon_2, \Delta_2]$ is introduced for fixed values of players precision parameters ε_1 and ε_2 and for fixed subdivisions $\Delta_1 = \{t_i\}$ and $\Delta_2 = \{t_j\}$ of the interval $[t_0, \vartheta]$. A pair of strategies (U, V) generates a nonempty compact (in the metric of $C[t_0, \vartheta]$) set consisting of ideal motions $x[\cdot, t_0, x_0, U, V]$.

We consider three variants of rules (II).

(II.a) Both the players choose their strategies simultaneously.

As solutions of the game in Variant (II.a) we use N-solutions and P^*-solutions defined as follows.

Definition 1. A pair of strategies (U^*, V^*) is a Nash equilibrium solution (N-solution) if for any strategies U and V the following inequalities are true

$$\max \sigma_1\big(x[\vartheta, t_0, x_0, U^*, V^*]\big) \le \min \sigma_1\big(x[\vartheta, t_0, x_0, U, V^*]\big)$$
$$\max \sigma_2\big(x[\vartheta, t_0, x_0, U^*, V^*]\big) \le \min \sigma_2\big(x[\vartheta, t_0, x_0, U^*, V]\big)$$

where max and min are taken over corresponding sets of limit motions. The set of N-solutions is denoted by $\mathcal{N}$.

Definition 2. N-solution (U^*, V^*) is modified Pareto solution (P^*-solution) if for any N-solution (U, V) one of the two following alternatives is valid

$$(1): \quad \sigma_i\big(x[\vartheta, t_0, x_0, U, V]\big) = \sigma_i\big(x[\vartheta, t_0, x_0, U^*, V^*]\big), \qquad i = 1, 2$$
$$(2): \quad \exists j \in \overline{1,2} : \sigma_j\big(x[\vartheta, t_0, x_0, U, V]\big) > \sigma_j\big(x[\vartheta, t_0, x_0, U^*, V^*]\big)$$

The only difference from the classical Pareto-solution (P-solution) introduced for multicriteria control problems is that P^*-solution is, by definition, N-solution. The sets of P^*-solutions and P-solutions are denoted by $\mathcal{P}^*$ and $\mathcal{P}$, respectively.

The sets $\mathcal{N}$ and $\mathcal{P}^*$ can be constructed in the following way. Consider auxiliary antagonistic differential games Γ_i, $i = 1, 2$ in which Player i minimizes the cost functional $\sigma_i(x[\vartheta])$ (2) and Player j, $j \ne i$ opposes him. It is known from (Krasovski and Subbotin, 1974; Krasovski, 1978, 1985) that under so-called condition of saddle point in the minor game both the games Γ_1 and Γ_2 have universal saddle points

$$\{\, u^i(t, x, \varepsilon), v^i(t, x, \varepsilon) \,\} \tag{3}$$

and continuous value functions $\gamma_i(t, x)$. The property of strategies (3) to be universal means that they are optimal for any initial position (t, x) not only for the fixed one (t_0, x_0).

Problem 1. For the control system (1) find the measurable functions $u(t)$ and $v(t)$, $t_0 \le t \le \vartheta$ which generate a trajectory $x(\cdot)$ satisfying the following inequalities

$$\gamma_i(t, x(t)) \ge \gamma_i(\vartheta, x(\vartheta)) = \sigma_i(x(\vartheta)), \qquad t_0 \le t \le \vartheta, \quad i = 1, 2 \tag{4}$$

Problem 2. For fixed $\lambda \in [0,1]$ find the solution of Problem 1 that minimizes the cost functional $\lambda\sigma_1(x(\vartheta)) + (1-\lambda)\sigma_2(x(\vartheta))$.

Let controls $u^*(t)$ and $v^*(t)$, $t_0 \le t \le \vartheta$ generate a trajectory $x^*(\cdot)$ of the system (1). Consider the strategies of P1 and P2 $U^0 = \{u^0(t,x,\varepsilon), \beta_1^0(\varepsilon)\}$ and $V^0 = \{v^0(t,x,\varepsilon), \beta_2^0(\varepsilon)\}$ where for all $t \in [t_0, \vartheta]$ we have

$$\begin{array}{lll} u^0(t,x,\varepsilon) = u^*(t), & v^0(t,x,\varepsilon) = v^*(t), & \text{if } \|x - x^*(t)\| \le \varepsilon \\ u^0(t,x,\varepsilon) = u^2(t,x,\varepsilon), & v^0(t,x,\varepsilon) = v^1(t,x,\varepsilon), & \text{if } \|x - x^*(t)\| > \varepsilon \end{array} \tag{5}$$

and the functions $\beta_1^0(\cdot)$ and $\beta_2^0(\cdot)$ are chosen so that the following inequality holds for $\varepsilon > 0$, $t_0 \le t \le \vartheta$

$$\left\| x[t, t_0, x_0, U^0, \varepsilon, \Delta_1, V^0, \varepsilon, \Delta_2] - x^*(t) \right\| < \varepsilon \tag{6}$$

The functions $u^2(\cdot,\cdot,\cdot)$ and $v^1(\cdot,\cdot,\cdot)$ are defined in (3). They can be interpreted as universal penalty strategies used when one of the players refuses to follow the trajectory $x^*(\cdot)$ at some moment of time t. Penalty strategies were applied in nonantagonistic differential games in (Kononenko, 1976). The pair of the strategies (U^0, V^0) (5), (6) generates a unique limit motion coinciding with $x^*(\cdot)$.

Theorem 1. Let controls $u^*(\cdot)$ and $v^*(\cdot)$ be a solution of Problem 1. Then the pair of the strategies (U^0, V^0) (5), (6) is an N-solution. Inversely, any N-solution is equivalent to an N-solution having the form (U^0, V^0) (5), (6) where $u^*(\cdot)$ and $v^*(\cdot)$ is a solution of Problem 1.

Theorem 2. Let controls $u^*(\cdot)$ and $v^*(\cdot)$ be a solution of Problem 2. Then the pair of the strategies (U^0, V^0) (5), (6) is a P^*-solution. Inversely, if the functions σ_i (2) are convex then any P^*-solution is equivalent to an P^*-solution having the form (U^0, V^0) (5), (6) where $u^*(\cdot)$ and $v^*(\cdot)$ is a solution of Problem 2.

Consider now the second variant of rules (II)

(II.b) The rules are the same as introduced in hierarchical Stackelberg game. They are the following. One player, called the leader, announces his strategy before the beginning of the game and another player, called the follower, knowing the leader's strategy chooses his rational strategy.

The definition of the concept "rational strategy" can be found in (Kleimenov, 1986). The same paper gives the definition of a solution of a hierarchical Stackelberg game with P1 as the leader (S_1-solution). The set of S_1-solutions is denoted by S_1 .

We define **Problem 3** as Problem 2 for $\lambda = 1$.

Theorem 3. Let controls $u^*(\cdot)$ and $v^*(\cdot)$ be a solution of Problem 3. Then the pair of the strategies (U^0, V^0) (5), (6) is an S_1-solution. Inversely, any S_1-solution is equivalent to an S_1-solution having the form (U^0, V^0) (5), (6) where $u^*(\cdot)$ and $v^*(\cdot)$ is a solution of Problem 3.

An analogous statement holds for solutions of a hierarchical Stackelberg game with P2 as the leader (S_2-solutions) and solutions of **Problem 4** which is Problem 2 for $\lambda = 0$. The set of S_2-solutions is denoted by $\mathcal{S}_2$.

It follows from Theorems 1–3 that

Theorem 4. $\mathcal{S}_i \subset \mathcal{P}^* \subset \mathcal{N}, \quad i = 1, 2$

The proofs of Theorems 1–4 can be found in (Kleimenov, 1986, 1987b).

Finally we consider the third variant of rules (II)

(II.c) The rules are such that we have a modified Stackelberg game with the cautions follower in the sense of (Kleimenov, 1987a).

The caution property for the follower means that his guaranteed result in corresponding antagonistic differential game Γ_i is monotonically not increasing along the trajectory generated by the solution of the game. The set of solutions of modified Stackelberg game with P1 as the leader (S_1^m-solutions) can be constructed on the basis of solutions of auxiliary Problem 3^m which differs from Problem 3 only in substitution of the following inequalities

$$\gamma_i(t_1, x(t_1)) \geq \gamma_i(t_2, x(t_2)), \qquad t_0 \leq t_1 < t_2 \leq \vartheta \tag{7}$$

for the inequalities (4).

It can be shown that S_1^m-solution is not P^*-solution, in general. However any S_1^m-solution is always an N-solution.

Trajectories generated by S_i^m-solutions satisfy Bellman's principle of optimality. However trajectories generated by S_i-solutions do not satisfy this principle, in general.

Remark 1. The sets $\mathcal{N}, \mathcal{P}^*, \mathcal{S}_i, \mathcal{S}_i^m$ contain, in general, more than one element. Therefore the coordination of players' actions is required to make physical realization of solutions possible.

3 A positional dynamic m-person game

Consider a control system described by the equation

$$\dot{x} = f(t, x, u_1, \ldots, u_m), \qquad u_i \in P_i, \quad x[t_0] = x_0, \quad t \in [t_0, \vartheta] \tag{8}$$

where $x \in R^n$ is a phase vector, $u_1, u_2, \ldots, u_m$ are vector controls governed by Players $1, 2, \ldots, m$, respectively. The sets P are compacts in R^{P_i}. The function f is continuous with respect to all arguments, satisfies the Lipschitz condition in x and a condition of extendability for solutions of the system (8) on the interval $[t_0, \vartheta]$.

The aim of Player i is to minimize the cost functional

$$I_i = \sigma_i(x[\vartheta]), \qquad i = 1, \ldots, m \tag{9}$$

where σ_i are continuous functions.

As stated above (Remark 1) even in a two-person game the coordination of players' actions is required for physical realization of solutions. That concerns the m-person game to an even greater degree. We assume in this section that there exists a certain coordinating organ not belonging to the system. This organ checks joint actions to realize some solution during the process of the game. If one player, say Player i, deviates from the solution then this organ informs all the players about his index i at the moment of the deviation. In (Kleimenov, 1982) such an assumption was formalized as follows. All the players get the information about the current value of a function $\alpha[\cdot]$ which is equal to zero when there is no deviation from the solution and is equal to i beginning with the moment τ when Player i deviates from the solution for the first time. Denote $\alpha^0[t] = \{0, \text{ if } t_0 \le t \le \vartheta\}$ and $\alpha^{i,\tau}[t] = \{0, \text{ if } t_0 \le t < \tau; \; i \text{ if } \tau \le t \le \vartheta\}$.

So we have the following informational assumption (I)

(I.2) Players $1, 2, \dots, m$ have the complete information of the current phase state $x[t]$ and of the current value of the function $\alpha[t]$ at time t.

A strategy of Player i is identified with a pair $U_i = \{\, u_i(t, x, \alpha, \varepsilon), \beta_i(\varepsilon) \,\}$ where $u(\cdot,\cdot,\cdot,\cdot)$ is any function depending on the position (t, x), a parameter $\alpha \in \{0, 1, \dots, m\}$ and a positive precision parameter ε and having values in the set P_i. The function $\beta_i(\cdot)$ is of the same type as in Sec. 2. For a fixed ε_i the value $\beta_i(\varepsilon_i)$ is the upper bound for the step of a subdivision of the interval $[t_0, \vartheta]$ which Player uses when forming approximate motions (Euler splines). An Euler spline corresponding to the function $\alpha[\cdot]$ is denoted by symbol $x[\cdot, t_0, x_0, \{U_i, \varepsilon_i, \Delta_i\}; \alpha[\cdot]]$. Further we assume that all the players choose one and the same value of their precision parameters, i.e. $\varepsilon_i = \varepsilon$, $i = 1, \dots, m$. For the function $\alpha[\cdot]$ a collection of strategies $(U_1, \dots, U_m)$ generates a set of ideal (limit) motions $x[\cdot, t_0, x_0, U_1, \dots, U_m; \alpha[\cdot]]$ (for details see Kleimenov, 1982).

(II.d) Players $1, 2, \dots, m$ choose their strategies simultaneously.

As solutions of the game we use N-solutions and P^*-solutions defined as follows.

Definition 3. A collection of strategies $(U_1^*, \dots, U_i^*, \dots, U_m^*)$ is an N-solution if for any $i \in \{i, \dots, m\}$ any $\tau \in [t_0, \vartheta)$ the following inequalities

$$\max \sigma_i\Big(x[\vartheta, t_0, x_0, U_1^*, \dots, U_i^*, \dots, U_m^*; \alpha^0[\cdot]]\Big) \le$$
$$\le \min \sigma_i\Big(x[\vartheta, t_0, x_0, U_1^*, \dots, U_i, \dots, U_m^*; \alpha^{i,\tau}[\cdot]]\Big)$$

are true for all the strategies U_i coinciding with U_i^* on the interval $[t_0, \tau)$. Here max and min are taken over corresponding sets of limit motions.

N-solution is called P^*-solution if it is unimprovable.

The set $\mathcal{N}$ on N-solutions and the set $\mathcal{P}^*$ of P^*-solutions can be constructed in the following way. Consider auxiliary antagonistic differential games Γ_i^*, $i = 1, \dots, m$ in which Player i minimizes his cost functional $\sigma_i(x[\vartheta])$ (9) and Players $1, \dots, i-1, i+1, \dots, m$ oppose him. Under so-called conditions of saddle points in the minor games the games Γ_i^* have universal saddle points in the classes of strategies not depending on parameter α

$$\Big\{\, u_i^i(t, x, \varepsilon), \; (u_j^i(t, x, \varepsilon), \, j = 1, \dots, i-1, i+1, \dots, m) \,\Big\} \tag{10}$$

and continuous value functions $\gamma_i^*(t, x)$, $i = 1, \dots, m$.

Problem 5. For the control system (8) find the measurable functions $u_1(t),\ldots,u_m(t)$ $t_0 \le t \le \vartheta$ which generate a trajectory $x(\cdot)$ satisfying the following inequalities

$$\gamma_i^*(t,x(t)) \ge \gamma_i^*(\vartheta,x(\vartheta)) = \sigma_i(x(\vartheta)), \qquad t_0 \le t \le \vartheta, \quad i=1,\ldots,m$$

Problem 6. For fixed $\lambda_i \ge 0$, $\sum_{i=1}^m \lambda_i = 1$ find the solution of Problem 5 that minimizes the cost functional $\sum_{i=1}^m \lambda_i \sigma_i(x(\vartheta))$.

Let controls $u_1^*(t),\ldots,u_m^*(t)$, $t_0 \le t \le \vartheta$ generate a trajectory of the system (8). Consider the strategies $U_i^0 = \{\, u_i^0(t,x,\alpha,\varepsilon), \beta^0(\varepsilon)\,\}$, $i=1,\ldots,m$ where

$$\begin{aligned} &u_i^0(t,x,0,\varepsilon) = u_i^*(t), \qquad && u_i^0(t,x,i,\varepsilon) \text{ are arbitrary} \\ &u_i^0(t,x,j,\varepsilon) = u_i^j(t,x,\varepsilon)\ (10), && j \ne i \end{aligned} \tag{11}$$

and the function $\beta^0(\cdot)$ is chosen so that the following inequality holds for $\varepsilon > 0$ and for all $t \in [t_0,\vartheta)$

$$\left\| x[t,t_0,x_0,\{U_i^0,\varepsilon,\Delta_i\};\alpha^0[\cdot]] - x^*(t) \right\| < \varepsilon \tag{12}$$

Let Players $1,\ldots,m$ come to the agreement to realize the collection of the strategies $(U_1^0,\ldots,U_m^0)$ (11), (12) and choose one and the same value ε of their precision parameters. We assume that coordinating organ declares a deviation from the solution if and only if the inequality (12) is violated for the first time. Then the collection of the strategies $(U_1^0,\ldots,U_m^0)$ (11), (12) generate a unique limit motion coinciding with $x(\cdot)$.

It follows from (Kleimenov, 1982, 1987b) that

Theorem 5. Let controls $u_1^*(\cdot),\ldots,u_m^*(\cdot)$ be a solution of Problem 5. Then the collection of the strategies $(U_1^0,\ldots,U_m^0)$ (11), (12) is an N-solution. Inversely, any N-solution is equivalent to an N-solution having the form $(U_1^0,\ldots,U_m^0)$ (11), (12) where $u_1^*(\cdot),\ldots,u_m^*(\cdot)$ is a solution of Problem 5.

Theorem 6. Let controls $u_1^*(\cdot),\ldots,u_m^0(\cdot)$ be a solution of Problem 6. Then the collection of the strategies $(U_1^0,\ldots,U_m^0)$ (11), (12) is a P^*-solution. Inversely, if the functions σ_i (9) are convex then any P^*-solution is equivalent to a P^*-solution having the form $(U_1^0,\ldots,U_m^0)$ (11), (12) where $u_1^*(\cdot),\ldots,u_m^*(\cdot)$ is a solution of Problem 6.

4 Conclusion

Thus the question considered in the present paper concern decision problems for positional two-person and many person nonantagonistic differential games. The most characteristic feature of the paper is application of the formalization and results of the theory of positional antagonistic differential games (Krasovski and Subbotin, 1974; Krasovski, 1978, 1985). This approach to the theory of nonantagonistic differential games has a number of advantages. One of them is that different solution types (Nash solutions, modified Pareto solutions and Stackelberg solutions) are considered within the framework of one and the same approach. Interrelations between these solution types are given. For each type of solutions the set of all solutions is put into one-to-one correspondence to the set of solutions of some nonstandard optimal control problem.

References

Kleimenov, A.F. (1982). Equilibrium coalitional mixed strategies in differential games of m players. *Problems of Control and Information Theory*, 11(2):85–95.

Kleimenov, A.F. (1986). Stackelberg strategies for hierarchical differential two-person games. *Problems of Control and Information Theory*, 15(6):399–412.

Kleimenov, A.F. (1987a). Modified Stackelberg strategies for hierarchical differential two-person games. *Problems of Control and Information Theory*, 16(2):73–87.

Kleimenov, A.F. (1987b). Nash, Pareto and Stackelberg solutions in nonantagonistic differential games. *Prikladnaja matematika i mehanika*, 51(2):209–215.

Kononenko, A.F. (1976). On equilibrium positional strategies in nonantagonistic differential games. *Dokl. Akad. Nauk SSSR*, 231(2):285–288.

Krasovski, N.N. (1978). Differential games. Approximation and formal models. *Matemat. Sbornik*, 107(4):541–571.

Krasovski, N.N. (1985). Control dynamic system. Nauka, Moscow (in Russian).

Krasovski, N.N. and Subbotin, A.I. (1974). Positional differential games. Nauka, Moscow (in Russian).

Generalized Reachable Sets Method in Multiple Criteria Problems

A.V. Lotov
Computing Center of the USSR Academy of Science
Moscow, USSR

1 Introduction

The Generalized Reachable Sets (GRS) method was developed as a method for investigation of open models, i.e. models with exogenous variables. Development of the GRS method started in late 60's and the first results have been published in early 70's (Lotov, 1972). The basic idea of the method can be formulated as follows. The properties of the open model under study are investigated by means of aggregated variables. The set of all combinations of values of aggregated variables which are accessible (or reachable) using feasible combinations of values of original variables is constructed. This set should be described in explicit form.

The GRS method was applied for investigation of dynamic models (Lotov, 1973b), for aggregation of economic models (Lotov, 1982), for coordination of economic decision (Lotov, 1983) and so on. Application of the GRS method to multiple criteria problems started in early 70's (Lotov, 1973a).

This publication is devoted to application of this method to the multiple criteria decision making (MCDM) problems. The exogenous variables hereafter are treated as decisions and the aggregated variables are treated as decision criteria. The GRS method in MCDM problems employs an explicit representation of the accessible set, i.e. the set of all accessible values of criteria. Construction of the accessible set in explicit form provides the possibility to study the MCDM problems in terms of a small number of criteria instead of hundreds and thousands of decision variables.

If the number of criteria is greater than two it is hardly possible to imagine a practical form of explicit representation of nonconvex sets in criteria space. Therefore we study the MCDM problems in the case when accessible set is convex and can be approximated by polyhedral set.

Note that in the multiple attribute decision making problems dealing with finite and relatively small number of alternatives usually apply decision matrix. The decision matrix describes the alternatives in terms of criteria values. The accessible set plays the same role for the DM problems with infinite number of alternatives. Construction of the accessible set permits to reformulate various existing MCDM dialogue procedures in simplified form and to suggest some new ones based mostly on the visualization of the accessible set.

2 Construction of accessible sets

2.1 GRS method for linear models

We start with the mathematical formulation of the problem for the most simple case, i.e. for linear problems. Let the mathematical model of the system under study be

$$x \in G = \{ x \in R^n : Ax \leq b \}, \tag{1}$$

where R^n is n-dimensional linear space of variables x (controls), G is the set of all feasible values of variables x, while A and b are the given matrix and vector respectively. Let $y \in R^m$ be the vector of criteria. The criteria y are connected with variables x by mapping $f : R^n \Rightarrow R^m$. If the mapping is linear it can be described by a given matrix F, i.e.

$$y = f(x) = Fx. \tag{2}$$

The GRS for the model (1) with the mapping (2) is defined as

$$f(G) = \{ y \in R^m : y = f(x),\ x \in G \}. \tag{3}$$

We obtain for linear case

$$f(G) = \{ y \in R^m : y = Fx,\ Ax \leq b \}. \tag{4}$$

The GRS method consists in analysis of the set $f(G)$ approximated in the form

$$f(G) = \{ y \in R^m : Dy \leq d \}, \tag{5}$$

where D is a matrix and d is a vector which should be constructed. The form (5) was choosen for practical reasons. In particular the form (5) gives the possibility to construct the slices of the accessible set very simply and rather quick.

2.2 Construction of the accessible set by means of convolution of systems of linear inequalities

A group of numerical methods was developed to construct the accessible set for the system (1), (2) in the form (5). These methods are based on the construction of projections of finite dimensional polyhedral sets into subspaces. Suppose we have some polyhedral set M belonging to $(p+q)$-dimensional linear space R^{p+q}. Suppose that this set is described in the form

$$Av + Bw \leq c, \tag{6}$$

where $v \in R^p$, $w \in R^q$, the matrices A, B and the vector c are given. The projection M_w of the set M into the space R^q of variables w is the set of all points w for which there exist such points $v \in R^p$ that the pair $\{v, w\} \in R^{p+q}$ belongs to M, i.e.

$$M_w = \{ w \in R^q : \exists v \in R^p : Av + Bw \leq c \}. \tag{7}$$

An example for $p = 1,\ q = 1$ is presented in Figure 1.

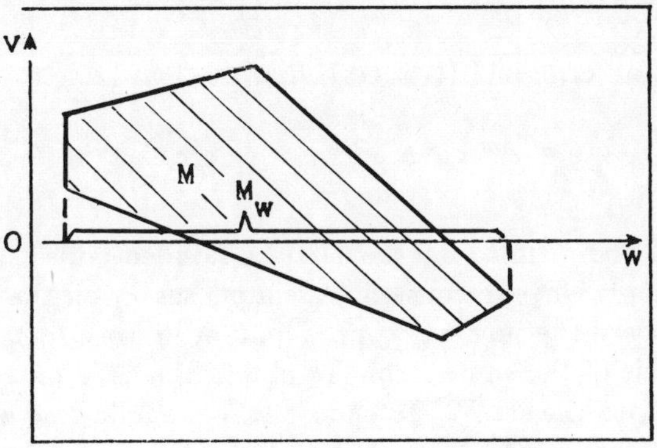

Figure 1.

To construct the GRS for the system (1), (2) let consider the set

$$Z = \{\{x, y\} \in R^{n+m} : y = Fx,\ Ax \leq b\}.$$

The projection of the set Z into the criteria space R^m coincides with the set $f(G)$.

The first method of the construction of projections of polyhedral sets given in the form (6) was introduced by Fourier (1826). The method was based on exclusion of variables from the system (6) by summation of inequalities multiplied by nonnegative values. Now it is called the convolution method (Chernikov, 1965). The construction by the Fourier method of the projection of the set presented in Fig. 1 is described in (Lotov, 1981a).

The convolution methods were modified (Motzkin et al., 1953 as well as Chernikov, 1965) and complemented by methods of exclusion of superfluous inequalities (Bushenkov and Lotov, 1980a, 1982). These methods were included into the first version of the applied programs system (Bushenkov and Lotov, 1980b). The experimental application of the methods proved that they are effective for small systems only (n =10–30). For models (1) with hundreds of variables the iterative methods of approximation of the accessible set were suggested.

2.3 Iterative methods of approximation of accessible set

The basic idea of the methods of iterative approximation of the accessible set consists in following (Bushenkov and Lotov, 1982 as well as Bushenkov, 1985). Two polyhedral approximations P_k and P^k of the accessible set, i.e. $P_k \subset f(G) \subset P^k$, should be given before the k-th iteration. The internal approximation should be presented in two following forms:

1. as the set of solutions for the system of linear inequalities

$$P_k = \{y \in R^m : (c_j, y) \leq d_j,\ j = 1, 2, \ldots, s\}, \tag{8}$$

where c_j are the vectors and d_j are the numbers calculated at the previous iterations, $(a,b) = \sum_{i=1}^{m} a_i b_i$.

2. as the convex hull of points (vertices) v_1, $v_2, \ldots, v_r$, i.e.

$$P_k = \left\{ y \in R^m : y = \sum_{l=1}^{r} \lambda_l v_l, \text{ where } \lambda_l \geq 0, \sum_{l=1}^{r} \lambda_l = 1 \right\} \tag{9}$$

The conversion from one form to another can be fulfilled only if the numbers s and r are rather small. This is why we construct a simple set P_1 on the first iteration. Then step by step we improve the internal approximation in both forms while each form is calculated on the basis of the same form. To obtain the set P_{k+1} on the basis of P_k we add a new vertex v_{r+1} to the set P_k. To choose v_{r+1} the following optimization problem should be solved for any vector c_j from the system (8)

$$(c_j, y) \to \max \qquad \text{where } y = Fx,\ Ax \leq b. \tag{10}$$

The most distanced solution of (10) is chosed for v_{r+1}.

To construct the set P_{k+1} in the form (8) it is possible to apply the convolution methods for which the dimension of the projection problem depends not on n but on m. If m =4–5 the dimension of the projection problem is usually not greater that 20–30. The problems of this kind can be solved by the methods described earlier (see for details Bushenkov, 1985).

After some iterations the sets P_k and P^k become so close that it is possible to stop the process of approximation. This method gives the possibility to approximate the accessible sets with thousands and millions of vertices. Some new modifications of the method are described in (Kamenev, 1986). The corresponding software providing the possibility to construct the accessible set for the models (1) with thousand of variables is described in (Bushenkov and Lotov, 1982, 1984).

If the directions of improvement of values of criteria are known the nondominated boundary of the accessible set is a matter of interest. In this case the accessible set complimented by all dominated points (so called Pareto hull of accessible set) can be constructed. The nondominated boundaries of accessible set and of its Pareto hull coincide, but the description of the Pareto hull is more simple usually. The Pareto hull of the accessible set for the model (1) can be constructed on the basis of the same methods as the accessible set.

The method discussed herein coincides in some details with the NISE method due to Cohon (1978). But the main features of our method consisting in application of the both forms of description of the set and in exclusion of variables help to avoid the difficulties which arise in the NISE method for $m > 2$.

2.4 Approximation of accessible set for more complicated models

The method described above can be easily reformulated for convex sets G. For this purpose it is sufficient to solve the convex optimization problems instead of linear problems (10).

To apply the GRS approach for the models in functional spaces (for example for controlled systems of differential equations) we substitute the original model by the finite dimensional (for example multistep) model and construct the accessible set for it. Problems of approximation are studied in (Lotov 1979, 1981a, 1981b).

For the multistep models it is possible to construct the reachable set, i.e. the set of all values of state variables which can be reached in the fixed time. The reachable sets for multistep models approximate the reachable sets for controlled systems of differential equations (Lotov 1972, 1975b).

3 Applications of the GRS method

3.1 Interactive procedures of decision making

Due to approximation of the accessible set in the form (5) it is possible to simplify and accelerate well known dialogue decision procedures. For this purpose it is sufficient to reformulate them in the form dealing with the criteria values only and to construct the accessible set. Some new visual procedures can be formulated as well. One of them (Kamenev and Lotov, 1985) consists in improvement of efficient point while the decision maker (DM) is dealing with two criteria only. The procedure is based on representation of two dimensional slices of the accessible set on display and is very simple for the DM and stable to his (or her) errors.

3.2 Demonstration of potential possibilities

The accessible set constructed in the form (5) can be treated as the aggregated description of potential possibilities inherent in decision situation. It is possible to describe them by visual presentation of various two dimensional slices of the accessible set. Since the accessible set is constructed in advance in the form (5) it takes only a few seconds to obtain on display a slice on request of the DM. A series of slices is presented in a few tens of seconds. Thus it is possible to inform the DM, experts and public opinion about the potential possibilities in clear graphical form. The efficient set is presented as the boundary of the accessible set.

This idea was introduced in 70's (Lotov, 1973a, 1975b). It was applied for analysis of the global systems (Moiseev et al., 1983; Bushenkov and Lotov, 1983) and of the long-term development of national economies (Lotov, 1973a, 1984a; Lotov and Ognivtsev, 1984; Chernykh, 1984). The GRS method was used as well for investigation of industrial planning (Egorova, Kamenev and Lotov, 1985), of regional economic-ecological systems (Bushenkov et al., 1982, 1986) and so on.

Examples of visualization of the accessible set are presented in Figures 2 and 3. Here we have two groups of slices of the accessible set for a model of a small agricultural region with ecological problems. The model with 460 variables and 672 linear constraints was studied on the basis of 4 criteria: (1) investment (*inv*); (2) additional income (y); (3) concentration of nitrates in deep aquifers (*cd*); (4) the fall of groundwater level (*hw*). In Fig. 2 slices in *hw*–*cd* space are presented while values of *inv* and y are fixed. The value *inv* is constant for all slices while the value of y is changing. In Fig. 3 there are slices in y–cd space while values of inv and hw are fixed. For slices 1 and 2 as well as for slices 3 and 4 inv is the same. Additional slices and detailed description of the model and of the results are given in (Kamenev et al., 1986).

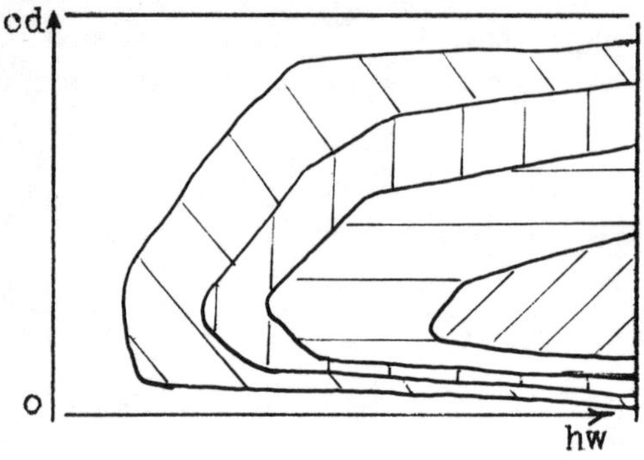

Figure 2.

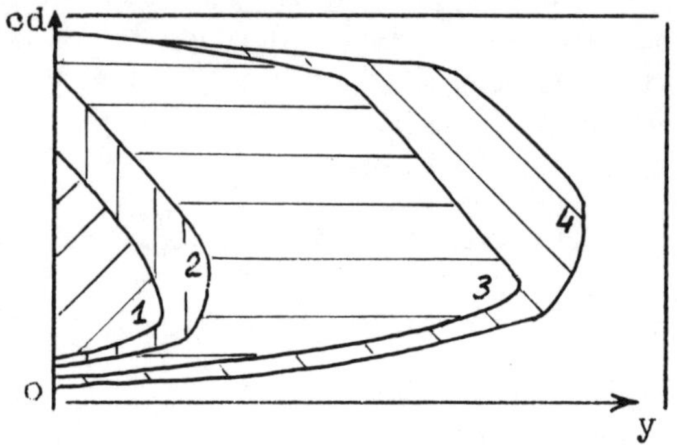

Figure 3.

3.3 The GRS method in decision and negotiation support systems

The GRS method can be effectively used in decision and negotiation support systems. In systems of these kinds the visualization of the accessible sets is applied to compliment and to simplify existing multicriteria methods. For example it is possible to combine it with methods for generating of efficient points. These points are choosen sometimes by chance (Steuer, 1986). Due to visualization of the accessible set it is possible to choose them consciously to be satisfied with a small number of the efficient points (Kamenev et al., 1986). Furthermore it is possible to apply the efficient points obtained hereby as goal (or reference) points in investigation of more complicated models. So it is possible to apply the GRS method to study simplified screening models in the DSS based on a system of models of various degree of complexity (Moiseev, 1981). This idea was applied to the long-term national planning (Lotov, 1984a). The most interesting slices can be reconstructed for more complicated linear models by parametric LP methods.

Application of the GRS method in DSS gives the possibility to discuss the problem under study avoiding the details. It is important that the method provides an objective information while the subjective preferences of the DM or negotiators are not studied. Due to this feature of the method it is possible to apply it in wide-spread situations where the idea of the DM is a convenient abstraction only. The GRS method presents an information on potential possibilities of the system under study and trade offs between criteria in graphical form which is clear for persons not trained in mathematics. By this the GRS method helps to involve public opinion into the decision making procedures.

The GRS method presents a new approach to the question of correspondence between personal and supercomputers in MCDM. In the GRS method due to division of the processes of construction and of analysis of the accessible sets the both types of computers can be used at appropriate place: capacity of a supercomputer can be effectively used to construct the accessible set and convenience of a personal computer can be utilized in analysis of the accessible set being constructed earlier in the form (5).

References

Bushenkov, V.A. (1985). Iteration method for construction of orthogonal projections of convex polyhedral sets. *USSR Computational Mathematics and Mathematical Physics*, Pergamon Press, 25(9).

Bushenkov, V.A., Ereshko, F., Kindler, J., Lotov, A. and de Mare, L. (1982). Application of the GRS Method to Water Resources Problems in Southwestern Skane, Sweden. WP-82-120. International Institute for Applied Systems Analysis, Laxenburg, Austria.

Bushenkov, V.A., Kamenev, G.K., Lotov, A.V., and Chernykh, O.L. (1986). Applications of the geometric method for the investigation of economic-ecological systems. In A.A. Samarsky, N.N. Moiseev and A.A. Petrov, eds., Mathematical Modelling. Processes in Complicated Economic and Ecological Systems. Nauka Publishing House, Moscow (in Russian).

Bushenkov, V.A. and Lotov, A.V. (1980a). An algorithm for analysis of independents of inequalities in linear system. *USSR Computational Mathematics and Mathematical Physics*, Pergamon Press, 20(3).

Bushenkov, V.A. and Lotov, A.V. (1980b). Methods and algorithms for analysis of linear systems based on constructing of GRS. *USSR Computational Mathematics and Mathematical Physics*, Pergamon Press, 20(5).

Bushenkov, V.A. and Lotov, A.V. (1982). Methods of Construction and Application of GRS. Reports on Applied Mathematics. Computing Center of the USSR Academy of Sciences, Moscow (in Russian).

Bushenkov, V.A. and Lotov, A.V. (1983). Analysis of potential possibilities of a region in multiregional multiindustrial model of world economy. In A.G. Granberg and S.M. Menshikov, eds., Multiregional Multiindustrial Models of World Economy. Nauka Publishing House, Novosibirsk (in Russian).

Bushenkov, V.A. and Lotov, A.V. (1984). POTENTIAL applied programs system. In Applied Programs Systems. Algorithms and Algorithmic Languages. Nauka Publishing House, Moscow (in Russian).

Chernikov, S.N. (1965). Convolution of finite systems of linear inequalities. *USSR Computational Mathematics and Mathematical Physics*, Pergamon Press, 5(1).

Chernykh, O.L. (1984). Analysis of Potential Possibilities of the Development of Economic Systems Taking Pollution Into Account. Reports on Applied Mathematics. Computing Center of the USSR Academy of Sciences, Moscow (in Russian).

Cohon, J. (1978). Multiobjective Programming and Planning. Academic Press, New York.

Egorova, N.E., Kamenev, G.K. and Lotov, A.V. (1985). Application of the GRS method in simulation system for industrial planning. In K.A. Bagrinovsky and T.I. Konnik, eds., Methods of Simulation of Economic Systems. Central Economic–Mathematical Institute of the USSR Academy of Sciences, Moscow (in Russian).

Fourier, J.B. (1826). Solution d'une question particulière du calcul des inégalités. In Nouveau Bulletin des Sciences par la Societé philomatique de Paris.

Kamenev, G.K. (1986). Investigation of Iteration Methods for Approximation of Convex Sets by Polyhedral Sets. Reports on Applied Mathematics. Computing Center of the USSR Academy of Sciences, Moscow (in Russian).

Kamenev, G.K. and Lotov, A.V. (1985). Interactive structured MCDM procedure based on GRS method. In Multicriteria Mathematical Programming Problems. Proc. of Seminar. Institute for Systems Studies, Moscow.

Kamenev, G.K., Lotov, A.V. and van Walsum, P. (1986). Application of the GRS Method to Water Resources Problems in the Southern Peel Region of the Netherlands. CP-86-19. International Institute for Applied Systems Analysis, Laxenburg, Austria.

Lotov, A.V. (1972). A numerical method of constructing reachable sets for linear systems. *USSR Computational Mathematics and Mathematical Physics*, Pergamon Press, 12(3).

Lotov, A.V. (1973a). An approach to perspective planning in the case of absence of unique objective. Proc. of Conf. on Systems Approach and Perspective Planning (Moscow, May 1972). Computing Center of the USSR Academy of Sciences, Moscow (in Russian).

Lotov, A.V. (1973b). A numerical method of studying the optimal-time continuity in linear systems and the solution of the Cauchy problem for Bellmans equation. *USSR Computational Mathematics and Mathematical Physics*, Pergamon Press, 13(5).

Lotov, A.V. (1975a). Numerical method for reachable sets construction in the case of linear controlled systems with phase constraints. *USSR Computational Mathematics and Mathematical Physics*, Pergamon Press, 15(1).

Lotov, A.V. (1975b). Economic Systems Analysis by means of Reachable sets. Proc. Conf. on Economic Processes Modelling. (Erevan, 1974). Computing Center of the USSR Academy of Sciences, Moscow (in Russian).

Lotov, A.V. (1979). On convergence of methods for numerical approximation of reachable sets for linear differential systems with convex phase constraints. *USSR Computational Mathematics and Mathematical Physics*, Pergamon Press, 19(1).

Lotov, A.V. (1980). On the concept of GRS and its construction for linear controlled systems. *Soviet Physics Doklady*, 25(2).

Lotov, A.V. (1981a). Reachable Sets Approach to Multiobjective Problems and its Possible Application to Water Resources Management in the Skane Region. WP-81-145. International Institute for Applied Systems Analysis, Laxenburg, Austria.

Lotov, A.V. (1981b). On the concept and construction of GRS for linear controlled systems described by partial differential equations. *Soviet Physics Doklady*, 26(11).

Lotov, A.V. (1982). Aggregation as approximation of the GRS. *Soviet Physics Doklady*, 27(8).

Lotov, A.V. (1983). Coordination of economic models with the help of GRS. In E.L. Berlyand and S.B. Barabash, eds., Mathematical Methods of Analysis of Interaction between Industrial and Regional Systems. Nauka Publishing House, Novosibirsk (in Russian).

Lotov, A.V. (1984a). Introduction into Mathematical Modelling of Economic Systems. Nauka Publishing House, Moscow (in Russian).

Lotov, A.V. (1984b). On evaluation of stability and on the condition number for the solutions set of the linear inequalities systems. *USSR Computational Mathematics and Mathematical Physics*, Pergamon Press, 24(12).

Lotov, A.V. and Ognivtsev, S.B. (1984). Application of coordination methods based on GRS in goal-program approach to economic planning. *Technical Cybernetics*, 2 (in Russian).

Moiseev, N.N. (1981). Mathematical Problems of Systems Analysis. Nauka Publishing House, Moscow (in Russian).

Moiseev, N.N. et al. (1983). Global Models. The Biospheric Approach. CP-83-33. International Institute for Applied Systems Analysis, Laxenburg, Austria.

Motzkin, T.S. et al. (1953). The double description method. In Contributions to the Theory of Games, vol. 2. Prinston University Press, Prinston.

Steuer, R. (1986). Multiple Criteria Optimization. Wiley, New York.

Analysis of Methods for Multicriterial Estimation and Choice for Discrete Problems with a Finite Set of Alternatives

L. Markova
Institute of Industrial Cybernetics & Robotics
1113 Sofia, Acad. G. Bonchev Str., Bl. 2, Bulgaria

1 Introduction

Recently, the interest towards the multicriterial programming problems bears momentum, since those problems are the main type of models used in multicriterial decision making (MCDM). This phenomenon is due to the fact that often the operational research of a given problem necessitates the consideration of several criteria in the models that are developed.

The methods for MCDM are diverse in their purpose, their ease of use, theoretical soundness and the estimations they yield. Problems for multicriterial optimization may be generally divided into two groups: problems which solution belongs to a continual set and problems which solution belongs to a discrete or even a finite set. Decision making processes differ in the way of local (partial) criteria representation, with regard to the additional information supplied by the decision maker (DM), and the estimations being received.

The great variety of methods gives sometimes as a result unsatisfactory compatibility between methods and problems. The experiments in which different methods were applied to one problem, clarify how the methods differ in their use and show how the choice of a method considerably affects the decision.

It is the purpose of this paper to show that the user of methods for multicriterial decision making faces a multicriterial problem when he chooses the appropriate method for multicriterial estimation and choice.

2 Preliminary information

To describe the choice of alternatives, one can use problems for multicriterial optimization of finite sets. The preliminary data have the form: given a set A of alternatives a_i ($a_i \in A$, $|A| = m$) which will be estimated and among them a choice will be made. The alternatives can be described by one set of characteristics (real numbers). All alternatives are estimated according to several partial criteria C_j and it is supposed that the criteria might be numerical functions of the characteristics or relations between the alternatives. The number of criteria is n.

Suppose that all partial criteria are to be maximized. Commonly, the alternatives are estimated by numerical functions and the output data are recorded in the form of a matrix $\|x_{ij}\|$, where i is the number of the alternative (number of the row) and j is the number of criteria (number of the column) and x_{ij} is the estimation of the i–th alternative by criterion with number j. It is assumed that there might be some additional information about the partial criteria — information about the levels (thresholds) of C_j or the relative importance, marked by the weighting factors or an order of these criteria. Additional information about the alternatives, expressing the preferences between them is also possible (we do not consider here such methods since they are not so appropriate for the practical cases of management decisions). The additional information is supplied by the decision maker and helps the process of decision making.

3 Analysis, estimation and choice of methods for multicriterial optimization for discrete problems with an explicitly given finite set of alternatives

We studied 15 methods for multicriterial estimation and choice for problems with a finite set of alternatives: dominance (Pareto) method; maximin method; minimal risk method; conjunctive method; disjunctive method; lexicographic method; Berezovsky–Kempner's method; Hannan's method; permutations method; linear assignment method; simple additive weighting method; hierarchical additive method; ELECTRE II; ideal point method; reference point method. Each method is described by 9 characteristics which have values 1 or 0, and show whether the respective method possesses a particular feature or not. Characteristics are denoted by B_i and the corresponding features are the following:

1. Methods using numerical functions as partial criteria.
2. Methods using relations between the alternatives as partial criteria.
3. Methods not using additional information about the partial criteria.
4. Methods using preliminary set levels (thresholds) of the partial criteria.
5. Methods using ordering of the partial criteria.
6. Methods using importance coefficient (weighting factor) of the partial criteria.
7. Methods which give as a final result a subset of alternatives.
8. Methods which give an order of alternatives.
9. Difficulties in obtaining the numerical results when enlarging the number of alternatives.

With the aforementioned features of the methods it should be taken into consideration that certain methods possess some of them and others don't. There is no common sense in searching for methods which possess all features.

For multicriterial choice of the 15 methods we will use the values of the 9 characteristics. In Table 1 every row contains the values of the characteristics of the respective method, 1 means that the method possesses the respective features, and 0 — that it does not. The column with number j in the table is denoted as follows: $B_j(i)$. The function $C_j(i)$ of the partial criteria has the form $C_j(i) = B_j(i)$, for $j = 1, 2, \ldots, 8$, and $C_9(i) = 1 - B_9(i)$.

	Methods	*No. of the respective characteristic*								
		1	2	3	4	5	6	7	8	9
1.	Dominance	1	1	1	0	0	0	1	0	1
2.	Maximin	1	0	1	0	0	0	0	1	0
3.	Minimum risk	1	0	1	0	0	0	0	1	0
4.	Conjunctive	1	0	0	1	0	0	1	0	0
5.	Disjunctive	1	0	0	1	0	0	1	0	0
6.	Lexicographic	1	0	0	0	1	0	1	0	0
7.	Berezovsky-Kempner's	1	1	0	0	1	0	1	0	1
8.	Hannan's	1	0	0	0	1	0	1	0	1
9.	Permutations	1	1	0	0	1	0	0	1	1
10.	Linear assignment	1	1	0	0	0	1	0	1	1
11.	Simple additive	1	0	0	0	0	1	0	1	0
12.	Hierarchical additive	1	0	0	0	0	1	0	1	0
13.	ELECTRE II	1	1	0	0	0	1	0	1	1
14.	Ideal point	1	0	0	0	0	1	0	1	0
15.	Reference point	1	0	0	0	0	1	0	1	1

Table 1: Characteristics of the multicriterial estimation and choice methods

With the so stated multicriterial problem, multicriterial choice of a method can be performed. The decision maker or the user of multicriterial analysis method, by means of appropriate setting of the preferences towards the characteristics of the methods, can choose a method corresponding to his point of view. Through several choices of the characteristics, the decision maker can obtain complete information about the features of the methods under consideration.

The dominance, maximin and minimum risk methods do not require additional information from the decision maker. The maximin and minimum risk methods do not use the whole information available in the matrix $\|x_{ij}\|$ and allow software realization which relatively easily works with a large number of alternatives. The dominance method allows simple software realization, but if $|A| = m$, the number of possible comparisons may be equal to $\binom{m}{2}$. These comparisons are performed easily if the whole matrix $\|x_{ij}\|$ is in the main memory but however, the time necessary for performing the operations grows fast with growing of the dimension of the problems which are solved. The dominance method does not require purely numerical criteria. If they are linear orders, they can be defined by ranks and after that it is possible to search for non-dominated alternatives.

The conjunctive and disjunctive methods use additional information which does not cause difficulties to the decision maker, besides that these methods allow simple software realization of the computation process when problems with large dimensions are considered.

The lexicographic, Berezovsky-Kempner and permutations methods use as preliminary data some orders of the partial criteria and the first two give the subsets of alternatives as an output result. The Berezovsky-Kempner, Hannan and permutations methods are characterized by durable computations when the number of subsets of alternatives is enlarged.

The linear assignment method, the simple additive weighting method, the hierarchical additive weighting method ELECTRE II, the ideal point method and the reference point method use weighting factors for presentation of the importance of the partial criteria. The linear assignment method and ELECTRE II work heavily with problems comprising of dozens of alternatives. The simple additive weighting method and the hierarchical additive weighting method do not differ in their formal characteristics, but the second method has the advantage that gradually it aggregates several criteria as well as their observation and estimation, which allows the user to avail himself of additional information, thus increasing the reliability of the decision making. Both methods are fast in respect of computing. The reference point method can be realized in such a way that if there isn't any alternative which estimates satisfy the set reference levels, then the whole non-dominated set is found and its elements are arranged along the distance to the reference point. That is why the speed of this method is comparative to the speed of Pareto's method.

4 Summary of the practical experience with concourse software system

The program for multicriterial estimation and choice of finite sets CONCOURSE, was developed at the Institute of Industrial Cybernetics & Robotics.

On the basis of the experience from the work with the software system CONCOURSE, and the analysis of the features of the methods used in it, one can choose methods for multicriterial estimation and choice depending on: whether it is enough to choose a subset of alternatives, or it is necessary to list all the alternatives, the type of the partial criteria and the number of alternatives.

Table 2 gives the numerical results from the experiments by the Pareto method, with examples with different dimensions, as well as the duration of every experiment. On the grounds of the analysis of the features of the multicriterial estimation and choice methods, three types of classification can be done:

1. Depending on the available information as a result from the work of the method — part of the methods propose to the decision maker a subset of alternatives

No. of alternatives	No. of characteristics	No. of criterial functions	Time
40	15	15	4'25"
100	15	15	35'
350	15	15	123'

Table 2: Experiments by Pareto's method with the program CONCOURSE

for further analysis and choice, and the other part propose a linear order of all considered alternatives.

2. The multicriterial decision making process can be performed considering some additional information known to the decision maker, or without using such information.

3. The partial criteria which are numerical functions contain more information about the alternatives, than the partial criteria, which are a relation between alternatives. In this sense, the results obtained through the method of aggregation of orders are more incomplete than those obtained through the method of aggregation of numerical functions.

Such an analysis of the features of the multicriterial estimation and choice methods helps the decision maker (user of a method) in the choice of the most appropriate method. A decision support system (DSS) for multicriterial estimation and choice can point out the method appropriate for a particular case, on the basis of the information available for solving a particular multicriterial problem and the form of the desired final result.

5 Criteria for choice of multicriterial decision making methods

The multicriterial decision making methods can be considered according to the following criteria (described in detail by Hobbs, 1984):

1. Whether a method is appropriate for a particularly chosen problem, depending on its formulation. This depends on the form, in which the functions of the partial criteria are described, and on the fact whether the decision maker uses additional information or not, the kind of this additional information, what kind of output information is necessary to be obtained.

2. Price and ease of use. This criterion reflects what efforts and knowledge are required for the application of a certain method, whether this method arises computational difficulties, especially when the set of alternatives is a large one.

3. Theoretical soundness. This criterion finds whether the method simulates the respective multicriterial decision making, to what an extent the axioms of the method are compatible with the structure of the decision. These criteria show the ability of the multicriterial decision making method to make a proper estimation of the alternatives. The compatibility of two methods with the same parameters or an estimation is a symptom of their theoretical validity. The great differences in the results show that the methods cannot be valid simultaneously. It must be taken into consideration, however, that the compatibility does not guarantee theoretical validity, e.g. both methods can have the same systematic mistake "noise".

The experiments with the multicriterial analysis methods demonstrate how the methods differ in respect of their applicability to the particular problems, ease of use, validity and the results they yield. Due to the difficult formalization of the above listed criteria, comparatively reliable estimation can be done by people with broad experience in the field of decision making methods and multicriterial programming.

6 Conclusion

Summing up the above mentioned we can conclude that the choice of a method for solving a multicriterial estimation and choice problem supposes the estimation of a lot of criteria, consequently, for the purpose of such a choice the multicriterial decision making methods can be applied. The choice of a method demands analysis of the properties of the method and analysis of the peculiarities of the problem under consideration.

It is advisable to develop open systems which allow the use of additional methods for multicriterial estimation and choice, thus, the variety of methods enhancing the reliability of the final decision making. A DSS which has different methods for multicriterial choice can have some tools for multicriterial estimation of these methods. Such DSS will give the user some possibilities for a founded choice of the appropriate method.

References

Berezovsky, B. A., Kempner, L. M. (1979). An approach for ordering the partial criteria with respect to their importance. *Autom. and Remote Control* (USSR), No. 4 (in Russian).

Hannan, E. L. (1981). Obtaining nondominated priority vector for multiple objective decision making problems with different combinations of cardinal and ordinal information. *IEEE Trans. on Syst. Man and Cybern.*, vol. SMC-11, No. 8.

Hobbs, B. F. (1984). Experiments in multicriterial decision making and what we can learn from them: an example. *Lecture Notes in Economics and Mathematical Systems (LNEMS)*, Berlin etc., Springer Verlag, vol. 242.

Hwang, C. L., Kwangsun, Y. (1981). Multiple attribute decision making. Methods and applications, *LNEMS*, Berlin etc., Springer Verlag, vol. 186.

Popchev, I., Guevsky, I., Danev, B., Metev, B., Slavov, G., Ionov, K. (1985). Technology for multicriterial estimation and choice. Bulgarian Industrial Association, Sofia, (in Bulgarian).

Popchev, I. P., Metev, B. S. (1985). Mathematical problems of multicriteria. In: Optimization decision making, microprocessors, systems. Bulgarian Academy of Sciences, Sofia, (in Bulgarian).

Popchev, I. P., Metev, B. S., Markova, L. P. (1987). Multicriterial estimation and ordering of a system software with multicriterial estimation, *Tehnicheska misal*, Sofia, No. 1, (in Bulgarian).

Popchev, I. P., Metev, B. S., Hristov, Ch. M., Markova, L. P. (1985). Interactive system for multicriterial estimation and choice. Bulgarian Academy of Sciences, Sofia, (in Bulgarian).

Two–Person Finite Games with Nature Participation and without Messages about its Choices

B. Metev* B. Danev** G. Slavov**

* *Institute of Industrial Cybernetics & Robotics, BAS*
1113 Sofia, Bulgaria
** *Bulgarian Industrial Association*
134 Rakovski Str.
1000 Sofia, Bulgaria.

1 Introduction

A finite game between two players is considered. Their payoffs depend of their choices, as well as on another parameter, too, which is chosen by the Nature. The game has fixed sequence of moves, both players have different information. The particularity is in the following: the second player (P2) knows the real choice s_c of the Nature, before to make his own choice, and the first player (P1) does not know s_c but he knows that s_c is known to P2. P1, having the first move, can suggest different strategies to P2. P1 can set his choice in dependence with different communications (messages) of P2 — for the second player's choice, for the Nature's choice, for both. The first case is considered here, i.e. P1 needs messages on P2 choice only, but not on the Nature choice. An approach for finding appropriate strategies for P1 using binary linear programming is proposed. Some possibilities to get estimates of his best guaranteed result are described.

2 Game description. Problem formulation

Two players (P1 and P2) participate in the game under consideration. P1 chooses $x \in X$, $|X| = m$, P2 chooses $y \in Y$, $|Y| = n$. The payoff function for P1 is $w_1 = f_1(x, y, s)$, and this for P2 is $w_2 = f_2(x, y, s)$. Here $s \in A$, $|A| = p$, s is chosen by the Nature. m, n, and p are natural numbers. w_1 and w_2 are real functions. P1 knows the sets X, Y, A and the functions w_1 and w_2. P2 knows the sets X, Y, A and w_2. The Nature chooses $s_c \in A$ before P1 and P2 to make their choices. P2 comes to know s_c and P1 does not know s_c. But P1 knows that s_c is known to P2. Each player wants to maximize his own payoff (or to get maximin) and this wish of P2 is known to P1.

P1, having the right of the first move, proposes to P2 a function $\tilde{x}(y)$ as a strategy, promising to choose $\tilde{x}(y_c)$, if P2 communicates y_c. Subsequently, P1 follows the proposed strategy. P2, knowing exactly s_c and the communicated strategy $\tilde{x}(y)$, chooses and communicates such y_c, which maximizes his own payoff. (P2 always communicates the chosen y_c). P1 knows this behaviour of P2 and, knowing w_2, can determine his own guaranteed result on the whole A for each strategy $\tilde{x}(y)$. The problem is to find such strategy $\tilde{x}(y)$, for which this guaranteed result is maximum.

The sequence of the moves in the game is as follows. First, the Nature chooses s_c and P2 comes to know s_c. Then P1 chooses $\tilde{x}(y)$ and communicates this function to P2. P2, knowing $\tilde{x}(y)$ and s_c, chooses and communicates y_c, maximizing his own payoff. P1 chooses $x_c = \tilde{x}(y_c)$ and both players get $f_1(x_c, y_c, s_c)$ and $f_2(x_c, y_c, s_c)$ respectively.

3 An expression for the maximin for P1

Each function $\tilde{x}(y)$ maps (point-to-point) the whole Y into some $\mathcal{X} \subseteq X$. Let $\widetilde{X}$ be the set of all such functions $\tilde{x}(y)$ and let u denote an arbitrary $\tilde{x}(y) : u = \tilde{x}(y) \in \widetilde{X}$. P2, knowing $u = \tilde{x}(y)$ and s_c, chooses and communicates such y_c, for which

$$f_2(\tilde{x}(y_c), y_c, s_c) = \max_{t \in Y} f_2(\tilde{x}(t), t, s_c)$$

Therefore it is necessary to know the sets

$$B(u, s_c) = \left\{ y / f_2(\tilde{x}(y), y, s_c) = \max_{t \in Y} f_2(\tilde{x}(t), t, s_c) \right\}$$

When $u = \tilde{x}(y)$ is chosen and $s_c \in A$ is fixed, P1 gets at least

$$\min_{y \in B(u, s_c)} f_1(\tilde{x}(y), y, s_c)$$

His guaranteed result on the whole A is

$$\min_{s_c \in A} \min_{y \in B(u, s_c)} f_1(\tilde{x}(y), y, s_c)$$

Therefore the problem is to find a strategy $\tilde{x}(y)$, which gives the following maximin:

$$R = \max_{\tilde{x}(y) \in \widetilde{X}} \min_{s_c \in A} \min_{y \in B(u, s_c)} f_1(\tilde{x}(y), y, s_c)$$

This is the maximal guaranteed result for P1.

4 Game analysis

Some notations, used in the previous section, are convenient to get an expression for the maximin for P1 as well as to move to continuous (semi-continuous) games, analogous to the described. It is possible to use, however, some other notations for the game under consideration in order to get formulations, convenient from the computational point of view.

We prefer here to denote the choice of P1 by $i \in I$, $|I| = m$, respectively $j \in J$, $|J| = n$ denotes the choice of P2. The Nature chooses $s \in A$, $|A| = p$. The payoff function for P1 is given by the series of matrices $\|a_{ij}^s\|$ $(i \in I, \ j \in J, \ s \in A)$. An analogous series $\|b_{ij}^s\|$ gives the payoff function for P2 (for the same i, j, s). All a_{ij}^s and b_{ij}^s are real numbers. We denote the searched strategy by $\tilde{\imath}(j)$. Each function $\tilde{\imath}(j)$ can be represented by a binary matrix $\|x_{ij}\|$ $(i \in I, \ j \in J)$. There is exactly one unity in each column of $\|x_{ij}\|$ (for each j), all other elements of $\|x_{ij}\|$ are equal to zero. We will use "the strategy $\|x_{ij}\|$" and "the strategy $\tilde{\imath}(j)$" as equivalents.

We do not have a relatively good algorithm for direct finding a best strategy, guaranteeing R to P1. We will consider here a replacing problem for finding a strategy, guaranteeing p_s to P1 and q_s to P2 for different $s \in A$. If this problem can be easily solved, varying p_s and q_s (for example under additional assumptions $p_s \equiv p_0$ and $q_s \equiv q_0$) leads to relatively good strategies for P1.

Thus, we suppose that the real number p_s and q_s are given. The following binary matrices $\|c_{ij}^s\|$ and $\|d_{ij}^s\|$ are introduced:

$$c_{ij}^s = \begin{cases} 1, & \text{if} \quad a_{ij}^s \geq p_s \\ 0, & \text{if} \quad a_{ij}^s < p_s \end{cases} \qquad (i \in I, \ j \in J, \ s \in A)$$

$$d_{ij}^s = \begin{cases} 1, & \text{if} \quad b_{ij}^s \geq q_s \\ 0, & \text{if} \quad b_{ij}^s < q_s \end{cases} \qquad (i \in I, \ j \in J, \ s \in A)$$

We will search for such a binary matrix $\|x_{ij}\|$, $i \in I$, $j \in J$ that satisfies the following restrictions:

$$\left| \begin{array}{lll} \sum_i x_{ij} = 1 & (\forall j \in J) & (1) \\ x_{ij} & \text{(if there exists some } s\text{, for which } d_{ij}^s = 1 \text{ and } c_{ij}^s = 0) & (2) \\ \sum_{i,j} x_{ij} \cdot d_{ij}^s \geq 1 & (\forall s \in A) & (3) \end{array} \right.$$

The equalities (1) are included, because there must be exactly one $i \in I$ for each $j \in J$. Equalities (2) do not permit $x_{ij} = 1$ if P2 can get 1 when P1 gets 0. We include one equality $x_{ij} = 0$ for each pair (i, j), if for this pair there exists one $s \in A$, for which $d_{ij}^s = 1$ and $c_{ij}^s = 0$. In this way we search for such strategies $\|x_{ij}\|$ only, which give the maximum to P2 in the places, where is the maximum for P1. The inequalities (3) guarantee that P2 can get 1 for each $s \in A$. If there is one $s \in A$, for which (3) does not hold, the choice of P2 at this s and this $\|x_{ij}\|$ is not dirigible. When, in addition, (2) hold, P1 gets 1 at each $s \in A$.

The system of restrictions (1), (2), (3) is linear one. The existence of one solution of this system can be checked by any standard software tool for linear (binary) programming problems. Each matrix $\|x_{ij}\|$, which is a solution of this system, is a strategy, which guarantees $p = \min_s p_s$ to P1 and $q = \min_s q_s$ to P2.

The number of the restrictions (1) is equal to n. The number of the restrictions (2) is not greater than $(m-1)n$. The number of the restrictions (3) is equal to p.

The conditions (restrictions) (1), (2), (3) are sufficient for the existence of a strategy, guaranteeing $p = \min_s p_s$ to P1 and $q = \min_s q_s$ to P2. They are not necessary, however. More exactly, there can be a strategy which guarantees the same p and q to P1 and P2, but for which there is one $s \in A$, such that the corresponding inequality (3) does not hold. This is possible when P2 gets 0 with each $j \in J$, but P1 gets 1 with each choice of P2 and with this strategy (and having suitable payoff function).

The shown way for obtaining replacing binary matrices is not unique. First we can suppose that initially $p_s \equiv p_0$ and $q_s \equiv q_0$. On the other hand we can use some reasons to form the binary matrices for P1 and after this we can use those new matrices to form the binary matrices for P2.

We have seen in the previous sections the possibility to use standard software tools for binary linear programming problems. A way to use the full capacity of such tools is including goal function under consideration. Lets consider the values (the numbers) $x_{ij} \cdot c^s_{ij} \cdot a^s_{ij}$. When $s \in A$ is fixed, these are the payoff for P1 which are not less than p_s and can be chosen by the strategy $\|x_{ij}\|$. It is possible to include the inequalities

$$x_{ij} \cdot c^s_{ij} \cdot a^s_{ij} \geq z \qquad (i \in I,\ j \in J,\ s \in S_1 \subset A) \tag{4}$$

Here S_1 contains these $s \in A$ for which P1 wants to maximize his own payoff. The number of restrictions (4) depends on $|S_1|$ as well as on the number of nonzero c^s_{ij} for $s \in S_1$. The wish to maximize the result for P1 for all $s \in S_1$, preserving the guarantees of p_s, can be expressed by the problem

$$\begin{gathered} \max z \\ \text{s.t. restrictions (1), (2), (3), (4)} \end{gathered}$$

Thus we have a standard binary linear programming problem. His solution $\|x_{ij}\|$ guarantees p_s to P1 for different $s \in A$ and probably higher payoff for $s \in S_1$. But, really, this is not a strategy, which maximizes the payoff for P1 at $s \in S_1$, because we have not taken into account the interest of P2 and his real choices.

Let $p = \min_s p_s$ and $q = \min_s q_s$. The strategy, which guarantees p to P1 and q to P2, will be called (p,q)-strategy. If there exist a (p,q)-strategy, there is no sense to look for (p_1,q_1)-strategy when $p_1 \leq p$, $q_1 \leq q$, because each (p,q)-strategy is a (p_1,q_1)-strategy, too. If there is no (p,q)-strategy, there is no (p_1,q_1)-strategy, too, for which $p_1 \geq p$, $q_1 \geq q$. This is due to the fact that the restrictions (2) for (p_1,q_1)-strategy give a subset of the set given by the same restrictions for the (p,q)-strategy. Such and similar reasons for existing or nonexisting of a good strategy can be used when looking for ways to maximize the payoff for P1.

It is possible to propose at least two ways for obtaining upper bounds for the maxmin R for P1 (in the game under consideration). First we can fix one $s \in A$ and find a strategy $\tilde{\imath}(j)$ which gives the highest guaranteed result to P1 for this s. This result is an upper bound for R. There exists corresponding exact, relatively fast, but unpublished algorithm, which does not use replacing binary matrices and finds the best result for P1 as well as one strategy, giving this result. For the corresponding continuous game there exist fundamental theorems of Yu.B. Germeier (1976). Second, a similar game is considered from Metev and Slavov (1986). In this game P1 proposes to P2 a strategy $\tilde{\imath}(j,s)$, i.e. P1 needs communications about the Nature choice, too. Because the strategy $\tilde{\imath}(j)$ is a special case of a strategy $\tilde{\imath}(j,s)$, the highest guaranteed result for P1 in the game with the strategy $\tilde{\imath}(j,s)$ is an upper bound for the highest guaranteed result for P1 in the game here considered.

5 Conclusion

A two-person finite game with payoffs depending on the Nature choice is considered. There is a fixed sequence of moves, the players exchange some information between them but this information does not concern the Nature choice. It is possible to use standard software tools in solving binary linear programming problems when searching for strategy which gives highly guaranteed result for the first player. Some ways to obtain upper bounds for the best guaranteed result for the first player are given.

References

Burkov, V.N. and Enaleev, A.K. (1985). Optimality of the open control principle. Necessary and sufficient conditions for information reliability in active systems. *Automat. and Remote control*, No. 3 (in Russian).

Germeier, Yu.B. (1976). Games with non-opposite interests. Science (Nauka), Moscow, (in Russian).

Kukushkin, N.S. and Morozov V.V. (1984). Theory of nonantagonistic games. University of Moscow, Moscow, (in Russian).

Metev, B.S. and Slavov, G.G. (1986). Two-person finite games with messages on the Nature choices. In: Large-Scale Modelling and Interactive Decision Analysis (Proceedings...), Lecture Notes in Economics and Mathematical Systems, Vol. 273, Springer-Verlag.

Sensitivity and Trade–off Analysis in Multiobjective Programming

Hirotaka Nakayama
Department of Applied Mathematics
Konan University
8–9–1 Okamoto, Higashinada, Kobe 658, Japan

Abstract

In multi-objective programming, the trade-off analysis is one of the most important tasks. There have been many devices in interactive programming methods so that the decision maker can make his trade-off easy. The purpose of this paper is to present a method for making trade-off easy by use of sensitivity analysis in linear programming. Some special consideration will be given on the sensitivity analysis at the degenerate optimal solution in LP which has been developed just recently.

1 Satisficing trade-off method for multi-objective programming

We consider the following multi-objective problem:

$$\text{(MOP)} \qquad \text{Minimize} \quad f(x) := \big(f_1(x), \ldots, f_r(x)\big)$$
$$\text{subject to} \quad x \in X \subset R^n.$$

Here the constraint set X may be represented by several functions

$$g_i(x) \leqq 0 \quad (i = 1, \ldots, m), \qquad h_j(x) = 0 \quad (j = 1, \ldots, s).$$

Throughout this paper, we impose the following assumption:

Assumption 1.1 The functions f_i $(i = 1, \ldots, r)$ and the set X are convex. For each effective domain *dom* f_i of f_i, the following holds:

$$X' := X \cap dom\ f_i \cap \ldots \cap dom\ f_r \neq \emptyset.$$

We shall use the following notations for an order for two vectors $y = (y_1, \ldots, y_r)$ and $z = (z_1, \ldots, z_r)$

$$\begin{array}{lll} y \geqq z & \Longleftrightarrow & y_i \geqq z_i, \qquad i = 1, \ldots, r \\ y \geq z & \Longleftrightarrow & y \geqq z \quad \text{and} \quad y \neq z \\ y > z & \Longleftrightarrow & y_i > z_i, \qquad i = 1, \ldots, r \end{array}$$

For the multi-objective programming problem (MOP), there does not necessarily exist a solution which minimizes all the objective function simultaneously. As the second best, therefore, we try to attain to the level where some of objective function can be improved only by sacrifice of some of other objective functions.

Definition 1.1 A vector x^* of X is called a strong Pareto solution to the problem (MOP), if the following relation holds:

$$f(x) \nleq f(x^*) \qquad \text{for any } x \in X.$$

On the other hand, x^* satisfying

$$f(x) \nless f(x^*) \qquad \text{for any } x \in X.$$

is called a weak Pareto solution.

For weak Pareto solutions, in general, some of objective functions can be improved more, while other objective functions are unchanged. Therefore, in practical decisions, strong Pareto solutions are preferred to mere weak Pareto solutions.

Since Pareto solutions constitute a subset of X in general, we introduce another value judgment so that an alternative may be singled out as a final decision. For this purpose, in practice, we usually take the value judgment of the decision maker. In this event, interactive programming methods, which look for an appropriate solution while eliciting some information on the value judgment of the decision maker, have been observed very effective. Among many kinds of interactive programming methods, the satisficing approach is very attractive because it requires the decision maker only very easy judgment, e.g. his aspiration level (Nakayama, 1984; Wierzbicki, 1986). We shall review the algorithm of the satisficing trade-off method in the following:

Step 1 (setting the ideal point). The ideal point $f^* = (f_1^*, \ldots, f_r^*)$ is set, where f_i^* is small enough, for example, $f_i^* \leqq \min\{f_i(x) \mid x \in X\}$. This value is fixed throughout the following process.

Step 2 (setting the aspiration level). The level $\bar{f}_i^k$ of each objective function f_i at the k–th iteration as asked to the decision maker. Here $\bar{f}_i^k$ should be set in such a way that $\bar{f}_i^k > f_i^*$. Set $k = 1$ for the first iteration.

Step 3 (weighting and finding a Pareto solution by the Min-Max method). Set

$$w_i^k = \frac{1}{\bar{f}_i^k - f_i^*}, \tag{1.1}$$

and minimize one of the following achievement functions over X:

$$\begin{aligned}
p_1 &= \max_{1 \leqq i \leqq r} w_i\big(f_i(x) - f_i^*\big) \\
p_2 &= \max_{1 \leqq i \leqq r} w_i\big(f_i(x) - \bar{f}_i\big) \\
q_1 &= \max_{1 \leqq i \leqq r} w_i\big(f_i(x) - f_i^*\big) + \alpha \sum_{i=1}^{r} w_i\big(f_i(x) - f_i^*\big) \\
q_2 &= \max_{1 \leqq i \leqq r} w_i\big(f_i(x) - \bar{f}_i\big) + \alpha \sum_{i=1}^{r} w_i\big(f_i(x) - \bar{f}_i\big)
\end{aligned}$$

Here we shall take P_1. Since the objective function P_1 is not smooth, its minimization is usually reduced to the following equivalent problem:

$$\text{(EQ)} \qquad \text{Minimize} \quad z$$
$$\text{subject to :} \quad w_i^k\left(f_i(x) - f_i^*\right) \leqq z, \qquad i = 1, \ldots, r$$
$$x \in X$$

Let x^k be a solution of (EQ).

Step 4 (trade-off). Based on the value of $f(x^k)$, the decision maker classifies the criteria into three groups, namely,

(i) the class of criteria which he wants to improve more,

(ii) the class of criteria which he may agree to relaxing,

(iii) the class of criteria which he accepts as they are.

The index set of each class is represented by I_I^k, I_R^k, I_A^k, respectively. If $I_I^k = \emptyset$, then stop the procedure. Otherwise, the decision maker is asked his new acceptable level of criteria $\tilde{f}_i^k$ for the class of I_I^k and I_R^k. For $i \in I_A^k$, set $\tilde{f}_i^k = f_i(x^k)$. Replace k by $k+1$, and go to Step 3.

For the satisficing trade-off method, the following is known:

- First of all, from Assumption 1.1 there exists some $x \in X$ such that $f(x)$ is finite, and hence there also exists $z \in R$ such that

$$w_i\left(f_i(x) - f_i^*\right) < z. \tag{1.2}$$

  Namely, the Slater's constraint qualification for Problem (EQ) holds under our assumption.

Theorem 1.1 Let $\tilde{x}$ be a solution to (EQ). Then there exists Lagrange multiplier $\tilde{\lambda} = (\tilde{\lambda}_1, \ldots, \tilde{\lambda}_r)$ such that

$$\sum_{i=1}^{r} \tilde{\lambda}_i = 1 \qquad \tilde{\lambda}_i \geqq 0, \qquad i = 1, \ldots, r, \tag{1.3}$$

$$\sum_{i=1}^{r} \tilde{\lambda}_i w_i \left(f_i(x) - f_i(\tilde{x})\right) \geqq 0 \qquad \text{for all } x \in X. \tag{1.4}$$

In addition, if $\tilde{x}$ is of the interior to the set X and each f_i has appropriate smoothness, then we have

$$\sum_{i=1}^{r} \tilde{\lambda}_i w_i \nabla f_i(\tilde{x}) = 0 \tag{1.5}$$

The Lagrange multiplier for (EQ) provides us very useful information.

Theorem 1.2 If all of the optimal Lagrange multipliers to the problem (EQ), $\tilde{\lambda}_i$ $(i = 1, \ldots, r)$, are nonzero, then the optimal solution to (EQ) is a strong Pareto solution. If some of $\tilde{\lambda}_i$ $(i = 1, \ldots, r)$ are zero, then the solution to (EQ) may not be a strong Pareto solution but merely a weak Pareto solution.

We can get a Pareto solution from a weak Pareto solution as follows:

$$
\begin{array}{lll}
(\mathrm{P}_\varepsilon) & \text{Maximize} & \sum_{i \in S} \varepsilon_i^2 \\
& \text{subject to}: & f_i(x) - \varepsilon_i^2 = f_i(\tilde{x}), \quad i \in S \\
& & f_i(x) = f_i(\tilde{x}), \qquad\quad i \notin S \\
& & x \in X
\end{array}
$$

where $S = \left\{ i \mid \tilde{\lambda}_i = 0, \ i = 1, \ldots, r \right\}$ and $\tilde{x}$ is a (weak) Pareto solution.

Theorem 1.3 If all ε_i for the solution to (P_ε) are zero, then $\tilde{x}$ itself is a strong Pareto solution. If there are some $\varepsilon_i \neq 0$, then the solution $\hat{x}$ to the problem (P_ε) is a strong Pareto solution.

Like this, we can get a strong Pareto solution from a given weak Pareto solution by solving an auxiliary optimization problem. However, in some cases such as structure design problems and camera lens design problems it is expensive to perform such an auxiliary optimization. In order to avoid such an additional scalar optimization problem, we can use scalarization function Q_1 or Q_2. The solution obtained by minimization of these scalarization function is assured to be a strong Pareto solution. Under this circumstance, however, even though the given aspiration level is feasible, the obtained solution is not necessarily satisfactory. On the other hand, the scalarization function P_1 or P_2 with the weight given by (1.1) provides us a satisfactory solution, only if the given aspiration level is feasible.

The above discussion shows that the information of Lagrange multiplier can be utilized for judging whether the solution to Problem (EQ) is a strong Pareto solution or a mere weak Pareto solution. In addition, we can use the information of Lagrange multiplier for trade-off. According to (1.5), $\beta_i = \lambda_i w_i$ represents the sensitivity of mutual affects among the criteria caused from the perturbation of f_i on the Pareto surface. Based on these information, the decision maker can know how much he has to sacrifice the criteria f_i $(i \in I_R)$ in order to assure the improvement of f_j $(j \in I_I)$. In the recent version of satisficing trade-off method, we can assign the amount of sacrifice automatically in the equal proportion to $\tilde{\lambda}_i w_i$ by using (1.4) or (1.5) as follows

$$
\triangle f_j = \frac{-1}{N \tilde{\lambda}_j w_j} \sum_{j \in I_I} \tilde{\lambda}_i w_i \triangle f_i \qquad j \in I_R \tag{1.6}
$$

where N is the number of elements of the set I_R. By doing this, in cases where there are a large number of criteria, the burden of the decision maker can be decreased so much. Of course, if the decision maker does not agree with this quota $\triangle f_j$ laid down automatically, he can modify them in a manual way.

2 Sensitivity analysis and trade-off analysis

In mathematical programming, the sensitivity analysis is considered as an investigation of affect to the objective function or the solution caused from a change of some parameters. On the other hand, the trade-off analysis is to judge how much he may relax other criteria in order to improve some of criteria holding the Pareto optimality. Clearly, the trade-off analysis can be considered to be a kind of sensitivity analysis. In this subsection, we shall show we can make the trade-off analysis more precisely by the use of sensitivity analysis in linear case.

Lemma 2.1 Under the assumption 1.1, the set $f(X) + R^r_+$ is convex. Furthermore, if the set X is convex polyhedral, and if the function f is linear, then the set $f(X) + R^r_+$ is also convex polyhedral.

It is well known that under the assumption 1.1 each Pareto solution can be characterized by the following problem

$$\begin{array}{lll} \min & f_k(x) & \\ \text{subject to} & f_i(x) \leqq \varepsilon_i \quad i = 1, \ldots, r & i \neq k \\ & x \in X. & \end{array}$$

In case of $k = r$, setting

$$F(\varepsilon_1, \ldots, \varepsilon_{r-1}) := \min \Big\{ f_r(x) \mid f_i(x) \leqq \varepsilon_i, \ \ i = 1, \ldots, r-1, \ \ x \in X \Big\},$$

we have the following theorem:

Lemma 2.2 *epi* $F = f(X) + R^r_+$

It should be noted that $(\tilde{\lambda}_1 w_1, \ldots, \tilde{\lambda}_r w_r)$ in Theorem 1.1 is a normal vector of the supporting hyperplane of $f(X) + R^r_+$ at $f(\tilde{x})$. Therefore, for $\tilde{\lambda}_r \neq 0$,

$$(-\tilde{\lambda}_1 w_1 / \tilde{\lambda}_r w_r, \ldots, -\tilde{\lambda}_{r-1} w_{r-1} / \tilde{\lambda}_r w_r)$$

is a subgradient of the function F at $\big(f_1(\tilde{x}), \ldots, f_{r-1}(\tilde{x})\big)$.

In trade-off, the amount of relaxation given by (1.6) is not sufficient in general, in particular, in nonlinear and convex cases. Therefore, we may modify it as follows:

$$\Delta f_j = \frac{-1}{N \tilde{\lambda}_j w_j} \sum_{j \in I_I} \tilde{\lambda}_i w_i \Delta f_i - \varepsilon, \quad \varepsilon > 0, \quad j \in I_R$$

However, in linear cases a more precise analysis is possible. We shall review the sensitivity analysis with respect to right hand side perturbation in linear programming:

(LP) $\qquad \min \ cx \qquad \text{subject to} \ \ Ax \leqq b, \quad x \geqq 0.$

Setting $f(b) := \min\big\{cx \mid Ax \leqq b, \ \ x \geqq 0\big\}$, the followings are well known:

Lemma 2.3 $f(b)$ is convex, and piecewise linear.

Lemma 2.4 π^1 is an optimal dual solution to (LP) (i.e., $\pi^1 b = \max\{\pi b \mid A^T\pi \leqq c, \pi \leqq 0\}$), if and only if π^1 is a subgradient of $f(b)$ at b^1.

Lemma 2.5 If and only if the solution to (LP) is primal nondegenerate, the associated dual solution is unique.

It can readily be derived from the above lemmas that if the optimal solution to (LP) with $b = b^1$ is nondegenerate, then $f(b)$ is differentiable at $b = b^1$ and $\partial f(b)/\partial b_i = \pi_i^1$. However, it is quite recent that the sensitivity analysis for degenerate solution in linear programming has been developed (Akgül, 1984).

Theorem 2.1 In the final (optimal) simplex tableau, let $\bar{a}^i$ be the i–th row vector of A, and let $\bar{b}$ be the right hand side constant of the constraints. In addition, set $T := \{i \mid \bar{b}_i = 0\}$, and let π^* be one of the optimal dual solution, then the general form of the optimal dual solution $\pi = (\pi_1, \dots, \pi_m)$ is given by

$$\pi_s = \pi_s^* + \sum\{t_i \bar{a}_s^i \mid i \in T\} \qquad s = 1, \dots, m \tag{2.1}$$

where t_i satisfies

$$\bar{c} + \sum\{t_i \bar{a}^i \mid i \in T\} \geqq 0. \tag{2.2}$$

Here it should be noted that a_s^i is a component of i–th row vector of A corresponding to the slack variables.

From Lemma 2.4 and Theorem 2.1, the directional derivative of $F(b)$ at $\bar{b}$ along u is given by

$$f'(\bar{b} : u) = \max\{\pi u \mid \pi \text{ satisfies (2.1) and (2.2)}\}.$$

We can make the trade-off for linear multiobjective programming problems more easily by using the above relation.

Recall that if $\lambda_r \neq 0$ for the Lagrange multiplier $(\lambda_1, \dots, \lambda_r)$ for the problem (EQ), the vector $(-\lambda_1 w_1/\lambda_r w_r, \dots, -\lambda_{r-1} w_{r-1}/\lambda_r w_r)$ is a subgradient of the function F. Given the amount of improvement $\triangle f_i$ $(i \in I_I)$, ask the decision maker which criterion is the most relaxable. Let f_s be the most relaxable criterion. For $k \neq s$, the amount of relaxation $\triangle f_s$ is assigned in a manner given by (1.6). For $\triangle f_s$, we utilize the sensitivity analysis.

Namely, suppose without loss of generality, $I_I = \{1, \dots, p\}$, $I_R = \{p+1, \dots, r\}$ and $s = r$. Then each $\triangle f_i$ is given by the following:

(i) $\triangle f_i$ $(i \in I_I)$ are given by the decision maker.

(ii) For $\triangle f_j$ $(j = p+1, \dots, r-1)$,

$$\triangle f_j = \frac{-1}{(r-1-p)\lambda_j w_j} \sum_{i \in I_I} \lambda_i w_i \triangle f_i \qquad j = p+1, \dots, r-1$$

The general form of optimal dual solution to the auxiliary problem (EQ) for the given linear multi-objective problem is given by

$$\lambda_s = \lambda_s^* + \sum\{t_i \bar{a}_s^i \mid i \in T\} \qquad s = 1, \ldots, r \tag{2.3}$$

where λ^* is an optimal dual solution, and t_i satisfies

$$\bar{c} + \sum\{t_i \bar{a}^i \mid i \in T\} \geqq 0. \tag{2.4}$$

Here, $\bar{a}$, $\bar{c}$ and T corresponds to the auxiliary problem (EQ) for the given linear multi-objective problem.

Therefore, let $u_i = \triangle f_i$ $(i = 1, \ldots, r-1)$ and $\Lambda = (\lambda_1 w_1/\lambda_r w_r, \ldots, \lambda_{r-1} w_{r-1}/\lambda_r w_r)$, then $\triangle f_r$ is decided by

$$\triangle f_r = \max\{-\Lambda u \mid \Lambda \text{ satisfies (2.3) and (2.4) }\}. \tag{2.5}$$

Since each λ_i is a function of t and satisfies

$$\Lambda u = \sum \lambda_i(t)\, w_i\, u_i / \lambda_r(t)\, w_r,$$

the problem (2.5) is a kind of fractional programming. Finally, considering that we have $t \geqq 0$ in the constraint (2.4), we can reduce (2.5) to the following form of fractional problem:

$$\text{(F)} \qquad \begin{array}{ll} \text{Max} & (pt + p_0)/(qt + q_0) \\ \text{subject to} & Dt - d \leqq 0 \\ & t \geqq 0 \end{array}$$

Here, t, p and q are respectively vectors with the dimension of the number of elements of T in (2.3) and (2.4).

In order to solve (F), transforming

$$s = t/\lambda_r(t) w_r, \qquad \sigma = 1/\lambda_r(t) w_r$$

and solve the following equivalent linear problem:

$$\begin{array}{ll} \text{Max} & ps + p_0\sigma \\ \text{subject to} & Ds - d\sigma \leqq 0 \\ & qs + q_0\sigma = 1 \\ & s,\ \sigma \geqq 0 \end{array}$$

where s and t are vectors with the same dimension and σ is a scalar.

3 Concluding remarks

It may seem to be difficult to decide $\triangle f_r$ in such a manner as the above. However, the dimension of t, that is, the number of elements of T (it may be considered to be the degree of degeneracy of the solution of the problem (EQ)), is not so large in practice, it is not so difficult to solve (F) or the equivalent linear problem. Moreover, in cases with a small $\| u \|$, the new aspiration level obtained in a manner as in this paper may be expected to be of Pareto surface. In general, this situation can be realized with a help of range analysis made often in LP. This encourages us to save our computation efforts for solving the auxiliary problem (EQ).

It is also possible to apply the parametric optimization for solving (2.5). At this circumstance, the author noticed through the discussion with Prof. Korhonen during the conference that the method presented here has a close relation with Pareto Race by Korhonen-Wallenius, 1987.

References

Akgul, M. (1984). A Note on Shadow Prices in Linear Programming, *J. Oper. Res.*, 35, pp. 425–431.

Korhonen, P. and Wallenius, J. (1987). A Pareto Rece, Working Paper F–180, Helsinki School of Economics.

Korhonen, P. and Laakso, J. (1986). Solving Generalized Goal Programming Problems using a Visual Interactive Approach, *European J. of Operational Res.*, 26, pp. 355–363.

Nakayama, H. (1984). Proposal of Satisficing Trade-off Method for Multiobjective Programming, *Transact. SICE*, 20, pp. 29–35 (in Japanese).

Nakayama, H. and Sawaragi, Y. (1984). Satisficing Trade-off Method for Interactive Multiobjective Programming Methods. In: Grauer, M. and Wierzbicki, A.P.(eds.) Interactive Decision Analysis, Proceeding of an International Workshop on Interactive Decision Analysis and Interpretative Computer Intelligence, Springer, pp. 113–122.

Nakayama, H. and Furukawa, K. (1985). Satisficing Trade-off Method with an Application to Multiobjective Structural Design, *Large Scale Systems*, 8, pp. 47–57.

Nakayama, H., Nomura, J., Sawada, K. and Nakajima, R. (1986). An Application of Satisficing Trade-off Method to a Blending Problem of Industrial Materials. In: Fandel, G. et al. (Eds.), Large Scale Modelling and Interactive Decision Analysis. Springer, Berlin, pp. 303-313.

Sawaragi, Y., Nakayama, H. and Tanino, T. (1985). Theory of Multiobjective Optimization, Academic Press.

Wierzbicki, A. (1986). On the Completeness and Constructiveness of Parametric, Characterization to Vector Optimization Problems. *OR Spektrum*, 8, pp. 73–87.

Choice of a Subset with Respect to Many Criteria

I. Popchev, B. Metev, L. Markova
Institute of Industrial Cybernetics & Robotics
1113 Sofia, Acad. G. Bonchev Str., Bl. 2, Bulgaria

1 Introduction

Let A be a finite set and let several binary preference relations on A be given. Then the problem of determining an order which aggregates the given relations is well known. With some additional assumptions we have the problem for Kemeny median. It is well known too, that in some cases the corresponding algorithms are time-consuming.

The following questions arise. If, instead of orders, we search for partitions on A into two parts — "good" elements and "bad" elements — can we get some computational advantages, preserving in some sense the value of the solution? On the other hand, if we use Kemeny median for choosing the first q elements, is there a possibility to construct a problem for direct finding of q "good" elements?

Suppose, that the complete binary preference relations, given on A, are interpreted as partial criteria. There are also corresponding weighting coefficients which are natural numbers. The choice of a subset is considered as a choice of partition on A into two parts with a given number of elements in the first one. For such an arbitrary partition on A a function of distances to the given relations is defined, with respect to the weighting coefficients. This is performed using the matrices, which correspond to these relations and partitions. We consider the problem for finding such a partition on A (into two parts), which minimizes this function on the set of all similar partitions on A with a fixed number of elements in the parts. It is possible to solve these problems using standard software tools.

2 Some preliminary notions

Let A be a set with a finite number of elements a_i, $a_i \in A$, $|A| = n$. A complete binary nonstrict preference relation on A is given by the matrix $U = \|u_{ij}\|$

$$u_{ij} = \begin{cases} 1, & \text{if} \quad a_i \succ a_j \quad (a_i \text{ is better than } a_j) \\ 0, & \text{if} \quad a_i \approx a_j \quad (a_i \text{ as good as } a_j) \\ -1, & \text{if} \quad a_i \prec a_j \end{cases} \qquad (\forall ij)$$

The following equations hold: $u_{ij} + u_{ji} = 0$, $u_{ii} = 0$ $(\forall ij)$. The set of all such binary relations on A is denoted by $\hat{S}$, the set of all corresponding matrices U is denoted by $\hat{V}$.

Several relations $R_k \in \hat{S}$ ($k = 1, 2, \ldots, r$) by the corresponding matrices U^k are given, corresponding weighting coefficients p_k (natural numbers) are given too.

Let $S_2 \subset \hat{S}$ denote the set of all possible partitions of A into two parts: A_1 and A_2. Such an arbitrary partition is interpreted in the following way:

$$\begin{array}{llll} a_i \approx a_j & \text{if} \quad a_i, a_j \in A_1 & \text{or} & a_i, a_j \in A_2; \\ a_i \succ a_j & \text{if} \quad a_i \in A_1 & \text{and} & a_j \in A_2. \end{array}$$

Let $V_2 \subset \hat{V}$ denote the set of all matrices U corresponding to the elements of S_2. On the other hand it is possible to represent each partition from S_2 by binary vector $\vec{t} = (t_1, \ldots, t_n)$, where

$$t_i = \begin{cases} 1 & \text{if} \quad a_i \in A_1 \\ 0 & \text{if} \quad a_i \in A_2 \end{cases}$$

T_2 is the set of all possible vectors $\vec{t}$. $|S_2| = |T_2| = 2^n$.

A well known way to get linear order on A, aggregating the given R_k, is using the matrix L:

$$L = \sum_{k=1}^{r} p_k U^k = \|l_{ij}\|, \qquad l_{ij} = \sum_{k=1}^{r} p_k u_{ij}^k$$

the numbers $s_i = \sum_j l_{ij}$ define a linear order on A:

$$\begin{array}{ll} a_i \succ a_j & \text{if} \quad s_i > s_j, \\ a_i \approx a_j & \text{if} \quad s_i = s_j. \end{array}$$

We call this order a WS-order (weighted-sum order).

It is known from Kemeny and Snell (1970), that for $U, V \in \hat{V}$ the function

$$\sigma(U, V) = \sum_{i,j} |u_{ij} - v_{ij}|$$

is distance in the set $\hat{V}$. Then it is possible to consider the following function $F(W)$ for an arbitrary $W \in \hat{V}$, when all matrices U^k corresponding numbers p_k are given:

$$F(W) = \sum_{k=1}^{r} p_k \cdot \sigma(U^k, W)$$

The relation (a partition), corresponding to the matrix which minimizes the function $F(W)$ (perhaps under some additional constraints) is the optimal one.

3 Problem formulation

In this paper we will study the minimization of $F(W)$ on V_2 under constraint $|A_1| = q$. Instead of $F(W)$ we minimize a corresponding pseudoboolean function given on T_2. Thus, each partition on A into two parts (A_1 and A_2, $|A_1| = q$), for which the corresponding W minimizes $F(W)$, contains a subset A_1, which is a possible solution.

Denote by U_g the set, containing p_k matrices U^k, $k = 1, 2, \dots, r$,

$$|U_g| = \sum_{k=1}^{r} p_k.$$

For an arbitrary $W \in \hat{V}$

$$F(W) = \sum_{k=1}^{r} p_k \cdot \sum_{i,j} |u_{ij}^k - w_{ij}| = \sum_{i,j} \sum_{k} p_k |u_{ij}^k - w_{ij}|.$$

Let

$$f_{ij}(w_{ij}) = \sum_{k=1}^{r} p_k |u_{ij}^k - w_{ij}|.$$

It is possible to use the numbers e_{ij}^+, e_{ij}^0, e_{ij}^- for more convenient representation of f_{ij}. e_{ij}^+ is the number of positive units in the i–th row and j–th column of all matrices from U_g. e_{ij}^0 and e_{ij}^- are the numbers of zeroes and negative units, respectively. Then

$$\begin{aligned} f_{ij}(1) &= e_{ij}^0 + 2e_{ij}^- &= b_{ij} \\ f_{ij}(0) &= e_{ij}^+ + e_{ij}^- &= c_{ij} \\ f_{ij}(-1) &= 2e_{ij}^+ + e_{ij}^0 &= d_{ij} \end{aligned}$$

If $R \in S_2$, the corresponding $W \in V_2$ and corresponding $\vec{t} \in T_2$ are linked by the following equations (for more information see Popchev and Metev, 1979)

$$w_{ij} = t_i - t_j \qquad\qquad (\forall i, j).$$

Then

$$\begin{aligned} f_{ij}(0-0) &= f_{ij}(1-1) = c_{ij}, \\ f_{ij}(0-1) &= d_{ij}, \\ f_{ij}(1-0) &= b_{ij}. \end{aligned}$$

Thus, we have the following representation:

$$\begin{aligned} f_{ij}(w_{ij}) &= f_{ij}(t_i - t_j) = \\ &= b_{ij}\Big[t_i(1-t_j)\Big] + c_{ij}\Big[t_i t_j + (1-t_i)(1-t_j)\Big] + d_{ij}\Big[(1-t_i)t_j\Big] = \\ &= c_{ij} + (b_{ij} - c_{ij})t_i + (d_{ij} - c_{ij})t_j + (2c_{ij} - b_{ij} - d_{ij})t_i \cdot t_j. \end{aligned}$$

It is possible to simplify the obtained function.

The equalities $e_{ij}^+ = e_{ji}^-$ $(\forall i, j)$ are true, because $u_{ij}^k + u_{ji}^k = 0$, $(\forall i, j, k)$; $e_{ij}^0 = e_{ji}^0$, too. Because

$$\begin{aligned} b_{ij} - c_{ij} &= e_{ij}^0 + e_{ij}^- - e_{ij}^+, \\ d_{ji} - c_{ji} &= e_{ji}^0 + e_{ji}^+ - e_{ji}^-, \end{aligned}$$

then

$$b_{ij} - c_{ij} = d_{ji} - c_{ji},$$

moreover

$$2c_{ij} - b_{ij} - d_{ij} = -2e_{ij}^0.$$

Thus, we have the following problem.

- Let the complete binary nonstrict preference relations $R_k \in \hat{S}$ $(k = 1, 2, \ldots, r)$ on A be given. All R_k are interpreted as partial criteria and they are represented by the corresponding matrices $U^k \in \hat{V}$. The corresponding weighting coefficients p_k and the natural number $q < n$ are given, too. Determine a subset $A_1 \subset A$, $|A_1| = q$, for which the following minimum is obtained

$$\min_{\vec{t} \in T_2} \sum_{i,j} \left[c_{ij} + 2(b_{ij} - c_{ij})t_i - 2e^0_{ij} t_i t_j \right]$$

  under the restriction: $\sum_i t_i = q$.

This is a quadratic pseudoboolean programming problem. There are different ways to analyse it, but the standard one is using linearization. It is possible to ignore the terms $e^0_{ij} t_i \cdot t_j$, for which $i = j$, because $e^0_{ii} = \sum_k p_k$ for all i and because $\sum_i t_i = q$. A common way for linearization is the following (Watters, 1967; Taha, 1982). Each t_i^2 can be replaced by t_i. The products $t_i t_j$ are substituted by the new variables t_{ij}. For each new variable t_{ij} it is necessary to add two new constraints

$$\begin{aligned} t_i + t_j - t_{ij} &\leq 1 \\ -t_i - t_j + 2t_{ij} &\leq 0 \end{aligned}$$

to those of the problem.

Thus, we get a standard linear binary programming problem. The number of additional variables is equal to the number of equivalences $a_i \approx a_j$, contained in the given R_k for different i, j.

If $|A| = n$ and the relations R_k contain equivalences $a_i \approx a_j$ for each two elements $a_i, a_j \in A$, the number of needed variables is equal to $\frac{n(n+1)}{2}$. There are standard relevant programs for IBM PC (and compatibles), allowing, for example, up to 100 binary variables.

4 Some additional information

The optimal subset, determined in the previous section, can contain elements dominated in Pareto sense. This can be demonstrated by examples for the case when all R_k are linear orders and the Pareto set is easy for defining.

If all R_k are strict preference relations, then $e^0_{ij} = 0$ for $i \neq j$ and $e^0_{ii} = \sum_k p_k (\forall i)$. Under restriction $\sum_i t_i = q$, we can ignore all terms of 2nd power in the minimized function. Thus, we have to minimize a linear pseudoboolean function under one restriction — equality. Popchev and Metev (1986) have shown that instead of solving such a problem, we can use the WS-order — the first q elements in this order give a subset, which minimizes the function $F(W)$ considered here. But, for the general case ($e^0_{ij} \neq 0$ for some $i \neq j$) this is not true. It is possible to show by examples that the subset of q elements, which are first in the WS-order, does not minimize the function $F(W)$.

It is easy to use the suggested method, because it needs standard software tools, only. The obtained subset can be an initial approximation in other methods for finding subsets with respect to many criteria.

References

Kemeny, J. G., Snell, J. L. (1970). Mathematical models in the social sciences, N.Y.

Linear Interactive Maximizing (Minimizing) System LINA-16. User's Guide. Bulgarian Academy of Sciences; Institute of Industrial Cybernetics & Robotics, May, 1986 (in Bulgarian).

Popchev, I. P., Metev, B. S. (1979). A choice of several elements with respect to many criteria which are relations. *Technicheska misal*, No.6, pp. 21–35, (in Bulgarian).

Popchev, I. P., Metev, B. S. (1986). Multicriterial choice of an "optimal" subset, *Syst. Anal. Model. Simul.* 3(2), pp. 167–169.

Taha, H. A. (1982). Operations research — an introduction. MacMillan Publishing Co., Inc. N.Y. Collier-MacMillan Publishers London.

Watters, L. J. (1967). Reduction of integer polynomial programming problems to zero-one linear programming problems. *Operat. Research,* 15(6) (Nov.-Dec.), pp. 1171–1174.

Degeneracy in Efficiency Testing in Bicriteria Integer Programming

R. Ramesh
School of Management
State University of New York at Buffalo
Buffalo, New York 14260

Mark H. Karwan
Department of Industrial Engineering
State University of New York at Buffalo
Buffalo, New York 14260

Stanley Zionts
School of Management
State University of New York at Buffalo
Buffalo, New York 14260

1 Introduction

This paper presents the theory underlying certain implementation features in an interactive solution framework for solving bicriteria integer programming problems. The solution framework is developed in (Ramesh et al., 1987). In this framework, a decision maker is assumed to have only an implicit utility function of the two objectives he wishes to maximize. The problem is solved by an interactive branch-and-bound method in which the decision-maker's preference structure is explored and determined using pairwise comparison questions.

The problem of concern is formulated as follows.

$$\begin{array}{lll} \text{Maximize} & g(Cx) & \text{(BCIP)} \\ \text{Subject to:} & Ax \leq b & \\ & x \geq 0, \ \text{integer} & \end{array}$$

where C and A are $n \times n$ and $m \times n$ matrices of criteria and constraint coefficients respectively. $b \in R^m$ is the vector of resources available, $x \in R^n$ denotes the vector of decision variables and $g(\cdot)$ is the implicit utility function of the decision maker which is assumed to be pseudoconcave and nondecreasing. The linear relaxation of problem (BCIP) is denoted as (BCLP).

The bicriteria problem has many special properties that can be successfully exploited in its solution (Ramesh et al., 1987) develop the theory underlying the bicriteria problem and present a solution framework incorporating several special features applicable only to the bicriteria problem. The problem (BCIP) is solved by employing the interactive multicriteria linear programming method of Zionts and Wallenius (1983) within a branch-and-bound framework. While solving this problem, certain cut constraints on the objective functions are derived from the decision-maker's responses. Further, the solution space is partitioned into sets that are efficient with respect to the incumbent, and the search is conducted separately in each set. In the bicriteria case, at most two such sets can be constructed and hence the exclusive search strategy is computationally viable. However, the cut constraints and the partitioning constraints lead to considerable degeneracy in the objective function space. This is because, these constraints are simple bounds on the objective functions. We show how this problem is handled in an implementation of the solution procedure for problem (BCIP) in this paper.

2 Efficiency procedure

In solving bicriteria problems, the objective functions are treated as variables and the cut constraints on the objectives are enforced as bounds on these variables. Similarly, partitioning the solution space is carried out by enforcing bound restrictions on the objectives. This however, gives rise to degeneracy in the objective function rows. The efficiency procedure has been modified to take this into account. The efficient extreme point solutions to the linear relaxation problem at any given node are classified into six categories for this purpose. The identification of adjacent efficient edges according to these categories is discussed below. This discussion is based on Figure 1 and 2.

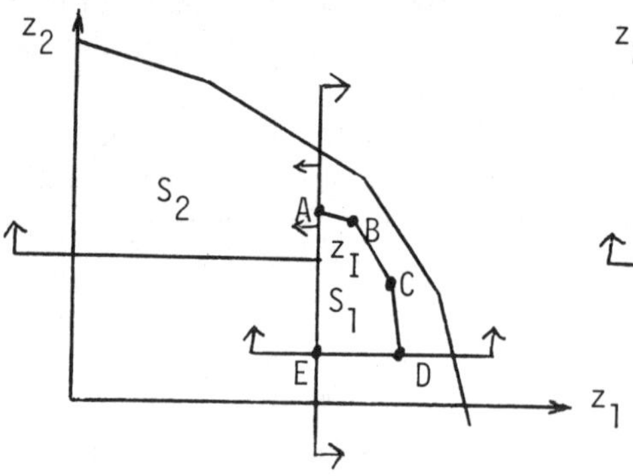

Figure 1. Categories in S_1.

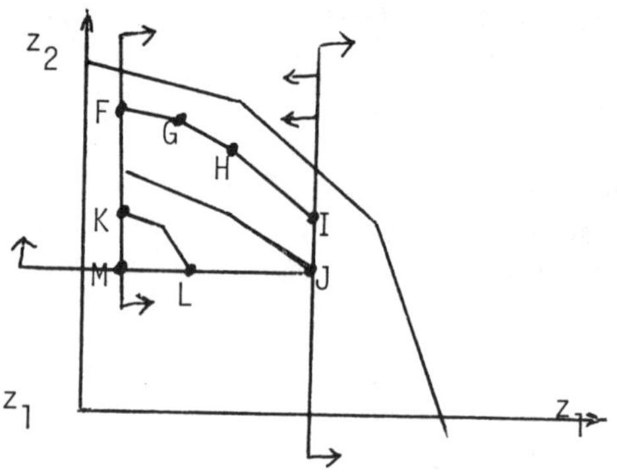

Figure 2. Categories in S_2.

Category 1

The variables z_1 and z_2 representing the objective functions are both basic and nondegenerate in the extreme point solutions in this category. Therefore, these solutions can have at most two distinct adjacent efficient extreme point solutions in the objective function space. Points B and C in Figure 1 and points G and H in Figure 2 belong to this category.

Category 2

The variable z_1 is at its lower bound and z_2 is basic nondegenerate in the extreme point solutions in this category. These points can have at most one distinct adjacent efficient extreme point solution in the objective function space. Points A and F in Figures 1 and 2 respectively, belong to this category. The identification of the adjacent efficient edges from points in this category is considered in the following cases.

Case 2a

In this case, z_1 is basic and degenerate. Let $(z_j^1 - c_j^1)$, $j = 1, \ldots, n$ denote the entries in the z_1-row and $(z_j^2 - c_j^2)$, $j = 1, \ldots, n$, denote the entries in the z_2-row. Let N_+ and N_- denote sets of nonbasic variables as follows:

$$N_+ = \Big\{ x_j \mid x_j \text{ is the nonbasic variable of column } j \text{ and } (z_j^1 - c_j^1) \geq 0 \text{ and } (z_j^2 - c_j^2) < 0 \Big\}$$

$$N_- = \Big\{ x_j \mid x_j \text{ is the nonbasic variable of column } j \text{ and } (z_j^1 - c_j^1) < 0 \text{ and } (z_j^2 - c_j^2) \geq 0 \Big\}$$

These sets are identified in the z_1 and z_2 rows as follows:

$$\begin{array}{cccc}
\hline
+\,+\,+\,+ & -\,-\,-\,- & +\,+\,+\,+\,+\,+\,+\,+\,+ & = z_1 \\
\hline
-\,-\,-\,- & +\,+\,+\,+ & +\,+\,+\,+\,+\,+\,+\,+\,+ & = z_2 \\
\hline
\underbrace{\qquad\quad}_{N_+} & \underbrace{\qquad\quad}_{N_-} & \text{Inefficient edges} &
\end{array}$$

Note that $(z_j^1 - c_j^1) < 0$ and $(z_j^1 - c_j^1) > 0$ is not possible since the current solution is efficient. It can also be seen that if the set N_- is empty, then the tableau is optimal with respect to z_1, and therefore, there is no adjacent efficient edge from the current solution. On the other hand, if N_- is not empty, then the adjacent efficient edge can be identified by employing the efficiency tests on the tradeoff vectors corresponding to the columns represented by the variables in N_-. However, introducing the nonbasic variable corresponding to the adjacent efficient edge into the basis will result in one of the following cases:

1. The entering variable takes a nondegenerate pivot. In this case, the adjacent extreme point solution obtained after the pivot is efficient.

2. The entering variable takes a degenerate pivot. In this case, a new basis representing the same extreme point is obtained by performing the degenerate pivot. The sets N_+ and N_- are reidentified from the new basis, and the efficiency procedure is repeated.

Case 2b

In this case, z_1 is nonbasic. Therefore z_1 is the candidate for entering the basis. Introducing any other nonbasic variable into the basis will either result in the same solution vector or lead to dominated solutions, since the current solution is efficient. Entering z_1 into the basis will result in one of the following cases:

1. z_1 takes a nondegenerate pivot. In this case, z_2 will decrease since the current solution is efficient. The adjacent extreme point solution obtained after the pivot is efficient.

2. z_1 takes a degenerate pivot. Hence after the pivot, z_1 is basic degenerate and z_2 is basic nondegenerate. This is the same situation as in Case 2a.

Category 3

The variable z_2 is at its lower bound and z_1 is basic nondegenerate in the extreme point solutions in this category. These points can have at most one distinct adjacent efficient extreme point solution in the objective function space. Points D and L in Figures 1 and 2 respectively, belong to this category. The identification of adjacent efficient edges form points in this category is performed on similar line to those in Category 2.

Category 4

Both variables z_1 and z_2 are at their respective lower bounds in the solutions in this category. Points E and M in Figures 1 and 2 respectively, belong to this category. It can easily be seen that these are the only feasible solutions to the linear relaxation problem, since they are efficient.

Category 5

This category is exclusive to partition S_2. The variable z_1 is at its upper bound and z_2 is basic nondegenerate in the solutions in this category. These points can have at most one distinct adjacent efficient extreme point solution in the objective function space. Point I in Figure 2 belongs to this category. If can be observed that this category is essentially the same as Category 2 except that z_1 is at its upper bound in this case. The identification of adjacent efficient edges from points in this category is considered in the following cases.

Case 5a

In this case, z_1 is basic and degenerate. It can be seen that if the set N_+ is empty, then the tableau is optimal with respect to z_2, and therefore, there is no adjacent efficient edge from the current solution. On the other hand, if N_+ is not empty, then the adjacent efficient edge can be identified by employing the efficiency tests on the tradeoff vectors corresponding to the columns represented by the variables in N_+. However, introducing the nonbasic variable corresponding to the adjacent efficient edge into the basis could result in a degenerate or nondegenerate pivot. These two cases are handled as in Case 2a.

Case 5b

In this case, z_1 is nonbasic. Therefore, z_1 is the candidate for entering the basis. Introducing any other nonbasic variable will either result in the same solution vector or lead to a dominated solution as in Case 2b. Entering z_1 into the basis will result in one of the following cases:

1. z_1 takes a nondegenerate pivot. In this case, if z_2 increases from its current value by entering z_1, then the pivot leads to the adjacent efficient extreme point. On the other hand, if z_2 decreases by entering z_1, then a dominated solution is obtained. This shows that there is no adjacent efficient edge from the current solution in this case.

2. z_1 takes a degenerate pivot. Hence after the pivot, z_1 is basic degenerate and z_2 is basic nondegenerate. This is the same situation as in Case 5a.

Category 6

This category is also exclusive to partition S_2. In this case, z_1 is at its upper bound and z_2 is at its lower bound. Point J in Figure 1 belongs to this category. It can be observed from Figure 2 that there can at most be one distinct adjacent efficient extreme point in this case. Identification of adjacent efficient edges from points in this category is considered in the following cases.

Case 6a

In this case, both z_1 and z_2 are basic and degenerate. It can be seen that if the set N_+ is empty, then the tableau is optimal with respect to z_2, and therefore there is no adjacent efficient edge from the current solution. Hovewer, if N_+ is not empty, then the situation is the same as in Case 5a and is therefore handled accordingly.

Case 6b

In this case, z_1 is nonbasic and z_2 is basic degenerate. Therefore, z_1 is the candidate for entering the basis. Introducing any other nonbasic variable into the basis will either result in the same solution vector or lead to a dominated solution, since the current solution is efficient. Entering z_1 into the basis will result in one of the following cases.

1. z_1 takes a nondegenerate pivot. Since z_1 is decreased from its upper bound, the value of z_2 will increase by entering z_1 into the basis if the element in the row in which z_2 is basic and the column in which z_1 is nonbasic is strictly positive. The adjacent extreme point obtained in this case is efficient. This is shown in the following diagram:

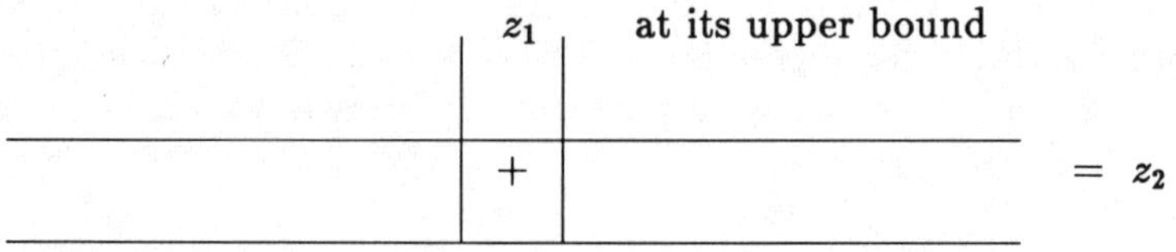

However, if this element is zero, then a dominated solution is obtained after the pivot. In this case, there is no adjacent efficient edge from the current solution.

2. z_1 takes a degenerate pivot. In this case if the element in the z_2-row and z_1-column is nonnegative, then degeneracy does not occur in the row in which z_2 is basic. Therefore, after entering z_1, both z_1 and z_2 are basic and degenerate, and the situation is the same as in Case 6a. However, if the element in the z_2-row and z_1-column is strictly negative, then z_2 will leave the basis if z_1 is entered. Therefore, trying to enter z_2 into the new basis will result in z_1 leaving it, leading to cycling between the two bases. Since entering any other nonbasic variable results in inefficient adjacent extreme point solutions, the procedure for the identification of the adjacent efficient edge from the current solution is not continued. A new efficient extreme point is generated by using a different set of multipliers and the Zionts-Wallenius procedure is continued from that solution.

Case 6c

In this case, z_2 is nonbasic and z_1 is basic degenerate. This case is similar to Case 6b and is therefore treated as similar lines. z_2 is the candidate for entering the basis. Entering z_2 will result in one of the following cases.

1. z_2 takes a nondegenerate pivot. Since z_2 is increased from its upperbound, the value of z_1 will decrease by entering z_2 into the basis if the element in the row in which z_1 is basic and the column in which z_2 is nonbasic is strictly negative. The adjacent extreme point obtained in this case is efficient. This is shown in the following diagram:

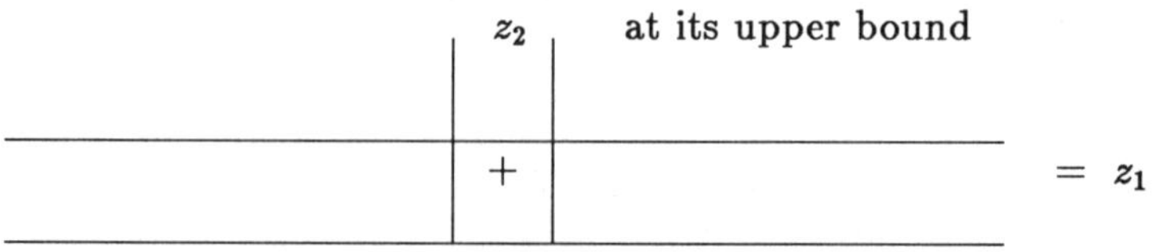

However, if this element is zero, then a dominated solution is obtained after the pivot. In this case, there is no adjacent efficient edge from the current solution.

2. z_2 takes a degenerate pivot. If the element in the z_2-row and z_1-column is nonpositive, then z_2 is entered into the basis and treated as in Case 6a. However, if the element is strictly positive, then degeneracy occurs in the row in which z_1 is basic and leads to cycling as in Case 6b. Therefore the efficiency procedure is terminated, and a new efficient extreme point is generated by using a different set of multipliers and the Zionts-Wallenius procedure is continued from that solution.

Case 6d

In this case, both z_1 and z_2 are nonbasic. If z_2 is entered into the basis, it will take a degenerate pivot, since the current solution is efficient. After entering z_2, z_1 is still nonbasic while z_2 is basic degenerate. This situation is the same as in Case 6a and is treated accordingly.

The efficiency procedure for bicriteria problems proceeds as follows: Initially the category of the current solution is determined. Based on this, the appropriate case is ascertained. The identification of the adjacent efficient edges is then carried out according to the above discussion.

3 Computational experience

The solution framework for problem (BCIP) has been programmed in FORTRAN V and implemented on the CDC–Cyber/730 at the State University of New York at Buffalo. (Ramesh et al., 1987) provide detailed computational experience with the various components of the solution framework. The bicriteria problem has been solved for problems with 10, 20 and 30 variables, and 4, 8 and 12 constraints, respectively. The decision maker is simulated on the computer using different utility functions. These functions are, quadratic (0.3, 0.7), quadratic (0.5, 0.5), fourth-degree (0.3, 0.7) and fourth-degree (0.5, 0.5), respectively. The figures within parentheses represent the weights on the objective functions in the respective utility functions. A completely randomized block design consisting of the problem size parameters and the utility functions is used. Twenty randomly generated problems were solved in each cell of this design. In this experiment, the number of questions asked of the decision maker was reduced between 10% and 15% by enforcing the cut constraints while solving the problem. Similarly, the number of questions was reduced between 20% and 25% by partitioning the solution space in the solution process. This reduction is significant, and hence results in decreased cognitive load in the decision making process. No significant changes in the solution time were observed with both the enforcement of cut constraints and partitioning the solution space. Since the reduction in the number of questions is significant when these two mechanisms are used, we conclude that these are effective mechanisms in facilitating the decision making process in solving bicriteria integer programming problems.

4 Conclusions

In this research, we have developed an efficient interactive solution framework for solving bicriteria integer programming problems. This framework has been developed for the large class of decision makers with underlying nonlinear utility functions. We present two components of this framework in this paper and discuss their implementation features. The implementation of these components leads to degeneracy in the objective function rows of the problem tableau. This problem has been effectively handled by appropriate modifications to the efficiency identification procedure. Our computational experience shows that these components can lead to a significant reduction in the number of questions asked. We conclude from this research that the two components are effective tools in minimizing the cognitive load in decision making while solving bicriteria integer programming problems. Possible areas of application are numerous. These include project selection, warehouse location, strategic planning and policy analysis, and many more.

Bibliography

Chalmet, L.G., Lemonidis, L. and Elzinga, D.J. (1983). An Efficient Algorithm for the Bi-Criterion Integer Programming Problem. Research Report No. 82–9. Department of Industrial and Systems Engineering, University of Florida, Gainesville.

Ramesh, R. (1985). Multicriteria Integer Programming. Unpublished Doctoral Dissertation, Department of Industrial Engineering, State University of New York at Buffalo.

Ramesh, R., Karwan, M.H. and Zionts, S. (1986). A Class of Practical Interactive Branch and Bound Algorithms for Multicriteria Integer Programming. *European Journal of Operations Research*, Vol. 26, No. 1.

Ramesh, R., Karwan, M.H. and Zionts, S. (1987). Interactive Bicriteria Integer Programming: Theory and Experimental Results. Working Paper No. 668, School of Management, State University of New York at Buffalo.

Zionts, S. (1979). A Survey of Multiple Criteria Integer Programming Methods. *Annals of Discrete Mathematics*, Vol. 5.

Zionts, S. and Wallenius, J. (1983). An Interactive Multiple Objective Linear Programming Method for a Class of Underlying Nonlinear Utility Functions. *Management Science*, Vol. 29, No. 5.

Trends in Interactive Multiple Objective Programming

Ralph E. Steuer
Department of Management Science
and Information Technology
University of Georgia
Athens, Georgia 30602, USA

Introduction

This paper discusses 25 topics that trace the past, present, and future development of interactive multiple objective programming. Grouped by decade, the topics are as follows:

- 1970s
  1. Linear Case
  2. Vector–Maximum Algorithms
  3. Vector–Maximum Codes
  4. Efficiency Versus Nondominance
  5. Interactive Procedures
  6. Filtering
- 1980s
  7. Integer and Nonlinear Cases
  8. Optimal Versus Final Solutions
  9. Nonconcavity of U
  10. Trajectory Applications
  11. Reference Point Procedures
  12. Unsupported Nondominated Criterion Vectors
  13. General Algorithmic Outline
  14. Cold Starting Versus Warm Starting
  15. Commercial–Grade Workhorse Software

16. DSS Implementations
17. Aspiration–Led Versus Algorithm–Led Reference Point Procedures
18. Consolidation
19. User Control

- 1990s

20. Switching
21. Preserving Convergence Achievements
22. Polyscreen Workstations
23. Group Decision Making
24. Network Optimization Applications
25. Supercomputers Versus Microcomputers

1 Linear case

Most of the work in multiple criteria optimization in the 1970s was on the multiple objective linear programming (MOLP) problem.

$$\begin{array}{ll} \max & \{c^1 x = z_1\} \\ \vdots & \\ \max & \left\{c^k x = z_k\right\} \\ s.t. & x \in S \end{array}$$

where k is the number of objectives and

$$S = \{x \in \Re^n \mid Ax = b, \;\; x \geq 0, \;\; b \in \Re^m\}$$

is the feasible region in *decision space*. Let $Z \subset \Re^k$ be the feasible region in *criterion space* where $z \in Z$ if and only if there exists an $x \in S$ such that $z = (c^1 x, \ldots, c^k x)$. *Criterion vector* $\bar{z} \in Z$ is *nondominated* if and only if there does not exist another $z \in Z$ such that $z_i \geq \bar{z}_i$ for all i and $z_i > \bar{z}_i$ for at least one i. The set of all nondominated criterion vectors is designed N and is called the *nondominated set*. A point $\bar{x} \in S$ is *efficient* if and only if its criterion vector $\bar{z} = (c^1\bar{x}, \ldots, c^k\bar{x})$ is nondominated. The set of all efficient points is designated E and is called the *efficient set*. Our interest in the efficient set E and the nondominated set N stems from the fact that a decision maker's (DM's) optimal point is efficient (Steuer, 1986b).

2 Vector–maximum algorithms

Sometimes an MOLP is written in *vector–maximum* form

$$v - \max\{Cx = z \mid x \in S\}$$

where "v − max" means that the endeavor is to maximize the vector $z \in \Re^k$, and C is the $k \times n$ *criterion matrix* whose rows are the c^i.

In an MOLP, the efficient set E is either

(i) all of S or
(ii) a portion of the surface of S.

Case (ii) is the usual situation. Algorithms for computing (characterizing) E are called vector–maximum algorithm (see Evans and Steuer, 1973; Yu, 1974; Zeleny, 1974; Isermann, 1977; Gal, 1977; Ecker, Hegner and Kouada, 1980).

3 Vector–maximum codes

There are two types of vector–maximum codes:

(a) algorithms that compute all efficient extreme points and all unbounded efficient edges

(b) algorithms that compute all efficient extreme points, all unbounded efficient edges, and all *maximally* efficient facets.

A maximally efficient facet is an efficient facet of S that is not contained in another efficient facet of higher dimension.

ADBASE (Steuer, 1986a) is a mainframe vector–maximum code of type (a). Introduced in 1974, ADBASE has undergone numerous revisions. For *international transportability*, ADBASE has been written in low level language Fortran IV. ADBASE is the most widely distributed mainframe vector–maximum code.

EFFACET (Isermann and Naujoks, 1984) is another Fortran vector–maximum code. It is of type (b). Because of the work involved in computing all maximally efficient facets, EFFACET is limited to vector–maximum problems of no more than 10 objectives, 40 constraints, and 60 variables. In addition to the mainframe version, a microcomputer version is available.

4 Efficiency versus nondominance

Efficiency is a decision space concept, and nondominance is a criterion space concept. That is, $\bar{x} \in S$ in decision space is efficient if and only if its criterion vector $\bar{z} \in Z$ in criterion space is nondominated. Points in S that are not efficient are *inefficient.* The criterion vector of an inefficient point is *dominated.* Whereas efficient points are *contenders* for optimality, an inefficient point can never be optimal.

5 Interactive procedures

Originally, it was thought that an MOLP could be solved by computing all efficient extreme points and then asking the DM to select the best one. However, after vector–maximum codes became available, it was found that MOLPs had far more efficient extreme points than anyone had imagined. For instance, a 5 objective, 50 constraint, and

100 structural variable MOLP can easily have over 2000 efficient extreme points. As a result, people's attention turned to ***interactive procedures*** for exploring the efficient set for the best solution. The most prominent interactive procedures to have been developed during the 1970s were:

1. STEM (Benayoun, de Montgolfier, Tergny and Larichev, 1971)
2. Geoffrion–Dyer–Feinberg Procedure (1972)
3. Zionts–Wallenius Procedure (1976 and 1983)
4. Steuer's Weighting Method (1977).

Another multiple criteria optimization method that was developed during the 1970s, that is neither a vector–maximum nor an interactive procedure, is the Surrogate Worth Tradeoff Method of Haimes, Hall, and Freedman (1975).

6 Filtering

Filtering (Steuer, 1986b) is a technique by which subsets of *dispersed* points can be selected from a larger finite set of points. The technique was developed to manage the large numbers of efficient extreme points generated in multiple objective linear programming.

Consider the following situation. We are exploring a neighborhood within the efficient set. We promise to bring the DM eight solutions representative of the neighborhood. Using a vector–maximum algorithm, we find that the neighborhood contains 40 efficient extreme points. Filtering would enable us to compute the eight most different (i.e. most dispersed) of the 40 for presentation to the DM.

7 Integer and nonlinear cases

As the 1970s drew to a close, research interest expanded to include multiple objective integer and multiple objective nonlinear programming:

$$\begin{array}{ll} \max & \{ f_1(x) = z_1 \} \\ \vdots & \\ \max & \{ f_k(x) = z_k \} \\ s.t. & \quad x \in S \end{array}$$

For the integer case, Bitran (1979) studied the vector–maximum generation of all efficient points, and Gabbani and Magazine (1981) and Karwan, Zionts and Villarreal (1981) studied interactive approaches. Nakayama, Tanino and Sawaragi (1980) and Sakawa (1982) studied interactive approaches for the nonlinear case.

8 Optimal versus final solutions

The ideal way to solve a multiple objective program would be to solve

$$\begin{array}{lll} \max & \{U(z_1 ... z_k)\} & \\ s.t. & f_i(x) = z_i & 1 \leq i \leq k \\ & x \in S & \end{array}$$

where $U : \Re^k \rightarrow \Re$ is the DM's utility function, because any solution that solves this program is an *optimal* solution of the multiple objective problem. Multiple objective programs, however, are not solved in this way because of the difficulty in obtaining an accurate enough mathematical representation of U. As a result, we use approaches that do not require explicit knowledge of the DM's utility function. Such methods produce *final* solutions. A final solution is either optimal, or close enough to being optimal, to satisfactorily terminate the decision process.

9 Nonconcavity of U

Most multiple criteria research is based on the assumption that the DM's utility function is *quasiconcave* (i.e. all of its level sets are convex). However, many DMs may have utility functions that are *not* quasiconcave. Consider a manager that "likes to do something well, or not at all". As shown in (Steuer, 1986b), such behaviour can lead to non–quasiconcave utility functions. If this is true, we must also pay attention to multiple criteria solution procedures that can address the non–quasiconcave utility function case.

10 Trajectory applications

Perhaps the most challenging applications are multiple criteria *trajectory* optimization applications. These are multiple criteria problems with ***multiple observation points*** (multi–time periods or multi–surveillance points). Suppose we have such a problem in which we wish to monitor k criteria over T observation points. In such problems we often have a goal level of achievement for each criterion at each observation point. Then, for each objective, the "path" of goal criterion values forms a *goal trajectory* over the T observation points. By the same token, for each solution, there is a "path" of criterion values for each objective over the T observation points. In these problems, the purpose is to find the solution whose k *criterion value trajectories* most closely match the k goal trajectories. To illustrate, we have the following:

- MANPOWER PLANNING (a multi–time period application)
  - min {overdeviations from salary budget}
  - min {underdeviations from strength–of–force requirements}
  - min {deviations from promotion targets}
  - min {underdeviations from length of service goals}

- RIVER BASIN MANAGEMENT (a multi–surveillance point application)
  - achieve {BOD standards}
  - achieve {nitrate standards}
  - min {pollution removal costs}
  - achieve {municipal water demands}
  - min {groundwater pumping}

11 Reference point procedures

Since 1980, most of the interest in interactive multiple objective programming has centered on the following *reference point* procedures:

1. Wierzbicki's Reference Point Method (Wierzbicki, 1980; Wierzbicki and Lewandowski, 1988).
2. The Tchebycheff Method (Steuer and Choo, 1983).
3. VIG: Visual Interactive Procedure (Korhonen and Laakso, 1986).

Actually, STEM of Section 5 is a reference point procedure. In STEM and in the Tchebycheff Method, the reference point $z^{**} \in \Re^k$ is calculated by the algorithm to dominate, and strictly dominate, all nondominated criterion vectors, respectively. In Wierzbicki's Method and VIG, z^{**} is specified by the DM at each iteration to reflect his or her updated aspirations. In Wierzbicki's Method, the Tchebycheff Method, and STEM, the reference point z^{**} is projected onto the nondominated set to produce *individual* criterion vectors. In VIG, the unbounded line segment, starting from the current point and passing through z^{**}, is projected onto the nondominated set to produce a *trajectory* of criterion values.

12 Unsupported nondominated criterion vectors

A nondominated criterion vector $\bar{z} \in Z$ is *unsupported* if and only if it does not maximize the *weighted–sum program*

$$\max\{\, \lambda^T z \mid\ z_i = f_i(x), \quad x \in S \,\}$$

for any $\lambda \in \Lambda = \left\{ \lambda \in \Re^k \mid\ \lambda_i \geq 0, \ \sum_{i=1}^k \lambda_i = 1 \right\}$ Otherwise $\bar{z}$ is *supported.*

Unsupported nondominated criterion vectors cannot be computed by the weighted–sums program because they lie in "nonconvex depressions" of the nondominated set. Although unsupported nondominated criterion vectors do not occur in MOLP, then often occur in multiple objective integer and multiple objective nonlinear programming. However, unsupported nondominated criterion vectors can be computed by the reference point procedures. This is because these procedures sample the nondominated set from z^{**} using L_∞ (Tchebycheff) based on distance measures and can thus "reach" into the nonconvex depressions. Along with their ability to compute nonextreme solutions in MOLP, we can see the power of the reference point methods.

13 General algorithms outline

All interactive multiple objective programming procedures more or less fit the following *general algorithmic outline*:

STEP 1: Get ready for 1st iteration.

STEP 2: Solve one or more single criterion optimization problems to sample the nondominated set.

STEP 3: Examine criterion vector results.

STEP 4: If DM wishes to continue, go to STEP 5. Otherwise, stop.

STEP 5: Get ready for next iteration and go to STEP 2.

Note that all steps, except Step 2, are free of heavy number–crunching demands.

14 Cold starting versus warm starting

Suppose we have a series of similar optimization problems. If the first is solved from "scratch" that problem is solved from a *cold start*. If a subsequent problem is solved from the optimal solution of a previously solved problem, that problem is solved from a *warm start*. The following suggests the kinds of savings that can be realized when solving a series of similar problems. Cold starting the first problem, suppose it takes 500 pivots. Warm starting the second problem, it may take 5 pivots to restore feasibility, and then 65 more pivots to achieve optimality, and so forth for all other subsequent problems. In this way, it may be possible to solve 5 to 10 problems in the time it takes to solve one from scratch.

15 Commercial–grade workhorse software

To address large problems, all of the interactive procedures of this paper have been designed to solve the optimization problems of Step 2 of the general algorithmic outline using commercial–grade products such as MPSX (IBM, 1979), MINOS (Murtagh and Saunders, 1980), and GRG2 (Lasdon and Waren, 1986). MPSX, although the international standard of linear and integer programming, is perhaps an example of the type of workhorse software *not* to use in interactive multiple objective programming. Its disadvantages are its high monthly fee, that external control is only allowed through PL/1, and that the user is denied access to the source code. MINOS and GRG2, on the other hand, can be obtained at cost, are written in Fortran, and are distributed with the source code. Thus, for international transportability, they can be modified and embedded in interactive procedures without license restrictions.

16 DSS implementations

Consider the four–part paradigm of a DSS (decision support system):

1. a database component,
2. a model component,
3. a solution procedure component,
4. a user–interface component.

While touching on components 2 and 4, the content of this paper primarily relates to 3, the solution procedure component. The general consensus is that the future of interactive multiple objective programming is in DSS implementations of this sort.

17 Algorithm–led versus aspiration–led reference point procedures

In the Tchebycheff Method, all the DM is required to do is select the most preferred from the group of solutions presented at each iteration. The algorithm then determines what neighborhood in the nondominated set is to be searched next. Hence the method is classified as an *algorithm–led* procedure. In Wierzbicki's Reference Point Method, the DM specifies an *aspiration* criterion vector at each iteration. The procedure then goes where the aspiration criterion vector sends it. Hence the method is classified as an *aspiration–led* procedure. Whereas STEM is an algorithm–led procedure, VIG is aspiration–led. Algorithm–led procedures are often very effective in the early iterations when the DM is still learning about the problem. Aspiration–led procedures are often most effective in the later iterations when the DM is trying to pinpoint a final solution.

18 Consolidation

Consolidation refers to the combining of different interactive procedures into a common computer package. This is possible because

(a) all of the interactive procedures of this paper follow the general algorithmic outline of Section 13
(b) all of the optimization problems of Step 2 are special cases of the *master sampling formulation*

$$
\begin{array}{llr}
\text{lex min} & \{\alpha, -\sum_{i=1}^{k} \lambda_i z_i\} & \\
\text{s.t.} & \alpha \geq \lambda_i (z_i^{**} - z_i) & i \in G \\
 & f_i(x) = z_i & i \in K \\
 & z_i \geq e_i & i \in H \\
 & x \in S & \\
 & z \in \Re^k, \text{ and } \alpha \in \Re \text{ unrestricted} &
\end{array}
$$

where $G \subset K$, $H \subset K$, and $K = \{1, 2, \ldots, k\}$. For instance, in the non-reference point procedures, the first lexicographic level and the first set of constraints would be vacuous. Of course, in all procedures, the λ_i's would be set in accordance with the rules of these procedures. Warm starting would be very desirable here, because the master sampling formulation changes little within each interactive procedure.

19 User control

User control refers to

1. control over the way the model is defined,
2. control over the solution procedure search for a final solution,
3. control over the way output is displayed.

The challenge in interactive multiple objective programming is to give excellent direction to the user, yet allow substantial user control. Without such direction and control, users will not be able to obtain what they expect when trying to deal with the types of complex applications typically encountered in multiple objective programming.

20 Switching

Although the literature has not yet seen any such applications, users of interactive multiple objective programming in the 1990s may wish to employ *switching*. Switching refers to the use of different interactive procedures on different iterations. For instance, a DM may wish to start with the Tchebycheff Method for one or two iterations, switch to VIG for the next one or two iterations, and then switch to Wierzbicki's Method for the last one or two iterations.

21 Preserving convergence achievements

Switching among interactive procedures iteration to iteration can be successfully negotiated if already attained convergence achievements can be preserved. This can be accomplished by preserving a *neighborhood* about the current point. This can be done by obtaining a weighting vector (denoted $\bar{\lambda}$) from the middle of the subset of weighting vector space pertaining to the current point. Then the set

$$\tilde{\Lambda} = \{ \lambda \in \Re^k | \ \lambda_i \in (\ell_i, \mu_i), \ \sum_{i=1}^{k} \lambda_i = 1 \}$$

where $0 \leq \ell_i$, $\mu_i \leq 1$ for all i, is centered about $\bar{\lambda}$ as well as possible. By specifying the size of $\tilde{\Lambda}$ relative to all of weighting vector space, the methodology of Steuer and Liou (1988) is able to compute the ℓ_i and μ_i for the specification of $\tilde{\Lambda}$. In this way, $\tilde{\Lambda}$ can be used to preserve a *neighborhood* about the current point when switching from one interactive procedure to another.

22 Polyscreen workstations

Although computer workstations with more than two screens have not been available as standard equipment, they certainly are feasible. The issue is "less display space and more windowing" versus "more display space and less windowing". Polyscreen workstations with up to six screens would enable us to see more and remember less (from windows that might otherwise be hidden or partially hidden). Having more on display at the same time would be especially helpful in trajectory applications because of the volumes of information generated. For example, at each iteration, two screens might be used to display criterion value range information for each objective over the nondominated set, model parameter values, and bounds values currently in effect on each variable. The remaining four screens might then be used to cross–reference different candidate solutions.

23 Group decision making

The interactive procedures of this paper have been more or less designed under the assumption that they would be used by a single decision maker or by a group of homogeneous decision makers. However, many of the applications in which multiple objective programming has great promise (e.g. in economic planning, energy planning, forestry, and water resources) involve groups of decision makers representing competing special interest groups. Consequently, it is important in the 1990s for researchers to develop and formalize group decision making protocols for use in such environments.

24 Network optimization applications

Consider the linear program (LP)

$$\max\{\, c^T x \mid \; x \in S\,\}$$

$$\text{s.t.}\;\; S = \{\, x \in \Re^n \mid \; Ax = b, \;\; x \geq 0, \;\; b \in \Re^m\,\}$$

If, apart from upper and lower bounds on the variables, A has

(i) no more than two nonzero elements per column
(ii) the nonzero elements are either 1's or $-$ 1's,

the LP is a *network*. Because of the special structure of A, networks can be solved using high–speed solution procedures (Kennington, 1980).

Let us now consider a multiple objective network. Unfortunately, with the interactive procedures discussed in this paper, the master sampling program of Section 18 is not a network because of the (non–network) *side–constraints*. However, with the development (which is currently in progress) of high–speed codes that can handle limited numbers of side–constraints in the master sampling program (Kennington and Aronson, 1987), multiple objective networks offer a growth area for applications in the 1990s.

25 Supercomputers versus microcomputers

Mainframe computers were mostly used in computational research in the 1970s. The 1980s have seen the microcomputer become dominant in multiple objective programming. However, the field must not ignore its large-scale potential and the fact that supercomputers are coming in the 1990s.

References

Benayoun, R., de Montgolfier, J., Tergny, J. and Larichev, O. (1971). Linear Programming with Multiple Objective Functions: Step Method (STEM), *Mathematical Programming*, Vol. 1, No. 3, pp. 366–375.

Bitran, G. R. (1979). Theory and Algorithms for Linear Multiple Objective Programs with Zero–One Variables, *Mathematical Programming*, Vol. 17, No. 3, pp. 362–390.

Ecker, J. G., Hegner, N. S. and Kouada, I. A. (1980). Generating All Maximal Efficient Faces for Multiple Objective Linear Programs, *Journal of Optimization Theory and Applications*, Vol. 30, No. 3, pp. 353–381.

Evans, J. P. and Steuer, R. E. (1973). A Revised Simplex Method for Multiple Objective Programs, *Mathematical Programming*, Vol. 5, No. 1, pp. 54–72.

Gabbani, D. and Magazine, M. J. (1981). An Interactive Heuristic Approach for Multi–Objective Integer Programming Problems, Working Paper No. 148, Department of Management Sciences, University of Waterloo, Waterloo, Ontario, Canada.

Gal, T. (1977). A General Method for Determining the Set of All Efficient Solutions to a Linear Vectormaximum Problem, *European Journal of Operational Research*, Vol. 1, No. 5, pp. 307–322.

Geoffrion, A. M., Dyer, J. S. and Feinberg, A. (1972). An Interactive Approach for Multicriterion Optimization with an Application to the Operation of an Academic Department, *Management Science*, Vol. 19, No. 4, pp. 357–368.

Haimes, Y. Y., Hall, W. A. and Freedman, H. T. (1975). Multiobjective Optimization in Water Resources Systems: The Surrogate Worth Trade–Off Method. Amsterdam: Elsevier.

IBM Document No. GH19–1091–1 (1979). IBM Mathematical Programming System Extended/370: Primer, IBM Corporation, Data Processing Division, White Plains, New York.

Isermann, H. (1977). The Enumeration of the Set of All Efficient Solutions for a Linear Multiple Objective Program, *Operational Research Quarterly*, Vol. 28, No. 3, pp. 711–725.

Isermann, H. and Naujoks, G. (1984). Operating Manual for the EFFACET Multiple Objective Linear Programming Package, Fakultät für Wirtschaftwissenschaften, Universität Bielefeld, Federal Republic of Germany.

Karwan, M. H., Zionts, S. and Villarreal, B. (1981). An Improved Multicriteria Integer Programming Algorithm, Working Paper No. 530, School of Management, State University of New York at Buffalo, Buffalo.

Kennington, J. L. (1980). Algorithms for Network Programming. New York: John Wiley & Sons.

Kennington, J. L. and Aronson, J. (1987). Private communications.

Korhonen, P. and Laakso, J. (1985). A Visual Interactive Method for Solving the Multiple Criteria Problem. *European Journal of Operational Research*, Vol. 24, No. 2, pp. 277–287.

Lasdon, L. S. and Waren, A. D. (1986). GRG2 User's Guide, University of Texas, Austin, Texas.

Murtaugh, B. A. and Saunders, M. A. (1980). MINOS/AUGMENTED User's Manual, Report SOL 80–14, Department of Operations Research, Stanford University, Stanford, California.

Nakayama, H., Tanino, T. and Sawaragi, Y. (1980). An Interactive Optimization Method in Multicriteria Decision Making, *IEEE Transactions on Systems, Man, and Cybernetics*, Vol. 10, No. 3, pp. 163–169.

Steuer, R. E. (1977). An Interactive Multiple Objective Linear Programming Procedure, *TIMS Studies in the Management Sciences*, Vol. 6, pp. 225–239.

Steuer, R. E. (1986a). Operating Manual for the ADBASE Multiple Objective Linear Programming Package, College of Business Administration, University of Georgia, Athens, Georgia.

Steuer, R. E. (1986b). Multiple Criteria Optimization: Theory, Computation, and Application. New York: John Wiley and Sons.

Steuer, R. E. and Choo, E.-U. (1983). An Interactive Weighted Tchebycheff Procedure for Multiple Objective Programming, *Mathematical Programming*, Vol. 26, No. 1, pp. 326–344.

Steuer, R. E. and Liou, F. H. (1988). Grid Point Weighting Vectors for Convergence Control in Multiple Objective Programming, to be presented at the International Conference on Multiobjective Problems in Mathematical Programming, October 26–28, 1988 Yalta, U.S.S.R.

Wierzbicki, A. P. (1980). The Use of Reference Objectives in Multiobjective Optimization, *Lecture Notes in Economics and Mathematical Systems*, No. 177, Berlin: Springer–Verlag, pp. 468–486.

Wierzbicki, A. P. and Lewandowski, A. (1988). Aspiration Based Decision Analysis and Support, Part I: Theoretical and Methodological Backgrounds, to be published at the International Institute for Applied Systems Analysis, Laxenburg, Austria.

Yu, P. L. (1974). Cone Convexity, Cone Extreme Points, and Nondominated Solutions in Decision Problems with Multiobjectives, *Journal of Optimization Theory and Applications*, Vol. 14, No. 3, pp. 319–377.

Zeleny, M. (1974). Linear Multiobjective Programming. *Lecture Notes in Economics and Mathematical Systems*, No. 95, Berlin: Springer–Verlag.

Zionts, S. and Wallenius, J. (1976). An Interactive Programming Method for Solving the Multiple Criteria Problem, *Management Science*, Vol. 22, No. 6, pp. 652–663.

Zionts, S. and Wallenius, J. (1983). An Interactive Multiple Objective Linear Programming Method for a Class of Underlying Nonlinear Utility Functions, *Management Science*, Vol. 29, No. 5, pp. 519–529.

Optimization of Hierarchical Systems with Multiple Objectives

Tetsuzo Tanino and Harukazu Satomi
Department of Mechanical Engineering II
Tohoku University, Sendai 980, Japan

1 Introduction

Optimization problems in the real world often have hierarchical structures and multiple objectives. For example, in a regional investment allocation problem, cities of subregions are lower level decision makers (DMs) and a prefecture consisting of them is an upper level DM. Moreover, each DM must take into account several objectives (criteria) such as economy, welfare, environment and so on. (Kobayashi et al., 1987).

In this paper we discuss optimization of hierarchical systems with multiple objectives. Assume that the system considered consists of two levels. The upper level optimization problem is given by

$$\begin{cases} \min\limits_{x} \; F(x, \hat{y}(x)) \\ \text{subject to} \;\; x \in X \subset R^n \end{cases}$$

where x is the upper level decision variable, F is a p-dimensional vector-valued function, and the vector $\hat{y}(x) = (\hat{y}^1(x), \dots, \hat{y}^N(x))$ is decided from the following N lower level optimization problems:

$$\begin{cases} \min\limits_{y^i} \; f^i(x, y^1, \dots, y^N) \\ \text{subject to} \;\; y^i \in Y_i(x, y^1, \dots, y^{i-1}, y^{i+1}, \dots, y^N) \subset R^{m_i} \end{cases} \qquad i = 1, \dots, N$$

Here y^i is the decision variable of the i-th subsystem in the lower level and f^i is a q_i dimensional vector-valued function.

In optimization of hierarchical systems, the upper level DM usually plays a role of coordinator. Hence we consider the above two-level optimization problem as an optimization (decision making) problem for the upper level DM. Two different approaches — a utility approach and an interactive approach — are taken according to whether the preference attitude of the DM is identified (i.e. the explicit utility function is obtained) a priori or it should be made clear in the process of decision making. We may classify our problems into the above-mentioned two cases from the viewpoint of the upper level DM. Moreover, as to the lower level optimization problems, we can consider the following two cases: the case in which a (unique) preferred solution for the lower level

DM can be obtained[1] and the case in which every Pareto optimal solution is accepted by the DM. After all, we consider the four cases described in the following table. This paper deals with these four cases in order.

Upper \ Lower	(Unique) preferred solution	Set of Pareto optimal solutions
Explicit utility function	Case 1	Case 2
Implicit utility function	Case 3	Case 4

Table 1: Classification of hierarchical multiobjective optimization problems.

2 Case 1: Upper level — explicit utility function Lower level — unique preferred solution

This section deals with the case in which the upper level utility function exists explicitly and each lower level multiobjective optimization problem has a (unique) solution via a utility function (scalarization). Throughout this paper we assume the following separability of the lower level problems for simplicity: each objective function f^i and constraint set Y_i are independent of y^j $(j \neq i)$, i.e. they are of the form $f^i(x, y^i)$ and $Y_i(x)$, respectively.

Let U be the upper level utility function. Since we assume the separability, every lower level optimization problem is of the same form, i.e. a minimization problem with respect to y^i depending on x. Therefore we may omit the superscript i, that is, we may assume that $N = 1$ for simplicity of description. Let u be a utility function or a scalarizing function in the lower level multiobjective problem. Then the whole hierarchical optimization problem is a scalar two-level minimization problem (Stackelberg problem) as follows:

$$\begin{cases} \min\limits_{x, \hat{y}(x)} \ \Psi(x, \hat{y}(x)) := U\big(F_1(x, \hat{y}(x)), \ldots, F_p(x, \hat{y}(x))\big) \\ \text{subject to} \quad x \in X \\ \qquad u\big(f_1(x, \hat{y}(x)), \ldots, f_q(x, \hat{y}(x))\big) = \min\limits_{y \in Y(x)} u(f_1(x, y), \ldots, f_q(x, y)) \end{cases}$$

The function F often depends rather on $f(x, \hat{y}(x))$ than directly on $y(x)$. If f is scalar-valued, we may assume $u(f) = f$ and hence $f(x, \hat{y}(x))$ is a so-called marginal function (optimal value function). The marginal function is not generally differentiable even when the functions in the original problem are all differentiable. However, several nice

[1] As Professor A.P. Wierzbicki pointed out, this case can be classified into two cases as in the upper level problems. However, in this paper, we focus on the case where the preferred solution of the lower level DM can be obtained by solving a scalar optimization problem.

results have been obtained concerning gradients, directional derivatives or generalized directional derivatives of the marginal function. Therefore the upper level optimization problem may be solved by using an appropriate nondifferentiable optimization method.

To the contrary, if f is vector-valued, $f(x, \hat{y}(x))$ is different from the marginal function $u(f(x, \hat{y}(x)))$ of the lower level problem. Hence we must discuss sensitivity analysis for the optimal solution $\hat{y}(x)$. Here we show the results for the case where Tchebycheff norm is used as the scalarizing function u and the constraint set $Y(x)$ is specified by inequalities. Namely we consider the following lower level optimization problem:

$$\begin{cases} \min\limits_{y} \max\limits_{i=1,\dots,q} & f_i(x, y) \\ \text{subject to} & g_j(x, y) \leqq 0, \quad j = 1, \dots, r \end{cases}$$

Here the origin is taken as the reference point for simplicity. This problem is equivalent to the following problem:

$$(P_x) \begin{cases} \min\limits_{y,z} z \\ \text{subject to} \quad f_i(x, y) - z \leqq 0, \qquad i = 1, \dots, q \\ \qquad\qquad\qquad g_j(x, y) \leqq 0, \qquad j = 1, \dots, r \end{cases}$$

The Lagrangian for the problem (P_x) is defined by

$$L(x, y, z, \mu, \lambda) = z + \sum_{i=1}^{q} \mu_i (f_i(x, y) - z) + \sum_{j=1}^{r} \lambda_j g_j(x, y)$$

We assume that the functions f_i $(i = 1, \dots, q)$ and g_j $(j = 1, \dots, r)$ are all twice continuously differentiable. Let x^* be a given value of the upper level decision variable, and $(y^*, z^*) \in Y(x^*) \times R$ be an optimal solution to the problem (P_{x^*}). Then, under some constraint qualification (e.g. linear independence constraint qualification in the theorems below), the following Kuhn-Tucker condition is satisfied:

$$\begin{array}{llll} \nabla_y L(x^*, y^*, z^*, \mu^*, \lambda^*) = 0, & & \sum\limits_{i=1}^{q} \mu_i^* = 1 & \\ \mu_i^* = 0, & f_i(x^*, y^*) \leqq z^*, & \mu_i^*(f_i(x^*, y^*) - z^*) = 0, & i = 1, \dots, q \\ \lambda_j^* = 0, & g_j(x^*, y^*) \leqq 0, & \lambda_j^* g_j(x^*, y^*) = 0, & j = 1, \dots, r \end{array}$$

where

$$\begin{array}{ll} I = \{i_1, \dots, i_h\} = \{ i \mid f_i(x^*, y^*) = z^* \}, & \tilde{I} = \{ i \mid \mu_i^* > 0 \}, \\ J = \{ j \mid g_j(x^*, y^*) = 0 \}, & \tilde{J} = \{ j \mid \lambda_j^* > 0 \}. \end{array}$$

We can obtain the following two theorems by applying the results of (Fiacco, 1983) and (Jittorntrum, 1984), respectively, to our problem.

Theorem 2.1. Assume the following conditions:

(a) Strict complementary slackness:

$$I = \tilde{I}, \qquad J = \tilde{J}$$

(b) Linear independence constraint qualification: The vectors

$$\begin{bmatrix} \nabla_y f_i(x^*, y^*) \\ -1 \end{bmatrix} \quad (i \in I), \qquad \begin{bmatrix} \nabla_y g_j(x^*, y^*) \\ 0 \end{bmatrix} \quad (j \in J)$$

are linearly independent.

(c) Second order sufficient condition for optimality (under (a)):

$$\left\langle v, \nabla^2_{yy} L(x^*, y^*, \mu^*, \lambda^*) v \right\rangle > 0$$

for any $v \neq 0$ such that

$$\begin{aligned} \left\langle \nabla_y f_{i1}(x^*, y^*), v \right\rangle &= \cdots = \left\langle \nabla_y f_{ih}(x^*, y^*), v \right\rangle \\ \left\langle \nabla_y g_j(x^*, y^*), v \right\rangle &= 0, \qquad j \in J. \end{aligned}$$

Then, there uniquely exist continuously differentiable vector-valued functions $y(\cdot)$, $z(\cdot)$, $\mu(\cdot)$, $\lambda(\cdot)$ defined on a neighbourhood of x^* such that

$$y(x^*) = y^*, \qquad z(x^*) = z^*, \qquad \mu(x^*) = \mu^*, \qquad \lambda(x^*) = \lambda^*$$

and $(y(x), z(x))$ is a strict local optimal solution to (P_x) and $(\mu(x), \lambda(x))$ is a corresponding Lagrange multiplier vector. Moreover

$$\begin{bmatrix} \nabla_x y_1(x^*)^T \\ \vdots \\ \nabla_x y_m(x^*)^T \\ \hline \nabla_x z(x^*)^T \\ \hline \nabla_x \mu_1(x^*)^T \\ \vdots \\ \nabla_x \mu_q(x^*)^T \\ \hline \nabla_x \lambda_1(x^*)^T \\ \vdots \\ \nabla_x \lambda_r(x^*)^T \end{bmatrix} = - \left[\begin{array}{c|c|ccc|ccc} \nabla^2_{yy} L^* & 0 & \nabla_y f_1^* & \cdots & \nabla_y f_q^* & \nabla_y g_1^* & \cdots & \nabla_y g_r^* \\ \hline 0 & 0 & -1 & \cdots & -1 & 0 & \cdots & 0 \\ \hline \mu_1^* \nabla_y f_1^{*T} & \mu_1^* & f_1^* - z^* & & 0 & & 0 & \\ \vdots & \vdots & & \ddots & & & \vdots & \\ \mu_q^* \nabla_y f_q^{*T} & \mu_q^* & 0 & & f_q^* - z^* & & 0 & \\ \hline \lambda_1^* \nabla_y g_1^{*T} & \lambda_1^* & & 0 & & g_1^* & & 0 \\ \vdots & \vdots & & \vdots & & & \ddots & \\ \lambda_r^* \nabla_y g_r^{*T} & \lambda_r^* & & 0 & & 0 & & g_r^* \end{array}\right]^{-1} \begin{bmatrix} \nabla^2_{xy} L^{*T} \\ \hline 0 \\ \hline \mu_1^* \nabla_x f_1^{*T} \\ \vdots \\ \mu_q^* \nabla_x f_q^{*T} \\ \hline \lambda_1^* \nabla_x g_1^{*T} \\ \vdots \\ \lambda_r^* \nabla_x g_r^{*T} \end{bmatrix}$$

where the abbreviated notations are used as follows:

$$\nabla_y f_i^* = \nabla_y f_i(x^*, y^*), \qquad \nabla_y g_j^* = \nabla_y g_j(x^*, y^*),$$

and so on.

Theorem 2.2. Assume the following conditions:

(a) Linear independence constraint qualification: The same as the condition (b) in Theorem 2.1.

(b) Strong second order sufficient condition for optimality: The same as the condition (c) in Theorem 2.1.

Then, there exist uniquely $y(\cdot)$, $z(\cdot)$, $\mu(\cdot)$, $\lambda(\cdot)$ on a neighbourhood of x^* such that

$$y(x^*) = y^*, \qquad z(x^*) = z^*, \qquad \mu(x^*) = \mu^*, \qquad \lambda(x^*) = \lambda^*$$

and $(y(x), z(x))$ is a strict local optimal solution to (P_x) and $(\mu(x), \lambda(x))$ is a corresponding Lagrange multiplier vector. Moreover there exist directional derivatives

$$y'(x^*; x) = v, \qquad z'(x^*; x) = w, \qquad \mu'(x^*; x) = \eta, \qquad \lambda'(x^*; x) = \xi$$

which are the unique solutions to the following system of equations and inequalities.

$$\begin{aligned}
&\nabla^2_{yy} L \cdot v + \sum_i \eta_i \nabla_y f_i^* + \sum_j \xi_j \nabla_y g_j^* = -\nabla^2_{yx} L^* \cdot x; \qquad \sum \eta_i = 0 \\
&\langle \nabla_y f_i^*, v \rangle - w = -\langle \nabla_x f_i^*, x \rangle \qquad \forall i \in \tilde{I} \\
&\langle \nabla_y f_i^*, v \rangle - w \leqq -\langle \nabla_x f_i^*, x \rangle \qquad \forall i \in I \setminus \tilde{I} \\
&\langle \nabla_y g_j^*, v \rangle = -\langle \nabla_x g_j^*, x \rangle \qquad \forall j \in \tilde{J} \\
&\langle \nabla_y g_j^*, v \rangle \leqq -\langle \nabla_x g_j^*, x \rangle \qquad \forall j \in J \setminus \tilde{J} \\
&\eta_i = 0 \quad i \notin I; \qquad \eta_i \geqq 0 \quad i \in I \setminus \tilde{I} \\
&\xi_j = 0 \quad j \notin J; \qquad \xi_j \geqq 0 \quad j \in J \setminus \tilde{J} \\
&\eta_i \left[\langle \nabla_y f_i^*, v \rangle - w + \langle \nabla_x f_i^*, x \rangle \right] = 0 \qquad \forall i \in I \setminus \tilde{I} \\
&\xi_j \left[\langle \nabla_y g_j^*, v \rangle + \langle \nabla_x g_j^*, x \rangle \right] = 0 \qquad \forall j \in J \setminus \tilde{J}.
\end{aligned}$$

3 Case 2: Upper level — explicit utility function Lower level — Pareto optimal solutions

In this section, it is assumed that the upper level DM has an explicit utility function and that the lower level DM has no utility (scalarizing) function and therefore he accepts any Pareto optimal solution. Moreover we assume that the upper level DM can select any decision of lower level according to his own preference so long as it is Pareto optimal.

Given a value of the upper level decision variable x, the set of all Pareto optimal solutions to the lower level optimization problem is denoted by $\hat{Y}(x)$. Then the upper level optimization problem is

$$\begin{cases} \min\limits_x \min\limits_{y \in \hat{Y}(x)} & \Psi(x, y) \\ \text{subject to} & x \in X \end{cases}$$

By the way, if the upper level DM cannot be concerned in the lower level decision, the upper level problem is

$$\begin{cases} \min\limits_{x} \max\limits_{y \in \hat{Y}(x)} \ \Psi(x, y) \\ \text{subject to } \ x \in X \end{cases}$$

which is not dealt with in this paper.

As in section 2, F (and therefore Ψ) is often a function of f. In other words, the upper level problem is given by

$$\begin{cases} \min\limits_{x, \hat{y}(x)} \ \Psi\big(x, f(x, \hat{y}(x))\big) \\ \text{subject to } \ x \in X, \quad \hat{y}(x) \in \hat{Y}(x) \end{cases} \tag{3-1}$$

In connection with the above problem (3-1), we consider the following problem:

$$\begin{cases} \min\limits_{x, y} \ \Psi(x, f(x, y)) \\ \text{subject to } \ x \in X, \quad y \in Y(x) \end{cases} \tag{3-2}$$

Then the following theorems hold (Shimizu, 1982).

Theorem 3.1. If Ψ is monotonically increasing with respect to f, an optimal solution (x^*, y^*) to the problem (3-2) is an optimal solution to the problem (3-1).

Theorem 3.2. (Revised). If Ψ is monotonically nondecreasing with respect to f and if $\hat{Y}(x)$ is externally stable (see Sawaragi et el., 1985), then an optimal solution to the problem (3-1) is also an optimal solution to the problem (3-2).

Hence we may solve the problem (3-2) instead of (3-1) under the assumption of monotonicity of Ψ with respect to f, which is rather reasonable from the practical viewpoint.

Even in a general case in which Ψ is a direct function of $y(x)$, if some appropriate parametrization for obtaining all the Pareto optimal solutions is possible, then the upper level problem is

$$\begin{cases} \min\limits_{x} \ \Psi(x, \hat{y}(x, \alpha)) \\ \text{subject to } \ x \in X, \quad \alpha \in A \end{cases}$$

where α is a parameter vector for scalarization of the lower level problem, A is the set of parameters and $\hat{y}(x, \alpha)$ is the optimal solution to the scalarized problem in the lower level given x and α. In order to solve this problem, sensitivity analysis of $\hat{y}(x, \alpha)$ with respect to (x, α) is important. Shimizu and Aiyoshi (1981) provided a useful method for solving a multiobjective resource allocation problem by using ε-constraint method as scalarization.

Another possibility for solving the upper level problem is to obtain the optimality conditions for the lower level problem and treat them as constraints in the upper level problem. (Tarvainen and Haimes, 1982).

4 Case 3: Upper level — implicit utility function Lower level — unique preferred solution

Next, we consider the case in which the utility function of upper level DM is known only implicitly and so an interactive optimization method is applied for finding the final preferred solution. Any interactive method includes repetition of the following two stages: the stage in which the DM provides some information on his preference and the stage in which computer generates a new Pareto optimal solution and any other related data based on the information given by the DM. The former stage is the same in our problem as in usual multiobjective optimization problems. In the latter stage we must solve problems explained in Case 1. Therefore, by solving these problems with the help of sensitivity analysis, we may apply interactive methods to problems in Case 3.

5 Case 4: Upper level — implicit utility function Lower level — Pareto optimal solutions

In this section we consider an interactive method for solving the upper level multiobjective optimization problem under the assumption that the lower level DM accepts every Pareto optimal solution. Namely, the whole problem is

$$\begin{cases} \min\limits_{x,\hat{y}(x)} F(x,y(x)) = \big(F_1(x,\hat{y}(x)),\dots,F_p(x,\hat{y}(x))\big) \\ \text{subject to } \; x \in X, \quad \hat{y}(x) \in \hat{Y}(x) \end{cases}$$

As in Section 3, we consider the case in which F is a function of f and so the problem is

$$\begin{cases} \min\limits_{x,\hat{y}(x)} F\big(x, f(x,\hat{y}(x))\big) \\ \text{subject to } \; x \in X, \quad \hat{y}(x) \in \hat{Y}(x) \end{cases} \tag{5-1}$$

In connection with the above problem, we may define the following problem:

$$\begin{cases} \min\limits_{x,y} F(x, f(x,y)) \\ \text{subject to } \; x \in X, \quad y \in Y(x) \end{cases} \tag{5-2}$$

Then we can prove the following two theorems as an extension of those in Section 3.

Theorem 5.1. Suppose that F is monotonically increasing with respect to f in the sense that $f^1 \leq f^2$ implies $F(x,f^1) \leq F(x,f^2)$, where $f^1 \leq f^2$ in and only if $f_i^1 \leqq f_i^2$ for all $i = 1,\dots,q$ and $f_i^1 < f_i^2$ for some i. Then any Pareto optimal solution to the problem (5-2) is a Pareto optimal solution to (5-1).

Theorem 5.2. Suppose that F is monotonically nondecreasing with respect to f and that $Y(x)$ is externally stable. Then every Pareto optimal solution to (5-1) is also a Pareto optimal solution to (5-2).

Hence we may solve a usual multicriteria decision making problem (5-2) instead of (5-1). Particularly, if F and f^j are of the same type (dimension), and if the interactive optimization method to be used and the form of F are compatible in the sense explained below, then we obtain interesting results.

As an example, let the reference point method be used as the interactive method for solving the upper level problem and the upper level objective function F_i $(i = 1, \ldots, p)$ is of the form

$$F_i = \max_j f_i^j \qquad (i = 1, \ldots, p)$$

where f_i^j $(j = 1, \ldots, N)$ is the lower level objective function of the same type as F_i $(i = 1, \ldots, p)$. A practical meaning of this form of F_i is that the upper level DM pays attention to the worst one of the lower level results. Let the reference point of the upper level be $\overline{F} = (\overline{F}_1, \ldots, \overline{F}_p)$ and we have the upper level Tchebycheff norm minimization problem as follows:

$$\begin{aligned}
&\min_x \min_{\substack{\{y^j\} \\ (j=1,\ldots,N)}} \max_i \left(F_i(x,y) - \overline{F}_i\right) = \\
&= \min_x \min_{\{y^j\}} \max_i \max_j \left(f_i^j(x,y^j) - \overline{F}_i\right) = \\
&= \min_x \min_{\{y^j\}} \max_j \max_i \left(f_i^j(x,y^j) - \overline{F}_i\right) = \\
&= \min_x \max_j \min_{y^j} \max_i \left(f_i^j(x,y^j) - \overline{F}_i\right)
\end{aligned}$$

Hence, when x is fixed, the minimization problem with respect to y^j

$$\min_{y^j} \max_i \left(f_i^j(x,y^j) - F_i\right)$$

is a Tchebycheff norm minimization problem in itself. We can compute directional derivatives of the optimal solution to the subproblem with respect to x as in Section 2 and therefore the whole minimization with respect to x is practicable.

6 Concluding remarks

In this paper we have discussed optimization of hierarchical systems with multiple objectives. We practically dealt with the cases in which lower subsystems are separable. If subsystems are not separable and there exist interactions among them, there arise conflicts among them. In other words, we face to game situations. However, suppose that an objective function of each subproblem is scalar-valued. Then, if the subsystems are cooperative and have some rule for compromise among them, the problem can be dealt with in the same manner as in Case 1 or 3 in this paper where the lower level DM decides his preferred solution by solving a multiobjective problem. Analogously, if the subsystems are noncooperative and therefore have to accept any equilibrium, the problem leads to that in Case 2 or 4 by regarding those equilibria as Pareto optimal solutions for one subsystem with multiple objectives. Therefore, discussion in this paper are also valid in those cases.

In general cases, hierarchical problems become more complicated and the upper level DMs are strongly required to play a role of the mediator and/or arbitrator. Necessity and importance of effective interactive decision support systems for those problems and of some fundamental mathematical tools such as sensitivity analysis and nondifferentiable optimization methods will increase in the future.

References

Fiacco, A.V. (1983). Introduction to Sensitivity and Stability Analysis in Nonlinear Programming. Academic Press, New York.

Jittorntrum, K. (1984). Solution point differentiability without strict complementality in nonlinear programming. *Mathematical Programming Study*, 21:127–138.

Kobayashi, K., Tanino, T., Wierzbicki, A.P., and Okumura, M. (1987). Multiactor decision analysis for regional investment allocation. In Y. Sawaragi, K. Inoue, and H. Nakayama, eds., Toward Interactive and Intelligent Decision Support Systems, Vol. 2, Springer-Verlag, Berlin.

Sawaragi, Y., Nakayama, H., and Tanino, T. (1985). Theory of Multiobjective Optimization. Academic Press, New York.

Shimizu, K. (1982), Theory of Multiple Objectives and Conflicts. Kyoritsu Press, Tokyo. (in Japanese).

Shimizu, K. and Aiyoshi, E. (1981). Hierarchical multi-objective decision systems for general resource allocation problems. *Journal of Optimization Theory and Applications*, 35(4):517–533.

Tarvainen, K. and Haimes, Y.Y. (1982). Coordination of hierarchical multiobjective systems. *IEEE Transactions on Systems, Man, and Cybernetics*, SMC-12(6): 751–764.

Towards Interactive Procedures in Simulation and Gaming: Implications for Multiperson Decision Support

Andrzej P. Wierzbicki
Institute of Automatic Control, Warsaw University of Technology
*Nowowiejska 15/19, 00–565 Warsaw, Poland**

1 Introduction

In multiperson decision analysis there are two basic types of decision situation. One is the case of ***collegial decisions***, where the nature or an institutional mechanism of decisions implies that only cooperative decisions are considered (such as in collegial discussions about joint budget allocation). Multiobjective decision analysis, cooperative game and bargaining theory have provided many tools for this case and several types of decision support systems have been already developed, see e.g. (Lewandowski and Wierzbicki, 1987; Bronisz, Krus and Lopuch, 1987). The other is the case of ***individual multiperson decisions*** where there is no institutional mechanism forcing the decision makers to make cooperative decisions, each of them can make individual decisions. This case has also motivated intensive studies in noncooperative game theory together with more experimental or computer tournament studies of strategies for repetitive games of social trap type, see e.g. (Rapoport, 1984; Axelrod, 1985); however, no clear implications for decision support have been derived from these studies.

On the other hand, a frequent tool of analyzing complex multiperson decision situations in modern systems analysis consists in building simulation models and performing gaming experiments with them. While such simulated gaming experiments have considerable educational and analytical advantages, not much has been achieved yet in equipping gaming and simulation models in tools of decision analysis and support. Without such tools, however, simulated gaming experiments model quite simplified decision situations, since analytical and computerized support is typically used in real life decisions if they are complex and important enough. The issue discussed in this paper is how to use various concepts and tools derived from game and decision theory to support decisions in simulated gaming.

*This research has been partly supported by the Polish research program grant RP.I.02 and partly by a cooperative research agreement with IIASA, Laxenburg, Austria.

2 Conflict escalation and rationality perceptions

In many simple game or *social trap* prototypes, such as *tragedy of commons* or *prisoner dilemma*, illustrated in its essential features in Fig. 1a, it is a known phenomenon that noncooperative (Nash) equilibria are not (Pareto) efficient. If such a game is played repetitively with an infinite or uncertain number of repetitions, the short-term maximizing rationality that leads to the noncooperative outcome becomes paradoxical. Instead of a single-step "rational" decision, we must look for a rational strategy that takes into account all history of previous decisions in the repetitive game. But such a strategy is nonunique, it depends on the strategy applied by the opposite player. Since this opposite strategy is typically not fully known and subject to changes, a reasonable approach is to choose strategies that perform well when confronted with a variety of strategies in frequent encounters.

This leads to the concept of *evolutionary rational* strategies — see (Axelrod, 1985). The most successful evolutionary rational strategies — exemplified by the TFT (Tit For Tat) strategy of Rapoport and its various modifications [1] — cannot be explained in the terms of simple maximization of gains. Amazingly, however, they can be explained in terms of *rational ethics*: an evolutionary rational strategy should be *nice*, that is, starting with cooperation, *righteous and provocable*, that is, quickly discriminating and retaliating attempts to doublecross it, *forgiving*, that is, reverting to cooperation after retaliation, and *consistently clear*, that is, easy to recognize in its straightforward honesty and consistency; it *should not be envious*, that is, should never try to get better than the opponent — instead, it accumulates positive results from cooperation with various confronting strategies.[2]

However, the game of the prisoner dilemma type is not the most dangerous of social traps. If the penalties for defection (or persistence, in another interpretation) of both sides increase, then the structure of the game changes and two separate noncooperative (Nash) equilibria appear, see Fig. 1b. This social trap is called the *battle of sexes* game, or the *game of chicken* and differs somewhat from the previous prototype. Theoretically, the result of one-shot game can be in either of the two noncooperative equilibria denoted by N1 and N2; psychologically, the temptation to persist and achieve a favourable equilibrium is even greater than the temptation to defect in the prisoner dilemma case. Thus, a rather probable outcome of such a game is a persistent disequilibrium outcome denoted by E; this is a prototype of conflict escalation processes caused by the nonuniqueness of noncooperative equilibria.

---

[1] The simple Tit For Tat strategy that was robustly most successful in evolutionary sense in various experiments performed by Axelrod consists in starting with cooperation and doing in the next rounds the same what the opposite strategy did last time; there are many more complicated but not as robustly successful variants of this simple strategy. The author of this strategy, Anatol Rapoport, observed in a private communication that even more robust would be a more forgiving strategy that starts with cooperation, retaliates when the other side tried to doublecross it, but after retaliation reverts to cooperation no matter what the other side did last time; this modification has not been investigated in Axelrod book.

[2] The amazing point are not the ethical principles, but the fact that Axelrod *has shown analytically their evolutionary rationality* in his excellent and astounding book. Thus, the book constitutes a major challenge to the very core of neopositivistic philosophy and supports the view of marxist philosophy that ethical rules are rational results of social evolution.

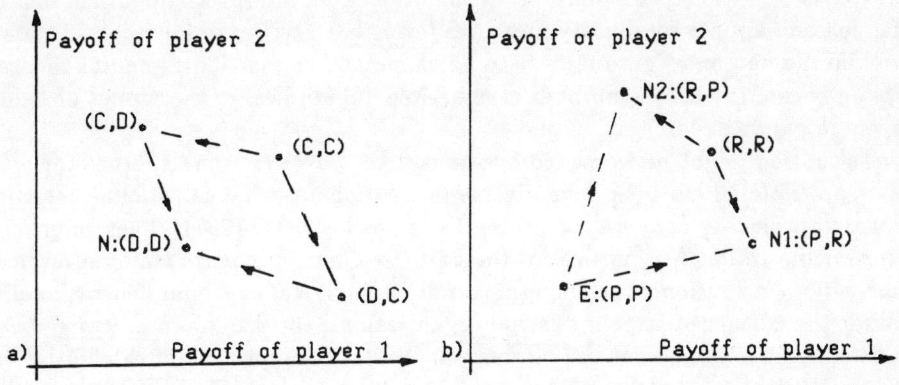

Fig. 1: a) the payoff space in a game of the prisoner dilemma type: C – cooperative move, D – defective move; b) the payoff space in a game of battle of sexes type: P – persistive move, R – relenting move.

When the battle of sexes game is played repetitively, however, the dynamics of such a game are very similar to these of the repetitive prisoner dilemma game: the temptation to persist might be greater, but the outcome of both side persistence might be more disastrous (which intelligent young couples soon learn after marriage; the nonintelligent ones divorce). Thus, a TFT-type strategy, perhaps with more forgiveness characteristics, is still the most rational in evolutionary sense. [3] The difficulty in promoting cooperative, relenting behavior in this case is related to the fact that it is easier to self-justify unrelenting, noncooperative behavior by its apparent "rationality"; conflict escalation processes can be often observed in real life.

The nonuniqueness of noncooperative equilibria is a very frequent phenomenon in realistic models of games, see (Wierzbicki, 1983), even in the cases of games with single-objective gains of each player — say, characterized by utility functions. If the interests of players are truly multiobjective and cannot be characterized by utility functions — e.g. because of cultural differences in their perceptions of rationality, see (Wierzbicki, 1984, 1987) — then the noncooperative equilibria of such games, defined as outcomes that are Pareto-efficient for each player while Nash-noncooperative between players, are almost always nonunique since such are Pareto-efficient outcomes for a single player.

[3] In this otherwise excellent book, Axelrod does not notice this distinction between the prototypes from Fig. 1a and 1b. In the definition of the prisoner dilemma game, he specifies the conditions that lead to the prototype 1a, but later he gives examples — such as the development of the "live and let live" system in World War I — illustrating actually the prototype 1b and speculates about increasing the penalties for defection as one of the methods to promote cooperative behavior. The results of the experiments described in his book would probably be only strengthened when including the prototype 1b, while the modification of TFT described in footnote 1 would possibly be the most successful evolutionary strategy. However, the emergence of cooperative strategies is not necessarily more easy in the prototype 1b; it might be more difficult in certain cases.

Thus, in realistic models of gaming situations there are often even infinite numbers of noncooperative equilibria. When playing such games repetitively, the *processes of conflict escalation* can develop, in which each player selects his own preferred equilibrium, expects a "rational" response from the other side, interprets the other side move as defection and applies retaliatory measures (even when trying to follow the TFT strategy), while the outcomes gradually become worse and worse. This general theoretical conclusion is confirmed by a number of experimental studies on the modes of behavior of players in gaming exercises.

This situation might be worsened by the fact that decision makers from various national or professional cultures have diverse perceptions of what is rational behavior or a rational approach to cooperation — see (Wierzbicki, 1984, 1987). They might follow the *maximizing rationality*, typical of the culture of entrepreneurs facing a large market, the *satisficing rationality* (sometimes misleadingly called "bounded rationality"), typical for the culture of large industrial organizations, the *goal- and program-oriented rationality*, typical for the culture of planning, or yet another type of calculative rationality. On the level of master experts in a given field, they can follow the deliberative, "soft" or *holistic rationality* of intuitive, heuristic decisions — see (Dreyfuss, 1984). In the case of repetitive decisions involving cooperation issues, they might follow the *evolutionary rationality* of readiness to cooperate, as suggested by Rapoport and Axelrod; but it requires a large degree of cultural tolerance to avoid interpreting the other side moves in terms of defection and necessary retaliation when these moves are truly motivated by differences in their perceptions of rationality.[4] Much more frequent than the evolutionary rationality is the *zero-sum rationality* of confrontation that interprets as positive each move that harms the other side (which is certainly true in chess and other confrontation games but far from being true in most social and international situations).

Therefore, the use of simulation models and gaming can serve various purposes, but one of the most prominent might be to expose the futility of simplified rationality perceptions in complex conflict situations, to teach evolutionary rationality and cultural tolerance. However, the pursuit of such goals requires that simulation games are played by participants representing various cultures and that an impartial game analysis unit — which might be a respected mediator or a computerized game analysis procedure — is involved in the evaluation of results achieved in gaming.

A helpful feature in such game analysis unit is the possibility to compute and compare current and minimal *conflict coefficients*. Conflict coefficients are simple means to characterize the degree of conflict and to identify conflict escalation in repetitive games and simulation gaming. Given an initial *status quo* outcome that is not Pareto cooperative, the degree of conflict in this point is assumed to be 2; compared to this value, the minimal degree of conflict can be determined. This is done by computing a

[4]Such differences occur even in scientific discussions, where an open criticism can be interpreted either as willingness to exchange different experiences and points of view and thus to cooperate, or as an ego-boosting attempt to harm the other side: all depends whether science and understanding are seen as a superior collective goal or as means to achieve other individual goals. Perhaps more illuminating is the example of cultural differences represented by various articles on geopolitical issues that can be read in even most informed journals of different superpowers: they often interprete the moves of the other side in terms of duplicity and the hunger of power, without seeing parallels to their own "rational" moves. Thus, cultural intolerance is certainly one of the most destabilizing factors in our world.

Pareto cooperative outcome of Raiffa–Kalai–Smorodinsky type and suitably transforming the distance of these outcomes in such a way that, independently of the number of players, the minimal degree of conflict is 1 for games with constant sum on Pareto surface and 0 if there is only one Pareto point and thus no conflict at all (provided that this cooperative point is actually selected). If a repetitive game is played starting with a given status quo outcome, the attained current degree of conflict greater than 2 characterizes conflict escalation. These concepts can be also generalized for games with multiple objectives and for cases of selecting a mediated outcome between nonunique noncooperative equilibria, see (Wierzbicki, 1987).

3 Decision support in gaming

Since simulation gaming and game-theoretical analysis have been pursued separately for quite a time, it is perhaps not astonishing that typical simulation games do not contain more sophisticated game analysis units. On the other hand, this might be considered as a serious deficiency of simulation games. In our times of approaching information society, any more serious decision is supported by considerable analysis performed either deliberatively by a group of experts or calculatively by computerized modelling. Therefore, it becomes gradually obsolete to insist that a participant of a computerized gaming exercise will make all his decisions without some support. Decision and game-theoretical analysis have developed a considerable body of results that can be utilized when constructing decision-support units for gaming participants. In fact, decision support systems have long been developed and applied both in single-person decision situations and in multiperson decisions of collegial type — see e.g. (Lewandowski and Wierzbicki, 1987). The question discussed here is what type of decision support functions and procedures can be developed for multiperson gaming situations.

3.1 Functions of decision support in simulation gaming

The main decision support functions in multiperson decision situations can be classified as follows. For a single player, the decision support system should provide the possibility of interactive, multiobjective decision analysis under given or assumed moves of other players. For all players jointly, the decision support system should provide conflict analysis and mediation procedures that might decrease the degree of conflict and lead to a cooperative outcome. When choosing basic concepts underlying the execution of such functions, we should keep in mind that the fundamental purpose of simulated gaming is learning, possibly in the situations of plural, cultural perceptions of rationality.

A basic concept of interactive decision analysis that takes into account learning aspects and plural perceptions of rationality is the *quasisatisficing framework of decision support*, see (Wierzbicki, 1984; 1986; Lewandowski et al., 1987). It is based on the following assumptions:

- People are too complicated to be modelled fully in a computer; thus, even if they do maximize some utility function, only rough approximations of such functions can be used in decision support.

- One of the most important aspects of any decision support is learning; thus, any approximation of a utility function must be nonstationary and we cannot impose stringent requirements of consistency on human decision makers since they have the right to change their minds while learning.

- In preparing decisions, people do form and adept *aspiration* and/or *reservation* levels concerning various decision attributes; thus, the simplest way to account for nonstationary preferences is to make utility approximations directly dependent on changing aspiration or reservation levels.

- For good additional reasons, such as avoiding social traps or conflict escalation, people do forego maximization and seek cooperative solutions, or apply special cooperative strategies; thus, the question — whether to forego maximization or not — should be decided consciously by the decision maker, not by the decision support system (as it happens in systems based on maximizing or satisficing rationality).

When following these assumptions, special nonstationary and rough approximations to utility functions — called *achievement functions* — have been developed, expressing the principle of optimization relative to aspiration levels or *reference point optimization*. These functions and principles can have also other interpretations, see (Wierzbicki, 1986), thus they can be used in supporting decisions of people following various perceptions of rationality. Achievement functions and reference point optimization have been used in many decision support systems — such as DIDAS or SCDAS, see (Lewandowski et al., 1987) — in the cases of single or collegial decision support. However, they can be also used to support interactive decision analysis for a single player in gaming, or even be extended to support conflict analysis and mediation support.

Another basic concept related to such extensions is the *axiom of limited confidence* as a basis for interactive mediation procedures in conflict situations, see (Bronisz et al., 1987). Having multiple objectives and a limited confidence in the intentions of other players as well as in their own ability to assess all uncertainties of a bargaining process, players should not agree to too large gains — counted from a status quo point — of any other side if they are not accompanied by proportional gains on their own objectives. It is rational for a player to demand that any tentative agreement of a negotiated joint decision should not give to any player more than a given part (the limited confidence coefficient, typically not greater than $1/n$ when n is the number of players) of possible individual gains. When accepting such principle, we obtain an axiomatically well-founded interactive process of fair mediation helping to decrease conflict degrees and achieve a cooperative decision.

3.2 Prototypes of model use and decision support procedures in simulation gaming

We focus here our attention on the cases where a computerized model of the gaming situation has been developed with some specific interpretations in real life. This model will be called the *substantive model of the game*; it should at least include decision variables for each player, possible outcome variables and mathematical relations between them.

A widely and almost solely applied prototype of model use in simulation gaming is just playing the simulated game without much decision support. In more sophisticated decision support systems for gaming, this option should be preserved, even if only to compare results with and without decision support.

A second prototype might include a basic game analysis module that should at least *compute current and minimal conflict coefficients*. In an initial period of gaming, a status quo outcome can be established; then the game analysis module would inform the players what is the minimal conflict coefficient compared to this status quo. In a further period of gaming, current conflict coefficients could be computed and displayed, together with various graphical images, to inform the players whether they escalate or deescalate conflict.

A third prototype might include *tentative arbitration module* that would compute, beside conflict coefficients, a one-shot cooperative solution (of Raiffa–Kalai–Smorodinsky type, or Nash cooperative type, etc.) and propose it to the players. They would not be obliged to accept the arbitrated solution, but the knowledge of such solution might have a considerable impact on their behavior.

A fourth prototype might include *interactive decision support systems for individual players*. Assuming some moves of other players, each player could select interactively his moves that best serve his multiple objectives (also in the dynamic trajectory sense, if the game has a dynamic character). A further degree of sophistication would allow each player to put himself tentatively in the position of other players, assume their objectives (which would not necessarily be assumed correctly, since each player might have the right of privacy of his analysis and, in particular, his objective selection). In this mode, he could analyse either noncooperative outcomes — simulating the behavior of each player and using the game analysis module — or cooperative outcomes — using the multiobjective decision support system augmented by additional objectives. The results of such analysis might give a basis for unsupported, verbal negotiations between players.

A fifth prototype would include, beside individual decision support systems, also an *interactive fair mediation module* based e.g. on the principle of limited confidence and a "single text" procedure, see e.g. (Raiffa, 1982). The full procedure of using this prototype might include all previous prototypes to prepare data for the mediation module. Thus, the module would be informed about the objectives of all players and also about their aspiration levels for these objectives, could establish confidence coefficients, compute and suggest to the players the corresponding decisions that would result in a proportional improvement of all objectives. The players would be asked to state whether they accept the proposed mediated decisions. If they all do, next round of mediated improvements could be computed; if some of them do not, they can revert to any of the previous prototypes.

There already exists theoretical background and even many tested software components for organizing a decision support system that would include all above prototypes. The structure of such a system is shown in Fig. 2. Much less advanced is the theory and software for the next, sixth prototype, where — for some reasons — players cannot agree on a cooperative solution and a mediation process is necessary leading to a mutually acceptable selection between nonunique noncooperative equilibria. Conceptually, one could proceed here as in the fifth prototype, while substituting the Pareto cooperative set by the Pareto frontier of the set of noncooperative equilibria; but the theoretical and software problems involved in making this concept operational are still quite considerable.

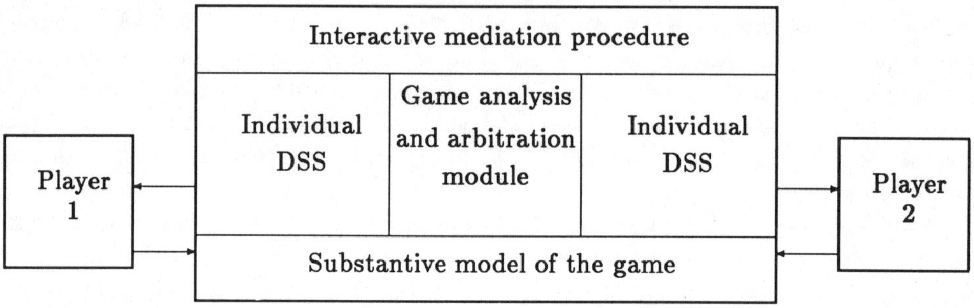

Fig. 2. The structure of a decision and mediation support system for simulation games.

References

Axelrod, R. (1985). The evolution of cooperation. Basic Books, New York.

Bronisz, P., Krus, L. and Lopuch, B. (1987). An experimental system supporting multiobjective bargaining problem: a methodological guide. In Lewandowski, A. and Wierzbicki, A. P., (eds.), Theory, Software and Testing Examples for Decision Support Systems, WP–87–26, IIASA, Laxenburg, Austria.

Bronisz, P., Krus, L. and Wierzbicki, A. P. (1987). Towards interactive solutions in bargaining problems. Submitted to Operations Research.

Dreyfus, S. E. (1984). Beyond rationality. In Grauer, M., Thompson, M. and Wierzbicki, A. P. (eds)., Plural rationality and interactive decision processes, Springer, Heidelberg.

Kalai, E. and Smorodinsky, M. (1975). Other solutions to Nash bargaining problem. *Econometrica* 43, pp. 513–518.

Lewandowski, A. and Wierzbicki, A. P. (1987). Interactive decision support systems — the case of discrete alternatives for committee decision making. WP–87–38, IIASA, Laxenburg, Austria.

Lewandowski, A., Kreglewski, T., Rogowski, T. and Wierzbicki, A. P. (1987). Decision support systems of DIDAS family (Dynamic Interactive Decision Analysis and Support). In Lewandowski, A. and Wierzbicki, A. P., (eds.), Theory, Software and Testing Examples for Decision Support Systems, WP–87–26, IIASA, Laxenburg, Austria.

Raiffa, H. (1953). Arbitration schemes for generalized two-person games. *Ann. Math. Stud.* 28, pp. 361–387, Princenton.

Raiffa, H. (1982). The art and science of negotiations. Harvard University Press, Cambridge, Massachusetts.

Rapoport, A. (1984) Uses of experimental games. In Grauer, M., Thompson, M. and Wierzbicki, A. P. (eds)., Plural rationality and interactive decision processes, Springer, Heidelberg.

Wierzbicki, A. P. (1983). Negotiations and mediation in conflicts, I: the role of mathematical approaches and methods. In Chestnut, H. et al. (eds)., Supplemental ways of improving international stability, Pergamon Press, Oxford.

Wierzbicki, A. P. (1984). Negotiations and mediation in conflicts, II: plural rationality and interactive decision processes. In Grauer, M., Thompson, M. and Wierzbicki, A. P. (eds)., Plural rationality and interactive decision processes, Springer, Heidelberg.

Wierzbicki, A. P. (1986). On the completeness and constructiveness of parametric characterization to vector optimization problems. *OR–Spektrum* 8, pp. 73–87.

Wierzbicki, A. P. (1987). Frameworks for rational decisions and conflict coefficients. IIASA Conference on Processes of International Negotiations.

Part 2

Theory, Methodology and Software for Decision Support Systems

An Experimental System Supporting Multiobjective Bargaining Problem

P. Bronisz, L. Krus, B. Lopuch
Systems Research Institute, Polish Academy of Sciences
Newelska 6, 01-447 Warsaw, Poland

1 Introduction

In most approaches (see Nash, 1950; Raiffa, 1953; Kalai and Smorodinsky, 1975; Roth, 1979), the bargaining problem has been considered in the case of unicriterial payoffs of players, i.e. when the preferences of particular players are expressed by utility functions. In many practical applications however, players trying to balance a number of objectives might have difficulties while constructing such utility functions. Moreover, the classic literature considers mostly axiomatic models of bargaining which yield one-shot solutions and do not result in procedures describing a process of reaching a binding agreement.

In this paper we consider n players each with m objectives. We are dealing with a multiobjective bargaining problem; in this problem, the players are faced with an agreement set of feasible outcomes, and any such outcome can be accepted as the result if it is specified by an unanimous agreement of all players. In the event that no unanimous agreement is reached, the players act independently; the joint outcome of such independent actions is called the disagreement solution. If there are feasible outcomes which all participants prefer to the disagreement solution, then there is an incentive to reach an agreement. In most situations, players differ in their opinions which outcome is most preferable, hence there is a need for bargaining and negotiation.

Dealing with multiple payoffs, we do not assume that there exist explicitly given utility functions of the players. In this paper, under a suggestion of Wierzbicki (1983), an interactive process is discussed starting from the disagreement solution and leading to a nondominated, individually rational solution belonging to the agreement set. During the interaction, players can express their preferences and can influence the course of the iterative process. The proposed process consists of two phases. In the first phase, the players act independently on their disagreements sets and select the disagreement solution. In the second phase, the cooperative action on the agreement set is considered.

On the basis of the proposed theory an interactive system has been built on simple example of joint realization of development program. The system has been done under a contracted study agreement with the Systems and Decision Sciences Program of the International Institute for Applied Systems Analysis. The system is implemented on professional microcomputers compatible with IBM-PC-XT (with Hercules or Color graphics card). It is written in Turbo Pascal utilizing Turbo Graphix Toolbox.

2 Problem formulation and definitions

Let $N = \{1, 2, \ldots, n\}$ be the finite set of players, each player having m objectives. A multiobjective bargaining problem can be described in the form

$$(S, S_1, S_2, \ldots, S_n)$$

where $S_i \in \Re^m$ is a disagreement set of the i–th player, $i \in N$, $S \subset \Re^{n*m}$ is an agreement set of all the players.

The bargaining problem has the following intuitive interpretation: every point x, $x = (x_1, \ldots, x_n)$, $x_i = (x_{i1}, \ldots, x_{im}) \in \Re^m$ in the agreement set S represents payoffs for all the players that can be reached when they do cooperate with each other (x_{ij} denotes the payoff of the j–th objective for the i–th player). If the players do not cooperate, each player $i \in N$ can reach the payoffs from his disagreement set S_i. The players are interested in finding an outcome in S which will be agreeable to all the players.

We employ a convention that for $x, y \in \Re^k$, $x \geq y$ implies $x_i \geq y_i$ for $i = 1, \ldots, k$, $x > y$ implies $x \geq y$, $x \neq y$, $x \gg y$ implies $x_i > y_i$ for $i = 1, \ldots, k$. We say that $x \in \Re^k$ is a weak Pareto optimal point in X if $x \in X$ and there is no $y \in X$ such that $y \gg x$; $x \in X$ is a Pareto optimal point in X if there is no $y \in X$ such that $y > x$.

In this paper, we assume that each player tries to maximize his every objective. As it was mentioned, the proposed interactive process consists of two phases. In the first phase, each player $i \in N$ acts independently of the others on his disagreement set S_i to select the most preferable point d_i. In the second, the players bargain over the agreement set S assuming that $d = (d_1, \ldots, d_n)$ is the status quo or disagreement point.

Let $\Re^k_x = \{y \in \Re^k : y \geq x\}$. We say that a set $X \subset \Re^k$ belongs to the class $\mathcal{B}^k$ if and only if X satisfies the following conditions.

(i) For any $x \in X$, the set $X \cap \Re^k_x$ is compact.

(ii) The set X is comprehensive, i.e. for any $x \in X$, if $y \in \Re^k$ is such that $x \geq y$, then $y \in X$.

(iii) For any $x \in X$, let

$$Q(X, x) = \{i : y \geq x,\ y_i > x_i \text{ for some } y \in X\}$$

Then for any $x \in X$, there exists $y \in X$ such that $y \geq x$, $y_i > x_i$ for each $i \in Q(X, x)$.

In the paper, we confine our consideration to the multiobjective bargaining problems satisfying: $S \in \mathcal{B}^{n*m}$, $S_i \in \mathcal{B}^m$ for $i \in N$.

Intuitively, condition (i) states that the set X is closed and upper bounded. Condition (ii) says that objectives are disposable, i.e. that if the players can reach the outcome x then they can reach any outcome worse than x. $Q(X, x)$ is the set of all coordinates in $\Re^k$, payoffs of whose members can be increased from x in X. Condition (iii) states that the set of Pareto optimal points in X contains no "holes". It is easy to notice that, for example, any convex set satisfies condition (iii).

3 First phase. Multiobjective decision problem

Let us consider the i–th player, $i \in N$. To simplify notation, let $X = S_i$ and $M = \{1, 2, \ldots, m\}$.

We define an affine transformation of $\Re^m$ by

$$T(\cdot, x^r, x^0) : \Re^m \longrightarrow \Re^m, \qquad T = (T_1, \ldots, T_m),$$

$$T_i(x, x^r, x^0) = (x_i - x_i^0)/(x_i^r - x_i^0) \qquad \text{for } i \in M,$$

where $x^0 \in X$, $x^r \in \Re^m$, $x^r \gg x^0$. The transformation T depends on two points settled by the player, the point x^0 define lower bounds on efficient outcomes (it may be, for example, the "nadir" point of X), the point x^r, called a reference point, reflects preferences of the player. The transformation T normalizes the problem in a sense that $T(x^0, x^r, x^0) = (0, \ldots, 0)$ and $T(x^r, x^r, x^0) = (1, \ldots, 1)$.

To select a Pareto optimal outcome in X according to x^0 and x^r, we utilize the Rawlsian lexmin principle (see Rawls, 1971; Imai, 1983). Let $\rhd^l$ be the lexicographical ordering on $\Re^m$, i.e. for $x, y \in \Re^m$, $x \rhd^l y$ if and only if there is $i \in M$ such that $x_i > y_i$ and $x_j = y_j$ for $j < i$. Let $L : \Re^m \longrightarrow \Re^m$ be such that for $x \in \Re^m$, there is a permutation on M, π, with $L(x) = \pi^* x$ and $L_1(x) \leq L_2(x) \leq \ldots \leq L_m(x)$. Then the lexicographical maxmin ordering on $\Re^m$ (with respect to x^0 and x^r), $\rhd$, is defined by

$$x \rhd y \equiv L\big(T(x, x^r, x^0)\big) \rhd^l L\big(T(y, x^r, x^0)\big) \qquad \text{for } x, y \in \Re^m$$

Let $F(X, x^r, x^0)$ denote the lexicographical maxmin outcome of X according to x^r and x^0, and is defined by

$$F(X, x^r, x^0) = x \equiv x \text{ is a maximal element in } X \text{ according to } \rhd .$$

Theorem 1. (Bronisz and Krus, 1987) For $X \in \mathcal{B}^m$, $x^0 \in X$, $x^r \in \Re^m$, $x^r \gg x^0$, $F(X, x^r, x^0)$ exists uniquely and is Pareto optimal in X.

Theorem 1 is a generalization of the result in (Schmeidler, 1969) for a nonconvex set X. The proposed approach is very closed to the achievement function concept (Wierzbicki, 1982) from the point of view of the user. Analogously, a special way of the parametric scalarization of the multiobjective problem is utilized to influence on the selection of Pareto optimal outcomes by changing reference points. However, in place of parametric scalarization through the order-approximating achievement function (for example, weighted sum of l_1 and l_∞ Tchebyshev norm), we propose the scalarization by the weighted l_∞ norm and then the lexicographical improvement of a weak Pareto point to a Pareto optimal outcome. The proposed solution, under not quite restrictive assumptions about the set X ($x \in \mathcal{B}^m$) can be determined in a simple way (even in a case of complicated nonconvex sets where the problem of maximizing the Tchebyshev norm can be ill-conditioned). The corresponding algorithm is based on several (at most m) directional maximizations using, for example a bisection method which works very quickly and effectively.

The procedure for locating the lexicographical maxmin outcome can be formalized as follows. If Q is a subset of M, let $e(Q) \in \Re^m$ be such that $e_i(Q) = (x_i^r - x_i^0)$ for $i \in Q$ and $e_i(Q) = 0$ for $i \notin Q$. Given $y \in X$ with $Q(X,y) \neq \emptyset$ define $x(X,y) \in X$ by $x(X,y) = \max_{\geq}\left\{x \in X : x = y + ae(Q(X,y)) \text{ for some } a \in \Re\right\}$. We construct a sequence $\{x^j\}_{j=0}^{\infty}$ such that $x^0 \in X$ is fixed by the player, and $x^j = x(X, x^{j-1})$ for $j = 1,2,\ldots$. Such sequence is exactly one and the following theorem can be proved (Bronisz and Krus, 1987). It is a generalization of the result in (Imai, 1983) for a nonconvex set X.

Theorem 2. For $X \in \mathcal{B}^m$, $x^0 \in X$, $x^r \in \Re^m$, $x^r \gg x^0$, let k be the smallest j with $x^j = x^{j+1}$. Then $k \leq m$ and $F(X, x^r, x^0) = x^k$ i.e. the sequence $\{x^j\}_{j=0}^{\infty}$ yields the lexicographical maxmin outcome in X in at most m steps.

4 Second phase. Cooperation

Let $d_i \in S_i$ be the lexicographical maxmin outcome in S_i calculated in the first phase by the i–th player, $i \in N$, and let $d = (d_1, d_2, \ldots, d_n)$ be the resulting disagreement solution or status quo point. Now we reduce the problem to the pair (S,d), where S is the agreement set. If the point d belongs to S and is not Pareto optimal point in S then there is an incentive to cooperation among the players; in the other case cooperation is not profitable. We assume that $d \in S$ and there exists $x \in S$ such that $x > d$.

We are interested in a constructive procedure that is acceptable by all players, starts at the status quo point and leads to a Pareto optimal point in S. The procedure can be described as a sequence, $\{d^t\}_{t=0}^{k}$ of agreement points d^t such that $d^0 = d$, $d^t \in S$, $d^t \geq d^{t-1}$ for $t = 1,2,\ldots$, d^k is a Pareto optimal point in S. (The assumption $d^t \geq d^{t-1}$ follows from the fact that no player will accept improvement of payoffs for other players at the cost of his concession). At every round t, each player $i \in N$ specifies his improvement direction $\lambda_i^t \in \Re^m$, $\lambda_i^t > 0$ and his confidence coefficient $\alpha_i^t \in \Re$, $0 < \alpha_i^t \leq 1$. The improvement direction λ_i^t indicates the i–th players preferences over his objectives at round t. The confidence coefficient α_i^t reflects his ability at round t to describe preferences and to predict precisely all consequences and possible outcomes in S (for more detailed justification, see Fandel, Wierzbicki, 1985; and Bronisz, Krus, Wierzbicki, 1987).

We propose an interactive negotiation process defined by a sequence

$$\{d^t\}_{t=0}^{\infty} \quad \text{such that } d^0 = d$$

$$d^t = d^{t-1} + \varepsilon^t * \left[u(S, d^{t-1}, \lambda^t) - d^{t-1}\right] \quad \text{for } t = 1,2,\ldots,$$

where $\lambda^t \in \Re^{n*m}$, $\lambda^t = (\lambda_1^t, \lambda_2^t, \ldots, \lambda_n^t)$ is the improvement direction specified jointly by all players, $u(S, d^{t-1}, \lambda^t) \in \Re^{n*m}$ is the utopia point relative to the direction λ^t at round t defined by

$$u(S, d^{t-1}, \lambda^t) = \big(u_1(S, d^{t-1}, \lambda_1^t), u_2(S, d^{t-1}, \lambda_2^t), \ldots, u_n(S, d^{t-1}, \lambda_n^t)\big)$$

$$u_i(S, d^{t-1}, \lambda_i^t) = \max_{\geq}\{x_i \in \Re^m : x \in S,\ x \geq d^{t-1},\ x_i = d_i^{t-1} + a\lambda_i^t \text{ for some } a \in \Re\}$$

Moreover, $\varepsilon^t = \min(\alpha_1^t, \alpha_2^t, \ldots, \alpha_n^t, \alpha_{\max}) \in \Re$, where $\alpha_{\max}^t$ is the maximal number α such that $d^{t-1} + \alpha\big[u(S, d^{t-1}, \lambda^t) - d^{t-1}\big]$ belongs to S.

Intuitively, the utopia point $u(S, d^{t-1}, \lambda^t)$ relative to the direction λ^t reflects the "power" of the particular players when the improvement direction λ^t is specified at round t. The individual outcome $u_i(S, d^{t-1}, \lambda_i^t)$ is the maximal payoff in S for the i–th player from d^{t-1} according to improvement direction λ_i^t, while ε^t is the minimal confidence coefficient of the players at round t (we assume that no player can agree on a coefficient greater than his) such that a new calculated agreement point belongs to S.

Theorem 3. (Bronisz, Krus, Lopuch, 1987) For an agreement set $S \in \mathcal{B}^{n*m}$ and a status quo point $d \in S$, let improvement directions of the players, $\lambda^t \in \Re^{n*m}$, $\lambda^t = (\lambda_1^t, \lambda_2^t, \ldots, \lambda_n^t)$, be such that $\lambda_{ij}^t > 0$ if coordinate ij belongs to $Q(S, d^{t-1})$ and $\lambda_{ij}^t = 0$ in the other case, for $t = 1, 2, \ldots$. Then the interactive negotiation process $\{d^t\}_{t=0}^{\infty}$ yields a Pareto optimal outcome in S. If k is the smallest t with $d^t = d^{t+1}$ then d^k is a Pareto optimal outcome in S. In other case, if there is a number $\alpha > 0$ such that $\alpha_i^t \geq \alpha$ for $i \in N$, $t = 1, 2, \ldots$, then the limit $\lim_{t\to\infty} d^t$ exists and it is a Pareto optimal outcome in S. Moreover, for each $t = 1, 2, \ldots$ and for each $i \in N$ there is a number β such that $d_i^t - d_i^{t-1} = \beta\lambda_i^t$, i.e. at each round t the improvement of players' payoffs is compatible with their improvement directions.

The interactive negotiation process, $\{d^t\}_{t=0}^{\infty}$ is a generalization of the iterative negotiation model for the unicriterial bargaining problem proposed and discussed by Bronisz, Krus (1986a) and Bronisz, Krus, Wierzbicki (1987).

5 A simplified model of a joint development program

The model relates to two countries (treated as players) which consider realization of a development program. The program requires some amount of resources of various kinds and gives as a result some volume of production. Each country can realize the project independently, or both the countries can decide on a joint development program. Joint program, due to scale effects, can allow for a decrease of required resources at a given production volume or an increase of the production under given resources in comparison to two independent programs.

In the model, two kinds of resources are considered : labor resources and capital assets. Each player is assumed to maximize the obtained production volume and to minimize the resources put in the joint program, but they can differ in preferences among the quantities. The problem consists in a choice of the production scale of the joint program and the sharing of the required resources and of the production volume — which should be agreeable and possibly close to the preferences of the players.

To deal with the case of maximization of objectives only, we assume that each player has given a disposable fund of capital assets $C_i \in \Re_+$, and a disposable labor resources $L_i \in \Re_+$, $i = 1, 2$, and tries to maximize slack variables $sc_i = C_i - c_i$, and $sl_i = L_i - l_i$, where c_i, l_i are the capital and labor resources, respectively, which should be put into the joint project by the i–th player.

The development program, which can be realized in various scales is described by two functions:

$$c : \Re_+ \longrightarrow \Re_+, \quad \text{and} \quad l : \Re_+ \longrightarrow \Re_+,$$

where $c(p)$ are capital assets required in the program of the scale or production volume p, $l(p)$ are labor resources required in the program. Assumed shapes of the are similar as obtained by Bronisz, Krus, (1986b) in an example of joint water resources project. In the model, the same forms of the functions are assumed for independently and jointly realized programs, but even in this case the problem is not trivial.

Each player $i = 1, 2$, maximizes three objectives: p_i, sc_i, sl_i. The disagreement sets are described by: $S_i \subset \Re^3_+$, $i = 1, 2$,

$$S_i = \left\{ (p_i, sc_i, sl_i) \in \Re^3 : c(p_i) \leq C_i - sc_i, \; l(p_i) \leq L_i - sl_i \right\}$$

The agreement set has the form: $S \subset \Re^{2\times 3}$

$$S = \Big\{ (p_1, sc_1, sl_1, p_2, sc_2, sl_2) \in \Re^6 : \; c(p_1 + p_2) \leq C_1 + C_2 - sc_1 - sc_2, \\ l(p_1 + p_2) \leq L_1 + L_2 - sl_1 - sl_2 \Big\}$$

On this example, the negotiation process proposed above has been included into an experimental system of bargaining support.

6 Short program description

The experimental system of bargaining support with multiple objectives has been built for simplified model outlined in the previous section. It can be considered as an illustration of the theoretical results related to the interactive process in multiobjective bargaining problem and its application in support of negotiations.

The system aids two players, each maximizing three objectives, to find an acceptable, cooperative, Pareto optimal solution in an interactive procedure. This is done in two phases:

first — a status quo is derived,

second — a cooperative solution is found.

The status quo is defined as being a composition of the outcomes preferable to players in the noncooperative case. The cooperative solution is found in an iterative process starting from the status quo point.

The first phase deals with the noncooperative case, in which the players look for preferable outcomes assuming independent realizations of the development programs. Each player tests efficient solutions and selects the preferable one. This is done in two steps. In the first step, the player defines reference points in his objective space according to his preferences. The system calculates related efficient solution using the approach described in Section 3. In the second step the player selects the preferable solution among the obtained efficient solutions.

The second phase deals with the cooperative case. It proceeds in a number of iterations. Each iteration consists of two stages:

first — both players define their desired, preferable directions for outcomes improvements,

second — the system calculates the cooperative outcome on the basis of the status quo point and directions of improvement specified by the players according to the solution concept presented in Section 4.

In the first stage each player tests directions that improve his outcome and selects a preferable one. This is done in three steps. In the first step, the player defines a step coefficient. In the second step, the player defines directions according to his preferences. Then the system calculates related improved outcomes, assuming the same improvement direction of the counterplayer as in the previous iteration. In the third step, the player selects a preferable direction among the tested directions.

Given the preferable directions of both players, the cooperative outcome is calculated in the second stage. The cooperative outcome is assumed as a new status quo point for the next iteration, and the process is repeated until an efficient cooperative solution is reached.

References

Bronisz, P., Krus, L. (1986a). A New Solution of Two-Person Bargaining Games. ZTSW–17–1/86, Report of Systems Research Institute, Polish Academy of Sciences, Warsaw.

Bronisz, P., Krus, L. (1986b). Resource Allocation and Cost Sharing in Common Enterprise. Game Approach, Proceedings of the Polish-DDR Symposium on Nonconventional Optimization, Prace IBS PAN, Warsaw.

Bronisz, P., Krus, L. (1987). A Mathematical Basis for System Supporting Multicriterial Bargaining. Archiwum Automatyki i Telemechaniki, Warsaw, Poland, (forthcoming).

Bronisz, P., Krus, L., Wierzbicki, A. P. (1987). Towards Interactive Solutions in Bargaining Problem, (forthcoming).

Bronisz, P., Krus, L., Lopuch, B. (1987). An Experimental System Supporting Multiobjective Bargaining Problem. A Methodological Guide. In: Lewandowski, A.,

Wierzbicki, A. P. (eds.), Theory, Software and Testing Examples for Decision Support Systems, WP–87–26, IIASA, Laxenburg, Austria.

Fandel, G., Wierzbicki, A. P. (1985). A Procedural Selection of Equilibria for Supergames, (private unpublished communication).

Imai, H. (1983). Individual Monotonicity and Lexicographical Maxmin Solution. *Econometrica*, Vol. 51, pp. 389–401.

Kalai, E., Smorodinsky, M. (1975). Other Solutions to Nash's Bargaining Problem, *Econometrica*, Vol. 43, pp. 513–518.

Nash, J. F. (1950). The Bargaining Problem, *Econometrica*, Vol. 18. pp. 155–162.

Raiffa, H. (1953). Arbitration Schemes for Generalized Two-Person Games. *Annals of Mathematics Studies*, No. 28, pp. 361–387, Princeton.

Rawls, J. (1971). A Theory of Justice, Cambridge: Harvard University Press.

Roth, A. E. (1979). Axiomatic Model of Bargaining. *Lecture Notes in Economics and Mathematical Systems*, Vol. 170, Springer-Verlag, Berlin.

Schmeidler, D. (1969). The Nucleolus of a Characteristic Function Game. *SIAM Journal on Applied Mathematics*, Vol. 17, pp. 1163–1170.

Wierzbicki, A. P. (1982). A Mathematical Basis for Satisficing Decision Making. *Mathematical Modelling*, Vol. 3, pp. 391–405.

Wierzbicki, A. P. (1983). Negotiation and Mediation in Conflicts I: The Role of Mathematical Approaches and Methods. Working Paper WP–83–106, IIASA, Laxenburg; also in H. Chestmat et al., eds: Supplemental Ways to Increase International Stability, Pergamon Press, Oxford, 1983.

Methodology for DSS and Expert Systems Development Using Distributed Data Bases

Bojil Dobrev
Institute for Information Technologies
Sofia, Bulgaria

Artificial Intelligence (AI) has been characterized as the science of ill-structured problems — and many modern management decisions surely fall into that category (Jordan, 1987). One definition of AI is: "Artificial Intelligence is the machine emulation of human perception, learning, planning, reasoning and decision making" (Jordan, 1985). Following this definition we can consider Decision Support Systems (DSS) and Expert Systems (ES) as derived from AI technologies. On the other side DSS and ES are in our opinion a logical extension of the Information Systems, based on the new quality and features of the hardware/software development. An Information System (IS) gives the answer to the question "WHAT", a DSS — to the question "WHAT–IF" and an ES answers to the question "IF–THEN". In the same time the ES has the role of a bridge between IS and DSS. It processes user requests and different data, stores users decisions and using this information the ES can produce new alternatives, comparing different rules and facts. So that an ES should integrate a part of the IS and DSS function, extending them using AI techniques.

Examples of typical architectures of DSS and ES show an important common element of both of them — *the Data Base*. Assuming that the Domain (or Internal) Data Base is more or less an integrated part of the DSS or ES, it is quite important to estimate the role of the External Data Base.

Every manager has many sources of information needed for decision making. In organizations with established Information Systems much of the needed information resides in IS and particularly in its Data Base(s). Furthermore, many of the inputs to managers are the results of processing and analysis of the information. Thus, it is not enough that an ES or DSS uses only a limited quantity of information — it must access the information in the IS as well. In many cases the External Data Base must content various kinds of such information as financial, marketing, forecasting, legal etc., which can be stored and maintained on different geographic places and is organized in a Distributed Data Base (DDB). A DDB is a set of logically integrated data, stored on different geographic places (Miller, 1978).

There are a lot of interface problems between AI and Distributed Computer Systems (*DCS*). As mentioned in (Stankovic, 1984), *DCS* research includes cooperative problem solving techniques of artificial intelligence and expert systems task is to effectively utilize the resources of the entire distributed system. ES can be a good tool for local Network control, for avoiding "deadlock" problems, for design of a Distributed Information System, including resource planning, project management etc. On the other side, DSS and ES development in a distributed environment is already a research and experimental task for many institutes and firms. DSS and ES in local Network and Distributed Knowledge Base are some of the up-to-date problems of research and development.

In this study we shall consider one particular problem of the relations between DSS/ES and DDB — the use of a DDB by DSS/ES from methodological point of view and a solution for DDB design a Global Distribution Model will be presented.

The methodology for DSS and ES development follows in general the methodology for IS development, based on the "life cycle" concept.

During the preliminary study it is recommended to concentrate on the links between AI tools and methods and methods and the required information. Main topics could be:

a) Detailed specifications of the information entities, their attributes and the relations between them.

b) Specification of the relations between Decision alternatives/Rules and the required information entities.

c) Determine the topology of the DSS/ES — allocation on one node or distributed allocation.

d) Specify requirements for information exchange between Domain (Internal) DB and External DB.

e) In case of existing DDB it is necessary to evaluate what part of the already distributed data is needed for a DSS/ES. In new applications it is also recommended to specify this part of the information, which could be used by the DSS/ES and take in account how often data are required, updated, retrieved, and used for DSS/ES independent user's applications.

i) And the last but not least it is obviously to have following organizational considerations in mind — a good work can be done only by the join efforts of Knowledge engineers, experts and DDB designers.

In the design stage important activities are:

a) to choose the approach for using DDB. Following considerations could be discussed:

   - Using a DDB directly for the DSS/ES functions, storing a Global Schema and all directories as a part of the Domain (Internal) DB or in the Knowledge Base. This approach could be recommended in the case of development a new application.
   - To create and external DB, dynamically updated from a DDB and to avoid the problems of interface between DSS/ES with a DDB, developing tools for integrating distributed data into an external DB in the terms of DSS/ES

and furthermore to develop a typical DSS/ES. This approach could be implemented in the case of existing DDB.

b) To choose the approach for integration on programming level. There are two primary approaches to integration. First, one can establish bridges from a stand-alone AI program to procedural programs and for data base access. Second, AI-based constructs can be incorporated into the programming languages used for system and application development. In our case it means an interface between the inference engine and the Distributed Data Base Management System. There has been far too little experimentation to determine which is the better approach; probably they both have their place (Jordan, 1987).

c) Synchronization between response time possibilities of the DDB and the performance requirements of the inference engine.

d) Optimal allocation of the DDB elements according to the requirements of the DSS/ES application.

Here is a proposal for one solution of the last problem based on a General Distribution Model (GDM) in the case of DSS/ES located at one node, using external information in a DDB. The application of the GDM is based on following assumptions. First, we shall name the information reports required by the user (in IS), Decision alternatives (in DSS) and Rules with the connected Facts with the term *APPLICATIONS* require *DATA*, which are organized in *FILES*, updated/retrieved by *TRANSACTIONS*, which are processed by *PROGRAMS* using *DICTIONARIES*. Third, we shall define following Problem Task: How to allocate applications, files, transactions, programs and dictionaries so that to achieve minimal total costs and each application can receive the necessary data for the required time.

The approach which is proposed for solving the problem consist in determine dependency between applications, files, transactions, programs and dictionaries and after that in defining their optimal allocation at the various nodes of a distributed network. The proposed global distribution model takes into account the dependency between model elements and is based on integer programming problems using an heuristic solution method.

Model elements are: A – Applications, F – Files, T – Transactions, P – Programs, D – Dictionaries. The number of nodes in a distributed computer network is N. Model solution uses three sets of zero-one variables, showing dependency between model elements and nodes. The first variables set shows if some element is allocated in j-node. We shall call them "condition variables".

$$\begin{aligned}
\varphi_{jn} &= (1,0), & \varphi_{jn} &= 1 \ \text{ when } A_n \text{ is allocated in } j\text{–node} \\
x_{ji} &= (1,0), & x_{ji} &= 1 \ \text{ when } F_i \text{ is allocated in } j\text{–node} \\
t_{jm} &= (1,0), & t_{jm} &= 1 \ \text{ when } T_m \text{ is allocated in } j\text{–node} \\
z_{jl} &= (1,0), & z_{jl} &= 1 \ \text{ when } P_l \text{ is allocated in } j\text{–node} \\
y_{jq} &= (1,0), & y_{jq} &= 1 \ \text{ when } D_q \text{ is allocated in } j\text{–node}
\end{aligned} \tag{1}$$

The second variables set includes so called "transfer variables". They represent the possibility for element transfer between two nodes and are presented as following:

$$x^i_{jk} = (1,0), \quad x^i_{jk} = 1 \quad \text{when } F_i \text{ is transferred from } j\text{-nodeto } k\text{-node}$$
$$t^m_{jk}, \ z^l_{jk} \text{ and } y^q_{jk} \quad \text{receive also a value of 1 when transaction, program or dictionary is transferred from } j\text{-node to } k\text{-node.} \tag{2}$$

Between the model elements exist "parents-children" relations. Each element can be connected to one or more other elements. We shall assume the following type of relations:

$$A(F,T,P), \quad F(T,P), \quad P(F,T,D), \quad T(F,P)$$

This relations are characterized by a set of "relation variables", which are represented by the following zero-one variables:

$$\alpha_{EE} = (1,0), \quad \alpha_{EE} = 1 \quad \text{when one element is related to another element For example : } \alpha_{ni} = (1,0), \ \alpha_{ni} = 1 \text{ when application } A_n \text{ uses file } F_i \tag{3}$$

Variables from set (1) and set (3) built a secondary "pair relation variables", showing if a pair of elements is allocated in node j. So for example $\lambda_{jni} = (1,0)$, $\lambda_{jni} = 1$, when A_n and F_i are allocated in node j. Similarly we can create the other variables:

$$\Psi_{jil}, \quad \lambda_{jnm}, \quad \Psi_{jim}, \quad \zeta_{jlm} \quad \text{and} \quad \xi_{jlq} \tag{4}$$

The condition of allocation A_n and F_i at the same time at node j will be true, if

$$\varphi_{jn} = x_{ji} = \alpha_{ni} = 1 \tag{5}$$

If $\varphi_{in} = 1$, $x_{ji} = 0$, $\alpha_{ni} = 1$, then file F_i is allocated at node k and (5) becomes

$$\varphi_{jn} = x_{ki} = \alpha_{ni} = 1 \tag{5'}$$

The "pair relation variables" are connected by a Boolean "AND" function, so that the allocation of all elements at j-node will be presented by following expression:

$$\varphi_{jn} = x_{ji} = z_{jl} = t_{jm} = y_{jq} = 1$$
$$\text{AND}$$
$$\alpha_{ni} = \alpha_{nl} = \alpha_{nm} = \beta_{il} = \beta_{im} = \gamma_{lm} = \gamma_{lq} = 1$$

The same condition can be also shown by one general variable:

$$X_{j(nilmq)} = \begin{cases} 1 & \text{when all elements are allocated at } j\text{-node} \\ 0 & \text{otherwise} \end{cases} \tag{7}$$

The objective function is to minimize total costs and response time for each application. Total costs are represented by the sum of processing costs at each node for one or more applications and communication costs for file, transaction program or dictionary transfer between nodes. Response time for each application includes the time period between a data request at given node and data receiving at the same node.

The method for model solution consists of two procedures:

Procedure 1: Determine the relations between each pair of elements and applications.

Procedure 2: Determine application, distribution and corresponding file, transaction, program and dictionary allocation at each node.

Procedure 1 consists in defining element dependency and as a result of its execution a set of "relation variables" (3) is generated, showing element relations by minimizing response time for each application. Procedure 2 uses an heuristic set of algorithms. Elements are reallocated for each application minimizing processing costs at each node. An application distribution minimizing total costs is obtained. After that a new distribution is done minimizing response time for each application. The iterative run of heuristic procedures is terminated when costs difference between nodes is less or equal to a predetermined value and the value of currently estimated total costs is less than previous by estimated values.

The proposed global model, compared with existing distribution models, has the advantage that Distributed Data Base elements allocation corresponds to user application distribution. This allows an user-friendly DDB design independent of network type and nodes number.

Conclusions

There are a lot of interface problems between DSS/ES and DDB and particularly in the methodology of their development. The problem of optimal data base allocation could be solved using the same techniques taking in account the specific DSS or ES requirements. In our case a Global Distribution Model is proposed. It provides such distribution of data, transactions, programs and dictionaries, that total costs can be minimized and each decision alternative or rule receives the necessary data for the required time.

Future research tasks could be the development of methodology and tools for interface between DSS/ES and DDB covering the whole scope of problems. The use of AI techniques in DDB design and performance and DDB design tools in DSS/ES development is one of the major trends in AI — and DCS research and development.

Literature

Jordan, J. A. (1987). The enterprise — wide Information Management Consultant. Proc. of AI Conference, May. Berlin.

Jordan, J. A. (1985). AI and Expert Systems. Proc. of the Malaysian National comp. Conf.

Miller, M. (1978). A Survey of DDB Management. *Information and Management*, Vol. 1, No. 6, Dec.

Stankovic, J. A. (1984). A Perspective on DCS. *IEEE Trans. on Comp.*, Vol. C–33, No. 12.

A Structure of the Interactive Optimization Systems

R. Kaltinska
Institute of Mathematics
Bulgarian Academy of Sciences
1113 Sofia, Bulgaria

1 Introduction

The great variety of computers and the high requirements to the temporary software put at least two principal problems to be solved:

- automation of software making in a given field, on a certain kind of computers;

- software portability, to some extent, on different kinds of computers.

The solution of these problems is of a great importance both for the software industry, which is supposed to satisfy rapidly and on high professional grounds the needs in different fields, and particularly for the experts in numerical methods, engaged in software making for different mathematical applications. There are some good solutions for a certain kind of basic software, for some logical-information problems, in the field of trade and administration (e.g. the integrated systems FRAMEWORK, SYMPHONY), etc.

This article considers the two problems already mentioned in the field of optimization problems (OP). In relation to the first problem a concept "interactive optimization complex" (briefly "complex") is introduced as a piece of software by means of which interactive optimization systems (IOS) can be made. The existence of complexes depends on the possibility an uniform method for structuring of IOS to be found. A method which is applicable on all kinds of computers to build complexes is briefly described herein. This method itself can be also treated as a solution of the second problem. Some brief information concerning one particular application of the method discussed, the interactive optimization complex OPTIMA based on CM-4 (PDP-11) minicomputer, is given.

2 Optimization problems and IOS

The nucleus of every IOS is the library of procedures based on numerical methods (procedures-methods). The connection user — IOS can be expressed as shown on fig. 1.

By "user interface" are formally designated all software facilities which an IOS provides to the user to solve his problem by means of library methods, i.e. to follow the two stages of a problem solution:

1. to formulate the problem
2. to compute it.

These stages are in principle independent. The problem formulation software consists of facilities to describe, edit and save the problems. Since the problem formulation for different mathematical fields is one and the same, they can share a common problem formulation software.

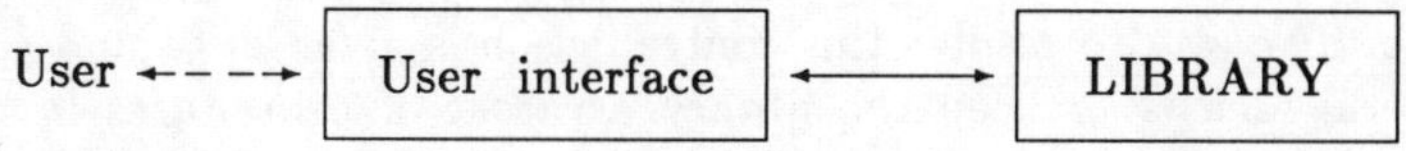

Figure 1

On the contrary, the computation process is closely connected with the mathematical methods used and usually requires some control. The latter is necessary because the universal methods for solving the great variety of optimization problem classes (OP classes) are not available. In such cases the efficient solution of optimization problems can be achieved only via direct interference in the computation process, i.e. via proper combination of various methods and control of the branching of the their algorithms.

Generally the requirements to the IOS can be summarized as follows:

A. Procedure libraries, including various efficient numerical methods, must be available.

B. Proper software support for every operation accompanying the problem solution must also exist.

C. A possibility has to be provided for use and combination of various components of A and B thus obtaining IOS of different kind and capacity.

D. Each IOS must exist also in the form of user callable procedure (procedure version of the interactive optimization system — PIOS).

The requirements C and D provide the IOS adjustability to a particular user environment. PIOS are applicable in practice in case when the optimization is only a part of more complicated problems.

3 Interactive optimization complexes

The "interactive optimization complex" is a piece of software which helps to create IOS. A family of IOS for different OP classes can be built on the basis of a complex for a certain kind of computers. The potential users of interactive complexes are experts who develop IOS. The complex automates their activity. Furthermore the IOS of a given family will facilitate the users because of their uniform behaviour and command language to operate with. One can easily work with all IOS of a given family if he has ever worked with any of its members. Examples of such complexes are the presented herein complex OPTIMA (§6) and the nonlinear programming complex DISO, now under development in the computer center at the Academy of Sciences in the USSR (for IBM PC).

Every complex is closely connected with the structure of the IOS, which are to be created by its means. The complex provides the "user interface" in all IOS so it must comprise both a command language for system-operator contact and an interpreter of this language. At the same time the said "user interface" of each IOS has to be oriented to the OP class, which IOS is intended for. At first sight there are two contradicting requirements. The way to resolve this contradiction is given in §4 and §5.

The general idea is to keep the library as a set of procedures in the traditional sense and to divide the "user interface" into "basic" and "oriented" parts. The "basic interface" comprises the features described above. The "oriented interface" adjusts the "basic interface" to the class of optimization problems solved by the procedures in the library.

The same idea is applicable to the problem formulation and the computation process which are in fact different things so they remain separated — each with "basic" and "oriented interface" of its own (§5). This approach leads naturally to a procedure version of the IOS, i.e. to the PIOS. The said idea is also applied in the computation process through uniforming of the process structure and creation of a proper hierarchy (§4).

The method to structure IOS (§4, §5) can be applied also in integrated systems — a piece of software for automatic IOS generation. Some of the reasons that OPTIMA is a complex, rather than an integrated system are due to the CM-4 specific features. The basic reason however, as we expect also for the DISO-complex, is a matter of principle. There is not enough experience in development and utilization of IOS. As it seems to us, the complexes are the necessary link between the individual IOS development and the automatic IOS generation, i.e. a bridge towards the integrated systems in the field of optimization.

4 A structure of the procedure version of the IOS (PIOS)

The PIOS carries out the computation process of optimization problems of the class, the IOS is intended for.

One specific feature of the methods for solving optimization problems of many classes is that they frequently need the solution of a number of subproblems of other OP classes. When organizing the interactive control over the PIOS it is necessary to reckon the optimization problems which take part in the computation process, the ties between them and the points of potential user interference. The interactive control can be unified if the following approach is applied:

a. To consider the computation process as a set of subprocesses. Each of them solves a particular class of optimization problems.

b. To isolate each of the subprocesses as an autonomous computation process, comprising an interactive control of its own (decentralization of the control by subprocesses).

c. To extract a common interactive control over all of the procedures-methods in a given subprocess (centralization of the control within the subprocesses).

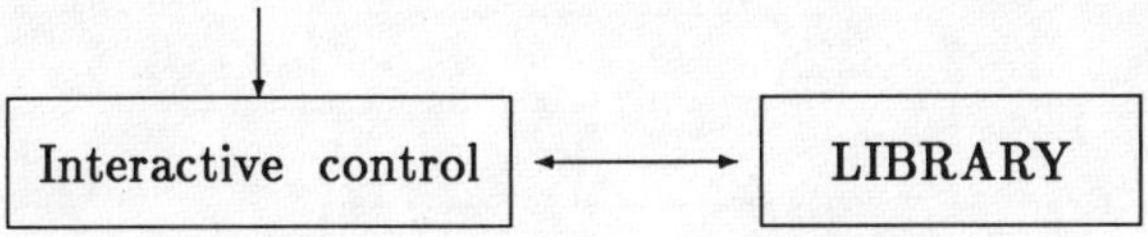

Figure 2

In this approach every subprocess is separated as a procedure library and a command unit, which executes the interactive control (fig. 2). The subprocess can be invoked only by calling its interactive control. Since the interactive control is extracted from the procedures-methods they will keep their traditional independence in respect to the outer program environment and their invariance in respect to the different kinds of computers.

The activities of the interactive control in all OP classes are in principle identical: to halt the acting procedure-method, to obtain some information about the computation process, to set some of its parameters to a proper value, to resume its work or to change the method. The specific features concerning the OP classes are the different terminology and parameters. Therefore the interactive control can be separated in (fig. 3):

- a base part, named DIALOGUE ("basic interface"), which performs the customary interactive control and therefore is independent of the OP classes. This part, once created, will fit all subprocesses.

- a problem oriented part, named MONITOR ("oriented interface"). Each subprocess has a MONITOR of its own which adjusts DIALOGUE to the corresponding OP class.

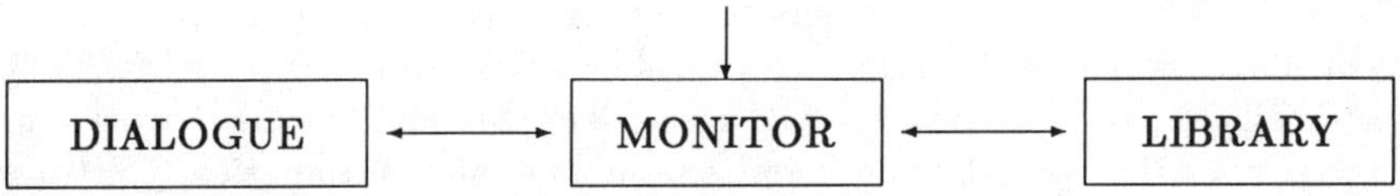

Figure 3

In this structure every subprocess is fully autonomous. Its software can be treated as a "brick", i.e. a constructive unit consisting of MONITOR and LIBRARY. Hence the complete software support of every computation process is built out of such uniform "bricks" plus the basic part, DIALOGUE. These "bricks" together with DIALOGUE can form, or be included in, an arbitrary program configuration. The ties between these constructive units and their mutual hierarchy are naturally built in the procedures-methods and/or in the monitors.

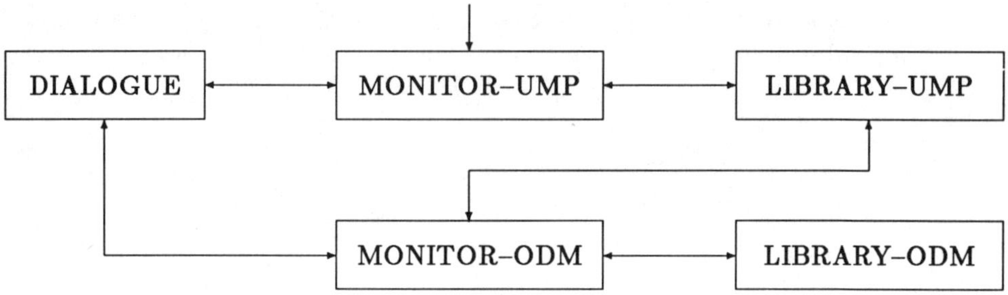

Figure 4

Let's give some examples. On fig. 4 it is shown the software structure of the unconstrained minimization problem (UMP). Many methods for solving UMP use one dimensional minimization (ODM) as an auxiliary optimization problem. So the structure in the common case will consist of two subprocesses — the UMP and the ODM. It is necessary an external call to MONITOR-UMP in order to invoke the UMP-computation process. MONITOR-UMP will carry out the dialogue in terms of the UMP until a reference to a LIBRARY-UMP occurs. Once called a library procedure will solve (if necessary) the ODM problem as a subproblem. It means that the procedure has to call MONITOR-ODM. The latter invokes the interactive control of the ODM computation process. In case when procedures using ODM methods are not available at LIBRARY-UMP, the computation process will consist only of the UMP-subprocess and its software will have the structure shown on fig. 3 (i.e. MONITOR-UMP and LIBRARY-UMP). When methods using the ODM are included the software support will retain the structure shown on fig. 4. Practically this means that a constructive unit (MONITOR-ODM and LIBRARY-ODM) is added to the software support.

An example of a computation process with a multilevel dialogue is shown on fig. 5. At each level i an optimization problem of the class named formally OP-i ($i = 0, \ldots, s$) is solved. To solve OP-0 problem an outer program unit has to call MONITOR OP-0. It adjusts DIALOGUE and by means of it carries on the dialogue in terms of the OP-0 problem until the current method from either LIBRARY OP-0 or MONITOR OP-0 calls MONITOR OP-1 to solve the OP-1 problem. MONITOR OP-1 works in the same way, etc. On exiting an arbitrary monitor the control is automatically returned to the calling module, i.e. the previous dialogue level.

In this approach the choice of the mathematical means to solve a certain class of optimization problems automatically defines the structure of the computation process as a whole. The reason lies in the detached interactive control of each subprocess. Thus the whole complexity of a computation process, consisting of many subprocesses with structurally complex mutual ties (their work sequence and hierarchical nesting), will not affect the interactive control at all. Otherwise, if a common interactive control for all subprocesses is present, there must be some means to take into account these mutual ties and hence the control will depend in a complicated way on every change in any of them.

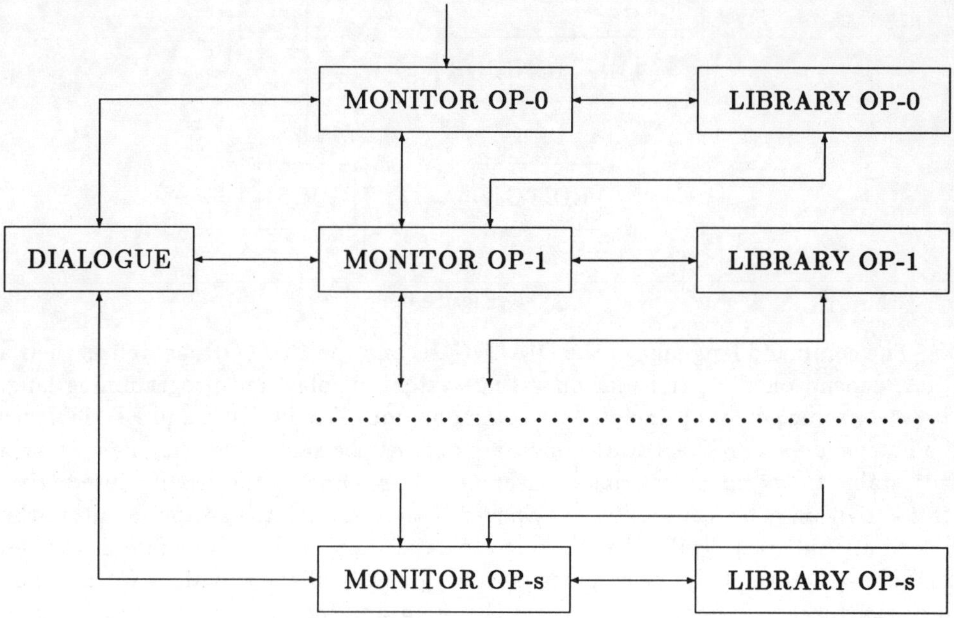

Figure 5

The structure of the computation process described above, actually presents a procedure version of an interactive optimization system (PIOS). On fig. 4 a PIOS for unconstrained minimization is shown. MONITOR-ODM, LIBRARY-ODM and DIALOGUE form a PIOS for one-dimensional minimization. The structure shown on fig. 5 represents an example PIOS for a class OP-0. From each level i ($i = 0, 1, \ldots, s$) downwards we obtain the structure of the PIOS for the OP-i class.

In the method of structuring described above, both the PIOS and its components are constructive units which can be properly combined dependent on particular needs (requirement C) or can be part of more complicated PIOS or other piece of software (requirement D).

5 A structure of the interactive optimization systems

The idea to unify software is applicable to the problem formulation, carried out by the basic part, EDITOR ("basic interface") and the problem oriented part, E-MONITOR ("oriented interface"). Thus the IOS for a certain OP class can be represented as shown on fig. 6. PIOS will provide the computation process for that class of problems.

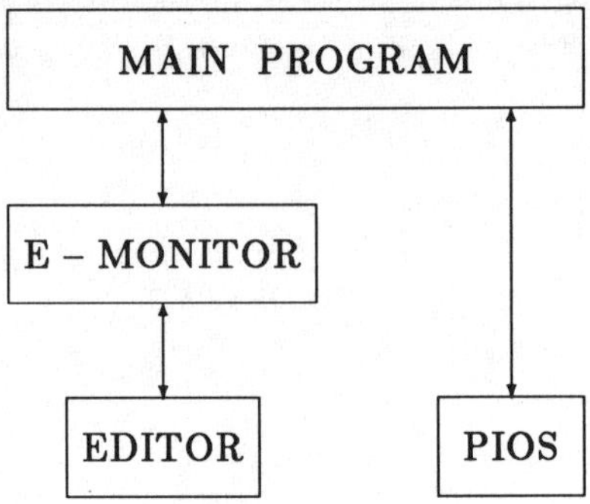

Figure 6

The command language of the DIALOGUE and the EDITOR, as well as their activities, depend on the particular operating system, display and programming language. However some general principles are common. Both DIALOGUE and EDITOR have to be independent in respect to the environment. At the same time they have to be easily adjustable to the specific terms of given OP classes and to the specific interactive control activities. This can easily be achieved if they are related to the monitors through informational arrays (tables) with concrete data, supplied by the monitors. Besides, the module structure of the basic parts is to be properly shaped to allow for the modules' inclusion/exclusion operations. As for the monitors, they have very simple and similar functions. Therefore both MONITOR and E-MONITOR can be written in the form of dummy procedures in the chosen programming language. Every particular monitor is obtained simply by filling the dummies with concrete information.

Some important features of the described IOS structure are:

- autonomy of all components, i.e. EDITOR, DIALOGUE, the monitors, the procedures of the libraries, the PIOS and the problem formulation itself, in respect to the environment. All these are procedures written in a particular programming language and are callable at any moment from any outer program unit.

- flexibility in use. All the components, due to their autonomy, are easily combined in various program configurations. An useful step to gain more flexibility is the separation of the problem formulation and the computation process. On the one hand, the basic part EDITOR is used to formulate arbitrary mathematical problems, so it can be applied to corresponding interactive systems. On the other hand, the problem formulation software can either be included or excluded, or replaced in the IOS, dependent on recent researches in the particular field, computer environment or some specific considerations.

- openness. Because of the autonomy of all the components their functions can easily be expanded or narrowed. In the basic parts and the libraries it is achieved by including/excluding modules and procedures, respectively. In the monitors the same applies to informational arrays and those statements which process them in dummy routines.

- uniformity of the software support and the command language. Except for the basic parts the software consists only of uniform monitors and procedures-methods. The unified command language performed by the basic parts, DIALOGUE and EDITOR, allows to unify the requirements to the procedures-methods, thus easing their programming or adapting.

According to the method of structuring described herein, an interactive optimization complex must comprise the "basic interface", DIALOGUE and EDITOR, and dummies of the "oriented interface" MONITOR and E-MONITOR. The creation of an IOS means to develop or adapt a proper methods library and fill the monitor dummies with concrete information.

6 The "OPTIMA" interactive optimization complex

The OPTIMA complex is made following the method described in §4 and §5 and is intended for the CM-4 (PDP-11) minicomputer, working under the RSX-11M operating system. The complex is written in FORTRAN except for one assembler module. OPTIMA includes "basic interface" DIALOGUE and EDITOR, dummies of MONITOR and E-MONITOR.

The EDITOR command language consists of menus and has complete capabilities to edit and save data. The DIALOGUE command language OPTIMA gives complete access to the computation process and takes into account the recommendations given by Golden and Wasil (1986) and by Sharda and Somarajan (1986). More particularly for every subprocess (dialogue level) by means of OPTIMA-commands it is possible: to get some help information; to select/change the current method; to invoke/abort the work of the current method at any moment; to get information for the current status of the computation process; to save/retrieve information into/from a file; to execute OPTIMA commands from a script file (batch mode work); to switch from interactive to batch mode and vice versa; to return to the parent subprocess; to have a proper error handling during an interactive session or in a script file; to issue a protocol of the interactive session, etc.

The script file can be created either during an interactive session or by means of an RSX-11M system's editor and may also contain user's comments.

The error handling means not only to detect an error and display the error message, but also an opportunity to correct it. Computation errors of the current method are also handled, e.g. division by zero, overflow, etc. When such an error occurs, the system begins a dialogue with the user.

By means of the interactive complex OPTIMA a family of IOS for CM-4 minicomputer is being created. By now it consists of seven IOS: the IOS ODM for one dimensional minimization; the IOS UPM for unconstrained minimization and when there are lower and/or upper bounds for the variables; the IOS QDM for quasiderivative function minimization; the IOS LTR to solve the linear transportation problem; the IOS HTR to solve the hyperbolic transportation problem; the IOS TRS to solve some classes of transportation problems; the IOS NSY to solve systems of equations with uncertain coefficients. According to the method of structuring described herein, the IOS UPM includes procedure versions of the IOS ODM (PIOS ODM), the IOS HTR includes the PIOS LTR and the IOS TRS includes both the PIOS LTR and the PIOS HTR.

References

Golden, B. L., Wasil, E. A. (1986). Nonlinear Programming on a Microcomputer. *Comput. and Ops. Res.*, vol. 13, No. 2/3, pp. 149–166.

Sharda, R., Somarajan, C. (1986). Comparative Performance of Advanced Microcomputer LP Systems. *Comput. and Ops. Res.*, vol. 13, No. 2/3, pp. 131–147.

Observations Regarding Choice Behaviour in Interactive Multiple Criteria Decision–Making Environments: An Experimental Investigation

Pekka Korhonen* and Jyrki Wallenius**
* *Helsinki School of Economics and Business Administration*
** *University of Jyväskylä, Finland*

1 Introduction

Many interactive procedures have been developed for solving optimization problems having multiple criteria. In such procedures, an exploration over the feasible or efficient region is conducted for locating the most preferred solution. As Steuer (1986) notes, interactive procedures are characterized by phases of decision-making alternating with phases of computation. Generally a pattern is established that we keep repeating until termination. At each iteration, a solution, or group of solutions, is generated for a decision-maker's (DM's) examination. Based on the examination, the DM inputs information to the solution procedure in the form of tradeoffs, pairwise comparisons, aspiration levels, etc. The responses are used to generate a presumably, improved solution, and so forth.

The nature and type of information requested from a DM differs from one procedure to another. Also, the mathematical assumptions upon which the procedures are based vary. In order to learn, what information could reliably be elicited from a DM and, which assumptions are plausible or reasonable from a behavioural perspective, we have carried out two laboratory experiments. Their purpose was to examine actual choice behaviour in interactive multiple criteria decision-making environments. In this paper, we review the main results and implications of these experiments. For additional details we refer to the original articles by Korhonen and Lantto (1986) and Korhonen, Moskowitz, and Wallenius (1987).

Different versions of a "free search" visual interactive reference direction approach, originally developed by Korhonen and Laakso (1986) to solving multiple objective linear programming problems, were implemented on an IBM/PC1 microcomputer. The experimental subjects were a group of management students who solved three realistic and relevant decision problems using the "free search" approach.

This paper consists of four sections. In the first section we have described the purpose of the study. The second section provides the details of the experiments and the third section the results. In the fourth section, the observed choice behaviour is discussed and explained.

2 Experiments

In this paper we describe two experiments, in which a group of management students at the Helsinki School of Economics and Business Administration solved three realistic and relevant decision problems. In the first experiment, 65 students solved a multiple objective linear programming problem (problem I below), and in the second experiment, 72 students solved two discrete alternative multiple criteria problems (problems II and III below). Most of the students were upper division undergraduates majoring in management science of accounting. They had prior experience in using microcomputers, interactive multiple criteria decision methods, and, specifically, the visual reference direction approach.

Description of the decision problems

Allocating One's Time (I). The first problem was a five objective linear programming problem for allocating one's time to study, work, and leisure. The objectives to be maximized were: total number of credit hours earned during a semester, income earned during a semester (FMK/month), leisure time (hours/day), work experience (measured as a function of working hours), and study performance (number of credit hours earned with excellent grades). (See Korhonen and Lantto, 1986.)

Choosing a Washing Machine (II). This problem was extracted from (Zeleny, 1982, pp. 210–211). The original decision problem consisted of 33 washing machines that were evaluated using four criteria: price, total washing time, electricity consumption, and water consumption. In our experiment, we used the first three criteria, which all were to be minimized. (See Korhonen et al., 1987.)

Buying a Home (III). The third problem consisted of choosing one out of 43 actual homes in the Helsinki metropolitan area. The data were collected from the main daily newspaper (Helsingin Sanomat) published in Helsinki. Five different criteria were used to evaluate the alternatives: price, location (measured on a 1–10 scale), area in square meters, number of rooms, and the condition of the unit (measured on a 1–10 scale). The context and the alternatives were defined so that all criteria except price were to be maximized. (See Korhonen et al., 1987.)

The visual interactive reference direction approach

The reference direction approach of Korhonen and Laakso (1986), with extensions and modifications by Korhonen and Wallenius (1987) and Korhonen (1987), was used as the research instrument.

The original approach for solving multiple objective linear programming problems is static by nature. Korhonen and Wallenius (1987) extended the original idea by developing PARETO RACE, a procedure for dynamically exploring the efficient frontier.

Recently, Korhonen (1987) developed a modification of the original method for solving discrete multiple criteria problems.

The procedures are not based on any assumptions regarding the properties of the value function. Using the procedures, a DM is free to examine any efficient solutions. Furthermore, this freedom is not limited by previous choices.

The main steps of the approach are as follows, but the details of the procedures vary:

0. Choose an arbitrary efficient solution as a starting point.

1. Determine a reference direction, that is a direction in which the DM's utility at least locally increases. If at a subsequent iteration the DM does not wish to change the reference direction, STOP. Otherwise, proceed to step 2.

2. Generate a subset of efficient solutions by projecting the reference direction on the set of efficient solutions. (See Wierzbicki, 1980; Korhonen and Laakso, 1986; Korhonen, 1987.)

3. Present the subset (as in the original approach or step by step as in PARETO RACE), generated in the previous step, to the DM graphically and numerically and ask him/her to choose the most preferred solution from this set; return to step 1.

There are several ways to specify a reference direction. In the first experiment, we compared five different techniques for specifying reference directions. They were: 1) the use of aspiration levels (Korhonen and Laakso, 1986), 2) the (modified) boundary point ranking method (BPR) (Hemming, 1978; Korhonen and Lantto, 1986), 3) the analytic hierarchy process (AHP) (Saaty, 1980), 4) the use of marginal rates of substitution (MRS) (Geoffrion et al., 1972), and 5) the use of unit vectors (Korhonen and Lantto, 1986).

Design

In the first experiment, the subjects were divided into groups of ten to sixteen students, although each subject was tested individually. If a subject had any problems in operating the system (that is, any of the five reference direction techniques), he/she was welcome to ask for advice from one of the assistants present. To prevent the subjects from benefitting from the results obtained with a previously used technique, a modified model was used for each trial. The models differed in the coefficients of the objectives. The order of using the models was fixed, whereas the order of using the five techniques was systematically varied. The direction finding routines were implemented on top of PARETO RACE, so that the step-size problem was solved by the dynamic line search procedure. Afterwards, each subject was subjected to an exit interview. To improve the reliability of the answers, the subjects were encouraged to keep notes during the session.

The subjects were asked to evaluate the techniques using several measures of performance (scales ranging from 1 to 7, 7 being the best). The measures are listed below.

1. Satisfaction with the solution obtained.
2. Confidence in the technique.
3. Ease of understanding the technique.
4. Ease of using the technique.
5. Correspondence between the subjects' responses and the implied search directions.
6. Information provided by the technique.
7. "Experienced" speed of convergence.

In addition, the number of iterations required by each technique was recorded.

In the second experiment, each subject solved (again, individually) two decision problems, first problem II, then problem III. The problems were perceived as being independent; hence, dependence effects, such as learning, were minimal. At the beginning of each session, the subjects were provided with one page problem descriptions. The discrete reference direction approach (Korhonen, 1987) was used as the research instrument. Only aspiration levels were used as the basis of determining reference directions, because of its superior performance in the first experiment. The subjects then made choices in each problem and were allowed to iterate as long as they desired. Their choices during the solution process were documented for subsequent analysis. After making decisions on the problems, they were subjected to an exit interview, reflecting on their choices, choice process, the procedure, etc.

3 Findings

The first experiment

A summary of the results of the first experiment is presented in Table 1. The preference ranking of the techniques was identical for each measure of performance. The use of aspiration levels was found superior. The runner-up was the analytic hierarchy process. The inferiority of the use of MRS did not come as a surprise. Despite its apparent theoretical soundness, the Geoffrion et al. (1972) procedure remains difficult to use, at least without any prior experience in its use. The modified boundary point ranking method performed quite well, partly because of improvements made to the original procedure. (Since the reference direction approach always proceeds from the currently best solution, the original BPR idea of generating directions did not work well and had to be modified. For additional details, see (Korhonen and Lantto, 1986.) In the unit vector technique, the generation of each new direction was counted as an iteration, even though the subjects may not have considered it a direction of improvement. Thus, its documented rate of convergence is negatively biased. Interestingly, when the subjects used some of the highest ranked methods, they made surprisingly few iterations (often less than five). With less attractive techniques, more iterations were needed.

The techniques: (in order of preference)	Total mean:	Average variance:	No. of mean:	Iterations st.dev.
1) aspiration levels	5.8	1.13	3.9	2.3
2) AHP	4.9	2.34	8.5	7.4
3) modified BPR	4.3	2.31	4.9	3.6
4) unit vectors	3.8	3.11	13.9	12.8
5) the use of MRS	3.1	2.98	13.0	8.4

Table 1: Summary of the results

Total mean: average of the means of the performance measures
Average variance: average variance within the groups

The second experiment

In the washing machine purchase problem (II), the average number of interactive iterations was 1.9, while in the home buying problem (III) it was 2.3. The difference in rate of convergence is presumably due to the greater number of choice criteria, and, apparently, the greater perceived relevance and interest of problem III. The subjects were aware that problem III was based on real data. The observed rapid degree of convergence of the reference direction approach on a preferred solution is consistent with the results of the first experiment. Thirty two percent and eighteen percent of the subjects in problems II and III, respectively, exhibited inconsistent or intransitive preferences at least once. Namely, at some point they would prefer choice A to B, even though they earlier preferred B to A. The percentage of intransitive cases is excessive considering the small number of average iterations. The transitivity axiom was violated in two different ways: a) *explicitly*, if the subject chose the same alternative as the best at least twice, but not at subsequent iterations; b) *implicitly*, if an alternative was chosen as the best subsequently, but not when it was available for the first time. The first type of violation results in, what we call, a cycle of Type A, and the second in a cycle of Type B. The observed frequencies are depicted in Table 2.

Type of Cycle	Problem II	Problem III
A	2	1
B	21	12

Table 2: Frequencies of cycles

4 Discussion

The main findings of our experiments can be summarized as follows:

1. Subjects' clear preference ranking of different reference direction techniques (first experiment).

2. A surprisingly rapid degree of convergence of the interactive procedures on a preferred solution (both experiments).

3. Intransitive behaviour of many subjects (second experiment).

It seems reasonable to assume that at any point in time the DM's perception of the constraint set and the value function would affect the determination of the reference direction. Therefore, we hypothesize that the DM seeks to achieve the optimum of his/her cognitive feasible set, that is the set of solutions the DM believes to be attainable. Hence, it follows that the DM would like to find a direction, which would lead directly from the current solution to this optimum.

Based on the above hypothesis, one can understand that the aspiration level procedure for determining reference directions turned out to be superior. Each vector of aspiration levels is, obviously, the optimum of the DM's cognitive feasible region. As the search process continues, the DM gains additional information about attainable solutions and his/her cognitive model converges towards the real model (provided that the model is believed). Thus the aspiration levels converge towards the optimum of the real model.

In AHP, in contrast to the Geoffrion et al. procedure, the DM considers marginal utilities instead of changes in the original criterion values. The evaluations are apparently easier to make, and thus the overall performance is better.

Our modification of the Boundary Point Ranking technique was relatively well accepted by the subjects. The reference direction is always close to the efficient frontier. Also, the BPR method gives explicit information about the solutions in the neighbourhood of the current solution and thus helps the DM to reduce his/her cognitive constraint set.

With the unit vector approach, the reduced freedom of the user to specify directions was considered a drawback. If the DM has an idea of a desired direction, it seems easier for him/her to explicitly influence the direction than to decide, if a computer generated direction is desirable or not.

A lesson from this experiment seems to be that a good reference direction technique is one that enables the DM to learn from the efficient solutions of the problem as freely as possible and thus helps to reduce the cognitive constraint set as quickly as possible towards the actual constraint set. This implies that the DM should be helped to generate directions close (and certainly not, orthogonal) to the efficient frontier.

A surprisingly rapid degree of convergence of the procedures on a preferred solution was established in both experiments, and especially in the second experiment. This phenomenon can be explained using prospect theory developed by Kahneman and Tversky (1979). In prospect theory, outcomes are expressed as positive or negative deviations (gains or losses) from a reference outcome. Although value functions differ among individuals (and criteria), Kahneman and Tversky proposed that they are commonly S-shaped; concave above the reference outcome and convex below it. Furthemore, according to prospect theory, value functions are commonly steeper for losses than for gains. Therefore, we may end up with a situation where a DM prefers A to B (if A is the reference outcome) and B to A (if B is the reference outcome), simply because subjects react more to negative than to positive stimuli. For additional details, see (Korhonen, Moskowitz and Wallenius, 1987).

The persistence of the intransitivities observed in our experiments is similar to those originally observed by Tversky (1969), among others. Moreover, Tversky (1969) has provided a choice theory that predicts and explains intransitive preferences between multidimensional alternatives. In the case where alternatives are evaluated based on comparisons of criterion-wise differences between alternatives, Tversky's additive difference model is applicable. If the difference functions (which determine the contribution of the particular subjective difference to the overall evaluation of the alternatives) are nonlinear, intransitivities may systematically occur. In interactive procedures (as in the reference direction approach), comparisons are made with respect to a so-called reference outcome (current solution). This clearly favors the use of an additive difference model, and hence accounts for the persistence of the cycles exhibited.

Tversky's (1969) difference model and Kahneman-Tversky's prospect theory (1979) together provide a simple explanation of choice behaviour observed in the second experiment. Obviously, there may exist other explanations. However, we feel that our explanation is plausible and that human subjects have conditional value functions that depend on the reference outcome. Additional, carefully designed experiments with interactive methods are needed to further substantiate our arguments.

Acknowledgment: The research was supported, in part, by grants from Y. Jahnsson Foundation, the Foundation of the Student Union of the Helsinki School of Economics, and Foundation for Economic Education.

References

Geoffrion, A., Dyer, J. and Feinberg, A. (1972). An Interactive Approach for Multi-Criterion Optimization, with an Application to the Operation of an Academic Department. *Management Science*, 19(4), pp. 357–368.

Hemming, T. (1978). Multiple Objective Decision Making under Certainty. EFI, the Stockholm School of Economics, Stockholm.

Kahneman, D. and Tversky, A. (1979). Prospect Theory: An Analysis of Decisions Under Risk. *Econometrica*, 47, pp. 262–291.

Korhonen, P. (1987). A Visual Reference Direction Approach to Solving Discrete Multiple Criteria Problems. Working Paper F-134, Helsinki School of Economics. Forthcoming in European Journal of Operational Research.

Korhonen, P. and Laakso, J. (1986). A Visual Interactive Method for Solving the Multiple Criteria Problem. *European Journal of Operational Research*, 24(2), pp. 277–287.

Korhonen, P. and Lantto, O. (1986). An Experimental Comparison of Some Reference Direction Techniques for MCDM-Problems. Working Paper F-142, Helsinki School of Economics.

Korhonen, P., Moskowitz, H. and Wallenius, J. (1987). Choice Behavior in Interactive Multiple Criteria Decision-Making. Working Paper, F-175, Helsinki School of Economics.

Korhonen, P. and Wallenius, J. (1987). A Pareto Race. Working Paper (DIS 85/86—13), Arizona State University. Forthcoming in Naval Research Logistics.

Saaty, T. (1980). The Analytic Hierarchy Process. McGraw-Hill, New York.

Simon, H. (1986). Alternative Visions of Rationality. In H. Arkes and K. Hammond, eds., Judgment and Decision Making. Cambridge University Press, Cambridge, pp. 97–113.

Steuer, R.E. (1986). Multiple Criteria Optimization: Theory, Computation, and Application, Wiley, New York.

Tversky, A. (1969). Intransitivity of Preferences. *Psychological Review*, 76, pp. 31–48.

Wierzbicki, A. (1980). The Use of Reference Objectives in Multiobjective Optimization. In G. Fandel and T. Gal, eds., Multiple Criteria Decision Making, Theory and Application. Springer-Verlag, New York, pp. 468–486.

Zeleny, M. (1982). Multiple Criteria Decision Making. McGraw-Hill, New York.

Solving Dynamic Multicriteria Linear Problems with HYBRID

Marek Makowski*
International Institute for Applied Systems Analysis
A-2361 Laxenburg, Austria

Janusz S. Sosnowski
System Research Institute
of the Polish Academy of Sciences
Newelska 6, 01-447, Warsaw, Poland

1 Introduction

The purpose of the paper is to describe methods used for formulation, solution and analysis of dynamic multiobjective linear programming problems with HYBRID package (see Makowski and Sosnowski, 1987). The method adopted in HYBRID for formulation and solution of a multicriteria problem is based on the reference point approach introduced by Wierzbicki (1980). In this approach a piecewise linear scalarizing function is defined. The function parameters are aspiration level for each criterion (reference points) and — possibly — weights. Minimization of the scalarizing function subject linear constraints is substituted by solution of an equivalent single-objective linear programming problem.

HYBRID allows for solving both static and dynamic LP problems. Static problems can be interpreted as problems for which a specific structure is not recognized nor exploited. But many real life problems have specific structure which — if exploited — can result not only in much faster execution of optimization runs but also remarkably help in problem definition and interpretation of results.

Many optimization problems in economic planning over time, production scheduling, inventory, transportation, control dynamic systems can be formulated as linear dynamic problems (see Propoi, 1978). Such problems are also called multistage or staircase linear programming problems (cf Fourer, 1982; Ho and Hanne, 1974). A dynamic problem can be formulated as an equivalent large static LP and any commercial LP code may be used for solving it, if the problem corresponds to single objective optimization. For multicriteria problems, a processor may be used for transformation of that problem to an equivalent LP one. The system DIDAS, described by Lewandowski

*On leave from Systems Research Institute of the Polish Academy of Sciences, Warsaw, Poland

and Wierzbicki (1987), is a package that is composed of preprocessor and postprocessor for handling transformation of multicriteria problem and processing results respectively (cf Lewandowski and Grauer, 1982). Those pre- and post-processor are linked with an LP package. HYBRID has generally similar structure. The main difference is that — instead of an LP package — another algorithm is applied, which exploits the dynamics of a problem. Similarly as some other systems of DIDAS family, HYBRID has the advantage of handling a problem as a dynamic one which results in an easy way of formulation of criteria and of interpretation of results, since one may refer to one variable trajectory contrary to a "static" formulation of dynamic problems which involves separate variables for each time period.

HYBRID is oriented towards an interactive mode of operation in which a sequence of problems is to be solved under varying conditions (e.g., different objective functions, reference points, values of constraints or bounds). Criteria for multiobjective problems may be easily defined and updated with the help of the package.

The HYBRID is available from SDS of IIASA in two versions: one for mainframes and one for PC. Each version requires a FORTRAN compiler that accepts full standard of FORTRAN–77. Implementation on a particular computer requires only changes in a routine that reads system date and time.

The package has been tested on VAX 11/780 (for f77 compiler under 4.2 BSD UNIX) and on a PC compatible with PC IBM/AT. The minimal configuration of PC consists of 512kB RAM. Intel coprocessor 80287 is strongly recommended (in fact required by some FORTRAN compilers).

2 Statement of problems

2.1 Multiobjective linear programming problems

HYBRID may be used for solving problems formulated in the following general form:

$$\min q \tag{2.1}$$

$$q = Cx \tag{2.2}$$

$$b - r \leq Ax \leq b \tag{2.3}$$

$$l \leq x \leq u \tag{2.4}$$

where C is a given $k \times n$ matrix of objective functions coefficients, $l, u \in R^n$ are given lower and upper bounds for variables $x \in R^n$, $b, r \in R^m$ are vectors of rhs and ranges, respectively.

Despite the fact that HYBRID accepts problems formulated in the above stated general form, problems that are dynamic by nature should be defined as such. The latter formulation allows for easier interaction with package, easier interpretation of results and results in faster execution of the package.

2.2 Dynamic multiobjective linear programming problems

Before discussing a general formulation of a dynamic problem that can be solved by HYBRID, let us first consider the classical formulation of a dynamic linear programming problem in the following form:

Find a control trajectory

$$u = (u_1, \ldots, u_T)$$

and a state trajectory

$$x = (x_1, \ldots, x_T)$$

satisfying the state equations with initial condition x_0

$$x_t = A_{t-1}x_{t-1} + B_t u_t - c_t \tag{2.5}$$

and constraints

$$d_{t-1} - r_{t-1} \leq F_{t-1}x_{t-1} + D_t u_t \leq d_{t-1} \qquad t = 1, \ldots, T \tag{2.6}$$

$$e_t \leq u_t \leq f_t \qquad t = 1, \ldots, T \tag{2.7}$$

$$F_T x_T \leq d_T \tag{2.8}$$

which results in Pareto-optimal solution in respect to the following K objectives:

$$\sum_{t=1}^{T} \left(a_t^i x_t + b_t^i u_t \right) \tag{2.9}$$

where: $i = 1, \ldots, K$ is a criterion index; $t = 1, \ldots, T$ denotes a period of time; state variables x_t, control variables u_t, both for each period, are elements of Euclidian spaces of appropriate dimensions; matrices A_t, B_t, D_t, F_t are assumed to be given; right-hand side vectors c_t and d_t, as well as range vector r_t and bounds for control variables e_t and f_t are given; initial condition x_0 is given.

In the above given formulation the state equation (2.5) is given in the normal form. However there exists many models which comprise state equations with distributed-lags on control and state variables, e.g. traffic network (cf e.g. Tamura, 1977), flood control models (cf e.g. Kreglewski et al., 1985), econometric models (cf e.g. Chow, 1975). Therefore HYBRID accepts the more general formulation of the dynamic problem in which equation (2.5) may be replaced by:

$$x_t = \sum_{i=t-1-p}^{t-1} A_{t-1,i}x_i + \sum_{i=t-q}^{t} B_{t,i}u_i - s_t, \qquad i = 1, \ldots, T \tag{2.10}$$

with initial conditions:

$$x_t = \bar{x}_t, \qquad t = -p, -p+1, \ldots, 0 \tag{2.11}$$

$$u_t = \bar{u}_t, \qquad t = -q+1, -q+2, \ldots, 0 \tag{2.12}$$

where s_t is a given vector.

In fact HYBRID accepts also constraints of type (2.5) and (2.10) where equality may be replaced by inequality condition (for such a case HYBRID generates appropriate slack variables).

2.3 Types of criteria for dynamic models

HYBRID allows for definition of criteria of various types. Beside of simple linear combinations of variables for particular time periods (cf eq. 2.9) a user may define nonlinear criteria of four types. Let x_{it} denotes i-th coordinate of the state vector x_t and $\{\bar{x}_{it}\}_{t=1}^{T}$ will be the reference trajectory for i-th state variable. For a given reference trajectory one may define criteria on the following three types (where $x_i \in R^T$ is a selected state or control variable, $\bar{x}_i$ — its reference trajectory):

$$q_k = \max_{t=1,\dots,T} (x_{it} - \bar{x}_{it}) \rightarrow \min \qquad \text{(Type SUP)}$$

$$q_k = \min_{t=1,\dots,T} (x_{it} - \bar{x}_{it}) \rightarrow \max \qquad \text{(Type INF)}$$

$$q_k = \max_{t=1,\dots,T} (abs(x_{it} - \bar{x}_{it})) \rightarrow \min \qquad \text{(Type FOL)}$$

The above types of criteria can also be defined for a control variable. For a state variable only a criterion of the following type may also defined:

$$q_k = \max_{t=1,\dots,T} (abs(x_{it} - x_{it-1})) \rightarrow \min \qquad \text{(Type DER)}$$

2.4 Finding Pareto-optimal solutions

A Pareto-optimal solution can be found by the minimization of the achievement scalarizing function in the form

$$\max_{i=1,\dots,K} (w_i(q_i - \bar{q}_i)) + \epsilon_m \sum_{i=1}^{K} w_i q_i \rightarrow \min \tag{2.13}$$

where: K — is the number of criteria; q_i — is the i-th criterion; $\bar{q}_i$ — is the aspiration level for i-th criterion; w_i — is a weight associated with i-th criterion; ϵ_m — is a given non-negative small parameter.

This form of achievement function is a slight modification of a form suggested by Lewandowski (1982). Note that for $\epsilon_m = 0$ only weakly Pareto-optimal points can be guaranteed as minimal points of this function. Therefore, the use of very small ϵ_m will result in practice (except of situations in which reference point has some specific properties) in almost weakly Pareto-optimal solution. On the other hand, too big values of ϵ_m could drastically change properties associated with the first part of the scalarizing function.

The method based on the reference point approach may be summarized in the form of the following stages:

1. The user of the model defines objective function q_i and aspiration levels $\bar{q}_i$, $i = 1, 2, \dots, K$.

2. The problem of minimizing the scalarizing function subject constraints is transformed into an auxiliary linear problem (see Makowski and Sosnowski, 1987). Solution of this auxiliary problem provides a Pareto-optimal point.

3. The user explores various Pareto-optimal points by changing either the aspiration level $\bar{q}$ or/and weights attached to criteria or/and other parameters related to the definition of the multicriteria problem.

4. The procedure described in points 2 and 3 is repeated until satisfactory solution is found.

The user may also estimate the bounds of Pareto-optimal set by selecting the option *utopia* in HYBRID which results in single-objective optimization with respect to a selected criterion. Repetition of calculation of utopia point for each criterion gives upper estimate of values of each criterion.

2.5 Formulation of dynamic problems accepted by HYBRID

Transformation of the problem of minimization of scalarizing function of single criterion LP problem (see Makowski and Sosnowski, 1987) results in a dynamic problem which no longer has the structure defined in the section 2.2. Therefore HYBRID has been modified to accept more general structure of a dynamic problem and still exploits dynamic nature of a problem being solved.

All variables are divided into two groups: decision variables u and variables x_t, the latter are specified for each period of time. A single criterion Dynamic Linear Problem (DLP) problem may be formulated as follows:

Find a trajectory x_t and decision variables u such that both:
state equations:

$$-H_t x_t + \sum_{i=0}^{t-1} A_{t-1,i} x_i + B_t u = c_t, \qquad t = 1, \ldots, T \tag{2.14}$$

with given initial condition x_0
and constraints:

$$d - r \leq \sum_{t=0}^{T} F_t x_t + Du \leq d \tag{2.15}$$

$$e \leq u \leq f \tag{2.16}$$

are satisfied and the following function is minimized:

$$\sum_{t=1}^{T} a_t x_t + bu \tag{2.17}$$

Components of vector u are called decision variables for historical reasons. Actually a vector u may be composed of any variables, some of them may be specified for each time period and enter criteria defined for a dynamic case. But some components of vector u may not be specified for any time period. A user may also specify variables independent of time. For the sake of keeping the formulation of the problem as simple as possible we have not introduced a separate name for such variables.

The structure of an DLP problem may be illustrated by the following diagram:

u	x_0	x_1	x_2	x_3	rhs	var.
B_1	A_{00}	$-H_1$	0	0	c_1	state eq.
B_2	A_{10}	A_{11}	$-H_2$	0	c_2	state eq.
B_3	A_{20}	A_{21}	A_{22}	$-H_3$	c_3	state eq.
D	F_0	F_1	F_2	F_3	d	constr.
b	0	a_1	a_2	a_3	—	goal

where H_t is diagonal matrix and 0 is a matrix composed of zero elements.

2.6 Remarks about formulation of a dynamic problem

HYBRID allows for solving both static and dynamic LP problems. Static problems can be interpreted as problems for which a specific structure is not recognized nor exploited. But many real life problems have specific structure which — if exploited — can result not only in much faster execution of optimization runs but also remarkably help in problem definition and interpretation of results.

Numerous problems have dynamic nature and it is natural to take advantage of its proper definition. HYBRID offers many options for dynamic problems, such as:

1. In many situations, the user may deal with generic names of variables. A generic name consists of 6 first characters of a name while 2 last characters corresponds to the period of time. Therefore, the user may for example refer to the entire trajectory (by generic name) or to value of a variable for a specific time period (by full name). Such approach corresponds to a widely used practice of generating trajectories for dynamic problems.

2. The user may select any of 4 types of criteria that correspond to practical applications. Those can be defined for each time period (together with additional "global" conditions), but this requires rather large effort. Therefore, for dynamic problems, criteria are specified just by the type of criterion and the generic name of the corresponding variable. Types of criteria are discussed in details later.

3. A problem can be declared as a dynamic one by the definition of periods of time. For a dynamic problem, additional rules must be observed. These rules correspond to the way in which the MPS file has to be sorted and to the way in which names for rows and columns are selected. These rules follow a widely accepted standard generation of dynamic problems.

3 General description of the package and data structure

The package is constructed in modules to provide a reasonably high level of flexibility and efficiency.

The package consists of three subpackages:

- Preprocessor that serves to process data, enables a modification of the problem, performs diagnostics and may supply information useful for verification of a problem. The preprocessor also transforms a multicriteria problem to a parametric single criteria optimization problem, helps in the interactive change of parameters, etc.
- Optimization package called solver of a relevant optimization problem (either static or dynamic)
- Postprocessor that can provide results in the standard MPS format and can also generate the "user file" which contains all information needed for the analysis of a solution; the later option makes it easier to link HYBRID to a specialized report-writer or a graphic package.

All three subpackages are linked by communication region, that contains all data packed in an efficient way. From the user point of view, HYBRID is still one package that may be easily used for different purposes chosen via specification file.

The chosen method of allocating storage in the memory takes maximal advantage of the available computer memory and of the features of typical real-world problems. In general, the matrix of constraints is large and sparse, while the number of all essential, non-zero coefficients that take different numerical values is much smaller than the number of all non-zero coefficients. A super-sparse-matrix technique is therefore applied to store the data that define the problem to be solved. This involves the construction of a table of these essential coefficients. In addition, all indices and logical variables are packed so that one four-byte word is being used for four indices (2 logical and 2 integer). All data is packed in blank common to minimize the storage area used.

Special commands of HYBRID support model verification and problem modification. This is necessary to facilitate scenario analysis and to reduce the problems caused by inappropriate scaling.

The data format for the input of MPS file and the output of LP results follows standards adopted by most commercial mathematical programming systems (cf e.g. Murtagh, 1981).

4 Outline of the solution technique for the auxiliary LP problem

The most popular methods for solving linear programming problems are based on the simplex algorithm. However, a number of other iterative non-simplex approaches have recently been developed (cf Mangasarian, 1981; Polyak and Tretiyakov, 1972; Sosnowski, 1981). HYBRID belongs to this group of non-simplex methods.

HYBRID uses a particular implementation of the Lagrange multiplier method for solving linear programming problems. General linear constraints are included within an augmented Lagrangian function. The LP problem is solved by minimizing a sequence of quadratic functions subject to simple constraints (lower and upper bounds). This minimization is achieved by the use of a method which combines the conjugate gradient method and an active constraints strategy.

In recent years many methods oriented for solving dynamic linear problems (DLP) have been developed. Most of those methods consists of adaptation of the simplex method for problems with a special structure of constraints. In HYBRID, a different approach is applied. A DLP, which should be defined together with a state equation, is solved through the use of adjoint equations and by reduction of gradients to control subspaces (more exactly, to a subspace of independent variables). The method exploits the sparseness of the matrix structure. The simple constraints (lower and upper bounds for non-slack variables) for control variables are not violated during optimization and the resulting sequence of multipliers is feasible for the dual problem. The global constraints (i.e. constraints other then those defined as simple constraints) may be violated, however, and therefore the algorithm can be started from any point that satisfies the simple constraints.

The solution technique briefly outlined above allows for solution of problems that are hardly to be solved by many other LP codes.

In order to provide general information about capabilities of HYBRID, the main options are listed below. HYBRID offers the following features:

- Input of data and the formulation of an LP problem follow the MPS standard. Additional rules (that concern only sequencing of some rows and columns) should be observed in order to take advantage of the structure of a dynamic problem. An experienced user may speed up computations by setting certain options and/or parameters (cf the HYBRID User Manual).

- Solution is available in the standard MPS format and optionally in a user file which contains all data that might be useful for postoptimal analysis and reports.

- A main storage area, called the *communication region*, contains all the information corresponding to a run. The communication region is stored on disk in certain situations to allow continuation of computations from failed (or interrupted) runs or to run a modified problem while using previously obtained information without the necessity of reading and processing the MPS input file.

- The multicriteria problem is formulated and solved as a sequence of parametric optimization problems modified in interactive way upon analysis of previous results.

- For static or dynamic problem, the solution technique can be chosen.

- The problem can be modified at any stage of its solution (i.e., by changing the matrix of coefficients, introducing or altering right-hand sides, ranges or bounds).

- A special problem scaling is implemented (as described by Makowski and Sosnowski, 1981).

- A comprehensive diagnostics is implemented, including the checking of parallel rows, the detection of columns and rows which are empty or contain only one entry, the splitting of columns, the recognition of inconsistencies in right-hand sides, ranges and bounds, and various other features that are useful in debugging the problem formulation.
- The package supports a display of a matrix by rows (printing the nonzero elements and names of the corresponding columns, right-hand sides and ranges), as well as a display of a matrix by columns (analogous to displaying by rows).
- A check of the feasibility of a problem prior to its optimization is optionally performed.
- The optimization problem solver uses a regularization of the problem (cf Sosnowski, 1981).
- More detailed information for an infeasible or unbounded problem is optionally provided by the package.

References

Chow, G.C. (1975). Analysis and Control of Dynamic Economic Systems. Wiley, New York.

Fourer, R. (1982). Solving staircase linear programs by the simplex method. *Mathematical Programming* 23, pp. 274–313, 25, pp. 251–292.

Ho, J.K. and Hanne, A.S. (1974). Nested decomposition for dynamic models. *Mathematical Programming* 6, pp. 121–140.

Kreglewski, T., Lewandowski, A. and Rogowski, T. (1985). Dynamic Extension of the DIDAS system and its Application in Flood Control. In M. Grauer, M. Thompson, A.P. Wierzbicki, eds., Plural Rationality and Interactive Decision Processes, Springer-Verlag.

Lewandowski, A. and Grauer, M. (1982). The reference point optimization approach — methods of efficient implementation. CP-8-S12, IIASA Collaborative Proceedings Series: Multiobjective and Stochastic Optimization Proceedings of an IIASA Task Force Meeting.

Lewandowski, A. and Wierzbicki, A. eds (1987). Theory, Software and Testing Examples for Decision Support Systems. WP-87-26, IIASA, Laxenburg, Austria.

Makowski, M. and Sosnowski, J. (1981). Implementation of an algorithm for scaling matrices and other programs useful in linear programming. CP-81-37, International Institute for Applied Systems Analysis, Laxenburg, Austria.

Makowski, M. and Sosnowski, J. (1987). A Mathematical Programming Package for Multicriteria Dynamic Linear Problems HYBRID; Methodological and User Guide to version 3.03. WP-87-00, IIASA, Laxenburg, Austria.

Mangasarian, O.L. (1981). Iterative solution of linear programs. *SIAM Journal for Numerical Analysis*, 18(4), pp. 606–614.

Murtagh, B.A. (1981). Advanced Linear Programming: Computation and Practice, Mc Graw-Hill, New York.

Polyak, B.T. and Tretiyakov, N.V. (1972). An iterative method for linear programming and its economic interpretation. *Economic and Mathematical Methods*, 8, pp. 740–751, (in Russian).

Propoi, A. (1978). Problems of Dynamic Linear Programming. RM-76-78, IIASA.

Sosnowski, J. (1981). Linear programming via augmented Lagrangian and conjugate gradient methods. In S. Walukiewicz and A.P. Wierzbicki, eds., Methods of Mathematical Programming, Proceedings of a 1977 Conference in Zakopane. Polish Scientific Publishers, Warsaw.

Tamura, H. (1977). Multistage Linear Programming for Discrete Optimal Control with Distributed Lags. *Autonomica*, vol. 13, pp. 369–376, Pergamon Press.

Principles of Multi–Stage Selection in Software Development in Decision Support Systems*

Marchev A. A., Motzev M. R.
Laboratory of Systems Analysis and Management
Economic University "Karl Marx"
Sofia, Bulgaria

1 Introduction

Nowadays there is a trend in the scientific world to use concepts like: decision support systems, simulation modelling, artificial intelligence, knowledge bases, formulation of hypotheses, selection procedures, etc., in a close connection when solving one and the same problem.

Gradually, such branches of scientific thought like simulation modelling, decision support systems and artificial intelligence get more closely connected with each other, and there comes into being a tendency of their consolidation and merging into one solitary branch.

The area of decision support systems is closely related to the simulation modelling. At least two very typical examples can be given:

1. The simulation model of a given complex system is used as a component part (constructive element) of a decision support system. This simulation model is used for conducting different simulation experiments connected with different versions of the generated decisions, and for evaluating their consequences.

2. The process of synthesizing a simulation model may be treated as a multi-stage decision making procedure, which includes: the generating of hypotheses, the choice of competing versions of the model (i.e. choice between different hypotheses), continuity and mutual dependence between decisions in successive stages of the process, etc. In this case, a system for automated construction of simulation models may be viewed as a peculiar decision support system.

In our work this connection between simulation modelling, decision support systems and artificial intelligence is quite strongly pronounced, on account of the use of such methods for automated construction of simulation models, which are based on a multi-stage selection procedure (MSSP).

*This project has been completed with the financial support of the Committee for Science at the Council of Ministers under contract No. 398/1987.

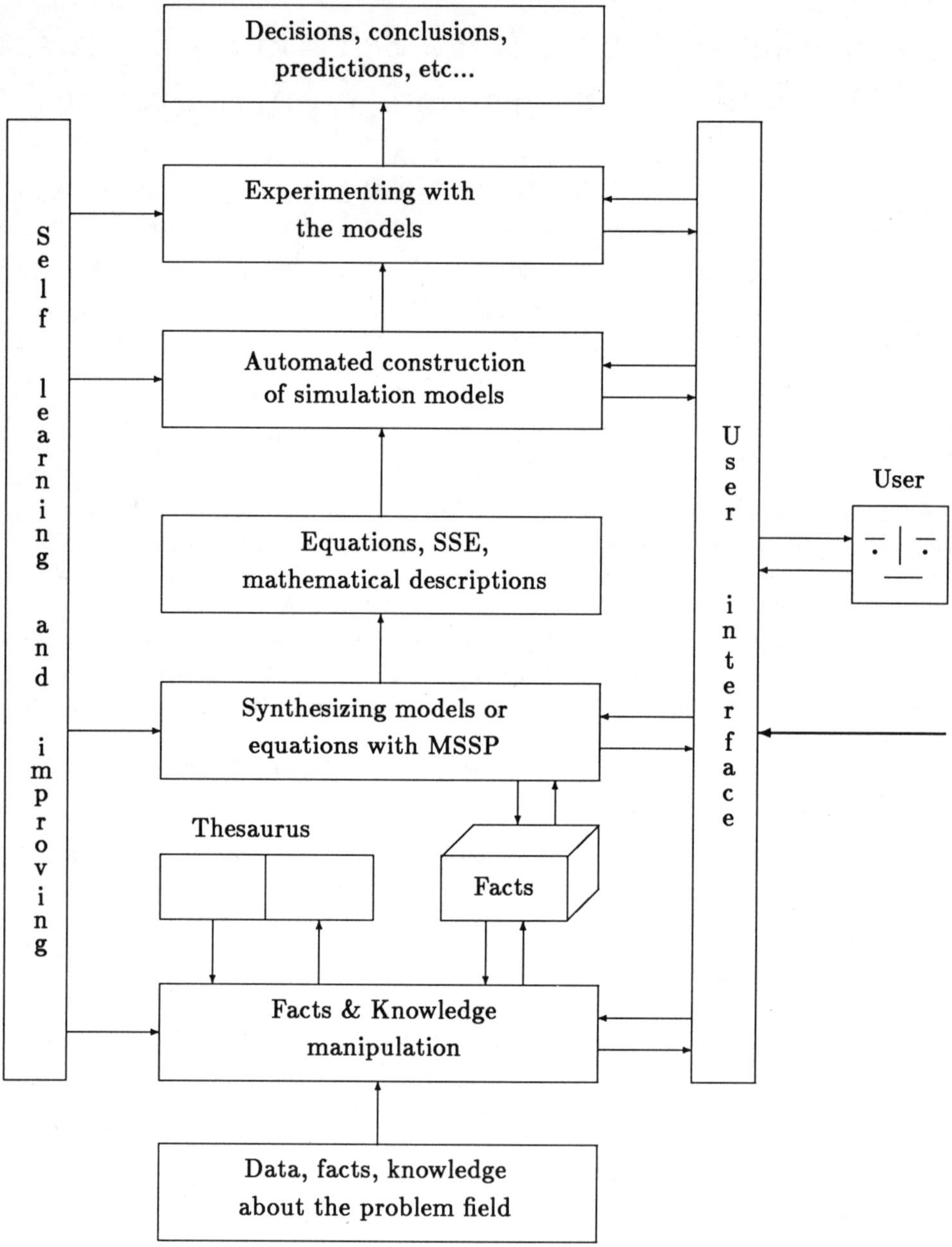

Figure 1. The structure of the software system

In this project some new principles for software development in Decision Support Systems are suggested. The main parts of the software system is presented on Figure 1.

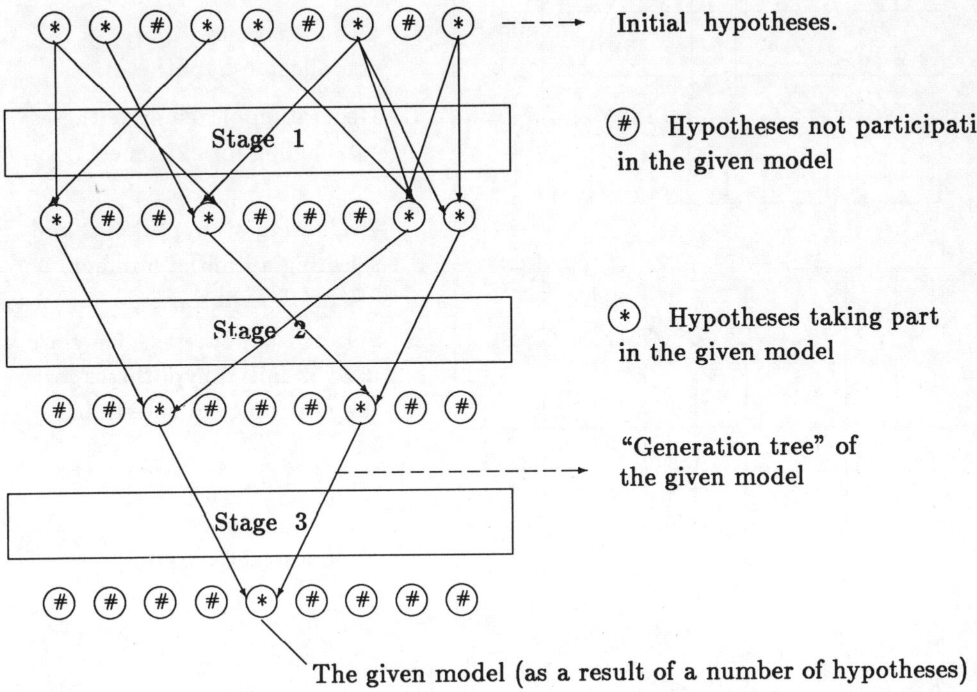

Figure 2. Multi-stage selection procedure.

Here we will pay attention to the part "Synthesizing models or equations with MSSP" (Figure 2.). The main idea is that at each stage of selection (Figure 3.) a number of hypotheses are generated. Each hypothesis is verified and evaluated and then it competes with other possible hypotheses "fighting for survival". After that only a few of them are selected as "best" in the sense of a predefined selection criteria. The so selected hypotheses are used for generating more complicated hypotheses at the next stage. The process of selection is started again, etc... The selection procedure ends with the achievement of a certain condition, limits or results.

Working permanently in an interactive mode the user has the possibility for a final choice of the best model and for some additional considerations (but after having the guarantee of evaluating a great number of possible models and the choice of a small number of good ones).

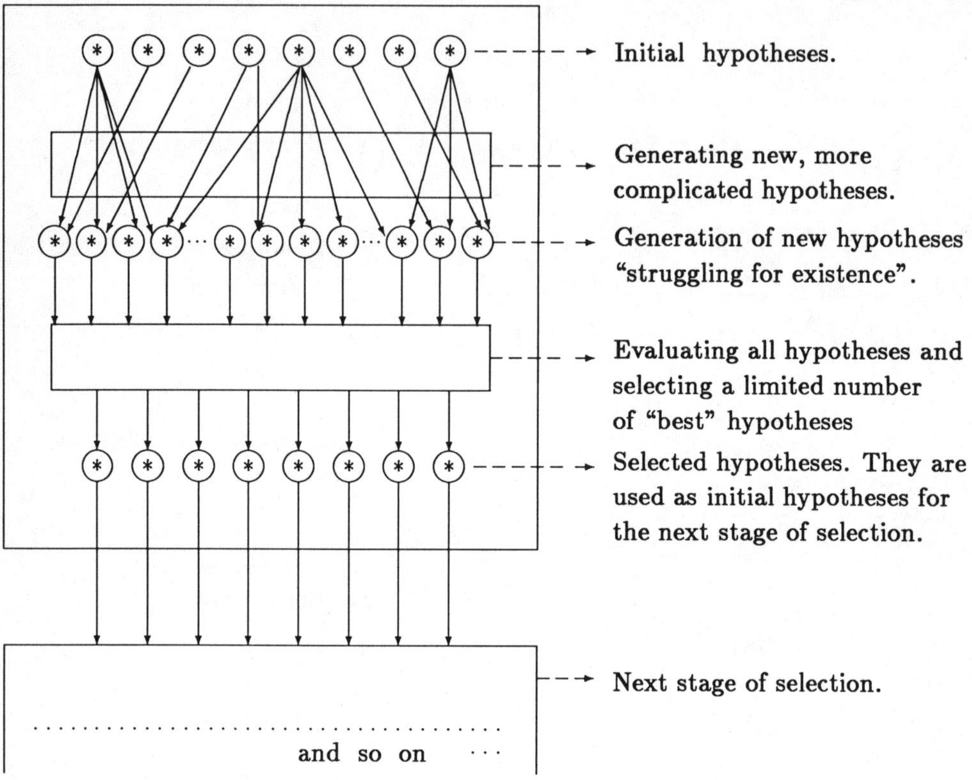

Figure 3. A single stage of selection procedure.

2 Multi-stage selection procedure (MSSP) for synthesizing simulation models in the form of simultaneous equations

In the MSSP which is designed for synthesizing simulation models in the form of a system of simultaneous equations (SSE) (Marchev and Motzev, 1983), we can differentiate three main parts:

I. In the first part, on the basis of existing real data, grouped in a table of observations of researched system, we make a first choice of significant factors, which will be included in the model. Then:

   I.1. The generating of the variety is done by including nonlinear transformations and taking into account the pre-history of the factors through heuristic considerations by the researcher and automatically using a computer program.

I.2. Each competing hypothesis represents a hypothesis of inclusion or non-inclusion of an additional factor in the table, that is, a hypothesis on the fact is this factor potentially important for the mathematical description of the research system.

I.3. The limit choice and the limiting of the variety is done using the criteria "correlation with a dependent variable", but can be supplemented with heuristic solutions given by the researcher. In all cases the preservation of the initial factors — "protection of the variables" is guaranteed.

II. The second part represents a procedure for multi-stage selection of each equation participating in the model. The form of the wanted equation is not predetermined. The task of finding the form and coefficients of each equation is divided in many tasks for determining the coefficients of equations with two variables — the principle of grouping variables. In this way, we make certain of obtaining statistically important coefficients, based on a limited number of observations (undersized samples of data). The form of the equation is determined by a few consecutive stages of selection.

II.1. The generation of the variety is done by introducing new intermediate variables for each stage and the creation of a new generation of intermediate equations function with two variables which include indirectly more and more complex combinations of the initial factors.

II.2. Each generated equation is considered as potential description of a given connection in the model, which competes with the other possible descriptions "fighting for survival".

II.3. After each selection stage, there is no choice of a unique equation, but a limited choice of a predetermined number of good equations is done — the principle of non-finalized solutions. This gives us the possibility to obtain a set of alternative good equations.

II.4. The estimation of the coefficient in each intermediate equation is done using the criteria of the average square error. The existing set of data is divided into two parts: a "teaching" set which is used for estimating the coefficient in the intermediate equations, and the control set used for evaluating the adequacy of the obtained equations — the principle of "Cross validation" choice of a good model.

II.5. The chosen equations in a given generation are used for generating new, more complex equations in the next generation. From these a predetermined number are chosen as good etc.

II.6. The selection procedure ends when certain conditions, limit or results are achieved, which the researcher wants to obtain based on a given number of selections, achievement of an average minimum for the generation error and others.

II.7. At the end of the second part of the MSSP automatically the full form of the best equations is restored. Each equation describing a given connection in the model has a given number of alternative variations.

III. In the third part of the procedure from the obtained equations a synthesis of the simulation model is done in the form of SSE:

III.1. The variety of alternative variants of the model, which represent SSE is obtained by combined, already chosen, best equations.

III.2. Each of the competing hypotheses represents a hypothesis for inclusion in the model of a given variant of the separate equation.

III.3. Each generated SSE is considered as a potential model which imitates the analyzed system.

III.4. The evaluation of these competing models is complexly done, using a great number of statistical criteria — coefficient of correlation, variation coefficient, average relative error, precision in forecasting and others.

III.5. The final choice of the best model is made by the researcher, who has the possibility to introduce some additional nonformalized considerations, but after having the guarantee of evaluating a great number of possible models and the choice of a small number of good ones.

We have to remark, that in difference to existing traditional methods (Malinvaud, 1969), when the structural and parametrical identification of SSE is done separately, in the described MSSP, this is done in a unified, highly automated procedure. In it, we have the possibility for imposing predetermined limits on SSE coefficients as in traditional methods. The difference is that an additional structural identification is done during multi-stage selection.

During this structural identification automatically some of the variables are removed and in the synthesized model remain only those, which are important. In this way, simultaneously the form of each equation is determined as well as the important variables participating and an estimation of the coefficients is done.

In addition the SSE coefficients can be obtained as time functions, which makes the MSSP applicable to nonstationary systems describing most economic processes.

3 Software

For the described procedure for automatic synthesis of simulation models, a great number of algorithms and programs have been designed. These are organized in the following program sets together with additional programs, applied program sets (APS):

- APS "ANALYSIS" — used for preliminary analysis of the dynamic role of variables in the designed model and the relation between them.

- APS "SELECTION" — it is used for synthesizing the equations in the designed model, using the multi-stage selection procedure.

Model Year of design	Main purposes Accuracy	Specific characteristics
SIMUR 0 (1977–1978)	First step of the SIMUR project. Traditional methods used. Accuracy = 14%.	A one–product macroeconomic model in the form of SSE with 5 equations. Contains 5 endogenous, 5 lag and 1 exogenous variables.
SIMUR I (1978–1980)	Analysis of possibilities for automatic synthesis of SSE during the run of multi-stage selection procedure. Accuracy = 2.7%.	A one–product macroeconomic model in the form of SSE with 5 equations. Contains the same set of variables.
SIMUR II (1981–1982)	Design and experimenting of a programming system for automatic holding of simulation experiments with SSE. Analysis of different criteria for the precision's estimating of SSE. Accuracy = 2.0%.	Aggregated macroeconomic model in the form of 12 interdepending simultaneous equations. Contains 12 endogenous, 5 exogenous and 26 lag variables with lag of up to 3 years.
SIMUR III (1983–1985)	Improving the MSSP for synthesis of SSE with many equations. Simulating and forecasting of main macroeconomic indexes. Accuracy < 1%.	Macroeconomic simulation model. Contains 39 equations and 39 endogenous, 7 exogenous and 82 lag variables with a time lag of up to 5 years.
SIMUR IV (1989)	Next step of the SIMUR project.	Multisector macroeconomic model. Contains more than 100 equations.

Table 1. The family of models "S I M U R"

- APS "TUNNING" — it is used for automatic tunning of undefined coefficients in the designed model and for automatic choice of equation blocks in SSE with the help of "competing" procedure between the model variation.
- APS "SIMUL" — it is used for complex evaluation of adequacy of the synthesized model using a great number of criteria and for conducting different simulation experiments with the model.

These APS cover the main tasks during automated design of simulation models.

4 Application

Together with the design of a procedure for automated synthesis of simulation models, we designed a family of macroeconomic models called SIMUR. The models from this family can be considered as a result and at the same time as a base for this procedure.

Each model from the SIMUR family is designed with a special purpose — experimentation and improvement of a given part of the MSSP for synthesis of SSE. The conclusions obtained from each experiment with a model are used on one hand for designing the next model and on the other for improving MSSP. In this way we have achieved a parallel development and interaction between the family of models SIMUR and the MSSP for synthesis of SSE.

Short information for the models is presented in table 1.

We have to remark, that during the design of new simulation models and with new acquired experience, we continuously enrich the set of algorithms and programs for automated synthesis of SSE.

5 Conclusions

This paper presents a new and perspective line in research and modelling of economic systems — using a multi-stage selection procedure for synthesis of simulation models. The proposed approach for automated design of simulation models gives us the possibility to shorten the time expenditure and efforts for the design of a simulation model and consequently widens the field of application of simulation modelling. The accumulated experimental data (Ivachnenko and Muller, 1984), (Marchev and Motzev, 1983) shows, that MSSP has great advantages over the existing methods — system dynamics, econometric approach, aggregated modelling etc.

In this connection, the presented approach has a large field of application and needs further development in the following main directions:

A. Further design of algorithms and programs for automated elaboration of simulation models.

   A very pressing practical problem in this direction is the design of a simplified version of the program system, which is intended for a personal computer. That is so, because of the fact that the now used program system is large and complex

— its' total volume is about 30 thousand program lines in the PL/1 language. It is designed for an IBM 4331 computer under the VM-370 operating system. At present this system has a multitude of abilities and parameters which are assigned in interactive mode, which fact often hampers more than aids the unprepared user. Moreover, it ties him to an outdated operating system and computer.

On account of all these reasons arises a practical necessity for the design of a simplified version of the program system, which is intended for a personal computer, and which reflects all the experience accumulated by our research group in the field of multi-stage selection procedures and algorithms, based on these procedures.

The existing situation doesn't exclude the possibility of using personal computers right now, if the following scheme is used:

I. The synthesis of the separate blocks in the model and of the model as a whole is done with the existing program system on a large computer.

II. The synthesized model, as well as the decision support system which uses it, are modified for use on a personal computer.

There is another possibility (currently elaborated upon), which consists of connecting a personal computer of the IBM/AT type to the IBM 4331 computer, in the form of an intelligent terminal.

B. The design of new simulation macroeconomic models. In this direction, special interest represents the design of the macromodels for different countries using the same set of variables. On the basis of this, it will be possible to make valuable comparisons and analysis of the common and specific characteristics reflected in the different models.

References

Ivachnenko, A. G. and Muller, J. A. (1984). Selbst-organisation von Vorhersage-modellen. VEB Verlag Technic, Berlin, Verlag Technika, Kiew.

Malinvaud, E. (1969). Methodes Statistiques de l'Econometrie. Dunod, Paris.

Marchev, A. A. and Motzev M. R. (1983). Simulation Macroeconomic Models Designed in the Form of Systems of Simultaneous Equations Synthesizing during the Run of Multi-Stage Selection Procedure. Scientific Papers of the Economic University "K. Marx", Vol.I, pp. 303–349, Sofia.

Some Aspects of the Integration Between DSS and Knowledge Based Systems

Victor Nitchev
Institute for Information Technologies
Sofia, Bulgaria

1 Introduction

Until recently, Decision Support Systems (DSS) were available only to those with access to large mainframes and minicomputers. Most DSS-packages were mainly research software type, practically unsupported and intended for experienced users.

The microprocessor technology brought significant changes. Many companies began to develop microcomputer versions of DSS-software. While the vast majority of the personal– and micro-computer users are not programmers but commercial program end users, the need for well designed and supported software arose over the DSS-area.

2 DSS-design problems

DSS-designers have to face a number of serious design problems. Despite the considerable progress, currently available microcomputers fall short of the memory and computational power needed to satisfy the requirements of a large-scale DSS (Reimann, Waren 1985). As a result, the designers often build separate DSS-modules instead of complete systems. The choice of an appropriate DSS-module among the available ones, its installation, the evaluation of the results — all these system functions remain uncovered and are normally leaved to the user. Thus the parts of the system are present, but the integrating link among them is missing.

Such an approach to the design of application systems is not new in the area of the personal computers. Healey (1985) notes, that "IBM's own PC-application programs are following the earlier, preintegration concept of a series of programs that are independent but use similar user interfaces".

As a consequence, the users have to undertake a great deal of the work. As Glatzer (1987) states, "to implement a DSS, users continue to tie software systems together, starting with corporate databases and moving to external databases, spreadsheets, and so on. The pipelines are usually in place, but there is no central repository. So users are making do in whatever way they can".

All these problems are especially difficult in the case of DSS microcomputers, but they represent also a more general tendency in the DSS-design. Ariav and Ginzberg

(1985) affirm that there has been no effective integration of the diverse elements of the DSS to date, and this lack of an unified approach to the subject has hampered efforts to develop a solid basis for DSS-design.

3 The role of the knowledge in the DSS-integration

It is clear that the problem of the integration of the elements of the DSS is a basic one in the DSS-design. As its solution is shifted on from designers to the users, they have to learn substantial information, concerning the operating system of the computer, the structure and operation of the DSS itself, the interpretation of the results, and so on. All this information is additional to the users, but they need it in order to manage the DSS-operation correctly and to obtain a useful level of interaction with the system.

In other words, the integration problem in the DSS arises due to the lack (at least in an explicit form) of all information, concerning the linkage of the available modules into an unified system (i.e., metainformation on the system's structure). It's missing also the information regarding the functioning of each system module (input data restrictions, theoretical base of the methods applied, ways of interpretation of the results and so on).

From the viewpoint of the conventional management information systems only the metainformation on the system's structure seems to be relevant to the problem of DSS-integration. In the case of DSS, however, the description of DSS-modules has the same importance, due to the highly interactive nature of the DSS. During the session with the system, DSS-users should have the possibility to simulate or model their problems as completely and accurately as possible and test the impact of different assumptions or scenarios (Reimann, Waren, 1985). This often requires the change of one method to another, or a number of repetitive steps during the interaction. In terms of the program implementation, this requires a transition from one DSS-module to another, based on the conditions of the processing. Such a transition can be made only on the base of exhaustive information about the process. So the information, describing the DSS-modules functions plays a direct role in the integration process.

All these information has to be included within the system in a certain way in order to achieve automatized integration. To expect to have all this information memorized by the users, or accessed through a set of manuals is a hopeless business even for a system of moderate complexity.

Current software engineering methods mark two possible ways for inclusion of that information within a whole system:

- distribution of the information among the separate program modules of the system;
- forming up a special module, where all integration information is represented in a special form, with the additional program tools for maintenance and interpretation of that representation.

As long as the integration information represents in fact *knowledge* about the system integration, the difference between the two approaches lies in the form of knowledge representation. In the first case, the knowledge is present within the system, but in a rather implicit form, which makes it directly nonaccessible to the user. The second approach, which is typical for the so called *Knowledge Based Systems (KBS)*, counts on knowledge, represented in an explicit form in a separate system module — Knowledge Base (KB).

The difference is not only formal; the type of knowledge representation determines the possibilities for system changes, improvements and further development. In the case of KBS it is possible to change the operation of the whole system (or parts of the system) changing the rules in the Knowledge Base. In the conventional programming systems re-specification of the system features normally leads to some recording of the programs.

The advantages and shortcomings of KBS are widely covered in DSS-literature (cf. Hayes-Roth, 1985). Modifications of such systems have found practical application in such fields as chemistry, biology, computer technology etc. The analysis of the integration problems in DSS-design shows that the KBS could contribute to the solution of that problems and to the improvement of the DSS in whole.

4 KBS as an integration link in DSS

Recently the question of relationship between DSS and KBS is often discussed in the DSS-literature. Because of the similarities many researchers postulate convergency in the development of both classes (Ariav, Ginzberg, 1985). Others declare the methods of KBS and Artificial Intelligence (AI) as the best suitable ones for DSS-development (Shen, 1987). There are also attempts to re-code existing methods, used in the DSS, in logic programming languages (such as PROLOG) and to obtain so called logical DSS as a result — though unefficient enough (Li, 1987).

Anyway, KBS should not be considered as a magical tool for producing "one-size-fits-all solution". It is doubtfull whether the mere "change" of the existing solutions with KBS-based ones will be the right answer to the DSS-problems. Much more realistic seems to be the perspective of the integration between the existing DSS and the KBS technology.

The discussion on the DSS-integration problems above prompts to the possibility of the integration of DSS-modules based on a KBS. In order to achieve better results, a balance between the detailed description of the knowledge and the computational efficiency should be pursued. It is important, however, to distinguish between the necessity of the description of some DSS-process within the KB, and the possibility of implementation of that process based on the KB-description. While the description is almost mandatory, the implementation through interpretation of the description can cause rather unefficiency than flexibility. This means, that all DSS-modules, performing well defined calculation or modelling operations, should remain practically unchanged within an integrated DSS. However, their descriptions should be included into the KB of the whole system and used in organisation of the links between DSS and KBS.

The following integration functions can be performed on the base of a KBS, used as an integrating link within a DSS:

- management of the system's user interface, in order to give the user the information needed in an unified form;

- management of the installation and starting procedures of the separate DSS-modules;
- evaluation of the results of the operation of the separate modules and automatic chaining from one module to another according to the rules and descriptions within the knowledge base;
- interpretation of the non-standard situations (including user and system errors).

Additional functions, facilitating the work of the users can also be performed on the base of the stored knowledge:

- issue of advices based on the knowledge about the characteristics of the system's modules (e.g., precision of the results, required processing time, theoretical limitations of the methods applied etc.);
- explanations about the course of the events and the expected results;
- advice information concerning the user's operations in a specific step of the process (tutorial information).

A significant advantage of this approach is the possibility to use currently existing (in the form of separate DSS-modules) software with little or no changes.

5 Implementation issues

The implementation of the approach described above imposes some requirements on the hardware and the system software. In order to maintain the reasonable efficiency level, the memory space of the computer has to be large enough to allow the simultaneous installation of both KBS and any of the DSS-modules. It is important to note that only *one* DSS-module at a time has to reside in the memory jointly with the KBS.

Since KBS has to carry out the management of the installation and starting procedures for any of the DSS-modules being integrated, the availability of the appropriate facilities in the operating system (OS) is premised. The KBS itself should not contain such facilities; it should only issue system calls to the OS, based on the rules and descriptions from the knowledge base. It's quite clear that the lack of such facilities in a specific OS can make the realisation of the concept impossible. In such cases building additional modules, carrying these functions, can be a solution.

Normally, no limitations on the use of different programming languages for both KBS and DSS-modules should be imposed. Moreover, the use of different language tools for the implementation is the more realistic case. The interface among different languages can be obtained through the OS.

Because of the necessity of building an unified user interface to the DSS, some restrictions on the internal structure of the DSS-modules can arise. It is advisable to remove the interface structures from the DSS-modules and to leave only the user interface of the whole system active. In case of well designed and structured DSS-modules their own user-interface parts could easily be adapted to the common system interface.

It is important to emphasize that the description of the user interface for each DSS-module within the common knowledge base can be a difficult task: in some cases the information used for user interface specification and description can constitute up to 40% of the whole KBS (Bobrow et al., 1986).

Last but not least the efficiency problems have to be mentioned. The efficiency of an integrated system depends very much on the efficiency of the implementation of the KBS itself. Here the use of advanced techniques for management of large knowledge bases will be of primary importance.

Another possibility for efficiency improvement could be the use of distributed processing, based on Local Area Networks (LAN) as an environment for the integration between DSS and KBS. The use of suitable system structures could help to avoid some of the hardware restrictions.

6 Conclusion

The approach of the use of a KBS as an integrating link in the building of DSS is an approach of more general character, overstepping the limits of the DSS-design. Applied to the DSS, it brings considerable flexibility of the solutions in compliance with the specific requirements and restrictions. All this allows to suppose that the research of the integration between DSS and KBS will bring substantial practical results.

References

Ariav, G., Ginzberg, M. (1985). DSS design: a systemic view of decision support. *CACM*, 28(10), pp. 1045–1052.

Bobrow, D., Mittal, S., and Stefic, M. J. (1986). Expert systems: perils and promise. *CACM*, 29(9), pp. 880–894.

Glatzer, H. (1987). DSS advances the art of thinking. *Software News*, 7(11), pp. 44–51.

Hayes-Roth, F. (1985). Rule-based systems. *CACM*, 28(9), pp. 921–932.

Healey, M. (1985). Toward a viable OS for the PC. *Datamation*, 31(17), pp. 92–100.

Li, Han-Lin (1987). Solving discrete multicriteria decision problems based on logic-based decision support systems. *Decision Support Systems*, 3(2).

Reimann, B. C., Waren, A. D. (1985). User-oriented criteria for the selection of DSS software. *CACM*, 28(2), pp. 166–179.

Shen, S. (1987). Knowledge management in DSS. *Decision Support Systems*, 3(1), pp. 1–11.

Methodological Background of the Dynamic Interactive Network Analysis System (DINAS)

W. Ogryczak, K. Studzinski, K. Zorychta
Institute of Informatics, Warsaw University
PL–00901 Warsaw, Poland

1 Introduction

This paper describes the methodological background of research performed at Warsaw University under the contracted study: "Theory, Software and Testing Examples for Decision Support Systems" supervised by the International Institute for Applied Systems Analysis (Ogryczak et al., 1987). The main goal of this work is development and implementation of the Dynamic Interactive Network Analysis System (DINAS) which enables the solution of various multiobjective transshipment problems with facility location using IBM PC/XT microcomputers. DINAS utilizes an extension of the classical reference point approach to handling multiple objectives. In this approach the decision-maker forms his requirements in terms of aspiration and reservation levels, i.e., he specifies acceptable and required values for given objectives. A special TRANSLOC solver was developed to provide DINAS with solutions to single-objective problems. It is based on the branch and bound scheme with a pioneering implementation of the simplex special ordered network (SON) algorithm with implicit representation of the simple and variable upper bounds (VUB & SUB).

2 The generalized network model

A network model of the problem consists of nodes that are connected by a set of direct flow arcs. The set of nodes is partitioned into two subsets: the set of fixed nodes and the set of potential nodes. The fixed nodes represent "fixed points" of the transportation network, i.e., points which cannot be changed. Each fixed node is characterized by two quantities: supply and demand. The potential nodes are introduced to represent possible locations of new points in the network. Some groups of the potential nodes represent different versions of the same facility to be located (e.g., different sizes of a warehouse). For this reason, potential nodes are organized in the so-called selections, i.e., sets of nodes with the multiple choice requirement. Each selection is defined by the list of included potential nodes as well as by lower and upper numbers of nodes which have to be selected (located). Each potential node is characterized by a capacity which bounds maximal flow through the node. The capacities are also given for all arcs but not for the fixed nodes.

A several linear objective functions are considered in the problem. The objective functions are introduced into the model by given coefficients associated with several arcs and potential nodes. They will be called cost coefficients independly of their real character in the objective functions. The cost coefficients for potential nodes are, however, understood in a different way than for arcs. The cost coefficient connected to an arc is treated as the unit cost of the flow along the arc whereas the cost coefficient connected to a potential node is considered as the fixed cost associated with the use (location) of the node rather than as the unit cost.

For simplicity of the model and the solution procedure, we transform the potential nodes into artificial arcs. The transformation is performed by duplication of all potential nodes. After the duplication is done all the nodes can be considered as fixed and each potential node is replaced by an artificial arc which leads from the node to its copy. Due to the transformation we get a network with the fixed structure since all the nodes are fixed. Potentiality of artificial arcs does not imply any complication because each arc in the network represents a potential flow. Moreover, all the bounds on flows (i.e., capacities) are connected to arcs after this transformation. Additional nonstandard discrete constraints on the flow are generated only by the multiple choice requirements associated with the selections. Cost coefficients are connected only to arcs, but the coefficients connected to artificial arcs represent fixed costs.

A mathematical statement of this transformed problem takes the form of the following generalized network model:

minimize

$$\sum_{(i,j)\in A\setminus A_a} f_{ij}^p x_{ij} + \sum_{(i,j)\in A_a} f_{ij}^p y_{ij} \qquad p = 1,2,\ldots,n_0 \tag{2.1}$$

subject to

$$\sum_{(i,j)\in A} x_{ij} - \sum_{(j,i)\in A} x_{ji} = b_i \qquad i \in N \tag{2.2}$$

$$0 \le x_{ij} \le c_{ij} \qquad (i,j) \in A \setminus A_a \tag{2.3}$$

$$0 \le x_{ij} \le c_{ij} y_{ij} \qquad (i,j) \in A_a \tag{2.4}$$

$$g_k \le \sum_{(i,j)\in S_k} y_{ij} \le h_k \qquad k = 1,2,\ldots,n_s \tag{2.5}$$

$$y_{ij} = 0 \text{ or } 1 \qquad (i,j) \in A_a \tag{2.6}$$

where

- n_0 – number of objective functions,
- N – set of nodes (including copies of potential nodes),
- n_s – number of selections,
- A – set of arcs (including artificial arcs),
- A_a – set of artificial arcs,
- f_{ij}^p – cost coefficient of the p–th objective associated with the arc (i,j),

b_i – supply-demand balance at the node i (supply is denoted as a positive quantity and demand as negative),

c_{ij} – capacity of the arc (i, j),

g_k, h_k – lower and upper number of (artificial) arcs to be selected in the k–th selection,

S_k – set of (artificial) arcs that belong to the k–th selection,

x_{ij} – decision variable that represents flow along the arc (i, j),

y_{ij} – decision variable equal 1 for selected arc and 0 otherwise.

The generalized network model of this form includes typical network constraints (2.2) with simple upper bounds (2.3) as well as a special discrete structure (2.5)–(2.6) connected to the network structure by variable upper bounds (2.4). While solving the model we have to take advantage of all these structures.

3 Interactive procedure for handling multiple objectives

There are many different concepts for handling multiple objectives in mathematical programming. We decided to use the so-called reference point approach which was introduced by Wierzbicki (1982). This concept was further developed in many papers and was used as a basis for construction of the software package DIDAS (Dynamic Interactive Decision Analysis and Support system). The DIDAS package developed at IIASA proved to be useful in analyzing conflicts and assisting in decision making situations (Grauer et al., 1984).

The basic concept of the reference point approach is as follows:

1. the decision-maker (DM) forms his requirements in terms of aspiration levels, i.e., he specifies acceptable values for given objectives;

2. the DM works with the computer in an interactive way so that he can change his aspiration levels during sessions of the analysis.

In our system, we expend the DIDAS approach. The extension relies on additional use of reservation levels which allow the DM to specify necessary values for given objectives (Wierzbicki, 1986).

Consider the multi-objective program associated with the generalized network model:

$$\begin{aligned} &\text{minimize} && q \\ &\text{subject to} && q = F(x,y), \quad (x,y) \in Q \end{aligned}$$

where

q represents the objective vector,

F is the linear vector-function defined by (2.1),

Q denotes the feasible set of the generalized network model, i.e., the set defined by conditions (2.2)–(2.6).

The reference point technique works in two stages. In the first stage the DM is provided with some initial information which gives him an overview of the problem. The initial information is generated by minimization of all the objectives separately. More precisely, a sequence of the following single objective programs is solved:

$$\min\left\{ f^p(x,y) + (r_0/n_0)\sum_{i=1}^{n_0} f^i(x,y) \;:\; (x,y)\in Q\right\} \qquad p=1,2,\ldots,n_0 \tag{3.1}$$

where f^p denotes the p–th objective function and r_0 is an arbitrarily small number.

The so-called decision-support matrix (or pay-off matrix)

$$D = (q_{pj})_{p=1,\ldots,n_0;\ j=1,\ldots,n_0}$$

which yields information on the range of numerical values of each objective is then constructed. The p–th row of the matrix D corresponds to the vector (x^p, y^p) which solves the p–th program (3.1). Each quantity q_{pj} represents a value of the j–th objective at this solution (i.e., $q_{pj} = f^j(x^p, y^p)$). The vector with elements q_{pp}, i.e., the diagonal of D, defines the utopia (ideal) point. This point, denoted further by q^u, is usually not attainable but it is presented to the DM as a lower limit to the numerical values of the objectives.

Taking into consideration the j–th column of the matrix D we notice that the minimal value in that column is $q_{pp} = q^u_p$.

Let q^n_j be the maximal value, i.e.,

$$q^n_j = \max_{1\le p\le n_0} q_{pj}$$

The point q^n is called the nadir point and may be presented to the DM as an upper guideline to the values of the objectives. Thus, for each objective f^p a reasonable but not necessarily tight upper bound q^n and a lower bound q^u are known after the first stage of the analysis.

In the second stage an interactive selection of efficient solutions is performed. The DM controls the selection by two (vector-) parameters: his aspiration level q^a and his reservation level q^r, where

$$q^u \le q^a < q^r \le q^n$$

The support system searches for the satisfying solution while using an achievement scalarizing function as a criterion in the single-objective optimization. Namely, the support system computes the optimal solution to the following problem:

$$\text{minimize} \qquad \max_{1\le p\le n_0}\left[u_p(q,q^a,q^r) + (r_0/n_0)\sum_{p=1}^{n_0} u_p(q,q^a,q^r)\right] \tag{3.2}$$

$$\text{subject to} \quad q = F(x,y) \quad (x,y)\in Q$$

where r_0 is an arbitrarily small number and u_p is a function which measures the deviation of results from the DM's expectations with respect to the p–th objective, depending on given aspiration level q^a and reservation level q^r .

The computed solution is an efficient (Pareto-optimal) solution to the original multiobjective model. It is presented to the DM as a current solution. The DM is asked whether he finds this solution satisfactory or not. If the DM does not accept the current solution he has to enter new aspiration and/or reservation levels for some objectives. Depending on this new information supplied by the DM a new efficient solution is computed and presented as a current solution. The process is repeated as long as necessary.

The function $u_p(q, q^a, q^r)$ is a strictly monotone function of the objective vector q with value $u_p = 0$ if $q = q^a$ and $u_p = 1$ if $q = q^r$. In our system, we use a piece-wise linear function u_p defined as follows:

$$u_p(q, q^a, q^r) = \begin{cases} a_p(q_p - q_p^a)/(q_p^r - q_p^a), & \text{if } q_p < q_p^a \\ (q_p - q_p^a)/(q_p^r - q_p^a), & \text{if } q_p^a \le q_p \le q_p^r \\ b_p(q_p - q_p^r)/(q_p^r - q_p^a) + 1, & \text{if } q_p^r < q_p \end{cases}$$

where a_p and b_p ($p = 1, 2, \ldots, n_0$) are given positive parameters. In particular, the parameters a_p and b_p may be defined (similarly as in Wierzbicki, 1986) according to the formulae

$$\begin{aligned} a_p &= a(q_p^r - q_p^a)/(q_p^a - q_p^u) \\ b_p &= b(q_p^r - q_p^a)/(q_p^n - q_p^r) \end{aligned}$$

with two arbitrarily given positive parameters a and b.

If the parameters a_p and b_p satisfy inequalities $a_p < 1$ and $b_p > 1$, then the achievement functions u_p are convex. Minimization of the function u_p is then equivalent to minimization of a variable u_p defined as follows:

$$u_p = v_p + b_p v_p^- - a_p v_p^+ \tag{3.3}$$

$$v_p - v_p^+ + v_p^- = (q_p - q_p^a)/(q_p^r - q_p^a) \tag{3.4}$$

$$0 \le v_p \le 1 \tag{3.5}$$

$$v_p^+ \ge 0, \quad v_p^- \ge 0 \tag{3.6}$$

4 General concept of the TRANSLOC solver

The TRANSLOC solver has been prepared to provide the multiobjective analysis procedure with solutions to single-objective problems. According to the interactive procedure described in Section 3 the TRANSLOC solver has to be able to solve two kinds of single-objective problems: the first one associated with calculation of the decision support matrix (problems (3.1)) and the second one associated with minimization of the scalarizing achievement function (problems (3.2)). Both kinds of the problems have, however, the same main constraints which represent the feasible set of the generalized network model. Moreover, the other constraints of both kinds of problems can be expressed in a very similar way.

Both the single-objective problems are typical mixed integer linear programs, i.e., they are typical linear programs with some integer variables (namely y_{ij}). Mixed integer linear programs are usually solved by branch and bound approach with utilization of the simplex method. The TRANSLOC solver also uses this approach. Fortunately, only very small group of decision variables is required to be integer in our model. Therefore we can use a simple branch and bound scheme in the solver.

Even for a small transshipment problem with facility location, the corresponding linear program has rather large size. For this reason it cannot be solved directly with the standard simplex algorithm. In order to solve the program on IBM PC/XT microcomputers, it is necessary to take advantage of its special structure.

Note that the main group of equality constraints (2.2) represents typical network relations. All these rows can be handled in the simplex method as the so-called special ordered network (SON) structure (Glover and Klingman, 1981, 1985).

The inequalities (2.3) and (3.5) are standard simple upper bounds (SUB) which are usually processed out of the linear programming matrix (Orchard-Hays, 1968). Similarly, inequalities (2.4) can be considered as the so-called variable upper bounds (VUB) and processed out of the matrix due to a special technique (Schrage, 1975; Todd, 1982).

Thus only a small number of inequalities has to be considered as typical rows of linear program. While taking advantage of this fact, the TRANSLOC solver can process transshipment problems of quite large dimensions. As a proper size of problems for IBM PC/XT microcomputers we regard:

- a few objective functions,
- about one hundred of fixed nodes,
- a few hundreds of arcs,
- several potential nodes (artificial arcs) organized in a few selections.

Initial experience with the TRANSLOC solver shows that such problems can be solved on IBM PC/XT microcomputers in a reasonable time.

References

Glover, F., Klingman, D. (1981). The simplex SON method for LP/embedded network problems. *Mathematical Programming Study*, 15, pp. 148–176.

Glover, F., Klingman, D. (1985). Basis exchange characterization for the simplex SON algorithm for LP/embedded networks. *Mathematical Programming Study*, 24, pp. 141–157.

Grauer, M., Lewandowski, A., Wierzbicki, A. (1984). DIDASS — theory, implementation and experiences. In: Grauer, M., Wierzbicki, A. P.(eds), Interactive Decision Analysis. Springer, Berlin.

Ogryczak, W., Studzinski, K., Zorychta, K. (1987). A solver for the transshipment problem with facility location. In: Lewandowski, A. and Wierzbicki, A. (eds.), Theory, Software and Testing Examples for Decision Support Systems. IIASA, Laxenburg.

Orchard-Hays, W. (1968). Advanced Linear-Programming Techniques. McGraw-Hill, New York.

Schrage, L. (1975). Implicit representation of variable upper bounds in linear programming. *Mathematical Programming Study*, 4, pp. 118–132.

Todd, M. J. (1982). An implementation of the simplex method for linear programming problems with variable upper bounds. *Mathematical Programming*, 23, pp. 34–49.

Wierzbicki, A. P. (1982). A mathematical basis for satisficing decision making. *Mathematical Modelling*, 3, pp. 391–405.

Wierzbicki, A. P. (1986). On the completeness and constructiveness of parametric characterizations to vector optimization problems. *OR Spektrum*, 8, pp. 73–87.

A Decision Support System Based on the Job Shop Problem in Real Manufacturing

Paolo Serafini
University of Udine, Italy

Walter Ukovich
University of Trieste, Italy

1 Introduction

The paper presents the general approach adopted to design a decision support system for the problem of scheduling the operations in the shop of a large manufacturing plant.

The general philosophy according to which the design is carried out consists essentially in formulating an abstract job shop problem and then using its output to generate an appropriate solution for the real scheduling problem.

Since there is no hope that the abstract job shop problem may ever adequately match all the relevant features of the real scheduling problem at hand, incongruities are unescapably generated this way (cf. for instance Gelders and Van Wassenhove, 1981).

Thus the aim of the design consists in bridging the gap existing between the abstract formulation and the real problem by exploiting the decision maker's problem knowledge and experience in an interactive way.

Other similar projects have been reported in the literature, although with different emphasis on different aspects, such as for instance setting some problem parameters like due dates (Viviers, 1983), or designing a suitable graphical user interface (Jones and Maxwell, 1986).

The present paper focuses mainly on general issues such as the overall architecture of the system and the motivations for it, the requirements it should meet and the functional structure according to which it should be organized. With this perspective in mind, some specific issues, such as algorithms or coding, are not dealt with here in detail.

Since the decision support system is tailored to cope with a specific production system, the latter is shortly presented at the beginning. Then the former is considered, and its structure and characteristics are presented. A special attention is dedicated to the optimization function and the features it should possess in order to provide effective elements to solve the real scheduling problem.

2 The production system

The production system we are considering has several peculiarities that deeply affect the production planning and scheduling problems. So in this section we briefly summarize some of its most relevant characteristics.

The produced items are electric machines (motors and generators, both a.c. and d.c.); each one of them is produced on the base of a specific customer order, and there is so a wide range of different product characteristics that in practice each order may be considered as requiring a different product. Moreover, very small lots, and often single items are normally required by each order, so that nearly each produced item is different from the other, and requires even to be designed, planned and scheduled individually.

The product structure is also rather articulated, and consists of several parts assembled together, which are in turn made up of other subassemblies, and so on up to a dozen depth levels. However, the operations on single parts largely prevail on the assembling operations in terms of time, machines and workforce required.

The production system is organized in departments, which perform a class of homogeneous activities (e.g. mechanical or electrical operations, testing, warehousing, etc.). The departments may be in turn divided in sections, devoted in general to operations to be performed on a same part type. So normally the operations on a same physical piece evolve within the same section; once they have been carried out, the piece is assembled and another series of operations takes place on the assembled unit, possibly in a different department.

The most heavily loaded department is the one performing the mechanical operations, and within it the section operating on medium- and small-size parts; such a section is the main subject of the work presented here. In order to grasp some quantitative aspects of the problems involved, we mention that this section has 32 machines and its average number of pending jobs (sequence of different operations, i.e. tasks, to be performed on a same part, generally by different machines) is of several hundreds, typically observed figures being in the range of 600–700.

3 The production planning system

The production planning function for the whole plant is performed by a MRPII system. It outputs a production plan for each department by first decomposing each product to be shipped in its constituents and then scheduling the operations necessary to produce them according to the production times fixed at the design stage. So in practice each department gets the list of the operations it should perform on a weekly basis. Since this constitutes the starting point for the detailed scheduling problem we are mainly interested in, it deserves to be analyzed in some depth, in particular for what concerns the way in which tasks are attributed to the machines and their leading times are evaluated.

The production planning system operates on an infinite capacity basis; in other words, the condition that the same machine cannot perform simultaneously different operations on different parts is simply disregarded. This would lead to unrealistically fast production plans if the actual operation times would be considered; so operation times are generously overestimated in order to take care of the limited availability of resources. In practice, the rather crude approximation is adopted of taking the time necessary to accomplish an operation, for planning purposes, equal to the effective time, expressed in workdays, rounded to the successive integer plus one day. It is clear that so a large tolerance allowed for the real operation times makes more complex the problem of scheduling the operations on the available machines. Moreover, the possibility of performing the same operation on different machines, possibly at different efficiency levels, is not considered at the production planning level, so the concrete scheduling problem also involves assigning the tasks to the machines.

Finally, the continuous nature of the process should be kept in mind, since orders may arrive at any time in the future within the horizon that has been already planned. Whereas at the planning level this just requires a re-planning procedure, at the scheduling level problems may arise from the fact that some tasks scheduled according to the previous plan may already be under operation.

4 The scheduling problem

The scheduling problem consists in determining when each planned operation has to be performed, if possible, within the planned period. The problem data concern the tasks to be executed and the resources (time, machine, workforce, etc.) available to carry them out. They may be categorized as follows:

- task resources: the resources required by each task are specified; all the possible alternatives are described explicitly;
- task sequences: the order in which the tasks of a job have to be performed is given;
- resource availability: the machine status (operating/down) and the time they are available (e.g. in number of shifts) is provided.

Whereas the planning problem in the plant we are considering is solved by a specific module of an MRPII system on an automatic information processing system, the scheduling problem was originally left to the skills and the experience of the production supervisors.

Due to the characteristics of the production system we are considering, the scheduling problem involves mainly the shop floor management, hence the section level of the shop organization; nevertheless, it is important to keep in mind the whole hierarchical organization of the shop, since the problem data come to the section level from the planning system through the shop and department levels, which may affect them in different ways: for example, by determining the resource availability or by setting priorities among the jobs. Moreover, the objectives of the production scheduling problem are considered in a different way at the different decision levels. In fact, all factors relative to a rational use of the resources are mainly of concern at the lower hierarchical levels, whereas more general aspects related to the productivity, such as respect of the planned due dates and the coordination among different departments have higher priorities at upper levels.

5 A decision support system for the production scheduling problem

The production scheduling problem just sketched in the previous section has several relevant features that make it very complicated in many senses: among them we may recall the necessity of dealing with many objectives, the different types of resources to be accommodated, the various skills or degrees of efficiency provided by different units, etc.

Moreover, the actual dimensions of the real problem to be tackled are so large that the decision makers cannot be reasonably supposed to master every slightest detail of the whole situation on hand; rather, their ability and experience allow them to operate on the base of few aggregate value judgments, thus providing common-sense solutions, but with no possibility of evaluating their fitness.

Furthermore, it must be stressed that a wide class of informal and hardly quantifiable elements play an important role to several crucial aspects of the problem, such as the priorities imposed among jobs or tasks, or unpredictable events, such as machine breakdowns requiring alternative routings, unavailability of tools or of NC machine tapes, lack of operators, etc. Again, all such aspects are faced in practice by the decision makers' ability; nevertheless, the nature and the characteristics of this problem suggest that there should probably be still further margins open for improved solutions.

Here is where the idea for a decision support system (DSS) comes in, as a tool for the decision maker to expand its decision capabilities. It should be pointed out that the DSS is intended not to replace the decision maker providing autonomous solutions, but rather to manage some well defined aspects whose characteristics (dimensions, data volume and availability, etc.) make them awkward to be dealt with manually, yet conveniently affordable by using automatic information processing means.

6 General requirements and structure for the decision support system

From a structural point of view, the DSS consists of different modules, each of which is dedicated to a specific function. We review in this section some aspects of the communication modules, whereas the optimization function will be analyzed more deeply in the next section.

One of the most relevant features the DSS should enjoy is the ability to exchange information in an effective way with the decision maker and the other systems of its environment: the one performing the planning function and the job shop monitoring system (not yet in operation to date). So appropriate interfaces must be provided to accomplish such tasks. Analyzing them is beyond the scope of this paper; nevertheless, some few remarks are appropriate in order to enlighten the overall philosophy of the system.

Information is flowing one way to the DSS from the production planning system and from the shop floor. In the former case the jobs to be scheduled and their features are obtained, and in the latter the piece and resource availability is monitored. (As it has been already mentioned, the information drawn from the shop floor is mainly relevant for production control purposes rather than for the production scheduling function.)

On the converse, the information is exchanged two-ways with the decision maker: the decision maker may provide some conditions on the scheduling problem and then gets the solution. It must be stressed that this is the only way the DSS outputs information: in fact, it is not supposed to affect directly neither on the shop floor nor on the production planning system.

As far as the user interface is concerned, some of its expected features are worth further consideration. First, the DSS should be highly interactive, in the sense that is should be able to deal with several kinds of conditions imposed by the user to the production scheduling problem at hand. Since such conditions may come to the attention of the decision maker by considering a solution just provided by the system, interactivity in this sense requires the ability of computing efficiently a new solution on the base of an already available one, which the conditions added by the user may have perhaps driven out of feasibility or of optimality.

Furthermore, the DSS must be fast in providing its answers. This is an obvious requirement to assure its effectiveness, but it has also deep consequences on the way it should be implemented. In fact, this implies that exact optimization methods may be not appropriate if they require large computation times. Since there is little hope to get efficient exact algorithms for such a complex and large kind of problems, sacrificing optimality to rapidity becomes unavoidable. So the DSS will necessarily use heuristics to provide suboptimal solutions to the scheduling problem.

7 The optimization module

The optimization module is the central part of the DSS. It produces a schedule for the tasks relative to the jobs released by the production planning system such that it is:

- feasible with respect to all the stated constraints and conditions; constraints refer either to the product structure (e.g. task sequence) or to the production plant (resource availability); conditions are further constraints imposed by the decision maker, e.g. to meet particular requirements, or to comply with some given precedences, etc.

- optimal, or at least "suitable" with respect to the different level objectives mentioned before.

Moreover, further desirable features the solution should enjoy are:

- stability: as the situation evolves (new orders arrive, operations progress, etc.), the solutions provided should change to meet the new requirements in a as smooth way as possible. In particular a new solution should not diverge dramatically from the previous one, unless the underlying situation has changed radically in the meantime; so the optimization module must be able to formulate efficiently a new solution based on a given one (possibly the previous one, or one proposed by the decision maker);

- robustness: the solution provided should not depend in a critical way on the specific data values provided, which may often be affected by uncertainties and errors.

Meeting the above requirements for the scheduling problem may be a very hard challenge, due to the features analyzed above (qualitative complexity, huge dimensions, non formalizable or quantifiable elements, etc.). The approach we take consists in formulating a simple, well-defined abstract problem which captures as many as possible (yet not necessarily all the) characteristics of the real scheduling problem; then the abstract problem is solved and its solution is used in turn to formulate an appropriate solution for the real scheduling problem.

Converting the abstract solution into a real one is the crucial point of the optimization module; besides by choosing an appropriate formulation for the abstract problem, its effectiveness may be accomplished in three different ways:

- by pre-processing the data for the real problem before they are fed to the abstract problem solver;

- by adopting a suitable solution method for the abstract problem in order to cope with some requirements of the real problem that haven't been formulated precisely in the abstract setting; this is particularly interesting if suboptimal solutions are searched by heuristic techniques;

- by post-processing the results obtained for the abstract problem; if a solution for the real problem cannot be derived, the data for the abstract problem may be modified through a feedback loop and the solution procedure may be iterated.

Accordingly, the optimization module will be logically and functionally organized in three parts: the core implementing the algorithm for the abstract problem and the pre- and post-processing elements.

The production scheduling problem is formalized as an abstract job shop problem. The version we adopt is stated as follows (cf. for instance Blazewicz et al., 1983):

A set of jobs is given, each of which consists of a sequence of tasks; each task is characterized by the time it requires and of the available machines on which it must be performed. Then a schedule is sought which must be feasible with respect to the task precedence and the machine availability constraints, and optimal in the sense of exhibiting the minimal overall makespan.

For this classical problem an efficient heuristic has been recently devised (cf. Adams et al., 1987). Lack of space doesn't allow to present it here, so the interested reader is referred to the quoted paper. Rather, it is interesting to analyze here in some detail some specific features of the problem at hand which called for significant adjustments both in the problem formulation and in its solution method. A thorough exposition of all the algorithmic details will appear in (Serafini et al., 1988).

8 Matching the real and the abstract problem

The job shop problem retains several relevant features of the real scheduling problem; nevertheless, it is important to analyze the differences between them in order to devise the most appropriate means to overcome them:

- the job shop problem considers a single objective, whereas the essence of the real problem is certainly multiobjective; as a consequence, optimality for the abstract problem is not essential; rather, a suboptimal solution showing a satisfactory performance also with respect to the other objectives of the scheduling problem would be more desirable. This affects the core of the optimization module and requires a careful specialization of the algorithm it uses. Actually the adopted heuristic behaves well in this respect.

- priorities among jobs or tasks are not considered by the job shop problem, whereas they are a crucial feature of the real problem. To overcome such a drawback, the data for the former are appropriately pre-processed by the decision maker by assigning all jobs to priority classes; then each class is scheduled in turn, starting from the one with higher priority. This procedure alters the classical structure of the job shop problem, introducing "forbidden periods", that is time intervals during which machines are not available because higher priority tasks have been already assigned to them. This requires appropriate modifications to the solution algorithm, that have been already carried out.

- the abstract problem deals with a single resource type, i.e. machines, whereas the real problem involves at least two main categories, that is machines and operators, and several minor ones, such as, for instance, tools, NC tapes, etc. Furthermore, each resource element may have different characteristics, which may also affect the effectiveness of the operations it may perform. As a consequence, a solution provided for the job shop problem may result nonfeasible for the real problem. Such a situation may be faced by post-processing the unfeasible solution, and possibly formulating additional constraints according to which the job shop problem must be then re-optimized. The additional constraints we are first considering at the moment consist in specific precedences between tasks. This does not complicate significantly the original algorithm.

- in the job shop formulation, each task is rigidly assigned to a specific machine, whereas the common practice normally allows some alternatives, although possibly with different efficiency degrees. However, such an incongruity may only affect the optimality and not the feasibility of the abstract solution, so a post-optimization procedure may be appropriate to deal with it. This is currently under investigation.

- the job shop problem requires that all the jobs are simultaneously available at the beginning of the process, whereas in the real situation orders may arrive at any time. Furthermore, production is normally in progress when the scheduling problem is being processed, so resources are not generally all available at the beginning of the scheduled period, but are released at the end of the current operations. The latter aspect may be dealt with again using forbidden periods, and the former one by re-optimizing when a large enough number of required but not yet scheduled jobs is attained.

We point out that the heuristic developed by Adams et al. (1987) and modified as outlined above performs satisfactorily. In fact instances of the size previously mentioned (about 30 machines, 100 jobs, 600 tasks) are solved in about one minute CPU. We consider this as a good starting point if we want add other features to the core algorithm.

9 Conclusions

As it has been anticipated, not all the relevant aspects relative to the project treated here are supposed to be presented in this paper. Nevertheless, the general philosophy and all the main ideas have been described, according to which the actual system has to be implemented. Such a careful preliminary analysis is certainly a necessary condition for a successful implementation. Moreover, it may provide interesting hints for similar projects in different conditions.

The realization of the optimization module is near to be completed to date. The other modules are somehow less critical, with the partial exception of the user interface, which may deserve some deeper analysis.

Needless to say, the ultimate evaluation of the project will be based on the way the system will be perceived by the decision makers and on the impact it will have on the production system. Obviously the actual decision makers are already engaged in the DSS project and most design characteristics are based on their suggestions.

References

Adams, J., Balas, E. and Zawack, D. (1987). The shifting bottleneck procedure for job shop scheduling. Management Science Report n.MSRR-525 (R), Carnegie Mellon University.

Blazewicz, J., Lenstra, J.K. and Rinnooy Kan, A.H.G. (1983). Scheduling subject to resource constraints: classification and complexity. *Discr. Appl. Math.* 5, pp. 11–24.

Gelders, L.F. and Van Wassenhove, L.N. (1981). Production planning: a review. *EJOR* 7, pp. 101–110.

Jones, C.H. and Maxwell, W.L. (1986). A system for manufacturing scheduling with interactive computer graphics. *IEE Transactions*, Sept., pp. 298–303.

Serafini, P., Ukovich, W., Kirchner, H., Giardina, F. and Tiozzo, F. (1988). Job shop scheduling: a case study. In F. Archetti, M. Lucertini, P. Serafini, eds., Operations Research Models in FMS, Springer, Vienna.

Viviers, F. (1983). A decision support system for job shop scheduling. *EJOR* 14, pp. 95–103.

DSS for Project Scheduling
A Review of Problems

Czeslaw Smutnicki
Institute of Technical Cybernetics
Technical University of Wroclaw
Wroclaw, Poland

1 Introduction

We consider the problem formulated by Anthonisse et al. (1987). A set of tasks, divided into several projects, is to be executed in certain production process. A set of limited resources (machines, equipment, personnel), available in various periods of time, is given in order to perform the tasks. The task processing times depend on resource allocation, and all the possible means of a task performing are known. All the constraints on production process are formulated as: resource constraints, object constraints, waiting time constraints, release time and dead line constraints. A multiobjective criterion is considered based on the penalty function with respect to given due dates of tasks.

The above model describes the functioning of an organisation that runs several projects ordered by customers, simultaneously. Decision making in the organisation is performed periodically and consist in designing a plan (tasks schedule) for a given production period.

The described model of the real life situation is not as general as we wish it should be. It is possible to create a more general one, however the discussed model seems to be enough difficult, from theoretical point of view, for solving.

2 From deterministic scheduling to DSS

When we analyse the problems stated above on the background of the deterministic scheduling theory we find them extremely hard. There exist no efficient tools for solving such a type of problems. One can solve them only when the size of problem instance is enough small (no more then 50 tasks); in other cases approximation methods are used. Therefore the detailed analysis should be carried out in order to indicate subareas of scheduling theory which can be applied in DSS.

The deterministic scheduling theory offers the following "tools": computational complexity theory, elimination criteria, polynomial algorithms, B–and–B algorithms, approximation algorithms, methods for finding lower bounds, solution evaluation methods. All this tools are shortly analysed and conclusions are presented.

The *complexity analysis* shows that the problem stated above is strongly NP-hard. Moreover, the problem of finding any feasible solution is NP-hard too. This means that we are forced to apply an enumerative method in order to find a feasible solution, but without guarantee of finding it in a reasonable time. On the other hand we may apply any fast approximation algorithm which, however, can generate infeasible solution. The DSS user should be informed about all the possible ways of solving the problem. In the case when DSS fails in obtaining a feasible solution, it may indicate the possible directions of problem modification (for instance deleting some tasks, varying dead lines, etc.).

The *elimination criteria* exist for some special cases of scheduling problems and allow us to reduce the set of feasible solutions. In such cases the solution search can be done easily. The following two examples show that, however, not all the known elimination criteria are useful for practical applications.

Example 1: Elimination criteria given by Szwarc (1978) for the $F \| C_{max}$ problem. Let assume that the ratio of number of arcs generated by elimination criteria to the number of all arcs in a full graph is represented by s. A simple experimental test (Table 1) shows that the number s drastically decreases with the increasing number of machines m, and hence the above criteria fail already for $m \geq 5$.

m	3	4	5	6	7
s	25%	5%	.5%	.1%	.0%

Table 1.

Example 2: The elimination criteria given by Carlier (1987) for the $J \| C_{max}$ problem. They are sufficiently good, because an algorithm in which they have been implemented, solves the famous instance 100|10|10 of $J \| C_{max}$ that haven't been solved for over 20 years (Muth and Thompson, 1963). The technique introduced by Carlier seems to be fruitful and should be extended on more general problems.

The *polynomial algorithms* exist only for a small class of scheduling problems (Rinnooy Kan, 1976; Gupta and Kyparisis, 1987), but the class of these algorithms seems to be very important, since all the solution methods for general scheduling problems are strongly based on fundamental results obtained for simple problems. Thus, polynomial algorithms are used as the auxiliary ones in more complex algorithms.

The *Branch-and-Bound methods* are formulated for finding optimal solution of strongly NP-hard problems. That methods are generally based on the active scheduling approach (e.g. Rinnooy Kan, 1976; Lenstra, 1976; French, 1982), cliques approach (Carlier, 1987) and critical path approach (Bouma, 1982; Grabowski et al., 1983). The computational experiments show that this type of method is "sufficiently good" only for the small size problems (no more then 100 tasks and 10 resources). The $1|r_j|L_{max}$ problem is the rare exception and has been solved by the B–and–B method (Carlier, 1982) for even 10000 tasks. However, in the general case, the method seems to be too complex and time-consuming for practical applications. Hence this type of algorithms is used only in special cases to improve solutions obtained in some other way.

The *approximation algorithms* are the most popular methods for solving the practical scheduling problems. There are based on the simple scheduling problems, relaxed problems, priority rules, local searching, and so on, and often run in a polynomial time. Panwalker and Iskander (1977) list about 80 different priority rules used in priority scheduling. In literature there exist many various specialized approximation algorithms; sometimes several ones for a problem. The algorithms differ one from other by complexity, solution times, solution quality, etc. It is clear that all these algorithms should be tested and areas of practical application should be precised.

The *lower bound* of a value of the goal function is, in many cases, necessary in order to evaluate the solution quality. Many various methods are used: linear programming, linear assignment, knapsack problem, simple scheduling problems, dual problems and so on. The algorithms for calculating the lower bound should run in a polynomial time.

The *solution evaluation methods* use the worst-case analysis, average analysis and massive experimental tests. The results are known, however, only for simple problems and simple algorithms.

From the above considerations the following practical conclusions arise. There exist no useful method for solving general multiobjective project scheduling problem. All the algorithms formulated for special cases should be taken into account in support system.

3 Architecture of DSS

On the base of the conclusions from the previous paragraph a structure of DSS is proposed in form shown in Figure 1. The function of particular system elements are discussed in the sequel.

All the information about the *production process* are collected by *data base manager* and stored in *data base*. The information consist of the following kind of data: (i) data for *projects* and *resources* (such parameters as: priority weights, release and due dates, dead lines, time periods of resource availability, etc.), (ii) the applied *decision* (with a full information about the decision situation) with respect to an actual state of production process, (iii) the future decision (*plan*) with respect to new states of the process, (iv) the history of the process i.e. decision situations and decisions that can be treated as the *base of experimental knowledge*. Data contained in data base are stored in a form convenient for managers i.e. technological cards, customer orders, charts, etc. A data base manager performs standard data base functions (i/o data, editing, selecting, reporting, etc.) and additionally transforms data stored in the data base to a standard form accepted by DSS and vice versa. It is assumed that the data base and the data base manager do not belong to DSS. This allows to link DSS with any existing data bases without additional limitations.

The DSS in the basic version consists of *solver* and *data processor* and fulfills elementary functions assumed by Anthonisse et al. (1987) (i/o data, updating data, consistency checking, manual scheduling, automatic scheduling, leading dialogue, etc). The presentation of information in a graphic form by *graphic processor* is an indispensable condition of carrying on the man-machine dialogue on the high level. The automatic scheduling is performed by the *solver* with application of the algorithms from *library of specialised scheduling algorithms*. The quality of obtained solution is estimated by the *evaluator* and algorithms from library. Every algorithm from library possesses the full information about numerical properties (solution time, memory requirements, guarantee of quality, etc.) and theoretical or empirical evaluation of practical usefulness for solving particular problems. In many cases the solution methods requires additional *operating data base* that stores a set of partial schedules and/or a set of alternative schedules.

In the discussed support system the activity is carrying on in one of the following scenarios:

(a) basing on the given data a problem is formulated. After that the *planist* designes the plan for a given production period. Plan is created in the iterative and interactive way with application of full knowledge of operator and the best available algorithm from solver and evaluator. The obtained plan can be accepted, evaluated or verified by the *customer service assistant* or by *manager*.

(b) several alternative plans are formulated as the result of planning process. Then the standard procedure of making choice, by the decision making group (planner, customer service assistant, manager), from given set of alternatives is carried on.

Let us note, that the automatic scheduling process requires making the decision which algorithm, from a given set, is the most useful to solving the given problem instance. One can assume that the measure of utility is a compromise evaluation between solution time and solution quality. In most of practical situations the evaluation is purely empirical and can be obtained in the solver learning process leading by the *teacher*. In the learning process a sequence of typical production process examples in generated by the *simulator*. Every example is solved by various algorithms existing in library and then the results are evaluated. The evaluation is made on the base of results from B–and–B algorithms or on the base of opinion of a group of experts. The learning process in DSS is performed out of the normal duties of the system.

Functional analysis of the system confirms existence of the following forms of interaction:

1. between DSS and planner, in planning process,

2. between DSS customer service assistant and manager, in the process of verifying the proposed plan,

3. between DSS and decision making group, in process of making choice from a given set of alternatives,

4. between DSS and group of experts, in the algorithm learning process.

Each of listed above interactions requires appropriate form of guiding the dialogue and appropriate form of presenting the information.

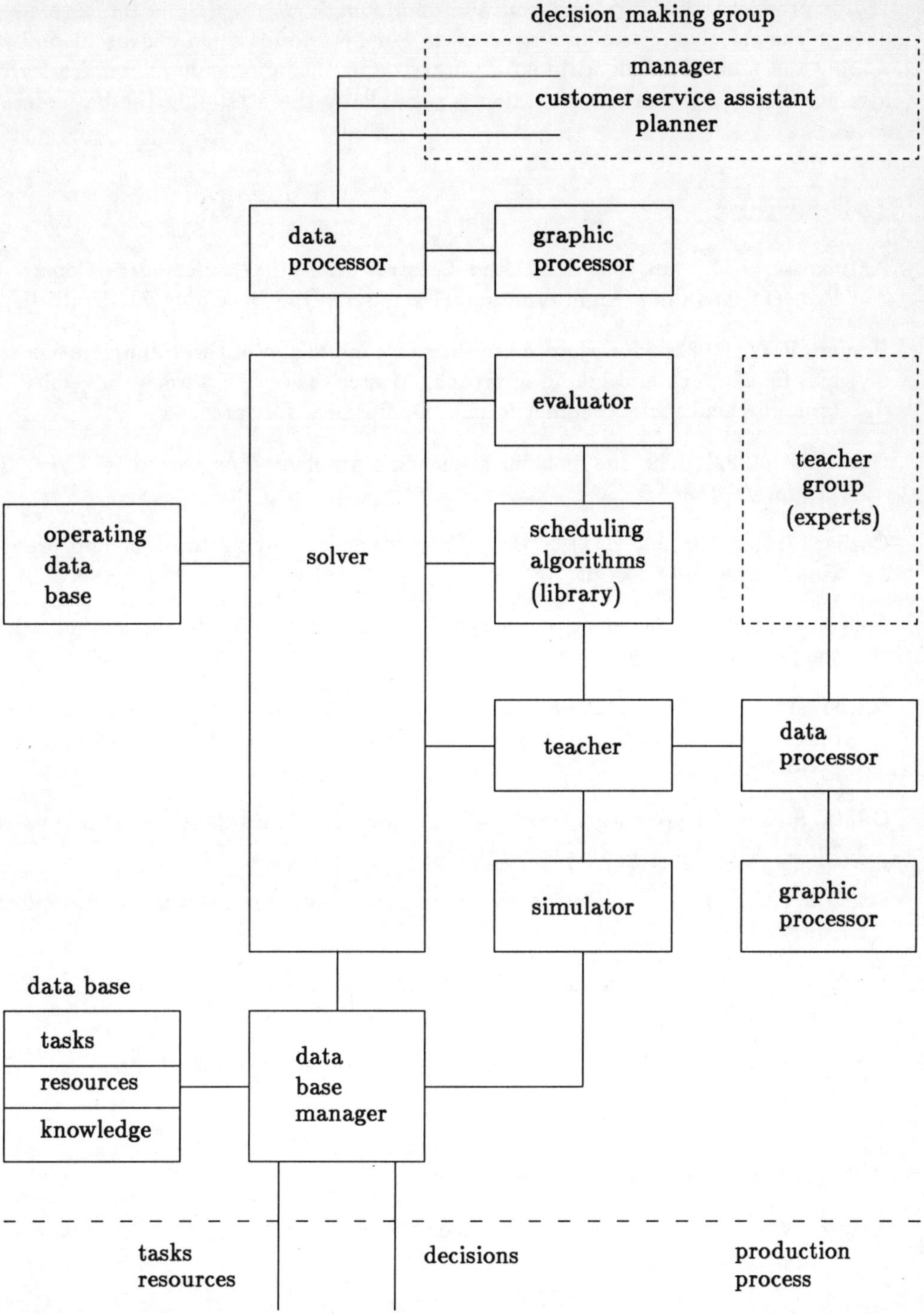

Figure 1: Architecture of DSS

The proposed DSS in thought as the developing system. In the basic version, it contains the solver and the data processor. Further modification can be made by increasing the number of algorithms in library or by including subsystems for learning the algorithms. The next modification is possible by the extending the basic decision model.

References

Anthonisse, J.M., van Hee, K.M. and Lenstra, J.K. (1987). Resource Constrained Project Scheduling: An International Exercise in DSS Development. Draft, IIASA.

Bouma, R.W. (1982). Job-shop scheduling: a comparison of three enumeration schemas in a branch and bound approach. Master's thesis. Erasmus University Rotterdam, Faculty of Econometrics and Operational Research.

Carlier, J. (1982). The one-machine sequencing problem. *European J. of Oper. Res.*, 11, pp. 42–47.

Carlier, J. and Pinson, E. (1987). An algorithm for solving the job-shop problem. Unpublished manuscript.

French, S. (1982). Sequencing and scheduling: an introduction to the mathematics of the job-shop. Wiley.

Grabowski, J., Skubalska, E. and Smutnicki, C. (1983). On flow-shop scheduling with release and due dates to minimize maximum lateness. *J. Oper. Res. Soc.*, 34, pp. 615–620.

Gupta, S.K. and Kyparisis, J. (1987). Single Machine Scheduling Research. *OMEGA Int. J. of Mgmt Sci.*, 15(3), pp. 207–227.

Lenstra, J.K. (1976). Sequencing by Enumerative Methods. Mathematish Centrum, Amsterdam.

Muth, J.F. and Thompson, G.L. (1963). Industrial scheduling. Prentice Hall, Englewood Cliffs.

Panwalker, S.S. and Iskander, W. (1977). A Survey of Scheduling Rules. *Oper. Res.*, 25, pp. 45–61.

Rinnooy Kan, A.H.G. (1976). Machine Scheduling Problems: Classification, Complexity and Computations. Nijhoff, The Hague.

Szwarc, W. (1978). Permutation Flow-Shop Theory Revisited. *Naval Res. Log. Quart.*, 25, pp. 557–570.

Software Engineering Principles in the Building of Decision Support Systems

Ivan Stanchev
University of Economics "Karl Marx"
Department of Systems Analysis and Management
Sofia, Bulgaria

In the beginning of the 60-ies, the methods and means of development of computer software were defined mainly by the strong desire for achievement of qualitatively new results in the application of computers, the efficiency of which was rather limited in comparison with the present one. The hardware determined strict limits for the development of the software and the costs of the machine-time and the memory that was used dominated over the expenses for programming.

After new computer generations were developed, the restrictions with regards to the software became smaller, and this made it possible to start the development of big and complicated software systems. Just at that moment, serious difficulties emerged in connection with the organizational planning and the realization of software projects that were complicated in content and very big in scope (Brooks, 1975).

These difficulties generally emerged as a result of the following circumstances:

- The deadlines and the expenses were planned by intuition and not on the basis of rational methods and technologies, which resulted in their multiple surpass when put to practice. This often caused the termination of certain projects, on which significant expenditures had already been made.

- In principle, no rules or procedures for the development of software existed and when attempts were made to organize the programmers' work, the prescriptions were ignored. This was even more valid when rationing the programmers' labour was concerned.

- The test programs did not allow precise and objective evaluation of the software functional characteristics, therefore the evaluations of their compatibility and reliability were completely subjective and, consequently, hard to adapt and given credit by the users.

- The working style of the programmers led to individualization of the software systems: the authors did not consent to criticism, the programmes were incomprehensive to the other specialists and that, on its part made their maintenance and development impossible when their producers were absent.

The participants in the international symposium on "Organization and Planning of Software Developments", held in Garmish (FRG) in 1968, in their search for a way out of the critical situation, use *the term "software engineering"* for the first time. By analogy with the engineering sciences, they suggest the use of definite principles and methods of production in working out the software systems.

In the beginning this concept was a set of ideas, as to how the programmers should start their work as constructor-engineers by making use of well-described methods and technologies and how the results of their work could be evaluated according to objective criteria. In the mid 70-ies, a significant number of developments existed that were related to software production (its management, planning of expenses, specification and documentation, validation and formal verification).

In the beginning of the 80-ies, a significant quantity of empirical information was piled up, thus giving grounds for comparative statistic analyses. A new notion EGOLESS–PROGRAMMING came into being (Weinberg, 1971), corresponding to a style of programming, as a consequence of which the software product was no more marked by its author's hand and, having been developed with respect to definite rules and standards, it became comprehensible for other programmers.

To summarize the large scope of the research and application activities in the field of software engineering in the last two decades, *three major trends* have to be mentioned. The first one is related to the *structuring of the process of software development*. The division of this process into stages, phases and separate groups of operations, brought about the emergence of separate modules with certain contents (activities and operations) that could be evaluated in advance according to their length, labour-consumption and value.

By a parallel analysis of the left and right parts of Table 1 it is easy to notice that the logical structure of the life-cycle of the product undergoes certain changes, dependent on the character of production (unique or batch) and this is true of the technical, as well as of the software products. Thus for example, the last phase does not exist with the batch production, but with the technical products the prototype product is refined with each new series, making it adequate to the changing marketing conditions.

The serial production of software products is very profitable (because of the extremely low cost and high reliability of disk copying), while the development and the improvement of the product lead to great expenses. That is why, the software products are usually offered on the market without any changes, which in turn creates a false impression of "immortality" of these products, regardless of their qualities and functions.

The second trend of the software engineering is related to the type of production itself, i.e. to *the kind and character of the programming languages, methods and techniques that are used*. A particularly important role in this trend was played by the methodology of STRUCTURAL PROGRAMMING, characterized by a sequential "step" detailing of the programs, by restricting the size of the separate modules, by using "clear" programming structures and deleting the instruction for jumping over from one place to another in the program.

In parallel to this, new programming languages were created and developed (MODULA-2, ADA, etc.) together with the respective translating and supporting pro-

Technical Product	Software Product
1. Defining the requirements and characteristics of the product	1. Systems analysis, defining the desired results and the existing limits
2. Projecting the product (general and constructive projects)	2. Preliminary design and specifying the subprograms and the program modules (a schematic presentation)
3. Detailed projecting	3. Working project (algorithmic description)
4. Preparation of the project	4. Coding and module test
5. The product is tried, evaluated and accepted by the user	5. Integrates (connection, editing and compilation) a complete text
6. Activities for maintenance and writing of the product	6. Accompanying of the software product (corrections, adaptation and development)

Table 1: Stages and Phases

grams, new DBMS and new program packets for work in a graphic mode, which not only turned into standard tools in the programmers' work, but also simplified and improved the relations among the end user and the computer system to a great extent. It is difficult to enumerate the software systems comprising the modern means of programming, having in mind that all available software systems for management of complex software projects have to be added to them (Lustman, 1985).

The third trend has to do with *the labour distribution in building and maintenance of a software system*. As early as in the beginning of the 70-ies, different variants were proposed for labour distribution within a team of programmers. The most interesting and efficient one of them suggests that this team's work be organized on the principles of a surgery team, according to which one person performs the operation and the rest assist him (Mills, 1971).

Figure 1 represents the structure of such a team, in which the part of the "surgeon" is played by the chief programmer who personally defines the functional specifics and indications of labour efficiency, works out the program: writes, encodes and tests, and prepares the documentation. The surgeon's "right hand", or still, as Brooks calls him, "the second pilot", is in the position to execute any of the above-mentioned activities, but he is not so experimented as the team leader. He is his permanent opponent and, in fact, guarantees the continuation of the performance upon the surgeon's exit.

The administrator takes over the hard and inefficient work from the surgeon, which, however, is indispensable for the organization and financing; the editor corrects, adds and clarifies the program documentation, controls the different versions of the product and their distribution. The other members of the team also have strictly defined

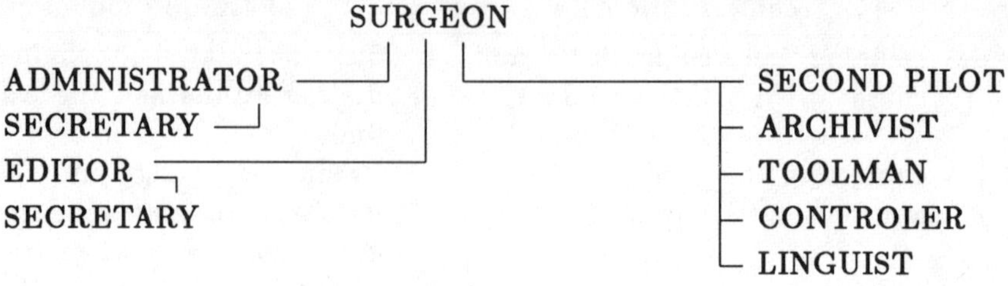

Figure 1

obligations that are to be performed in the process of the general development. Mills stresses on the fact that his concept turns programming from "an individual into social activity", which presupposes that all results be open and accessible for all members of the team, as common property is. The tests of the "surgery team" principle confirm its efficiency and give, as Brooks points out (Brooks, 1975), very positive results.

With the development of the interactive systems for data processing and decision making new duties open up. For instance, to work out the interface between the dialogue manager and the end user, two new positions are formed: applied programmer and dialogue author (Bevan and Murray, 1985). The first one is responsible for the efficiency of the algorithms and models that are included in the software system and specifies the necessary structure for data presentation. The second one constructs and describes the dialogue and therefore he occupies a key position in the development of the overall system. Like in film production, the dialogue author — in software engineering — determines the degree of the product's take-in by the end user in advance (see Figure 2).

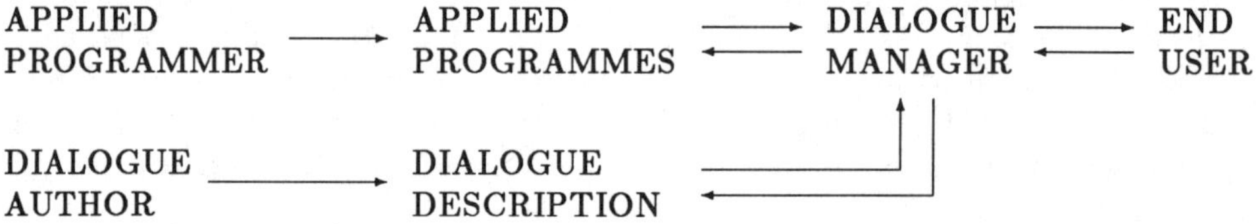

Figure 2

The classic "engineering approach", which has been established in the process of designing conventional systems for electronic data processing, cannot be applied successfully in the design and introduction of Decision Support Systems (DSS). The individual style and methods of decision making in a specific enterprise play significant role in projecting and especially in the introduction of DSS. Because of these and other reasons (the specific character of the concrete problems to be solved, the different degree of training of staff in the various organizations has, etc.), it may be necessary to introduce some changes in the approach in DSS design by making use of the *principles of consulting in the economic enterprises.* According to this new approach, the data processing specialists and the specialists in projecting and introducing DSS models work in collaboration with the decision makers (secondary and high management) and *develop DSS on the basis of the real needs, possibilities and experience that the use of the user of the system has.*

The purpose of this is to create the primary information, software and technical support for the solution of the problem, i.e. to present the user with the most essential data, methods and models that he is able to master quickly and effectively in the process of decision making. His evaluation of their usefulness is the main criterion for further development and improvement of the DSS.

This approach can be called **evolutionary**, *as the building of the system is based on the available methods and ways of decision making, for which models are designed and computer data is supplied.* In the process of these activities, requirements for more data and additional problems and tasks, realized by the user, lead to further development and improvement of the system. Another approach is possible, of course, when the construction of the DSS starts from the very beginning (zero-based), but with this approach the development of the system can continue for months and years and besides, it requires high degree of specialization and ability on the part of the designers (Carlson, 1979). The evolutionary approach makes the design of DSS an easier job, as well as quicker and cheaper, and even more so in case parts of available information systems or DSS are used. The problem here is the need to observe a number of limitations, as the problems of the new system which are solved have to be in correspondence with the existing system. The modification in this case are carried out with the help of a special program and technical means, called DSS generators. The construction of the generators and the applied products is accomplished with the so-called DSS tools that include languages of special purpose, specialized technical means and software systems.

The *active participation of the user* is of primary importance for the further success of the system when the evolutionary approach is applied. The designing itself and *the user interface depend on the qualification of the users and the frequency of the system's use.* These two criteria are the basis for choosing the mode of interface work, which is to be used (e.g. dialogue management through a menu or a question/answer).

The process of building a DSS can be divided into three phases: pre-designing, designing and introducing.

The pre-designing phase (see Figure 3) contains two interconnected cycles of activities. One of them starts with the studying and defining the existing needs, interests and readiness for application of this new system by the users. The specialists must find out what the specific problems are that the decision makers need support for finding solutions and what their general expectations of a DSS are. The users' motivation has to be taken as a variable, as the task of the specialists themselves is to provoke interest and readiness for introduction of DSS by suggesting alternative decisions for the content and functions of the system. This problem is solved in an iterative way by a repeated cyclic performance of the separate activities from the first phase.

Besides this, the first cycle contains:

- definition of the goals of DSS development;

- identification of the available resources (finance, personnel, etc.);
- working out of alternatives for the system, decomposition of the goals, defining the expenses, the expected results and real limitations that will accompany the introduction of the system.

The last activity is an element of the second cycle, it accomplishes the connection between the two cycles and is, in fact, a final module of the realization of the pre-projecting phase. In order to execute this final module, it is necessary to execute, too, the activities of the second cycle:

- defining, analysing and documenting the existing process of decision making;
- defining the "key" decisions;
- formulating the "normative" and "descriptive" models;
- choosing particular areas for development and introduction of DSS.

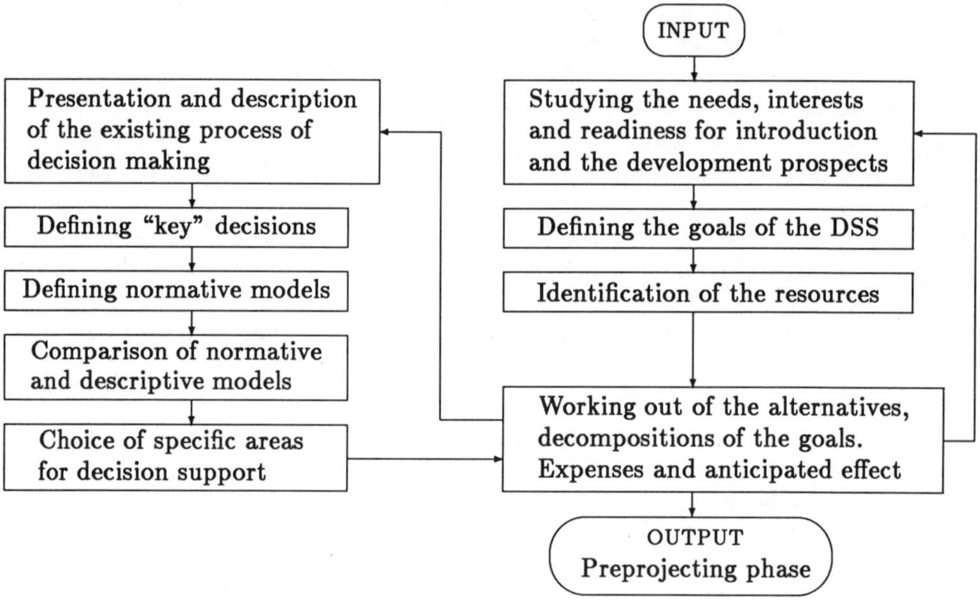

Figure 3: Scheme of the Preprojecting Phase[1]

The second cycle is closed by the need of a more detailed study of the process of decision making (Bahl and Hunt, 1984), resulting from the user's evaluation of the proposed alternatives and anticipated results.

[1] After Keen P., Morton S., Decision Support Systems: an Organizational Perspective, Addison-Wesley Publ. Co, Reading, Mass., 1978

In a number of cases the first cycle is closed by the need for the user to re-evaluate his view of the system, or when it is necessary to modify the goals and resources in order to achieve the required balance. The output of the last module, leading to the projecting phase, is realized after the final decision making about the content and functions of the systems, the resource needed and the final effect of its development.

These decisions, as well as the whole pre-projecting phase, are of grave importance for the further activities in developing the system. Even here the size of the practical changes in organization are defined, which grow bigger by moving further form the descriptive models towards the normative ones. This rule, established by practice, allows an even search for the best variant for developing DSS according to the real circumstances and needs.

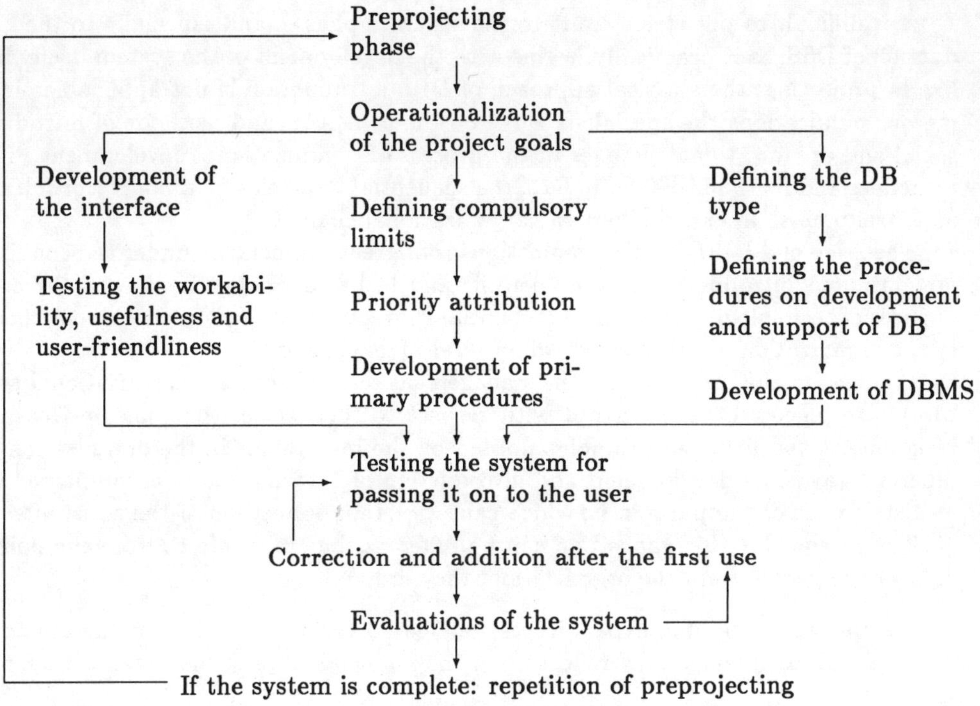

Figure 4: Scheme of the Projecting Phase[2]

The projecting phase (see Figure 4) is also of an iterative character. It contains parallel activities for:

- defining and building the database, the procedures for their updating, the choice and adapting of the necessary software support for their management (DBMS — data base management systems);

[2]Same as Figure 3.

- structuring the interface (the system of connections) among the separate elements of DSS and testing its "workability", "usefulness" and "user-friendliness";
- defining the compulsory, initiating and routine procedures, attribution of priorities and development of "menus".

After the parallel execution of these activities and testing the system as a whole (again with the active participation of the user) it usually becomes necessary to make certain specifications and improvements, stemming from the analysis and evaluation of the preliminary work of the system and the comparison of the results obtained to the goals defined in the preceeding phase. When the specialists and the users decide that the system is fully "complete", its further development and perfection can start by returning to the activities from the previous phase.

It is difficult to put strict limits to the separate phases, and especially to the introduction of DSS, as it practically begins with the development of the system itself. Here, like in projecting, the classical approach of DPS introduction is not applicable. In numerous publications the specialists agree on the principles and methods of introducing social and organizational changes in the process of organizational development. These principles and methods define, in fact, the sequential interrelation among "consultants" and "customers" in carrying out the organizational changes.

The issue of adaptivity of organizations is of great importance under the conditions of continuous introduction of the scientific and technical achievements and the consequences of technological, technical and social character that lead to permanent changes in the organization of production, labour and management.

Changes in the organization (in management technology and organizational structure) take place all the time, but with respect to their scale, they can be treated as insignificant and to be accordingly adopted by the individuals in the organization in a different way. The development and introduction of DSS is usually accompanied by a re-distribution of the parts in it, which causes certain opposition of the assistants.

The reasons for this opposition can be different, but most often, from the point of view of the people from the organization, they are:

- expectations for big expenditures, related to the transition from the old to the new system, which may reflect upon the financial state of the organization;
- threat of a rise of certain positions of the personnel in the organization, who have to change their functions with the re-distribution of rights and obligations;
- threat for the high degree of integration attained in the organization, i.e. for the established order and way of work in a certain joint team;
- fear of uncertainty in the behaviour of the separate individual which grows even bigger if frequent changes are introduced. This uncertainty is connected with potential changes of the social environment, of the conditions for work and its safety.

The reasons enumerated above, are of a psychological character, but many more reasons exist, which, together with the social and psychological character, can have an underlying economic character (payment, social advantages, general financial state of the organization, etc.).

A keypoint in the modern organizational theory is the overcoming of the resistance against organizational changes. For the theoretic consideration of the problem and for the search of means for their solution, a concept for organizational development is formed (French and Bell, 1973). Its primary sources are related to the theories devoted to the problems of raising the qualification of managers. Besides, it forms its basic principles for characterizing the DEVELOPING ORGANIZATION:

- it is adaptive, it quickly adjusts to the new goals and the changes of the environment;
- its members consciously collaborate among themselves and manage the changes, avoiding their destructive influence over the organization;
- it has favourable conditions for further rise and qualification of its members;
- it is characterized by open internal communication and mutual trust among its members, which contributes to the constructive decision making;
- as a rule, all levels take part in decision making, so everyone realizes his commitment in planning and management of the development of the organization.

The concept of organizational development is closely related to the problem of MANAGEMENT CONSULTING (the place, the role and the way of work of the management consultant), as the overcoming the resistance within the organization, is usually supported by external experts working in the area of organizational development and DSS development.

Organizational development is aiming at not only solving short-term organizational problems, but it is a rather complicated process of training in practical skills for solving the problem (including the learning of specific methods of organizational development). This process has a great mobilizing power, as it involves the "claimants" themselves, as the consequences of all decisions reflect on the whole organization. That is why the specialists of DSS introduction adopt the scheme for organizational changes as corresponding to the iterative character of the process in evolutionary DSS development.

I can conclude thus. On one hand, regardless of the progress in methodological support of software engineering (Fairley, 1985; Sommerville, 1985), still we are witnesses of a significant lag behind the classical engineering disciplines. *General standards and regulations in DSS methodology are missing; standardization must refer not only to norming the technical and economic indicators of the software systems, but also to technology of software development.*

Canonizing is related to basic knowledge mostly. Until a short time ago, there was no methodology or learning aids whatsoever for training system programmers as software engineers. *The expenses for instrumental tools greatly surpassed the expectations.* Less experimental developments in this area are financed and the comparative research of workable methods is so labour-consuming, that it can be done only in extremal projects (e.g. space research). Most available tools are compatible to definite computers and operational systems and that is the reason why they cannot be integrated and compared in the general case.

On the other hand, the change of the concept for DPS and DSS development destroys the already classical principles of software engineering. Thus, for example, *the application of the classic concept of separate phases and stages in sequence, does not work with DSS*. This is evident in Figures 3 and 4.

The roles are re-distributed in the organization of the team's work, a significant part of it being overtaken by the consultants, and the end-user becomes an active figure in the overall process of DSS development and introduction.

Thirdly, *with DSS development, individualization again predominated over unification* (determined by the unique character of the systems), a fact which reflects upon the choice of programming tools. The OBJECTIVE-ORIENTED PROGRAMMING is now established as a new, workable and better approach.

All this supposes a through re-assessment of the principles, methods and means of software engineering and requires the development of a solid methodical support in DSS development.

References

Bahl, H.C. and Hunt, R.G. (1984). A Framework for Systems Analysis for DSS. Volume 7, North-Holland.

Bevan, N. and Murray, D. (1985). Man-Machine Integration, State of the Art Report. Pergamon Iniotech Ltd., England.

Brooks, P.F. (1975). The Mythical Manmonth. Addison-Wesley Publ. Co., Reading, Mass.

Carlson, E.D. (1979). An Approach for Precision Support Systems. *Data Base*, Winter.

Fairley, R.E. (1985). Software Engineering Concepts. Mc Graw Hill, N.Y.

French, W.L. and Bell, C.H. (1973). Organizational Development. Prentice Hall Inc., Englewood Cliffs, New Jersey, USA.

Lustman, F. (1985). Managing Computer Projects. Reston Publ. Co., Reston, Virginia.

Mills, H. (1971). Chief Programmers Teams, Principles and Procedures. IBM Federal Systems Division Report FSC 71-5108, Gaithersburg, Md.

Sommerville, I. (1985). Software Engineering. Addison-Wesley, Woringham, England.

Weinberg, G.M. (1971). The Psychology of Computer Programming. Van Nostrand & Reinchold, New York.

Procedure for Multi-Criterial Multi-Expert Decision-Making

B. Vachev*, P. Tsvetanov**, P. Yordanov, M. Ruicheva
* *Higher Institute for National Economy, Varna, Bulgaria*
** *Institute for Nuclear Research and Nuclear Energy, Bulgarian Academy of Sciences, Sofia, Bulgaria*

1 Introduction

The procedure of decision-making realizes the process of decision-making in the system of analysis of the strategy of energy development of Bulgaria. The methodology and methods of the system of analysis of the strategy of energy development have been developed by Tsvetanov (1980, 1981, 1987). The main aims of the system are as follows: assessment of scale and structure of long-term energy demand; determination of the dynamics and structure of energy supply development; determination of mutual requirements of the energy sector and its interconnected branches; study of the effect of energy upon the growth and proportions of economic development (structural changes in case of non-energy-intensive development included); formation of the leading directions of scientific and technical progress.

2 Research procedure of the system of analysis of strategic development

The research procedure is based on the properties of the national energy complex, the features of the decision-making process, the critical study of uncertainty, the approaches and methods of decision-making in the conditions of uncertainty and the specifics of the system of models for long-term forecasting. It is built upon the system of models and covers all stages of long-term forecasting (Tsvetanov, 1980). The procedure (Fig. 1) consists of the following basic stages: formation and description of the development scenarios; formation and analysis of variants; choice of variants.

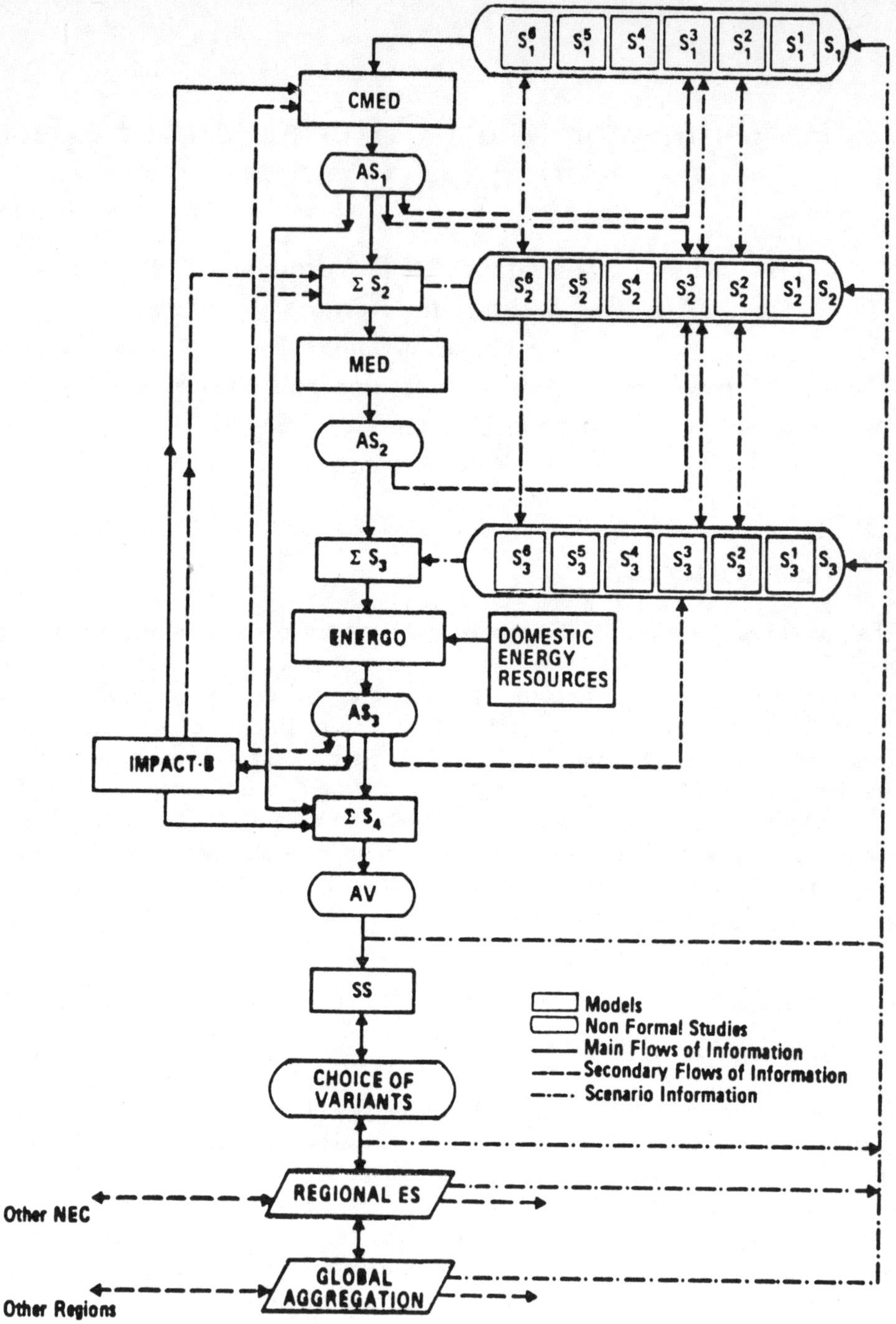

Figure 1: Main stages of the procedure for analysis of the long-term energy development of Bulgaria.

3 Multi-expert procedure of scenarios formation and description

Scenarios formation is based on the structuring of: scenario set, the scenarios themselves and scenario indicators. Structuring is based on the following: inertia monouevrability in the development of the environment and the national energy complex; features (eg. structural and functional decomposition) of the system of long-term forecasting models; degree of similarity among the scenarios; introducing of a subjective-probabilistic measure and measure of preference.

The formation and description of the scenarios comprises several basic steps: preliminary studies and analysis; hierarchic structuring of the scenario basis (of the parameters governing the system); formation of the scenario tree of the external conditions, the social-economic and energy policies; assessment of the uncertainty and quantification of the scenarios; generation of scenarios.

A method for assessment of the uncertainty and quantification of the scenarios consisting of two main parts has been developed:

- *Classification of scenario indicators (in terms of degree of controllability)*: uncontrollable; controllable; partially controllable.

- *Assessment of uncertainty (Fig. 2)*:

  - formation of the corridors of change of the scenario indicators:

    $\underline{s}$, $\overline{s}$ – possible lower and upper boundaries;

    $s_{\underline{\beta}}$, $s_{\overline{\beta}}$ – most probable boundaries (for the uncontrollable indicators);

    $s_{\underline{\alpha}}$, $s_{\overline{\alpha}}$ – most preferred boundaries (for the controllable indicators);

    $s_{\underline{\beta}}$, $s_{\overline{\beta}}$ – for the partially controllable indicators;

    $s_{\underline{\alpha}}$, $s_{\overline{\alpha}}$, s_v, s_p – most probable and preferred values of the scenario indicators.

  - formation of a subjectively probabilistic measure and measure of preference of the scenario indicators.

This approach is based on the representation of the scenario indicators as fuzzy sets by a function of belonging (1) (Fig. 2).

$$\mu_{S'}(s_i) = \begin{cases} [(s_i - \overline{s})/(s_v - \overline{s})]^{\overline{w}} , & s_i \in (s_v, \overline{s}]; \\ , & s_i = s_v \in [s_{\underline{\beta}}, s_{\overline{\beta}}] \subset [\underline{s}, \overline{s}]; \\ [(s_i - \underline{s})/(s_v - \underline{s})]^{\underline{w}} , & s_i \in [\underline{s}, s_v); \end{cases} \qquad (1)$$

$$\mu_{S'}(s_i) : S \to [0,1].$$

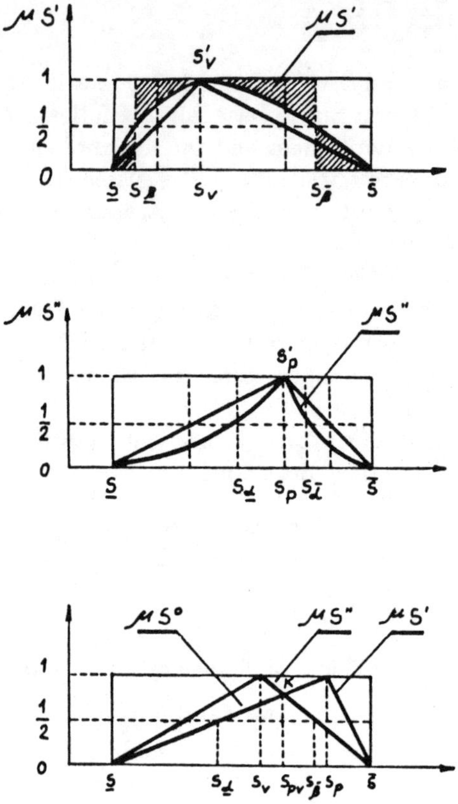

Figure 2: Functions of belonging of the fuzzy sets of the uncontrollable, controllable and partially controllable scenario indicators.

where:

S' – fuzzy set of the most probable value of the uncontrollable indicator;

δ – factor of non-linearity;

S'' – fuzzy set of the most preferred values of the controllable indicator (set by a function analogical to (1));

S^0 – fuzzy set of the most probable and preferred value of the partially controllable indicator; set as a section of the sets S' and S'' with the following function of belonging:

$$\mu_{S^0}(s_i) = \min\left(\mu_{S'}(s_i), \mu_{S''}(s_i)\right) \tag{2}$$

The most preferred and most probable value of the partially controllable indicator s_{pv} is obtained as a solution of the non-linear equation

$$\mu_{S'}(s_{pv}) = \mu_{S''}(s_{pv}) \tag{3}$$

The application of the method for formation of scenarios, consideration and decrease of uncertainty (Tsvetanov, 1985; Vachev, 1987) results in: fuzzy sets respectively of the most preferred, most probable and most preferred and most probable values of the scenario indicators; coefficient of uncertainty of a verbal formulation of the scenarios and index of uncertainty for each scenario indicator; other concrete values of the scenario indicators; summed up assessment of the scenario in terms of probability and preference.

The experts generate concrete values of the scenario indicators around their extremal values in conformity with the tree of verbal formulations of the scenarios and together with the respective corridors of scenario indicator change.

4 Multi-criterial multi-expert choice of variants

The criteria of choice of variants used in research procedure are on four levels: strategic; economic; energy and ecological, system.

The procedure realizing the choice of variants comprises four main steps: formulation of task; expert assessment; computer procedure; analysis and choice of variants.

The method of choice of variants (Vachev, 1987) realizes the developed new concept for formation of fuzzy sets for preference referring to the usefulness of the changes of value of a certain indicator depending on its initial value. On this basis the criteria of selection are represented as fuzzy sets and are specified by their functions of belonging in graphic interactive regime. The non-applicability of the method of weight coefficients for obtaining generalized criteria of decision-making has been proved. It can be used only when the coefficients of non-linearity of the functions of belonging of the fuzzy sets of the various criteria are equal to 1, i.e. in the linear case.

The fuzzy relations of preference among the criteria and among the variants (for a given criterion) are determined by the functions of belonging of the fuzzy sets of the criteria in the following way:

- non-rigorous strong linear fuzzy relation of preference among the criteria x and $y - \mu_R(x_i, y_i)$ (depending in their values x_i and y_i) is determined by the formula

$$\mu_R(x_i, y_i) = \begin{cases} 1 & , \quad \mu_x(x_i) \geq \mu_y(y_i); \\ 1 - [\mu_y(y_i) - \mu_x(x_i)] & , \quad \mu_y(y_i) \geq \mu_x(x_i); \quad x_i, y_i \in [0,1]. \end{cases} \tag{4}$$

- non-rigorous strong linear fuzzy relation of preference among the variants a and b in terms of criterion (indicator) $x - \mu_R^x(a, b)$ is determined by the formula:

$$\mu_R^x(a, b) = \begin{cases} 1 & , \quad \mu_x(a) \geq \mu_x(b) \\ 1 - [\mu_x(b) - \mu_x(a)] & , \quad \mu_x(a) \leq \mu_x(b). \end{cases} \tag{5}$$

An extension of Orlovski's method (1981) for of three relations of preference of the sets X, L, and M, respectively of the variants, experts and criteria has been worked out and three fuzzy relations of preference have been obtained:

- among the experts $\mu : L \times L \rightarrow [0,1], \ \{\mu_{pq}\}$;
- among the criteria $\eta : M \times M \times L \rightarrow [0,1], \ \{\eta^p_{jf}\}$;
- among the variants $\rho : X \times X \times M \times L \rightarrow [0,1], \ \{\rho^{jp}_{ir}\}$.

Variants with the highest degree of non-dominarability in the set X have been chosen. The algorithm of the method is as follows:

1. The fuzzy relation of preference Ω in the sets of the expert-criterial assessments has been established, i.e. as a relation of preference between E_pK_j and E_qK_f; $p,q = \overline{1,L}, \ j,f = \overline{1,M}$, where E_pK_j is the expert's assessment p in terms of the criterion j:
$$\Omega : (M \times L) \times (M \times L) \rightarrow [0,1]$$
$$\Omega(E_pK_j, E_qK_f) = \begin{cases} \eta^p_{jf} & , \quad p = q, \ \forall j,f; \\ \mu_{pq} & , \quad j = f, \ \forall p,q; \\ \eta^p_{jf} & , \quad \mu_{pq} > \mu_{qp}, \ p \neq q, \ j \neq f; \\ (\eta^p_{jf} + \eta^q_{jf})/2 & , \quad \mu_{pq} = \mu_{qp}, \ p \neq q, \ j \neq f; \\ \eta^q_{jf} & , \quad \mu_{pq} < \mu_{qp}, \ p \neq q, \ j \neq f; \end{cases} \tag{6}$$

2. A fuzzy sub-set of non-dominarable variants (for a given expert-criterial assessment P) with the following function of belonging is formed:
$$\rho^{n.d.}(x,P) = 1 - \sup_{y \in X} \left[\rho(y,x,P) - \rho(x,y,P)\right] \tag{7}$$

3. A fuzzy relation of preference among the variants in the set X induced by the functions $\rho^{n.d.}$ and the fuzzy relation of preference Ω is formed:
$$\delta(x_i,x_r) = \sup_{P,Q \in EK} \min \left\{\rho^{n.d.}(x_i,P), \rho(x_r,Q), \Omega(P,Q,x_i,x_r)\right\} \tag{8}$$
where EK is the set of combinations of experts and criteria $E_pK_j, \ p = \overline{1,L}$, $j = \overline{1,M}$ (set of expert-criterial assessments) and $\Omega(P,Q,x_i,x_r)$ is the relation of preference between the expert-criterial assessments P and Q for concrete values of the criteria (j,f) for the variants x_i and x_r corresponding to P and Q.

4. The function of belonging of the fuzzy set of the non-dominarable variants is calculated:
$$\delta^{n.d.}(x_i) = 1 - \sup_{x_r \in X} \left[\delta(x_r,x_i) - \delta(x_i,x_r)\right] \tag{9}$$

5. The most preferred variant is chosen in accordance with a decisive rule selected by a given set of decisive rules.

5 In conclusion

The formulated unified procedure of multi-expert multi-criterial decision-making is part of the overall research procedure of the system for long-term forecasting of the national energy development. It has a dialog interactive character and its working out aims at achieving better compliance with the potentialities of the experts and the decision-makers. The procedure makes possible the adequate consideration and decrease of uncertainty which has a different character at different stages of the process of decision-making.

The procedure is realized on a 16-bit PC IBM PC/XT as part of the program-computing complex of the system for analysis of the strategy of energy development.

References

Orlovski, C.A. (1981). Problems of Decision-Making in Cases of Unclear Initial Information. Nauka, Moscow (in Russian).

Tsvetanov, P.C. (1980). System Analysis in the Energy Sector. Proceedings of the Bulgarian Academy of Sciences, 4, pp. 16–30 (in Bulgarian)

Tsvetanov, P.C. (1981) System for Models for Assessment of Long-Term Development of the Energy Complex of Bulgaria. Proceedings of IIASA/IFAK Symposium on Modelling of Large-Scale Energy Systems. Pergamon Press.

Tsvetanov, P.C., Vachev, B.I. and Boyadzhiev, D.K. (1985). Method of Formation of a Scenario of the System for Long-Term Forecasting of the Development of the National Energy Complex. Proceedings of the Higher Institute of National Economy D. Blagoev, Varna, 2, pp. 75–85 (in Bulgarian).

Tsvetanov, P.C. (1987). A Method for Taking into Account the Interrelation in the Development of the National Energy and Economy. In A.A. Makarov and D.B. Wolfberg, eds., Tendencies of Development and Methods of Forecasting in the CMEA Member-Nations (in print). Energoatomizdat, Moscow (in Russian).

Vachev, B.I. (1987). Consideration of Uncertainty in Studying Long-Term Development of the Energy Complex of the P.R. of Bulgaria. Abstract of Ph.D. Thesis, Sofia (in Bulgaria).

The Design of Interactive Decision Support Systems

A. H. Vellekoop
M.I.S.-Department, Erasmus University Rotterdam
Rotterdam, Netherlands

C. G. E. Boender, A. H. G. Rinnooy Kan
Econometric Institute, Erasmus University Rotterdam
Rotterdam, Netherlands

1 Introduction

In the Netherlands there is a national research project to design "Decision Support Systems" (DSS). This research project is subsidized by the National Facility of Informatics (NFI). Several universities and companies participate in this project. One of the sub-projects is a co-operation between the Erasmus University of Rotterdam and the dredging company Royal Boskalis Westminster.

It is this project which is the subject of this paper. In the first part of the paper we present our view of DSS. On this view the total project is based. In the next section the decision situation is described, following a more detailed discussion of one of the modules of the total system.

2 Interactive decision support systems

A definition of a DSS that is acceptable to everybody is not available at this moment. The reason for this is that DSS are being studied by various scientific disciplines. Each of these disciplines emphasize different aspects of DSS based on their own background to the subject. It is not our intention to give a definition of a DSS, but we want to present our view of the matter.

We believe that the main goal of a DSS is to improve the quality of the decisions to be made. A DSS is seen as a subclass of information systems. Such computerized systems are desirable in those situations in which the solution of a complex decision-making problem calls for a comprehensive input of the insights, expertise and preferences of the decision maker. The decision maker must have the freedom to choose the level of support he needs for his problem.

He must be able to take a position between two extremes. In the first extreme the computer program does nothing more than register and analyze the data given by the user (the computer acting as "assistant"). The other extreme is the situation in which the complete solution of the problem is left entirely to the computer program (the computer acting as "advisor").

The reason that a DSS must be a highly interactive computer program is to make sure that maximal use is made of the decision maker's knowledge of the problem.

Seen in this light the following three functions are the minimal requisites of a DSS:

(a) Computing the effects of decisions proposed by the decision maker;

(b) Generating decisions which are "optimal" with respect to a criterion specified by the decision maker;

(c) Sensitivity analysis of the decisions by computing the effects of changes in parameters.

In order to realize these three functions in an efficient way, it is necessary to use the facilities of man-machine interaction on the one hand and quantitative mathematical models on the other hand. The type of decision-making problems can be on a strategic, tactical or operational level in a variety of practical situations. In general these problems will be too complicated to be described in one mathematical model. Therefore it is necessary for all relevant mathematical models to be integrated in one DSS.

3 The decision situation

The main activity of Boskalis Westminster is contracting for and executing dredging works. The decision-making situation which will be supported by the DSS is the tendering process which has to be carried out before acquiring a new job.

This process is characterized as a forecasting problem. The estimator has to predict productions and costs of a project that might be carried out some time in the future. This estimation problem can be extremely difficult when it is based on scarce and uncertain information.

Therefore it is very important that analyses are made of the risks involved for all possible alternatives. Usually, the company who offers the lowest tender price acquires the new job. Therefore the company is looking for that alternative which has low costs and low risks.

The tendering process can be divided into several phases (see figure 1). The first phase is the interpretation of the geological information of the area to be dredged. Calculation of the quantities and evaluation of the characteristics of all the different and relevant soil layers must be made. This involves not only estimating averages of these values, but also the evaluation of the risks of these parameters. A new method, based on the theory of stochastic processes, is being developed to help the estimator as much as possible. In the next section this DSS–module is worked out in more detail as an example.

As soon as the soil evaluation phase is ended, a decision has to be made as to how the job will be carried out. This involves the selection of the necessary equipment, the design of a working method for the job and the calculation of the production capacities.

Several mathematical models are available for these calculations and a method will be developed to integrate the risks of the soil information with the production estimates.

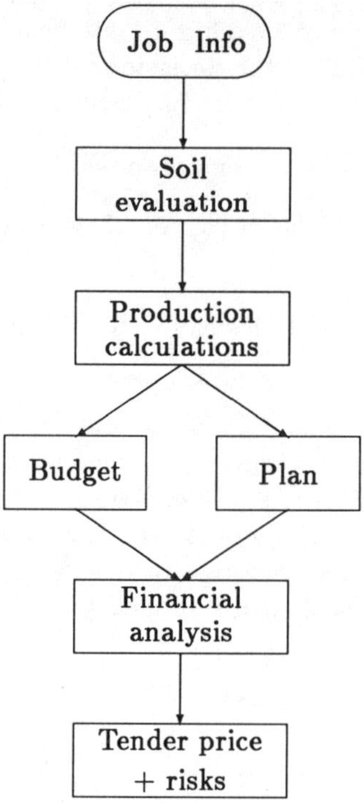

Figure 1. Flow chart depicting the decision-making process during estimation

After this phase a cost estimate is made for each alternative. A plan of the work is formulated and finally a financial analysis of all relevant costs is made. In this financial analysis the costs of each activity of the job is combined with the timeplanning of the activities. Given these costs, planning and a payment schedule (according to which the client will pay for the job) it is possible to calculate all the financial costs or revenues by a given tender price.

The DSS–module for this phase calculated not only the financial consequences by a given tender price, but also the optimal tender price for which the financial consequences are in accordance with the preferred profit of the estimator for the job. If the tender price is chosen too high, there will be an unwanted financial profit at the end of the job and therefore the tender price can be lowered, giving a higher chance of acquiring the new job. If the tender price is chosen too low, there will be an unwanted financial loss at the end of the job and therefore the tender price should be taken higher.

The main goal of the DSS, as said before, will be to help the estimator find that alternative which has the best composition of low costs and minimal risk. If the risk of this best alternative is still too high, the DSS must advise whether it is useful to gather extra information to reduce the risk. Therefore it is necessary that the final risk of the tender estimate can be traced back to the individual factors that induce this risk.

4 The soil evaluation

In the soil evaluation phase we are confronted with the following questions. Given a number of measurements (borehole information) of the thickness of a particular soil layer (e.g. sand) in different locations:

1. What is the *spatial distribution* of the soil layer?
2. What is the *total quantity* of soil in the layer over a certain area?
3. What is the *uncertainty* of this estimated volume?
4. Are *extra expensive* boreholes necessary to improve upon this estimate?
5. If so, *how many* boreholes should be taken and *where* should they be located *to reduce the uncertainty* as much as possible and what is the *expected reduction*?

In order to answer these questions the thickness of the soil layer is seen as a function over a two-dimensional domain. At each location of a measurement point the function value is known. The problem now becomes the problem of finding a suitable interpolating function in two dimensions. Desirable properties for such a function are that it should pass through all the specified measurement points exactly and that it should be continuous is all its derivatives.

Question 3 motivated us to consider the thickness of the soil layer as a realization of a *stationary Gaussian stochastic process*. This means that the unknown function is assumed to be embedded in a large class of functions over which a probability distribution is defined. Given such a (prior) probability distribution and the measurement points the conditional (posterior) probability distribution can be determined. The expected value of this posterior distribution is the interpolating function we are looking for. The variance of this estimated curve can also be computed. With this statistical information it is possible to give an adequate answer to the questions mentioned above. The suggested method can even be extended to three or more-dimensional domains. Therefore it is also possible to use this method to model other characteristics (e.g. the hardness) of the soil layer.

Gaussian stochastic processes are characterized by the mean– and covariance function:

$$u(x) = \varepsilon[f(x)] \qquad (x \in \Re^D) \tag{1}$$

$$r(x,y) = \varepsilon\Big([f(x) - u(x)] \cdot [f(y) - u(y)]\Big) \quad (x, y \in \Re^D) \tag{2}$$

A Gaussian stochastic process is called stationary if its covariance function only depends on $h = x - y$, and if the mean function is equal to a constant. Conversely, we can define a stationary Gaussian stochastic process by specifying a constant u, and a covariance function $r(h)$. Then, due to a famous result of Kolmogorov (1933), there exists a stationary Gaussian stochastic process possessing u and $r(h)$ as mean– and covariance functions.

Several restrictions on possible forms of $r(h)$ are necessary to make sure that a proper stochastic process is defined. Each covariance function must have the fundamental property of being of non-negative definite type. In (Cramér and Leadbetter, 1967) it is shown that this property of being of non-negative definite type is in fact a characteristic property of the class of all covariance functions. An important result due to Bochner (1933) states that a function on $\Re^D$ is of non-negative definite type iff it is the characteristic function of a D–dimensional distribution function.

This means that possible covariance functions are for instance,

$$r(x-y) = \sigma^2 \cdot \prod_{d=1}^{D} \exp\left\{ -\left|\frac{x^d - y^d}{\alpha^d}\right| \right\} \tag{3}$$

$$r(x-y) = \sigma^2 \cdot \prod_{d=1}^{D} \exp\left\{ -\frac{1}{2}\left(\frac{x^d - y^d}{\alpha^d}\right)^2 \right\} \tag{4}$$

$$r(x-y) = \sigma^2 \cdot \prod_{d=1}^{D} \frac{1}{1 + \left(\frac{x^d - y^d}{\alpha^d}\right)^2} \tag{5}$$

where x^d denotes the d–th component of the vector x.

In figure 2 these three covariance functions (divided by σ^2) are plotted against the distance h for the one-dimensional case. The scaling parameter α^D of the covariance functions in this figure are chosen in such a way that all three functions go through the point (1, 0.9).

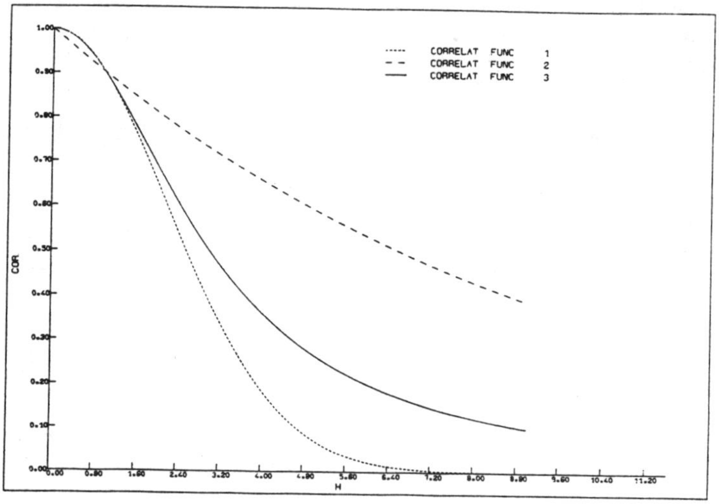

Figure 2. Covariance functions divided by σ^2.

From the theorems of Cramér and Leadbetter (1967) it follows that the realizations of the stochastic process with covariance function (3) are continuous with probability 1. The realizations of the stochastic processes with covariance function (4) and (5) can be proven to be continuously differentiable infinitely often with probability 1, so that these processes are good mathematical models for the soil layers of interest.

A Monte Carlo realization of the stochastic process with covariance function (5) is plotted in figure 3. This covariance function is of special interest to our problem, because the posterior expected integral over an interval $A \in \Re^D$ and its variance can be calculated analytically. At the moment this is the only known covariance function for which this is possible. In (Boender et al., 1988) the analytical formulas are presented to calculate these quantities.

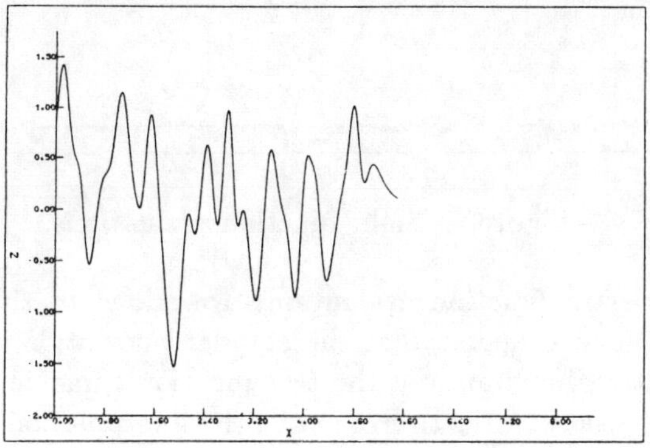

Figure 3. Realization with covariance function (5).

In the figure 4, 5 and 6 we used this covariance function as an illustrative example on a test function on which only a limited number of function evaluations were used to predict the function. In figure 4 only six function evaluations were used by the model

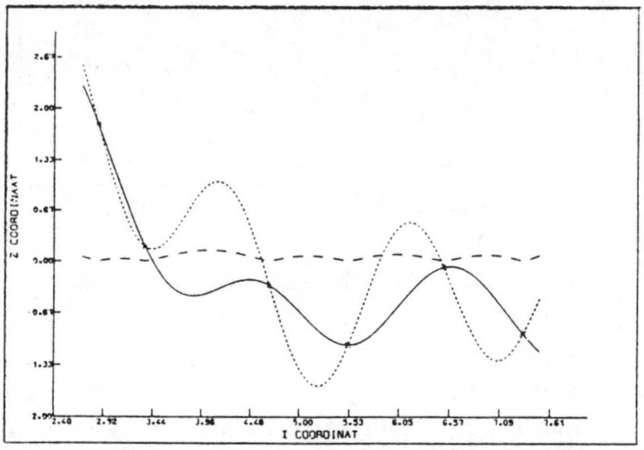

Figure 4. Six function evaluations.

The dotted line is the test function and the solid line is the best interpolating function given the six function evaluations. The standard deviation is also plotted in the figures. It can be seen that the interpolating function goes through the known function values and in those points the standard deviation is zero.

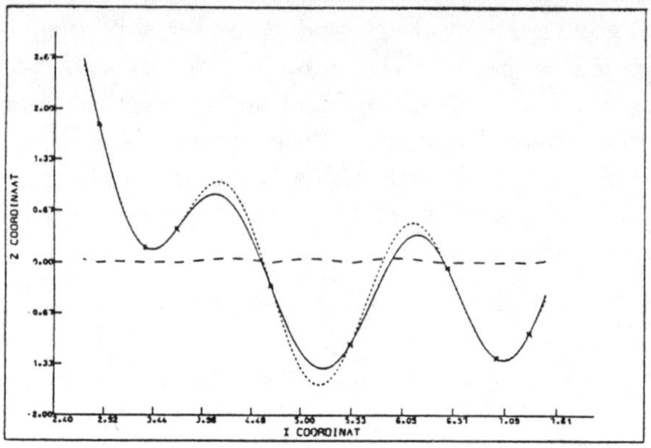

Figure 5. Eight function evaluations.

In figure 5 two extra function evaluations are added to the six function values. The model has the good property that the standard deviation is zero in those points where the interpolating function and the test function coincide and is positive where the estimation is not exact. After twelve points the interpolation is exact (see figure 6).

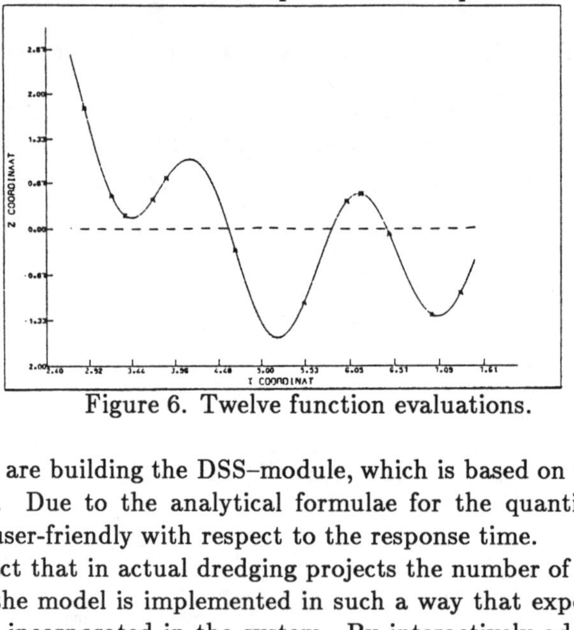

Figure 6. Twelve function evaluations.

Currently we are building the DSS–module, which is based on the statistical model described above. Due to the analytical formulae for the quantities of interest, the systems is very user-friendly with respect to the response time.

Due to the fact that in actual dredging projects the number of measurement points is very limited, the model is implemented in such a way that expert-knowledge about soillayers can be incorporated in the system. By interactively adding so-called fictive measurements, it is possible to estimate the unknown parameters of the covariance function. At the moment we are extending the model to make it possible that different measurement errors in the borehole information and the subjective error in the fictive measurements can be taken along in the model. The user can interactively construct different models for unknown soillayers by changing or adding fictive measurements until he is satisfied with the results of the model.

Another way to influence the results of the system is by changing the α^d parameters of the model. By trying out several kind of levels of the α^d the user changes the interpolating function, until it coincides with his knowledge of the given soillayer at hand.

As a conclusion we notice that in the given problem the theoretical model was not strong enough to solve the problem alone. The knowledge of the soil expert was not enough either. But by integrating both it was possible to do the job. That is what DSS is all about!

References

Bochner, S. (1935). Monotone Funktionen Stieltjesche Integrale und Harmonische Analyse, *Mathematische Annalen*, 108.

Boender, C. G. E., Rinnooy Kan, A. H. G. and Vellekoop, A. H. (1988). A Random Field Model for Estimating the Context of Soillayers, Applied Mathematics Letters.

Cramér, H. and Leadbetter, M. R. (1967). Stationary and Related Stochastic Processes, Wiley, New York.

Kolmogorov, A. N. (1933). Grundbegriffe der Wahrscheinlichkeitsrechnung, *Erg. Mat.*, 2.

Part 3a

Applications of Decision Support Systems

Real-Life Applications of Multiple Criteria Decision Making Technology

B. Danev*, I. Popchev**, G. Slavov*

* *Bulgarian Industrial Association, 134 Rakovski Str., 1000 Sofia, Bulgaria*

** *Institute of Industrial Cybernetics & Robotics, BAS, 1113 Sofia, Bulgaria*

1 Introduction

If we ask the scientists and the decision makers what they consider a Decision support system to be, we shall receive two not quite identical answers.

The Decision Support Systems (DSS), though quite widely developed in contemporary research, are not so widely used to resolve current problems in business or other spheres of the social practice. Without attempting to give a comprehensive explanation, we would summarize some views popular among the decision makers, concerning these phenomena, as follows:

First. Most decision problems are related to ill-defined, fuzzy or weak-structured tasks. They possess specific characteristic features and cannot be developed immediately, in "decision making urgency" frames, by computer assistance.

Second. Decision makers (DM) are not well acquainted with the achievements of decision theory, structural identification, optimization problems, game theory, interactive methodology, etc., or with the mechanisms of their implementations either.

Third. There is no good linkage between decision makers and DSS's and the end users usually find it difficult to exploit in crossfertilizing way the computers' advantages at fast, iterative, reversible, complex computation and the strongest point of human beings: heuristic thinking.

There is a great variety of DSS's classifications: (Sawaragi, 1986; Naisbitt, 1982; Van Hee, 1986; Lewandowski et al., 1986). We shall follow the most practical (Sawaragi, 1986) classification, according to which DSS could be divided into two main groups: mathematical modelling and multiple criteria decision making systems.

The application of the mathematical modelling systems is limited due to no less than two of the above mentioned reasons.

We would like to argue that multiple criteria decision making (MCDM) systems at the contemporary "evolutionary" stage of decision support system development are closer to real-life decision problems. Usually decision makers try to select a decision alternative corresponding to their requirements, i.e. the multiple criteria task naturally emerges due to the multiplicity of the decision maker's requirements.

The topic of the paper is real-life applications of MCDM technique in the Bulgarian economy practice.

What is to be considered "a real-life application"? We assume that real-life applications are the applications, that will have a measurable economic or social impact.

We would like also to stress that all further "well sounding" remarks are considerations rather than conclusions or recommendations and they are closer to the decision maker's experience than to pure academic knowledge.

2 Decision making technology and directions of application

The implemented Decision Making Technology, based on the MCDM technique was described in (Popchev et al., 1985; Danev et al., 1986; Popchev and Danev, 1987). The Technology comprises several stages performed interactively and incorporates several basic modules of different information origin. Some of them are independent computational procedures or open information processes, others are man-machine or expert procedures. This Technology could be easily adapted to the specific features of a definite task.

The technology kern module is DSS "MULCRE" (Popchev et al., 1985) or Interactive DSS (IDSS) "microMULCRE" (Danev et al., 1986)[1]. The purpose of these DSS is multicriteria comparative evaluation and/or multicriteria choice between/from a finite set of feasible elements (objects, alternatives).

In the current versions, the available multicriteria evaluation methods can be divided into three groups:

(i) Alternatives (objects) ranking according to the calculated estimation: simple additive weighing, hierarchical additive weighing, maximin.

(ii) Obtaining a subset of alternatives (objects): conjunctive method, nondominated set (Pareto), subset of a nondominated set (Hannan; Berezovski and Kempner).

(iii) Obtaining a subset and further ranking of this subset: reference point method.

Some of the real-life applications, by means of the DSS "MULCRE" and the IDSS "microMULCRE", in the last five years are listed in Table 1.

[1]IDSS "microMULCRE" is developed under contract with International Institute of Applied System Analysis

Table 1: Real-life applications

Year	No.	Project	No. of alter-natives	No. of cha-ract.	No. of crite-ria
1	2	3	4	5	6
1983	1.	Nation-wide competition between proposal for the establishment of small and medium scale enterprises (SME) for the production of consumer goods (Decree 12 of 1980 of the Council of Ministers).	370	23	12
	2.	Evaluation of the product structure of enterprises within the Ministry of Light Industry	302	54	54
	3.	Analysis of the efficiency and the long-term prospects of export commodities	20	147	48
1984	4.	Nation-wide competition between proposals for rendering credits for fulfillment of counter-plans	998	62	14
	5.	Nation-wide competition between proposals for establishment of SME (Decree 33 of 1984 of the Council of Ministers).	563	100	21
	6.	Nation-wide competition between proposals for rendering of credits to the economic partnerships	117	25	14
	7.	Competition, organized by the State Committee for Science and Technology, between enquires for the purchase of licenses	10	7	7
	8.	Competition, organized by the State Committee for Science and Technology between enquires for the purchase and production of pilot equipment	39	10	10
	9.	Analysis of the efficiency of the branches of Bulgarian economy	103	9	8
	10.	Competition between enquires for participation in the Program for automation of the continuous technological processes in Bulgaria	36	24	24

1	2	3	4	5	6
	11.	Nation-wide competition between proposals for the establishment of SME (Decree 33 of 1984 of the Council of Ministers)	194	100	21
	12.	Nation-wide competition between enquires for investments in execution of Decree 6 of 1985 of the Council of Ministers	90	100	21
1985	13.	Competition for investment credit allocation for projects, included in the economic enterprises counter-plans	196	25	14
	14.	Competition for distribution of investment credits for the establishment of SME for the production of new materials	19	24	12
	15.	Choice of optional decision for automated utility control system	7	48	12
1986	16.	Nation-wide competition between proposals for the establishment of SME (Decree 33 of 1984 of the Council of Ministers)	237	100	21
	17.	Analysis of the efficiency of chemical export commodities	72	70	27
	18.	Nation-wide competition for state financing of research projects	863	47	27
1987	19.	Nation-wide procedure for determining non-efficient enterprises	2000	24	16
	20.	Nation-wide competition between proposals for the establishment of SME (Decree 33 of 1984 of the Council of Ministers)	72	100	21

The titles are a direct translation from Bulgarian and follow the formal documents, some of them are state decrees or special regulations.

The main directions of the reported real-life applications are shown on the Fig. 1.

From theoretical point of view, some of the directions overlap, but we adopt a decision maker's understanding. Decision makers usually identify the problems with formal technique and final results.

The reported applications are mainly in the business sphere — (BIA, 1983; BIA, 1984; BIA, 1985; BIA, 1986).

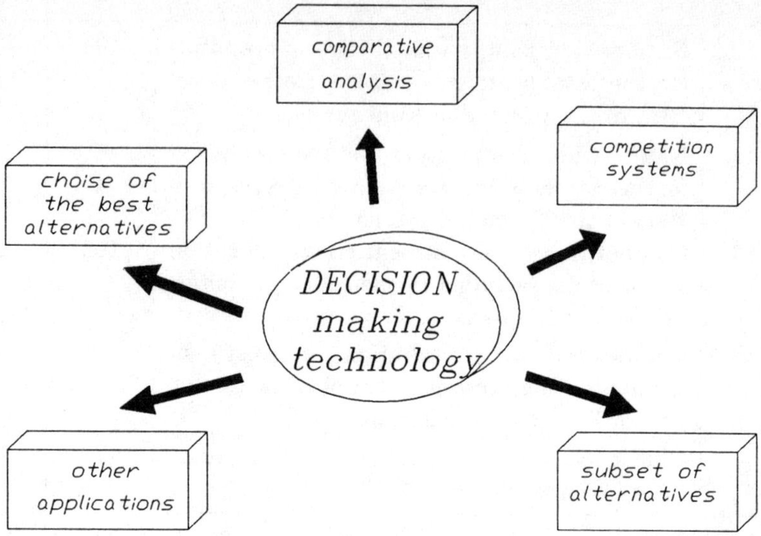

Figure 1: Directions of applications

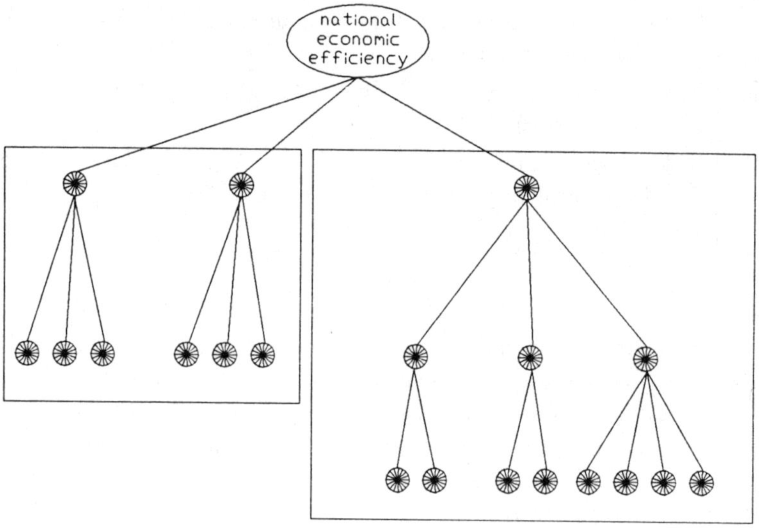

Figure 2

3 Comparative analysis

In this line of applications two main types of tasks are solved — direct and reverse ones. Those of the first type are tasks for multicriteria evaluation of elements of a finite set. Partial criteria are numerical functions. Various normative methods realized in IDSS "microMULCRE" are used. Such tasks are solved in applications 2, 3, 9, 17 of the given Table. They cover evaluation of the product structure, export commodities, the national economy branches, etc. The tasks of the second type are in a sense opposite to the ones of the first type. The main problem is the following. On the basis of multicriteria evaluation, possibilities for suitable changes in the characteristics of alternatives are searched in order to improve their positions in the subsequent ranking. Some mathematical tasks that are to be solved in this case are described in (Danev, 1986). Application 9 of Table 1 is an example of solving tasks of this type. 96 branches of the national economy have been analyzed. Here, for the purpose of illustration, is given the data for the aggregated task for 18 branches. The complete tree of partial criteria is shown in fig. 2. The following two figures 2.a and 2.b are the corresponding windows from fig. 2 and the particular criteria are indicated in them.

Most of the formal criteria are quantitative and account for the direct as well as indirect results of the particular branches in accordance with the established economy structure and the concrete interfield relations. The ranking according to the global evaluation of the 18 branches is given in Table 2.

Alternatives	Ranking	
BIA		
UTILITY INDUSTRY	7.07	1
FORESTRY	6.78	2
OTHER SECTORS OF PRODUCTION	5.97	3
MACH.BLDG., EL. & ELECTRONIC IND.	5.89	4
CHEMICAL & RUBBER IND.	5.76	5
LEATHER & SHOE INDUSTRY	5.60	6
COMMUNICATIONS	5.49	7
FERROUS METALLURGY, MINING	5.38	8
PLANT GROWING	5.18	9
TEXTILE & KNITWEAR INDUSTRY	5.15	10
TAILORING INDUSTRY	5.13	11
TRADE & DISTRIBUTION	5.09	12
TRANSPORT	5.04	13
POWER GENERATION	4.87	14
PRINTING & PUBLISHING	4.86	15
WOOD PROCESSING	4.72	16
GLASS & CHINA INDUSTRY	4.67	17
LIVESTOCK BREEDING	4.60	18

Table 2

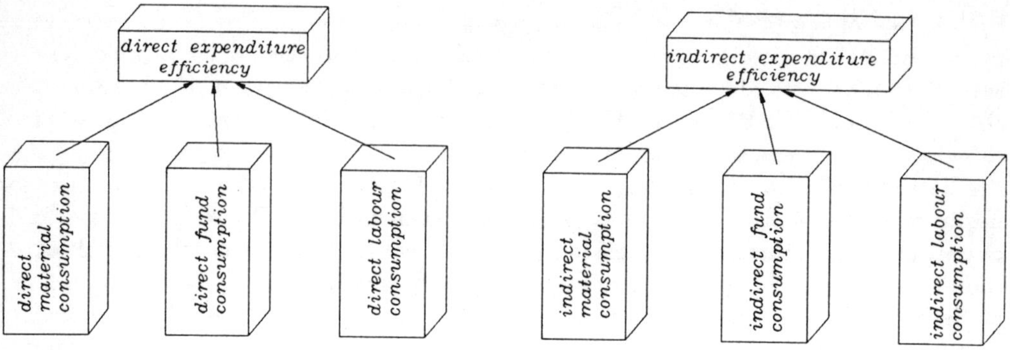

Figure 2.a

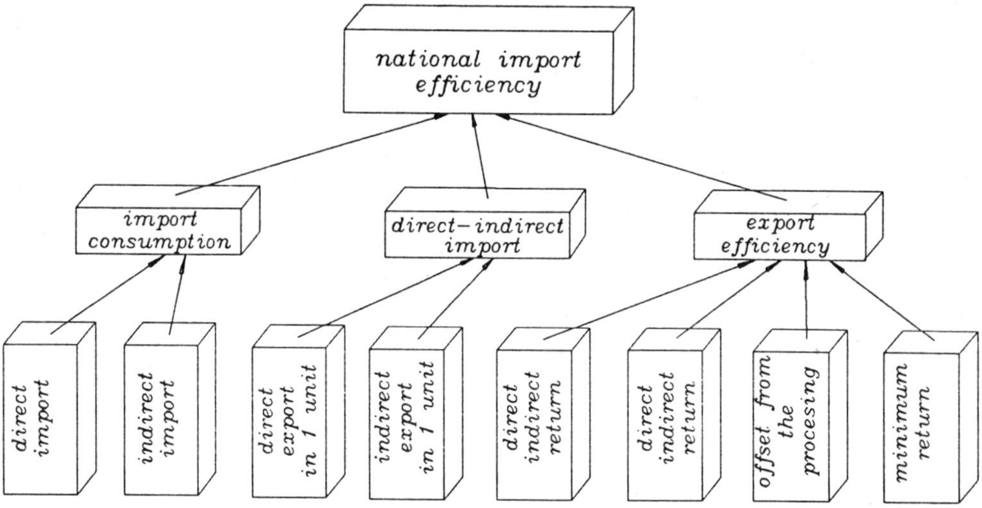

Figure 2.b

Two of them (plant growing and livestock breeding) are compared according to all 14 criteria (fig. 3).

The partial criteria are normalized, which means that they must be maximized. On the basis of these results the DM could take an appropriate decision in order to improve the performance in both branches.

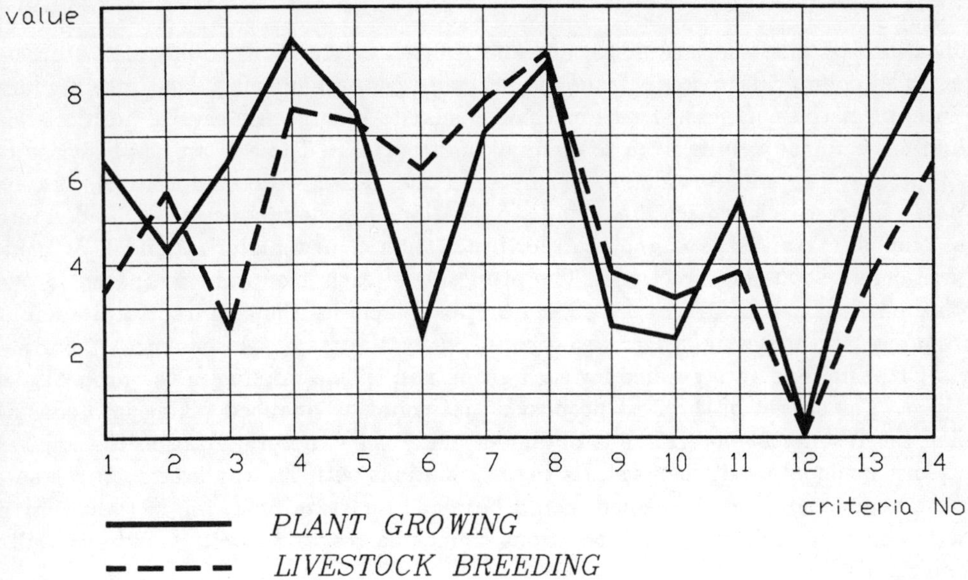

Figure 3

4 Choice of the best alternatives

The essence of this set of applications is the necessity of choosing (only) one alternative. The concrete problems to be solved are quite often unique and a second solution of the problem is not provided. Application 15 of Table 1 is of such a type. 7 alternatives with 46 characteristics have been considered and 12 formal criteria have been used. A combination of normative methods has been used — first finding out nondominated elements and second choosing one of them on the basis of simple additive weighing.

5 Subset of alternatives

The applications of this type are numerous (1, 4, 5, 6, 7, 8, 11, 12, 13, 14, 16, 20 of Table 1). The tasks of this type are regular in economy practice and that is why such tasks are quite frequently solved in certain spheres. For example, the resource allocation competitions for establishment of small and medium-scale enterprises are annually announced and performed. Financial resources are allocated in nearly all applications of this type. For nation-wide competitions, the rules are regulated by state normative documents. The formal procedures include a particular sequence of normative methods. With that approach the results of one method are used as initial data for the following one. The results from the application of these procedures is a solid basis for the real final decision.

6 Competition systems

Applications of this type are quite new and are related to more sophisticated procedures. The complication stems from the necessity of mechanisms taking into account the interest of the partners. These mechanisms could incorporate several multicriteria evaluations and the results from the gaming approach. In Table 1 two applications of this type (18, 19) are shown. For example, in the nation-wide competition between proposals for research projects financing (application 18), the proposals are divided into three groups: state tasks, technologies for production of new materials and R & D investigations in strategic directions. The proposals of each group are compared to one another on the basis of 27 criteria. Each proposal includes the required total amount of resources and a part of them being supplied by the state. A sequence of normative MCDM methods are applied for each group and thus a ranking of the proposals is obtained. The subset of the best proposals that could be financed taking into consideration the resources constraints is obtained. Only then the organization that makes the resource allocation decisions starts the negotiations with the applicants. As a result of these negotiations, an agreement could be made for state financing of the winning projects. In this agreement the conditions cannot correspond exactly to the initially announced data.

A rather more complicated procedure is used in application 20 for determining the nonefficient small enterprises. Based on the evaluation of all enterprises (not only small ones) in a definite sector, a hypothetical enterprise is formed. The aim is to separate a subset of enterprises which have a global estimation lower than the hypothetical enterprise global estimation. The small enterprises which are a part of the defined subset are determined as nonefficient. The procedure continues with new competitions for renovation, restructuring or reorganization of each enterprise, determined as nonefficient. The results of these competitions is a selection of the best proposals, i.e. the described methods and means of the second direction of applications are used.

The financial resources allocated by means of the above technology during the last 5 years are shown in fig. 4.

A general tendency towards increasing this amount can be noticed. The sharp rise in 1987 can be explained by the fact that in one of the competitions the resources for the five-year-period have been allocated.

7 Conclusion

As a conclusion we can say that the application of DSS in solving real-life problems of human activity, is a task of no less importance than creating the systems themselves. Decision makers usually want to change the technology or some other characteristic features of the system so that it would "correspond to their own personality".

Out of experience it can point out that the confidence and certainty in the DSS real potentiality increase considerably after each successful real life application.

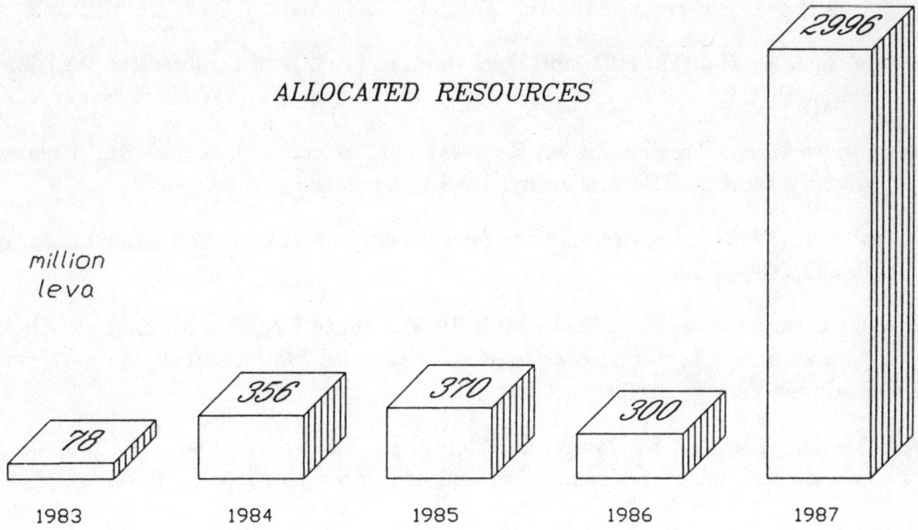

Figure 4

References

Bulgarian Industrial Association (1983). Annual Report of the Economic Research Center and the Center for Industrial Development, Sofia, (In Bulgarian).

Bulgarian Industrial Association (1984). Annual Report of the Economic Research Center and the Center for Industrial Development, Sofia, (In Bulgarian).

Bulgarian Industrial Association (1985). Annual Report of the Economic Research Center and the Center for Industrial Development, Sofia, (In Bulgarian).

Bulgarian Industrial Association (1986). Annual Report of the Economic Research Center and the Center for Industrial Development, Sofia, (In Bulgarian).

Danev, B., Slavov, G. and Metev, B. (1986). Multicriteria Comparative Analysis of Discrete Alternatives. In: Toward Interactive & Intelligent DSS (Proceedings...), Kyoto, Japan. *Lecture Notes in Economics and Mathematical Systems*, vol. 273, Springer-Verlag, Berlin.

Danev, B., Slavov, G. and Boshnakov, G. (1987). Interactive Decision Support System "microMULCRE". In: Methodology and Software for Decision Support System (Proceedings...), Albena, Bulgaria. *Lecture Notes in Economics and Mathematical Systems*, in this vol., Springer-Verlag, Berlin.

Georgiev, R. and Danev, B. (1986). Multicriteria Evaluation of Technological Interrelations between Industrial and Agricultural Sectors of the Bulgarian Economy. 7-th World Congress of the Int. Economic Association, New Delhi, India.

Goicoechea, A., Hansen, D.R. and Duckstein, L. (1982). Multiobjective Decision Analysis with Engineering and Business Applications. John Wiley & Sons, N.Y.

Lewandowski, A., Kreglewski, T., Rogowski, T., Wierzbicki, A. (1986). Decision Support Systems of DIDAS Family. IIASA, Laxenburg, Austria.

Naisbitt, J. (1982). Megatrends: Ten New Directions Transforming our Lives. Warner Books, New York.

Hwang, C. and Yoon, K. (1981). Multiple Attribute Decision Making. Methods and Applications. *Lecture Notes in Economics and Mathematical Systems*, vol. 186, Springer-Verlag, Berlin.

Popchev, I., Guevsky, I., Danev, B., Metev, B., Slavov, G., Ionov, K. (1985). Multicriteria technology for evaluation and decision making, BIA, Sofia.

Popchev, I. and Danev, B. (1987). Competition systems and innovations. Joint BAS–NAS seminar: "New Technology and Society", Washington D.C., USA.

Rietveld, P. (1980). Multiple Objective Decision Methods and Regional Planning, North Holland Publ. Comp., Amsterdam.

Roy, B. and Vincke, Ph. (1981). Multicriteria Analysis: Survey and New Directions, *Eur. J. of Oper. Res.*, No. 8, pp. 207–218.

Sawaragi, Y. (1986). Towards Interactive and Intelligent Decision Support Systems. In: Toward Interactive & Intelligent DSS (Proceedings...), Kyoto, Japan. *Lecture Notes in Economics and Mathematical Systems*, vol. 273, Springer-Verlag, Berlin.

Van Hee, K. (1986). Operation Research and Artificial Intelligence Approaches to Decision Support Systems. International Seminar: New Advances in Decision Support Systems, IIASA, Laxenburg, Austria.

Wierzbicki, A.P. (1980). The Use of Reference Objectives in Multiobjective Optimization. In: G. Fandel and T. Gal, eds., Multiple Criteria Decision Making — Theory and Application, (Proceedings), *Lecture Notes in Economics and Mathematical Systems*, vol. 177, pp. 468–486, Springer-Verlag, Berlin.

A Decision Model for Bank Asset Liability Management via MCDM

Dieter Langen
Institute for Statistics and Mathematical Economics
University of Karlsruhe, Kollegium am Schloß
Bau III. D–7500 Karlsruhe 1, FRG

1 Motivation and problem description

In the last years the banking business has become more and more complex. New financial instruments, substantial risks connected with all kinds of banking business, volatile interest rates, market-oriented private and corporate customers and the internationalization and globalization of the national business systems have resulted in the biggest challenge to banks since the great depression in 1929. The need for overall strategic (asset liability (A/L)) management has become very obvious while the bank managers still have to deal with partial approaches leading to suboptimal overall solutions and strategies and often just act as "firefighters".

The idea of our model was to create and build a model and decision support system which is able to comprise and to consider the most important quantifiable bank objectives and provide the user(s) with one (or several) solution(s) as a basis for further decision making. Since you deal with future and thereby uncertain events there is never anything like "the" best solution but only "a" best solution for the predicted future scenario, the chosen parameters and the set and importance of the chosen objectives. Therefore the system has to be interactive to be able to react easily on all required problem changes but besides having the necessary freedom to formulate his own specific model the DM should be restricted to an overall (sub-) model environment.

2 The model

There have been numerous publications on financial modelling in the past (for good overviews see Cohen, 1980; Santomero, 1984 and Schmidt, 1983) and some even dealt with bank A/L-management but almost all of them just concentrated on partial banking problems. Little academic work has been done so far for a global reconciliation and even the existence of efficient solution algorithms for overall bank planning optimization models which can adequately handle the problems mentioned has been recently denied (Schmidt, 1983, p. 312). Therefore we tried to consider all major quantifiable banking problems and objectives in an integrated approach which has to be solved by a suitable (combination of) optimization algorithm(s).

The main model assumptions are the following: The bank is a (German) universal bank operating nationally and internationally in its home currency (HC, e.g. Deutsch Mark). It pursues several, conflicting objectives and faces legal (e.g. banking laws) and other constraints. The different A/L-positions are homogeneous among each other with respect to all model and scenario parameters. Considering uncertainty of future events and developments we assume that the bank can estimate scenarios of future outcomes of the uncertain parameters and the associated probabilities. Any bonds in the bank's portfolio are not sold before the end of maturity.

As decision variables we take the (new) A/L-positions of business to be started in the next planning period (index "new") but we also have to consider (old) A/L-positions of business started in the past (index "old") which cannot be changed anymore.

Gain. Our first objective is the **maximization of the bank's gain or returns.** We basically define gain as net return of the interest business since it is almost impossible to connect any costs other than refinancing costs with a certain A/L-position and since the (negligible) yield from commissions is not sufficiently influentable. Formally:

$$f_1 \; : \; \Re_+^{n+m} \rightarrow \Re, \quad \text{continuous} \tag{1}$$

$$\begin{aligned} f_1(\underline{x}^{\text{new}}, \underline{y}^{\text{new}}) \; := & \; \sum_{i=1}^{n} rx_i^{\text{new}} \cdot x_i^{\text{new}} + rx_i^{\text{old}} \cdot \bar{x}_i^{\text{old}} \cdot (1 - a_{1,i}^{\text{old}}) \\ & - \sum_{j=1}^{m} ry_j^{\text{new}} \cdot y_j^{\text{new}} + ry_j^{\text{old}} \cdot \bar{y}_j^{\text{old}} \cdot (1 - b_{1,j}^{\text{old}}) \rightarrow \max \end{aligned}$$

The gain is defined as the difference of the sum of the effective net interest earned and the one paid for by the bank. x_i/y_j denote A/L-positions, rx_i/ry_j the effective net interest rates of x_i/y_j and $a_{1,i}^{\text{old}}/b_{1,j}^{\text{old}}$ the percentage of $\bar{x}_i^{\text{old}}/\bar{y}_j^{\text{old}}$ (constant) that matures in the first planning period. Therefore our objective is to maximize the average annual interest income by the bank.

Effective net interest rates are uncertain and in order to consider the different criteria of the A/L-positions correctly they comprise effective interest rates (e_{rx_i}/e_{ry_j}), effective credit loss rates (xcr_i) and currency factors (FC_{rx_i}, FC_{ry_j}):

$$rx_i = e_{rx_i} - xcr_i +/- FC_{rx_i}; \quad ry_j = e_{ry_j} +/- FC_{ry_j}. \tag{2}$$

For fixed interest rate A/L–positions e_{rx_i}/e_{ry_j} are constant and for HC–business FC_{rx_i}/FC_{ry_j} are 0 (if one does not consider credit losses and/or FC-changes one compares the A/L-position on a wrong basis).

Balance volume. As a second objective we take the **maximization of the bank's balance** (or business) **volume** which by various reasons (e.g. an indicator for market power, customer popularity, management performance and ability to place corporate bonds) is important for the bank's standing. Formally:

$$f_2^1 \; : \; \Re_+^n \rightarrow \Re_+, \quad \text{cont.}; \qquad f_2^2 \; : \; \Re_+^m \rightarrow \Re_+, \quad \text{cont.};$$

$$f_2^1(\underline{x}^{\text{new}}) := \sum_{i=1}^{n} x_i^{\text{new}} + \bar{x}_i^{\text{old}} \cdot (1 - a_{1,i}^{\text{old}}) \rightarrow \max \tag{3}$$

or

$$f_2^2(\underline{y}^{\text{new}}) := \sum_{j=1}^{m} y_j^{\text{new}} + \bar{y}_j^{\text{old}} \cdot (1 - b_{1,j}^{\text{old}}) \rightarrow \max \tag{4}$$

The bank business volume function can be formulated in almost the same way including also off-balance sheet positions.

Credit risk. The third objective is the **minimization of credit losses.** Although already considered with respect to the gain objective this is not enough. Besides (nat'l and int'l) credit risks our bank faces country risk and regularly has to take risk precautions for defaulted credits which for various reasons (e.g. possible bankruptcy of the bank or cancellation of dividends, public standing) have to be kept as small as possible in order to avoid negative consequences (e.g. customer money withdrawals, higher refinancing interest rates, drop of the bank's stock price, lower credit and stock ratings, etc.). Formally:

$$f_3 : \Re_+^n \rightarrow \Re_+, \quad \text{cont.}; \tag{5}$$

$$f_3(\underline{x}^{\text{new}}) := \sum_{i=1}^{n} xcr_i^{\text{new}} \cdot x_i^{\text{new}} + xcr_i^{\text{old}} \cdot \bar{x}_i^{\text{old}} \cdot (1 - a_{1,i}^{\text{old}}) \rightarrow \min$$

A similar objective function could be formulated for off-balance sheet positions, especially important for new financial instruments. The objective also considers when credit loss assessments of old credits change due to unforeseen events or developments.

Interest rate risk. As a fourth major objective we consider the **minimization of interest rate risk.** A great deal of banking profits usually result from structural disparities (short- vs. long-term) between asset and liability positions. The banks which let those disparities get out of hand can suffer huge losses when the interest rates in connection with different maturity dates of A/L-positions increase or decrease rapidly or even change their structure (normal to inverse or vice versa). Structural imbalances are not wrong by definition since there are also interest rate chances. While these as well as variable interest rate risk and "interest rate breath" are often neglected by other approaches (e.g. duration concepts) **we define interest rate risk** as a decrease of the interest revenues from one period to another due to interest rate changes which is basically a gap management approach. Formally:

<u>$t = 1$:</u>

$$f_{4,1} : \Re_+^{n+m} \rightarrow \Re, \qquad \text{cont.}; \tag{6}$$

$$\begin{aligned} f_{4,1}(\underline{x}^{\text{new}}, \underline{y}^{\text{new}}) \;:=\; & \Big(\sum_{i=1}^{n} a_{1,i}^{\text{old}} \cdot \bar{x}_i^{\text{old}} \cdot e_{r\bar{x}_i^{\text{old}}} - x_i^{\text{new}} \cdot e_{rx_i^{\text{new}}}\Big) \\ & - \Big(\sum_{j=1}^{m} b_{1,i}^{\text{old}} \cdot \bar{y}_j^{\text{old}} \cdot e_{r\bar{y}_j^{\text{old}}} - y_j^{\text{new}} \cdot e_{ry_j^{\text{new}}}\Big) \rightarrow \min \end{aligned}$$

$\underline{t > 2:}$ $$f_{4,t} : \Re_+^{n+m} \rightarrow \Re, \qquad \text{cont.}; \tag{7}$$

$$f_{4,t}(\underline{x}^{\text{new}}, \underline{y}^{\text{new}}) := \Big[\sum_{i=1}^{n} a_{t,i}^{\text{old}} \cdot \bar{x}_i^{\text{old}} \cdot (e_{\overline{rx}_i^{\text{old}}} - e_{rx_i{}^t}) + a_{t,i}^{\text{new}} \cdot x_i^{\text{new}} \cdot (e_{rx_i{}^{\text{new}}} - e_{rx_i{}^t})\Big]$$
$$- \Big[\sum_{j=1}^{m} b_{t,j}^{\text{old}} \cdot \bar{y}_j^{\text{old}} \cdot (e_{\overline{ry}_j^{\text{old}}} - e_{ry_j{}^t}) + b_{t,j}^{\text{new}} \cdot y_j^{\text{new}} \cdot (e_{ry_j{}^{\text{new}}} - e_{ry_j{}^t})\Big] \rightarrow \min$$

Hereby e_{rx_i}/e_{y_j} (constant for fixed-term A/L) denote the effective interest rates of old/new A/L-positions for period $t = 1$, i.e. the coming period, while $e_{rx_i{}^t}/e_{ry_j{}^t}$ stand for the effective interest rate of the respective A/L-position in period t.

The basic idea is that the maturing amounts of all A/L-positions have to be reinvested resp. refinanced for the same interest rates as before so that there exist no risks nor chances. A higher refinancing and/or a lower reinvestment interest rate mean decreasing interest returns and thereby risk while lower refinancing and/or higher reinvestment interest rates mean increasing interest returns and thereby chances. The sum of all risk/chance effects is the net interest rate risk (> 0) or chance (< 0) in a period.

Although we don't plan future A/L-positions beyond the next period we still take the effects of the decision variables on the future business into account thereby mitigating possible myopia. In order to avoid interest rate risk the bank has to close all positive gaps during the planning horizon T, e.g. minimizing the overall interest rate risk function for periods $t = 1, \dots, T$ measured as the maximum possible (discounted) risk (repricing gap) in one single period. Formally:

$$f_4 : \Re_+^{n+m} \rightarrow \Re, \quad \text{cont.}; \tag{8}$$

$$f_4(\underline{x}^{\text{new}}, \underline{y}^{\text{new}}) := \max\Big\{ f_{4,1}(\cdot,\cdot) \cdot (1+i)^{-t+1}, \dots, f_{4,T}(\cdot,\cdot) \cdot (1+i)^{-T+1} \Big\} \rightarrow \min$$

Options and futures are not considered in this stage of the model.

Other objectives. While in another version of the model we also considered the usage of foreign currency (FC) business which leads to currency or exchange rate risk **other quantitative objectives**, e.g. to keep certain balance sheet ratios, can easily be included (as objective or as constraint) but will not be discussed here. Qualitative bank objectives, e.g. enlarging the number of branches or the customer service, cannot be pursued in such a quantitative model.

Constraints. The **constraints** are basically legal (e.g. principles I–III of the German Banking Law ("KWG"), reserve requirements, etc.), policy or market (e.g. financial, accounting and management constraints, lower and upper growth limits through market forecasts) and model constraints (e.g. the balance equation).

3 Uncertainty and target risk

All objectives but f_2 contain uncertain parameters whose outcomes are known to the decision maker in form of scenarios given by the bank itself. To transform this stochastic into a deterministic problem you need an evaluation or decision method ("risk evaluation"). We evaluated five major concepts of risk measures (decision methods) with respect to their applicability for our model: expected utility (or utility dominance), stochastic dominance, probability dominance, three parameter (3-PRM) and bipolar risk measures (e.g. prospect ranking vectors (PRV)).

The first three ones are theoretically good risk measures but require such a lot of assumptions and/or additional data that they are practically unusable. For expected utility you need to specify a utility function which is almost impossible over multiple objective functions and decision variables and for stochastic and probability dominance you need to know all possible A/L-portfolio alternatives (totally unrealistic). Besides they are both basically a ranking measure.

Three parameter risk measures (Stone, 1973) with mean variance as the oldest approach consist of two objective functions:

i) usually the expected value function of the corresponding uncertain function (to be maximized or minimized);

ii) a function that considers the possible deviation from the expected value in i) or any other target value (target or estimation risk):

$$L(h, \alpha, \lambda) = \int_{-\infty}^{\lambda} | t - h |^{\alpha} \, dF(t).$$

By varying the triple (h, λ, α) you also get well-known moments like the variance $\big(\mu(F(t)), \infty, 2\big)$, the neg. semivariance $\big(\mu(F(t)), \mu(F(t)), 2\big)$, etc. H, λ and α determine the DM's attitude towards a target or reference level h (e.g. the expected value), the outcomes to be included (λ) and the relative importance of large versus small deviations (α, grade of risk aversion).

The **PRV-concept** (Colson, 1980) basically is nothing else than the 3-PRM but it is defined by the bipolar risk theory, i.e. instead of just one target risk measure it considers at least two: one for the negative deviations from EV (the actual risk or the 'risk pole' to be minimized) and one for the positive ones (possible chances, e.g. the pos. semi-variance, i.e. the 'speculative pole', to be maximized, see Colson, 1987).

From the practical point of view 3-PRM and PRV are the only suitable concepts for our problem.

The DM resp. the bank now has to decide in the model formulation step which one of the different model components, i.e. objectives and target risk measures, it would like to have simultaneously optimized. Thereby the chosen risk measure crucially depends on the bank's attitude towards risk (not necessarily pure risk aversion). A strongly risk averse bank e.g. may favor the 3-PRM approach with just one target risk measure and a higher α, less risk averse banks may choose the PRV approach with a positive and a negative target risk measure and reasonably low α's and a risk-neutral bank may just optimize the expected values.

4 Solution algorithm

We have the following general vector optimization or MCDM problem:

$$F : \Re^n \to \Re; \qquad F(\underline{x}) = \min\left(f_1(\underline{x}), \ldots, f_k(\underline{x})\right) \tag{9}$$

subject to:

$$\begin{array}{ll} g_i(\underline{x}) \leq 0 & \text{for } i = 1, \ldots, m; \\ h_j(\underline{x}) = 0 & \text{for } j = 1, \ldots, p; \\ x_l \leq b_l,\ x_l \geq a_l & \text{for } l = 1, \ldots, n; \\ \underline{x} \geq 0 & \underline{x} = (x_1, \ldots, x_n) \in \Re^n; \end{array}$$

whereby $\underline{x}$ is an n-dimensional decision variable vector and there are k objectives, m inequality, p equality and n box constraints. In order to get a solution resp. an efficient point of the MCDM-problem you can either set upper bounds to all but one objective and minimize the remaining one or you can create an overall objective (distance) function which includes all the obj. functions $f_k(\underline{x})$ and determines the efficient point by minimizing this function with respect to a chosen reference point (compromise solution). Since our problem is too complex to provide the complete set of efficient solutions the DSS is interactive, delivers one efficient point at a time and thereby gives the DM the possibility to gradually screen the solution space and finally to reach the efficient point which maximizes his unknown utility function.

The DSS is based on a testing version of the non-linear DIDAS-NL program (Lewandowski, 1985) but it contains several additional interactive features and program improvements. The basic decision method is the reference point method by Wierzbicki (1980, 1986). It works with the conjugate gradient method in connection with the shifted penalty algorithm for all constraints and gradient projection for linear constraints. The original MCDM-problem is reduced to a single (distance) objective problem using a scalarizing achievement function (SAF) for the different objectives (for an exact description of the method see Lewandowski, 1985).

In our problem one objective function (f_4) and some risk measures, e.g. the neg. semivariance $\left(\sum_k \max^2\left(0, E(t_k) - t_k\right) \cdot P(t_k)\right)$, are non-differentiable functions of the type $\min \max_i(f_i)$. Since the DSS only works with differentiable functions (or constraints) we transform the problem $F, f_i : \Re^n \to \Re$, $F(\underline{x}) := \max_i\left(f_i(\underline{x})\right) \to \min$ into $\bar{F}, f_i : \Re^{n+1} \to \Re$, $\bar{F}(\underline{x}, x_{n+1}) := x_{n+1} \to \min$ subject to $x_{n+1} \geq f_i(\underline{x})$ for $i = 1, \ldots, m$. This substitutional problem can be applied to all non-differentiable (convex or non-convex) objectives and constraints of the aforementioned type (e.g. see Psenicnyj, 1982).

5 Description and features of the decision support system IDSSBALM

At present **IDSSBALM** basically is a traditional decision support system (DSS) whereby a DSS is defined as an interactive, computerized system which uses dialogue, databases and (mostly mathematical) methods to help DMs with the recognition of problems and the preparation, choice and implementation of decisions, strategies and/or alternatives (e.g. Jarke, 1987).

Right now one can distinguish between two principle versions of IDSSBALM: the current (implemented) and a future (final) version. In the current one the user basically has to perform three tasks before working with the DSS:

i) collect the necessary data,
ii) make his choice of the possible model components, i.e. objectives, constraints, etc.,
iii) store the problem (raw) data in certain data files: the general problem specifications (e.g. number of objectives, (in)equality constraints, etc.) in SPECS.DAT, the spec. problem specifications (e.g. the linear coefficients, bounds, starting point, etc.) in MODEL.DAT and a (short) FORTRAN program containing the definition and the gradients of *all* objectives and *all* non-linear constraints (similar as in DIDAS-NL).

Nevertheless almost all problem description parameters can be interactively changed. In addition the user has the chance to conduct sensitivity analysis which is fairly easy for (lower or upper) bounds of decision variables, the right hand side of constraints and objectives and different objective setting whereby he can switch to a different set within MODEL.DAT (specifying a different BOU/RHS name) or the FORTRAN program (different problem number). For different scenarios however he still has to undergo the model building procedure from the beginning.

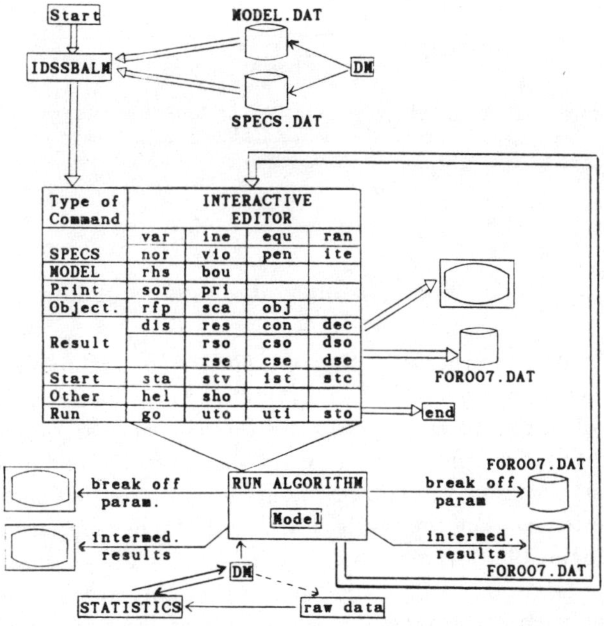

Figure 1: (Logical) Structure of IDSSBALM

The normal way to use the DSS is the following: the DM inputs raw data (e.g. the uncertain parameters) into STATISTICS and makes his choice(s) of objectives and constraints. Using the output of STATISTICS he then writes the FORTRAN program MODEL and specifies the two input files MODEL.DAT and SPECS.DAT.

Interacting with the program the DM has several types of command possibilities: SPECS and MODEL (change problem parameters or sets). PRINT (specify output media and the desire for intermediate results). OBJECT (change reference points or scaling factors), RESULT (display different kinds of results), START (manipulate starting points), OTHER (get help, show parameters) and RUN (compute solution or utopia points) commands.

The DSS does not (yet) contain a knowledge base. Our model which is a 'top down' approach for high level strategic planning (Dolk, 1986) and which can be split into several sub-models (for objectives and risk measures) is custom-built. The data still have to be collected externally but in an applied bank version the data collection process should be done internally whereby the central strategic planning unit could be freed from data research and could concentrate on model building and planning.

In a future version the model building step should be integrated:

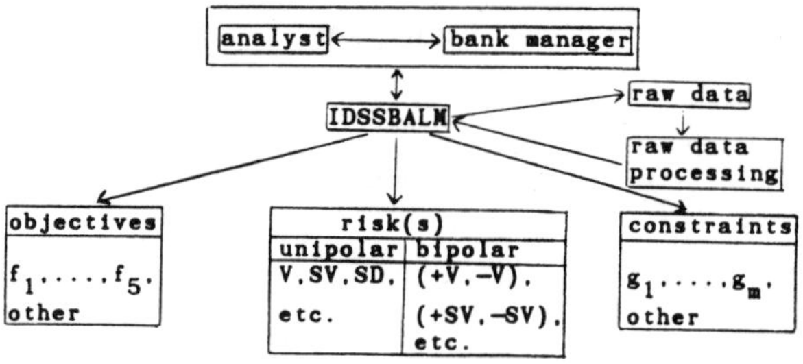

Figure 2: Integrated model building

After internal data processing the DM, either a financial analyst (interpreter, intermediary; trained in mathematical programming) or a bank manager, could specify his model and problem structure by quite flexibly choosing among the different submodel possibilities without writing a program (in the current version the analyst is definitely needed, at least to input the correct model formulation). Thereby the bank manager might be able to conduct the model building himself using automatic model building tools (Binbasioglu, 1986) to make a choice from the offered submodel possibilities. Since 'interactive' so far in our DSS 'only' means that the DM can make a decision on the selection of (efficient) alternatives based on his preferences and change problem specifications it might also be worthwhile to help the DM in his model building process, e.g. by asking him a catalogue of questions (e.g. about his grade of risk aversion) and letting the system develop the model, in a way of extended support.

The basic idea for the present interaction with IDSSBALM is that two types of users can work with it:

i) the sophisticated user (financial analyst) who knows the influence of the different parameters and wants to change them according to his needs,

ii) the merely practical bank-oriented user, i.e. the bank manager himself, who is able — after the problem has been specified respect. the model has been formulated — to get the different efficient alternatives by just varying the reference points.

The DSS is implemented on a VAX 8900 in FORTRAN. For problems of a small example size (3 objectives, 10 constraints, 23 variables) you need about 500–7.000 (on average 2.500) iterations to reach an efficient point depending on the chosen parameters and the starting point (average waiting time 3–6 sec.). For larger and more complex problems this time span can somewhat grow but it is still within an acceptable range.

IDSSBALM is different from DIDAS-NL in several aspects. At first it contains quite a few program changes, improvements and additional interactive command types, e.g. PRINT, RESULT, START, OTHER and a few options of the other types. Although the solver principally has not been changed IDSSBALM is more user-friendly and provides results in a more meaningful way (there is a new, improved DIDAS-NL PC-version (Kreglewski, 1987) but our model is too large to be run on a PC for a suitable problem size) although its comfort might still be improved (e.g. with a screen able to run in graphics mode).

In addition DIDAS-NL is a general non-linear MCDM DSS while IDSSBALM considering model and DSS is tailored to a special problem environment (due to space restrictions a data example of the model cannot be provided here).

6 Conclusion

IDSSBALM, principally still belonging to the family of DIDAS programs, is an (interactive) decision support system which is able to consider today's urgent bank planning problems and objectives and comprise them in a way which is attractable for an experienced and inexperienced (practical) user. The model contains several submodels which can be composed in a quite flexible manner. Taking care of uncertainty and letting the user apply his own approach and (intuitive) opinion about the major objectives, his attitude towards risk (which does not have to be consistent) and his (implicit) utility function within the model environment allows him to find his own best solution to the problem by specifying his preferences. Thereby IDSSBALM is a valuable decision aid.

References

Binbasioglu, M. and Jarke, M. (1986). Domain Specific DSS Tools for Knowledge-Based Model Building. *Decision Support Systems*, 2, pp. 213–223.

Cohen, K. J., Maier, S. and van der Weide, J. (1980). Recent Developments in Management Science. Vol. 22, No. 10 (Oct.), pp. 1097–1119.

Colson, G. (1987). The Biopolar Theory of Risk in Finance: A Tutorial. Paper presented at the 2. Meeting of the Euro Working Group on Financial Modelling, Paderborn, FRG, Nov. 19–20.

Colson, G. and Zeleny, M. (1980). Uncertain Prospects Ranking and Portfolio Analysis under the Conditions of Partial Information. Oelgeschläger, Gunn & Hain, Cambridge, MA., A. Hain.

Dolk, D. R. (1986). Data as Models: An Approach to Implementing Model Management. *Decision Support Systems*, 2, pp. 73–80.

Jarke, M. (1987). Kopplung qualitativer und quantitativer Theorien in der Entscheidungsunterstützung. Fakultät für Mathematik, und Informatik, Universität Passau, MIP–8716.

Kreglewski, T., Paczynski, J. and Wierzbicki, A. (1987). A Version of Nonlinear DIDAS for an IBM PC Computer. Lecture held at the IIASA Int. Workshop on Methodology and Software for Interactive Dec. Support in Albena, Bulgaria, Oct. 19–23.

Lewandowski, A., Kreglewski, T. and Rogowski, T. (1985). DIDAS-NL — A Nonlinear Version of DIDAS System. In: Lewandowski, A. and Wierzbicki, A. (eds.), Software, Theory and Testing Examples in Decision Support Systems, IIASA, pp. 128–141.

Psenicnyj, B. N. and Danilin, J. M. (1982). Numerische Methoden für Extremalwertaufgaben. Deutscher Verlag der Wissenschaften, Berlin.

Santomero, A. M. (1984). Modelling the Banking Firm — A Survey. *Journal of Money, Credit and Banking,* Vol. 16, No. 4 (Nov), part 2, pp. 576–602.

Schmidt, R. (1983). Neuere Entwicklungen der modellgestützten Gesamtplanung von Banken. *Zeitschrift für Betriebswirtschaft*, 53. Jg., Heft 3, pp. 304–318.

Stone, B. K. (1973). A General Class of Three-Parameter Risk Measures. *Journal of Finance* 28, pp. 675–685.

Wierzbicki, A. (1980). A Mathematical Basis for Satisficing Decision Making. IIASA WP–80–90.

Wierzbicki, A. (1986). On the Completeness and Constructiveness of Parametric Characterizations to Vector Optimization Problems. *OR Spektrum*, Vol. 8, No. 2, pp. 73–88.

Decision Support System for R&D Management Problems

Alexey B. Petrovsky
Institute for System Studies, USSR Academy of Sciences
Moscow, USSR

One of the major functions of bodies directing research activities is to define and pursue a *scientific and technological policy* which involves:

- multiaspect analysis of the current state-of-the-art and trends in science and technology development;
- formulation of a system of long-range and short-term goals facing science and technology, to meet the needs of society and development of science per se;
- selection and all-round evaluation of the research areas contributing to the accomplishment of the goals set, and determination of priority areas;
- analysis and estimation of scientific and technological potential, its consistency with the problems solved, determination of the required resources and their allocation to contributors;
- R&D coordination with regard to the cross-impact of different disciplines, their contribution to solution of scientific and practical problems;
- advancement of research activities, promotion of the formulated policy implementation;
- monitoring the scientific policy implementation, evaluation of progress in the goals accomplishment, exercising necessary adjustments.

Scientific and technological policy is represented in the form of advanced and current plans, programmes, projects, statements. Formulation and implementation of scientific and technological policy take form of decision making processes which provide for the accomplishment of all general and partial functions of organizational management.

Forecasting and planning R&D on the nationwide and sectoral levels belong to the so-called ill-structured problems of unique choice (Larichev et al., 1987). These problems have common features such as a comprehensive nature of alternatives difficult for assessment; presence of various aspects to be taken into account; nonrecurrence of the choice situation making it impossible to act "by analogy"; unsufficient determination of decision making sequences; necessity of using expert information and taking into account the preferences of decision makers.

Consideration and structurization of R&D forecasting and planning problems are connected with processing and analyzing various information on up-to-date situation and trends of science development. One of the promising approaches in management automation is design of *Decision Support Systems* which help decision makers to utilize data, objective and subjective models, knowledge for analyzing and solving ill-structured and unstructured problems (Sprague, 1980).

DSS MEDIAN was worked out by Petrovsky et al., (1984) for solving three types of R&D management tasks:

- recurring tasks with regular forms of input and output documents;
- inquiry tasks;
- analytical and investigational ill-structured tasks.

The main "objects of control" in problem-oriented organization of R&D are scientific programmes and comprehensive scientific problems covering large areas of science. Usually they have complex hierarchical structure and are divided into several problems, subproblems, directions, themes integrated by common purposes. Among tasks solved by DSS MEDIAN are:

- formulation of annual R&D plans;
- formulation of scientific programmes;
- multiattribute assessment of scientific problems;
- modelling an information structure of a comprehensive scientific problem, etc.

DSS MEDIAN information base consists of special documents which describe the planned and conducted R&D and include multiaspect information of accounting, topical and criterial nature. The main components of the system information base are a text-base, a data-base, a model-base and a rule-base. A text-base comprises R&D names and abstracts. A data-base consists of names of researchers and organizations dealing with R&D, dates of R&D beginning and end, sources of budgeting and other accounting data. A model-base includes information models of problem object fields, estimations of R&D "information values" and other models. A rule-base determines criteria for taking documents to problem field, compiling frequency dictionaries of terms, estimating the quality of DSS adjustment to problem object field, etc. An analogous approach to structurization of DSS information base was suggested by Bellew (1985).

The system is based on the following principles:

- dialogue interaction between the user and the system;
- ability to process formalized and nonformalizable (text) information;
- independence of routine software procedures on tasks solved;

- interactive mode of system adjustment to a concrete problem field.

Formulation of scientific programmes is connected with analyzing various information on R&D to be conducted in different institutions and organizations. A considerable part of such information is contained in R&D documents mentioned above. In order to develop a scientific programme it is necessary to search for and integrate a great number of R&D projects related to programme matter. DSS MEDIAN is to help a programme manager to structure his information needs, to quickly process a bulk of R&D documents, to obtain documents relevant to his needs (Petrovsky et al., 1986).

Above all DSS is adjusted to the programme object field. The DSS adjustment is a procedure of ordering general document file X by a degree of document correspondence with the programme in accordance with the programme manager's preferences. First, an arbitrary set of documents X is picked out from general file X. This "probe" file X_0 is considered as a fuzzy set $X_0 = \{x, \mu(x)\}$ containing elements (documents) x with different degrees of correspondence with the programme.

The degree of document correspondence with the programme $\mu_p(x)$ is determined by the programme manager or experts using ordered scale with the following verbal estimations:

A – R&D topic is completely corresponding to the programme,

R&D must be included in the programme;

B – R&D topics corresponds to the programme to a certain degree,

R&D can be used in the programme;

C – R&D topic is poorly corresponding to the programme,

R&D can probably be used in the programme;

D – R&D topic is not corresponding to the programme.

Values of membership function $\mu_p(x)$ are received by averaging expert assessments. Note that the suggested algorithms of non-structured information processing have a low sensitivity to concrete values of membership function $\mu_p(x)$.

According to the programme manager's preferences "probe" document file X_0 is divided in two fuzzy subsets. First file X_p consists of documents x "near" to programme field R_p interesting for the user. Second file X_q consists of documents x belonging to field R_q that is "far" from field R_q:

$$X_p = \{x, \mu_p(x)\} \qquad \mu_p(x) \geq \Theta_p > 0,$$
$$X_q = \{x, \mu_q(x)\} \qquad \mu_q(x) = 1 - \mu_p(x) \geq \Theta_q > 0.$$

Then documents from "probe" file X_0 are analyzed automatically using a special procedure of Problem-Oriented Sorting Text (POST). As a result frequency dictionaries of words or terms ("lexical units") are built for two fields R_p and R_q; values of "informativeness" of lexical units and their combinations are calculated; lexical units and their combinations the most informative for programme field R_p are determined.

By making use of the values of informativeness of lexical units and their combinations in texts of documents "information weights" of documents from general file X are calculated. An "information weight" of a document is determined by the quantity of informative lexical units in its text and characterizes a document's relevance to information needs of the user. According to their information weights all documents from general file X are ordered by degrees of their correspondence with the programme.

The quality of DSS adjustment to the programme object field is estimated by minimizing a distance between the expert and computer ordering. The final step of system adjustment is the construction of a binary matrix B (documents — lexical units) used on the stage of a programme analysis.

A dialogue procedure of analyzing problem-oriented file of R&D documents comprises several steps:

- formulation of an inquiry in natural language using words and their combinations;
- formalization of an inquiry using a dictionary of lexical units for the programme object field;
- processing a binary matrix B and an output of brief information on the relevant documents found;
- precising inquiry;
- processing general document file X and an output of document's texts and other factographical information.

It should be noted that an output of documents is executed from the ordered file. So documents having the highest degree of correspondence with the programme come first. The programme manager can abort an output when he/she receives a sufficient number of relevant documents. The described approach has been used for a formulation of the medical part of scientific programme on biotechnology. Using DSS MEDIAN the programme manager analysed large files of R&D documents and received the information on R&D and possible participants of the programme earlier unknown to him.

Modelling an information structure of a comprehensive scientific problem or a programme is aimed at investigating a typology of objects considered and representing essential information in a more compact and obvious form. The development of a comprehensive scientific problem or implementation of a programme is characterized by a continuous change of information connections between R&D directions, arising new approaches and priorities. DSS MEDIAN is to help managers to analyse a structure, intensity and dynamics of interactions between different components of the complex problem, to obtain useful information on the real distribution of efforts and their coordination.

The comprehensive problem G is considered as a set of several scientific problems $\{g_i\}$. Every problem g_i is a fuzzy set $g_i = \{x, \mu_i(x)\}$ containing elements (documents) x with different degrees of correspondence with problem g_i. The procedure of DSS adjustment to the problem object field is similar to the one discussed earlier. Experts estimate a degree of document correspondence $\mu_i(x)$ with problem g_i using an ordered scale analogous to the above scale. DSS information base adjusted to the problem field G is represented as a document file X ordered by the degree of document correspondence $\mu_G(x) = \max \mu_i(x)$.

A simulation of the problem information structure is based on approaches characteristic of structural methods for data processing. An information structure of comprehensive problem G is represented by a connected graph with nodes corresponding to problems g and arcs corresponding to information links between problems. The intensity of the information connection between two problems is estimated by an expression taking into account degrees of documents correspondence with problems and values of information links between documents relating to the problems considered. The value of information link between two documents depends on a number of lexical units (words, terms or descriptors) in their texts and is determined by the modified Tanimoto-Rodgers ratio.

For investigating the problem information structure dynamics in any time period the intensities of interconnections between different problems are calculated for each annual interval. Changes of information structure and values of link intensities are represented in table and graphic forms on display.

The analysis of dynamics of information interactions between scientific problems provided an opportunity for identifying groups of active (increasing intensity of links) and passive (decreasing intensity of links) problems inside the comprehensive scientific problem and also for determining a group of autonomous scientific problems poorly communicating with each other. Using DSS MEDIAN and the above approach the Scientific Board on medical radiology has worked out proposals on the correction of the problem management system and new organizational procedures on R&D planning and coordination.

References

Bellew, R. K. (1985). Evolutionary Decision Support Systems: An Architecture Based on Information Structure. In: Methlie, L. B. and Sprague, R. H. (eds.), Knowledge Representation for Decision Support Systems. North-Holland, Amsterdam.

Larichev, O. I., Petrovsky, A. B., Moshkovich, H. M. (1987). Methodological Approaches to the Assessment of Research and Development Activities. Proc. Int. Symp. Planning and Programming of Science and Technology Development, Moscow, March 1986. Institute for System Studies, Moscow.

Petrovsky, A. B., Sternin, M. Yu., Morgoev, V. K., Putintsev, A. N. (1984). Decision Support System for R&D Forecasting and Planning. Proc. All-Union. Conf. Theory, Methodology and Practice of System Studies. Section 10. Moscow, January 1985. Institute for System Studies, Moscow (in Russian).

Petrovsky, A. B., Putintsev, A. N., Sternin, M. Yu., Morgoev, V. K., Ostroumova L. M. (1986). Interactive Decision Support System for R&D Coordination Problems. In:

Emelyanov, S. V. and Larichev, O. I. (eds.), Systems and Methods of Decision-Making Support. Institute for System Studies, Moscow, (in Russian).

Sprague R. H. (1980). A Framework for Research on Decision Support Systems. In: Fick, G. and Sprague, R. H. (eds.), Decision Support Systems: Issues and Challenges. Pergamon Press, Oxford.

Multi-Objective Optimization in River Water Quality Management by Means of the DSS REH

P. Rathke, R. Straubel, A. Wittmüss
Academy of Sciences
Central Institute of Cybernetics and Information Processes
Berlin, GDR

A. Gnauck
Water Authority of Berlin
Institute of Water Management, Berlin, GDR

1 Introduction

The complexity and the variety of questions and problems on both water quality and quantity have increased to such an extent that planning frameworks and management policies must be fine tuned to resource availability. Thus, the decision making process has become exceedingly complex and will become more so in the future. Conceptually man has used always models to make decisions. Water quality management, even in its simplest state, is coupled with different processes which are influenced by a lot of uncertain variables, by high-dimensional disturbances and by restricted information structures. The economic consequences of management alternatives are difficult to predict correctly. The problems are further compounded because of the difficulties associated with satisfactory aggregation of social benefits and costs for different trade-offs.

Water quality models play a vital role both in the design of alternative waste abatement measures and in the evaluation of alternative sanitation programs. Pollution regulations are specified either in terms of river quality or in terms of effluent standards. In the first instance, given a set of river standards, there is a large number of combinations of treatment levels at specific discharge points which will meet the requirements. In the second case, the water authority responsible for setting the effluent standards must also recognize that the river has a limited assimilative capacity, and eventually adjusts effluent standards according to conditions in the river. In either case, a decision model is necessary in order to screen the array of possible courses of action.

2 River water quality simulation models

Most of the river water quality problems are generated by matter which is discharged into the river as a consequence of human activities. Many of these problems are related to the interactions between the discharged matter and river organisms. In river water quality modelling major emphasis is laid on eutrophication and self-purification (Straškraba and Gnauck, 1985). Therefore, water quality simulation models may be distinguished by the type of waste modeled (Biswas, 1981): models for biodegradable wastes and models for conservative non-degradable wastes.

Degradable waste concentrations can be described mathematically by considering the natural purification role of dissolved oxygen (DO) in water bodies. The DO concentration of a water body is a general measure of pollution in situations of non-toxic exposure. But there are many variables by which it can be directly or indirectly affected. Because a complex relationship exists between the biochemical oxygen demand (BOD) of the waste discharged and the DO concentration at points downstream of the discharge, this relationship has become one of the main indicators governing water quality management and control of water resources. DO-BOD models have become wide-spread in water quality modelling studies after the classical paper written by Streeter and Phelps (1925). The basic equations were modified by a number of scientists which have incorporated additional processes acting on DO (Gromiec, 1983). The model theory is based on the assumption that there are only two major processes take place: BOD and DO are being removed by bacterial oxidation of the organic matter, and DO is being replaced by atmospheric reaeration by gas absorption through the air-water interface. Deoxygenation and reaeration are considered as first-order reactions with constant reaction rates. Streeter-Phelps-models are used for various purposes relating to analyses of influencing parameters of water quality. The practical applicability and validity of such a model is delimited by the choice of its structure. Therefore, purpose and essential influence variables should be clearly defined and verified by measured data before computerized treatment of data collections is actually started.

The primary mechanisms for conservative non-degradable wastes are transport and dilution. The simulation models are appropriate for describing temporal and spatial changes of suspended solids with low settling rates, various dissolved organic chemicals, heavy metal ions, radioactivity, chlorides etc. Since dilution is the only means of reducing the concentration of non-degradable pollutants, the downstream concentration of these substances can readily be predicted if the flow pattern is specified.

3 The decision support system REH

The literature on optimization models for water quality management mainly deals with some form of cost minimization designed to meet river water quality and effluent standards. Then decisions are made by scenarios resulting from simulation models. Generally, real decisions are characterized by alternatives of action, by consideration of multiple goals, by selection of one element of the set of alternatives (the actual decision) and by individual weighting of one single goal related to the preference structure of the decision maker. The decision making process is then given by a choice of one objective allowable kind of action related to a subjective valuated compromise on partly satisfaction of conflicting goals (Pareto, 1896; Straubel and Wittmüss, 1983; Wittmüss, 1985). The individual weighting of the goal functionals often depends from their actually reachable values. In search of all possible alternatives for controlling a dynamic process or a dynamic system the use of computers will be very helpful.

In the most cases interactive computer programs are hierarchically structured. The decision support system REH developed by Straubel and Wittmüss (1986) is written in FORTRAN 77 language. It shows the following structure (table 1):

Program package level	Characterization/Remarks
Preparation level	General arrangements for computing, Input of external process model parameters, Input of parameters for optimization runs.
Learning level	Study of the time behaviour of the process model, Investigation of the influence of different control strategies on the process model time behaviour in dependence of changing external parameters and of the performance of the goal functionals, Learning how to choose a suitable control strategy by game theoretic methods.
Testing level	Realization check for reachability of control targets related to the goal functionals, Search for a special control strategy to reach given targets within a choosen time horizon, Computation of the individual optima of the goal functionals.
Optimization level	Computation of Pareto-optimal solutions by ranking the goal functionals, by relaxation method or by computation of the set of compromise points with decreasing apriori knowledge of the decision maker.

Table 1: Hierarchical structure of the DSS REH

The DSS REH works in an interactive dialogue form. No special requirements are necessary for the type of process equations and for the mathematical formulations of the goal functionals. Nonlinear process equations with time delay of any order, non-convex or non-concave goal functionals and also disconnected reaches of control variables are accepted for computation. Time-dependent restrictions of the control variables in form of lower and upper bounds and other implicit formulated restrictions between state and control variables are taken into account additionally.

4 Application of DSS REH to river water quality management

In opposite to the use of water quality simulation models only a few applications of decision support systems for solving water quality problems exist (Hahn and Cembrowicz, 1981; Cembrowicz, 1984; Krawczak and Mizukami, 1985; Kaden and Kreglewski, 1986). For a particular river basin a modified Streeter-Phelps-model was implemented in the DSS REH to get Pareto-optimal solutions for controlling waste water input from point sources and to get informations for extending sewage treatment plants in the river basin by limited budgets.

4.1 Characteristics of the river basin

A river basin in the hilly mountain region in the south of the German Democratic Republic was choosen as test area. Because only a one-dimensional model was used, segmentation was done in longitudinal direction by 11 segments only. Segmentation cuts are performed in such a way, that the ensuing segments represent river stretches with close to homogeneous characteristics (figure 1). The global parameters describing DO-producing and DO-consuming reactions as well as pertinent hydraulic parameters (flow rate, flow velocity etc.) considered as constant for each segment. Segments are also determined by tributaries and essential waste water inputs.

Inputs of organic load are located at the beginning of a segment (if any), where a segment is considered as a continuous stirred tank reactor with complete mixing approximately. Water quality variables observed are given at the beginning and at the end of each segment. Then the output of the i-th segment will be the input of segment $(i+1)$.

Two hydrologic standard situations were taken into account for water quality management: mean flow conditions and mean low flow conditions. The optimization results presented in this text are valid for mean flow.

4.2 The DO-BOD simulation model SPROX

Following the notation given by Beck and Young (1976) some input parameters have to be known: discharge rates and cross-sectional areas (or flow velocities), total amounts of DO and BOD transported in the river or introduced into the river and parameters describing DO consumption and DO input segment-wise. For each segment a set of ordinary differential equations can be formulated as follows:

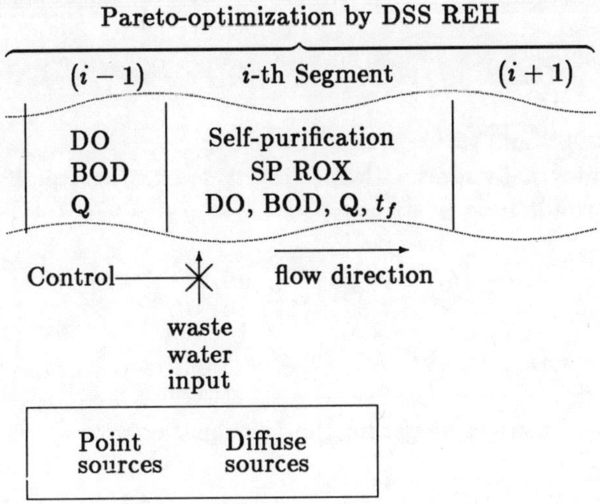

Figure 1: Schematic representation of the segmented river

DO – equation:

$$\begin{aligned} \dot{c}_1^{(i)} &= -\left(K_2(t) + A^{(i)}\right)c_1^{(i)} - K_1(t)c_2^{(i)} + A^{(i)}c_1^{(i-1)}\left(t - t_f^{(i)}\right) \\ &\quad + K_2(t)c_{1S}(t) + B_1^{(i)}u^{(i)}(t) \end{aligned} \tag{1}$$

BOD – equation:

$$\dot{c}_2^{(i)} = -\left(K_1(t) + A^{(i)}\right)c_2^{(i)} + A^{(i)}c_2^{(i-1)}\left(t - t_f^{(i)}\right) + B_2^{(i)}u^{(i)}(t) \tag{2}$$

where the dot notation is referred to the time derivation and c_1-DO concentration, c_2-BOD concentration, c_{1S}-(temperature-dependent) DO saturation concentration, K_1-BOD decay rate constant, K_2-reaeration rate constant for DO, $A^{(i)} = Q^{(i)}/V^{(i)}$ is constant for each segment with Q is the mean volumetric flow rate and V is the mean volume of a segment.

The DO saturation concentration within a segment is given by a third order polynomial equation (Thomann, 1972):

$$c_{1S}(t) = 14.65 - 0.41022 \cdot TW + 0.007991 \cdot TW^2 - 0.0000474 \cdot TW^3, \tag{3}$$

where the annual time course of water temperature TW is modelled as a sinusoidal function (Gnauck et al., 1987):

$$TW(t) = 13.16 + 10.23\cos(2\pi(t - 213)/365). \tag{4}$$

The coefficients B_j $(j = 1,2)$ are defined as follows: $B_j^{(i)} = \mathrm{QE}_{\max}^{(i)}/V^{(i)}c_{jE}^{(i)}$, with QE denotes the additional volumetric flow rate and c_{jE} denotes additional inputs of DO and BOD concentrations due to waste water and/or tributaries, respectively.

The solutions of the linear differential equations (1) and (2) can be formulated under the assumption of constant K_1- and K_2-values for each segment. For equ. (2) one gets

$$c_2(t) = e^{-A_1^{(i)}t} c_2^{(i)}(0) + \int_0^t \left(A^{(i)} c_2^{(i-1)}(t' - t_f^{(i)}) + B_2^{(i)} u^{(i)}(t')\right) * e^{-A_1^{(i)}(t-t')}\, dt', \quad (5)$$

with $A_1^{(i)} = K_1^{(i)} + A^{(i)}$ and $A_2^{(i)} = K_2^{(i)} + A^{(i)}$.

Replacing the integral by sums with fixed intervals Δt, then equ. (2) can be expressed by the following formula for any time step t_k:

$$c_2^{(i)}(t_k) = e^{-A_1^{(i)}t_k} c_2^{(i)}(0) + 1/A_1^{(i)} \left(\sum_{j=1}^{k} \left(A^{(i)} c_2^{(i-1)}(t_j - t_f^{(i)}) + B_2^{(i)} u^{(i)}(t_j)\right) * \left(e^{-A_1^{(i)}(t_k - t_j)} - e^{-A_1^{(i)}(t_k - t_{j-1})}\right)\right). \quad (6)$$

An analogous expression will be get for the DO equation.

4.3 Computation of the individual optima of the goal functionals

According to the choosen model structure the goal functionals for control of waste water input into the investigated river (model REHSPROX) were formulated by the following expressions:

$$\max_u \sum_i \sum_t \mathrm{DO}^{(i)}(t); \qquad \min_u \sum_i \sum_t \mathrm{BOD}^{(i)}(t); \qquad \max_u \sum_i \mathrm{QE}^{(i)}(t). \quad (7)$$

Solving the design problem for extension of sewage treatment plants (model SPROXEC) the third objective was replaced by $\min_u \sum_i \mathrm{costs}^{(i)}(t)$. The computation results of the individual optima are assorted in table 2.

Management task	Run No.	DO	BOD	Costs
Design of sewage	1	<u>10.4</u>	62.6	17.4
treatment plant	2	10.4	<u>62.6</u>	17.4
	3	5.9	169.0	<u>0.0</u>

Table 2: Coordinates of the individual optima

The coherence of the goal functionals related to the design problem can clearly be seen from figure 2. A minimum concentration of BOD in each segment can be reached by a maximum value for the costs.

In table 3 all computed Pareto-points for the investigated problems are given. Only five optimal points could be found by computer runs for the development of a control strategy of waste water input, while for the design problem a broader basis to make decisions is to be given.

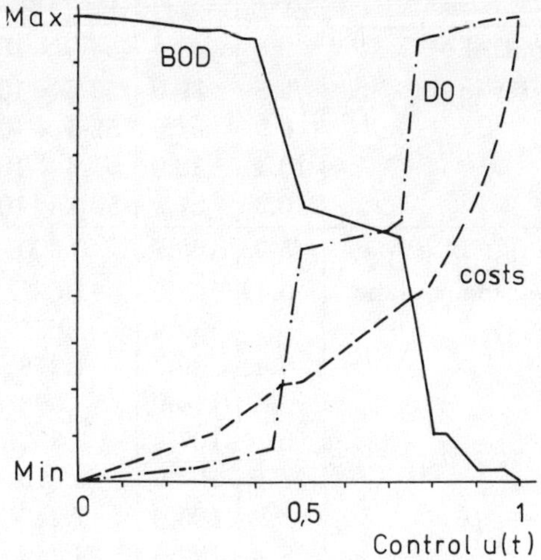

Figure 2: Schematic representation of the compromise strategy for solving design problems of sewage treatment plants in a river basin

An example of the optimization results is shown in figure 3. In the upper part the annual time behaviour of DO and in the lower part the annual time behaviour of BOD can be seen. The increase of BOD concentration in the third segment is caused by an high waste water input. While the DO curve shows an acceptable time behaviour, critical BOD values can be observed in the upper part of the river during summer and autumn.

5 Conclusions

The investigations of a river basin by water quality simulation models allow statements for single essential variables of water quality. The combination of a decision support system with a special process model gives a good chance to check our thinking on development of control strategies for environmental protection and how to formulate goal functionals in water quality management. This is not only a theoretical question more than a practical one.

References

Beck, B. and Young, P. (1976). Systematic Identification of DO-BOD Model Structure. *Journal of the Environmental Engineering Division*. Proc. ASCE, 102(EE5), pp. 909–927.

Task	DO	BOD	QE/Costs
Control of waste water input	9.6	43.4	54.9×10^6
	9.8	39.0	53.8×10^6
	9.9	34.6	52.4×10^6
	10.1	30.9	51.3×10^6
	10.3	27.9	50.1×10^6
Design of sewage treatment plant	5.9	168.7	0.000
	6.1	159.5	1.621
	6.3	139.9	2.657
	6.4	130.7	4.278
	6.6	110.9	5.098
	6.7	107.4	5.802
	7.1	104.9	6.170
	7.8	103.0	7.240
	8.7	102.0	8.450
	9.5	95.1	9.660
	9.8	85.8	11.280
	10.1	76.6	12.810
	10.3	69.6	15.200
	10.4	62.6	17.420

Table 3: Compromise sets of the investigated water quality management tasks

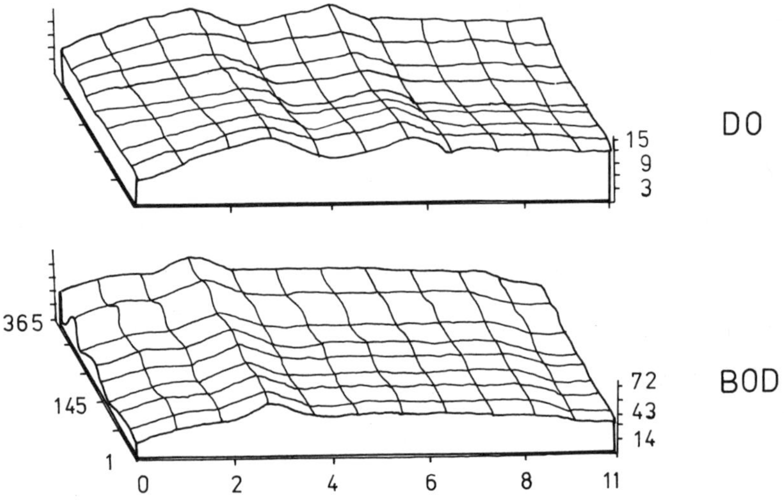

Figure 3: Optimization results for DO and BOD by DSS REH

Biswas, A.K. (Ed.) (1981). Models for Water Quality Management. McGraw-Hill, New York.

Cembrowicz, R.G. (1984). Bewirtschaftungspläne, Teil VIII: Entscheidungsmodelle in der Wassergütewirtschaft — ein Teilaspekt der Pilotstudie Bewirtschaftungsplan Leine. *Deutsch. Gewässerkundl. Mitt.* 28(5/6), pp. 146–158.

Gnauck, A.H., Winkler, W., Groth, K., Komoss, F. and Six, E. (1987). Modellierung und Simulation des Phytoplanktongehaltes in einem eutrophen Fliessgewässer. *Acta hydrochim. hydrobiol.* 15(2), pp. 149–159.

Gromiec, M.J. (1983). Biochemical Oxygen Demand — Dissolved Oxygen: River Models. In S.E. Jorgensen (Ed.), Application of Ecological Modelling in Environmental Management. Part A. Elsevier, Amsterdam.

Hahn, H.H. and Cembrowicz, R.G. (1981). Model of the Neckar River, Federal Republic of Germany. In A.K. Biswas (Ed.), Models for Water Quality Management. McGraw-Hill, New York.

Kaden, S. and Kreglewski, T. (1986). Decision Support System MINE: Problem Solver for Nonlinear Multi-Criteria Analysis. CP-86-05. International Institute for Applied Systems Analysis, Laxenburg, Austria.

Krawczak, M. and Mizukami, K. (1985). River Pollution Control as a Conflict. In K. Malanowski and K. Mizukami (Eds.), Constructive Aspects of Optimization. Polska Akad. Nauk, Instytut Badan System., Ser. Badan. Systemowe, Tom 6, Warsaw.

Pareto, V. (1896). Cours d'Economie Politique. Pouge, Lausanne.

Straskraba, M. and Gnauck, A. (1985). Freshwater Ecosystems. Modelling and Simulation. Elsevier, Amsterdam.

Straubel, R. and Wittmüss, A. (1983). Ein interaktives Entacheidungsmodell zur optimalen Steuerung eines Systems mit mehreren Zielfunktionen. *Messen-Steuern-Regeln* 26(1), pp. 2–4.

Straubel, R. and Wittmüss, A. (1986). Das Programmsystem REH zur rechnergestützten Entscheidungshilfe. *ZKI-Informationen* 2/86. Akademie der Wissenschaften, Berlin.

Streeter, H.W. and Phelps, B. (1925). A Study of the Pollution and Natural Purification of the Ohio River. *Publ. Health Bull.* 146, pp. 1–25.

Thomann, R.V. (1972). Systems Analysis and Water Quality Management. McGraw-Hill, New York.

Wittmüss, A. (1985). Scalarizing Multiobjective Optimization Problems and an Interactive Approach for Multiobjective Decision Making. In A. Sydow, M. Thoma and R. Vichnevetsky (Eds.), Systems Analysis and Simulation. Vol. I, Akademie-Verlag, Berlin.

Part 3b

Computer Implementation of Decision Support Systems

Interactive Decision Support System MICRO–MULCRE

B. Danev, G. Slavov, G. Boshnakov
Bulgarian Industrial Association
Sofia, Bulgaria

1 Purpose of the program

The purpose of IDSS MICRO–MULCRE is multicriteria comparative evaluation and/or multicriteria choice between/from a finite set of feasible elements (alternatives, objects).

2 Methodological and theoretical backgrounds

In the current version the available multicriteria evaluation methods can be divided into two groups:

1. Alternatives (objects) ranking according to the calculated estimation: simple additive weighting, maximin,

2. Obtaining a subset of alternatives (objects): conjunctive method, nondominated set (Pareto).

The methods could be used separately or in consecutive order given by the user.

3 Description of the implementation

The current version of the program is capable of solving problems with maximum of 50 columns and 50 rows. The interface is based on menu techniques. Language: TURBO PASCAL 3.01A. Operating system: MS DOS 3.10 or higher version.

4 Hardware requirements

IDSS MICRO–MULCRE operates on IBM–PC, XT, AT or compatible computers with 640 KB memory, 1 disk drive, color monitor and printer.

5 Availability of the program

The current version was developed in accordance with a contract (Ist stage) with the International Institute for Applied Systems Analysis, Laxenburg, Austria. IDSS MICRO-MULCRE is distributed by IIASA and Bulgarian Industrial Association, 134 Rakowski Str., 1000 Sofia, Bulgaria.

Software System STRUCTURE

Nikolai Dushkov, Ivan Stanchev
Sofia, Bulgaria

1 Purpose of the program

Software system STRUCTURE is designed to support decision makers in the construction of optimal structures of interrelations among the elements of a certain system which is subjected of a team of experts. The elements (objects) comprising the system under study can be of the following types:

- aims which the decision maker is aiming at,
- alternatives, choosen by the decision maker for achieving his goal(s),
- criteria for evaluation of the decision maker's activities,
- consequences resulting from the choice and applications of one or more alternatives.

2 Methodological and theoretical backgrounds

The objects that are obtained usually are linked by relation of dependence. A relation of dependence between two objects exists when the achievement of one brings about the increase or decrease of the degree of achievement of the other.

Apart from the sign (+ or −), the relation of dependence has one more feature called *power of dependence* which is the degree at which the existing of one object would increase (or decrease) the degree of existing the other.

Besides direct relation between objects, there are indirect relations comprising of more than one direct relation (chains of relations). When the power of such an indirect relation is measured, it can prove grater than the direct relation existing between them. Because of this the decision maker needs, in the process of constructing and analyzing the system, information about the significant powerful direct and indirect relations existing in each couple of objects, as well as about the maximum power of direct or indirect relation in each couple of objects.

3 Description of the implementation

In Software System STRUCTURE a mathematic apparatus is used with the help of which the relations of dependence are constructed on the basis of ordinal information about the power of relations of influence. It is typical of this case that the power of influences' evaluations are formulated with phrases in natural language, adequate to the terminology used by the decision maker and corresponding to the specifics of the problem under study. A spreadsheet technique is used when the evaluations are entered (and modified) and the results are displayed as the oriented weighted graphs the vertices of which correspond to elements of the system and the arcs represent the computed power and direction of maximal influences between the elements.

4 Hardware requirements

Software System STRUCTURE operates on IBM–PC, XT, AT or compatibles under the MD DOS version 3.0 and higher and requires 256K RAM, color graphic monitor and hard disk. If possible, a printer with graphic capabilities can be added.

5 Availability of the program

The program is property of IIASA. To obtain a further information, please contact N. Dushkov, RDL PROGRAMA, Acad. G. Bonchev Str., BL 8, Sofia, Bulgaria.

IOS — Interactive Optimization System

Emil Kelevedziev
Institute of Mathematics, Bulgarian Academy of Sciences
Sofia, Bulgaria

1 Purpose of the program

IOS is an interactive system which will support the decision maker in solving optimization problems. Such problems are common in areas as production planning, resource allocation etc. The main feature of the different classes of the mathematical optimization problems is the lack of universal solving method. For this reason the IOS includes a library with various methods. Often, in the process of solving a particular problem, it is necessary to replace one method by the another or to change the values of method's parameters etc. Our aim is to facilitate the nonexperienced user in his work with the software — the dialogue is led in terms of his language and in a correspondence with his experience.

2 Methodological and theoretical backgrounds

IOS is based on the following principles:

- Orientation to user's professional background and availability of the program tools which permit description and a thorough editing of the problems in a way natural to the user,
- Process orientation, i.e. a possibility for thorough intracement and control of the process of problem solving, which is the advantage of the interactive optimization systems,
- The library of IOS is open for including new numerical algorithms as well as for excluding certain ones due to the system adaptation to a practical set–up.

3 Description of the implementation

IOS is implemented in Pascal language and includes:

- A system for unconstrained function minimization and function minimization with lower and upper bound for variables,

- A system for solving linear programming problems,
- A symbol transformation system providing a description of the problem by means of formulae and algebraic computation of partial derivatives,
- A table editor of fixed type data,
- A screen editor for control of computation, choice of method and analyzing the progress of optimization process.

4 Hardware requirements

The program runs on an IBM–PC, XT, AT or compatibles and require 640K RAM and at least one floppy disk. A color monitor is recommended.

5 Availability of the program

Please contact the Institute of Mathematics, Bulgarian Academy of Sciences to obtain further information.

VIG — A Visual Interactive Approach to Goal Programming

Pekka Korhonen
Helsinki School of Economics
Finland

1 Purpose of the program

Most management problems typically have multiple criteria and are semistructured. Such problems are common in strategic planning, financial planning, personnel allocation, resource allocation, advertising, and pricing.

VIG is a dynamic, visual, and interactive system which will support the user in structuring and solving multiple criteria decision making and planning problems. It helps to analyse the consequences of decisions either as flexible goals (objectives) or rigid goals (constraints). The system enables the user to obtain a holistic perception of semistructuted problem and to examine the trade–offs between conflicting goals by visual interaction.

2 Methodological and theoretical backgrounds

Visual interaction is implemented using *Pareto Race*. In *Pareto Race* the user can freely search efficient solutions of a multiple objective linear programming problem, in a dynamic way. Visual as well as detailed numerical information is presented simultaneously.

The foundation of VIG originate in the visual reference direction approach. By projecting a reference direction onto the efficient surface, a subset of efficient solutions are generated and presented for evaluation.

3 Description of the implementation

The current version of the system is capable of solving problems with a maximum of 96 columns and 100 rows, from which at most 10 may be defined as objectives and constraints during a session.

The interface is based on the main menu, spreadsheets and visual interaction, making it very user friendly. Computer graphics and colors play a central role in the design of the interface. These features make it easy to construct, modify and solve the model, enabling the user to concentrate on his decision problem.

4 Hardware requirements

VIG runs on an IBM–PC, XT, AT or compatible computers and requires 256K RAM. A color graphic monitor is recommended.

5 Availability of the program

The system is distributed by NumPlan, P.O. Box 00421, Helsinki, Finland. Please contact the company to obtain more information.

IAC–DIDAS–N — A Version of Nonlinear DIDAS for an IBM–PC Computer

Tomasz Kreglewski, Jerzy Paczynski, Andrzej P. Wierzbicki
Institute of Automatic Control, Warsaw University of Technology
Warsaw, Poland

1 Purpose of the program

The IAC–DIDAS–N is an interactive decision analysis and support system for multicriteria analysis of nonlinear models. It is equipped with a nonlinear model generator and editor that supports, in an easy standard of a spreadsheet, the definition, edition and symbolic differentiation of nonlinear formulae and of other parts of nonlinear models for the multiobjective decision analysis.

2 Methodological and theoretical backgrounds

The multicriteria optimization is based on the reference point approach. The optimization runs helping the interactive, multiobjective decision analysis are performed with the help of the solver, that is, a version of nonlinear programming algorithm especially adapted for multiobjective problems. This algorithm is based on the shifted penalty functions and the projected conjugate direction techniques.

3 Description of the implementation

The current version can handle problems with up to 26 independent variables, 26 parameters and 26 outcome functions. Each outcome can be defined as a constraint (with upper and lower bounds) and/or as an objective that may be maximized, minimized or stabilized. Bounds on efficient outcomes (utopia and nadir points) can be easily calculated. Formulae for derivatives are currently kept in an internal form; to be viewed or modified, these formulae should be processed with the nonlinear model generator integrated with the DIDAS–N package.

4 Hardware requirements

IAC–DIDAS–N runs on IBM–PC, XT, AT and compatibles (with Hercules Graphic Card, Color Graphic Adapter or Enhanced Graphic Adapter and, preferably, with a numeric coprocessor and a hard disk) and requires 512K of RAM. There are two versions of the program available — one of them taking advantage of the numeric coprocessor, the second utilizing the emulator library. Model files for both versions are compatible, however the inevitable loss of accuracy occur while transferring data from the coprocessor version of the program to the emulating version.

5 Availability of the program

Please contact IIASA or Institute of Automatic Control, Warsaw University of Technology, ul. Nowowiejska 15/19, 00–665 Warsaw, Poland.

DISCRET — Package for Multicriteria Problems with Discrete Alternatives

Janusz Majchrzak
Systems Research Institute
Polish Academy of Science
Warsaw, Poland

1 Purpose of the program

Decision problems in which from the explicitly listed set of feasible alternatives one alternative has to be selected with respect to several criteria are common in many areas of management, planning and engineering etc. DISCRET is an interactive package which will support the decision maker in learning more about the problem and his own preferences during the decision making process based on the holistic perception of the problem.

2 Methodological and theoretical backgrounds

DISCRET is based on a fast technique for selecting either the set of nondominated (Pareto optimal) alternatives from the explicitly listed set of feasible alternatives or a representation of the nondominated alternatives set. Other options allow to keep or reject duplicate alternatives and to select weakly nondominated alternatives. The reference point approach is implemented to support the decision maker in the final stage of the decision making process.

3 Description of the implementation

The current version of the package is capable of solving problems with maximum 20 criteria and with the number of alternatives multiplied by actual criteria number not greater than 16000. However, larger problems can be solved with partition option implemented. Interaction is based on menus, spreadsheets and is supported by graphical presentation of result (two criteria projections and *slices*).

4 Hardware requirements

DISCRET runs on IBM–PC, XT, AT and compatibles and requires 640K RAM and at least one floppy drive. A color monitor is recommended.

5 Availability of the program

Please contact IIASA or the author — Systems Research Institute, Polish Academy of Sciences, ul. Newelska 6, 01–447 Warsaw, Poland.

DINAS — Dynamic Interactive Network Analysis System

Wlodzimierz Ogryczak, Krzysztof Studzinski, Krystian Zorychta
Institute of Informatics, Warsaw University
Warsaw, Poland

1 Purpose of the program

The program enables the solution of various multiobjective transshipment problems with facility locations. For a given number of fixed facilities and customers and for a number of potential facilities to be optionally located DINAS provides the user with a distribution pattern of a homogeneous product under a multicriteria optimality requirement. As a result the user gets optimal locations of the potential facilities and a system of optimal flows of the product between nodes of the transportation network.

2 Methodological and theoretical backgrounds

DINAS is based on an extension of the reference point optimization. The basic concept of that approach is as follows:

- the user forms his requirements in terms of aspiration and reservation levels, i.e. he specifies acceptable and required values for given objectives,
- the user works wit the computer in an interactive way so that he can change his aspiration and reservation levels during the session.

DINAS searches for the satisfying solution while using an achievement scalarizing function as a criterion in a single objective optimization.

3 Description of the implementation

The program consists of three parts:

- the network screen editor for data input and results examination,
- the TRANSLOC solver for single objective minimization,
- the main interactive procedure for handling multiple objectives.

The current version of the program is capable of solving problems with a few objective functions, about one hundred of fixed nodes, a few hundreds of arcs and several potential nodes organized in a few selections.

4 Hardware requirements

DINAS runs on an IBM–PC, XT, AT and compatibles equipped with Hercules or color graphic card and requires 640K RAM and a hard disk and at least one floppy drive.

5 Availability of the program

The program is distributed by IIASA, Laxenburg, Austria. For further informations please contact SDS Program at IIASA or Institute of Informatics, Warsaw University, PKiN 850, 00–901 Warsaw, Poland.

Nonlinear Model Generator

Jerzy Paczynski, Tomasz Kreglewski
Institute of Automatic Control, Warsaw University of Technology
Warsaw, Poland

1 Purpose of the program

The Nonlinear Model Generator is an auxiliary tool for the nonlinear multiobjective decision support system IAC–DIDAS–N, used for advanced model analysis and in case of numerical problems during optimization phase. It can be also used independently in order to gain insight into the analytical structure of a nonlinear model, forms of formulae for derivatives and into numerical range of outcomes and their derivatives.

2 Methodological and theoretical backgrounds

The program performs symbolic calculation to present formulae for all partial derivatives used in the calculation of gradients of all outcome variables in a nonlinear model. Formulae can be viewed and even modified (by performing *what if* analysis). Values of outcomes and derivatives are also calculated in a usual spreadsheet manner.

3 Description of the implementation

The current version can handle problems with up to 26 independent variables, 26 parameters and 26 outcome functions. Model files are compatible with the IAC–DIDAS-N program.

4 Hardware requirements

The program runs on IBM–PC, XT, AT and compatibles (with Hercules Graphic Card, Color Graphic Adapter or Enhanced Graphic Adapter and, preferably, with a numeric coprocessor and a hard disk) and requires 512K of RAM. There are two versions of the program available — one of them taking advantage of the numeric coprocessor, the second utilizing the emulator library. Model files for both versions are compatible, however the inevitable loss of accuracy occur while transferring data from the coprocessor version of the program to the emulating version.

5 Availability of the program

Please contact IIASA or Institute of Automatic Control, Warsaw University of Technology, ul. Nowowiejska 15/19, 00–665 Warsaw, Poland.

MDS — An Interactive System for Multicriteria Evaluation of Alternatives

Peter Parizek, Tomas Vasko
Institute for Applied Cybernetics
Bratislava, Czechoslovakia

1 Purpose of the program

Multicriteria decision support in ranking a finite set of alternatives is a very common problem in management practice.

MDS is an interactive microcomputer — oriented software package for multicriteria analysis and evaluation of alternatives. The purpose of the system is to support decisions in a large set of problems in the area of multicriteria evaluation of alternatives for both individual and group decision making. The system makes no restrictions on the character and type of attributes and alternatives.

2 Methodological and theoretical backgrounds

The MDS system supports decisions in selection and ranking of alternatives of a certain problem according to attributes which can be mutually opposite, of different measuring units or incomparable. This system supports decisions of one decision maker or group of decision makers. The number of users and problems solved is unlimited. On the other hand, exact relations and access rules between the problems and the users must be exactly defined.

3 Description of the implementation

The number of attributes and alternatives for a given problem is finite but unlimited with respect to memory constraints of the PC. The attributes can be quantitative, qualitative or considered as aspiration levels. Quantitative attributes are characterized by name, measuring unit, upper and lower bounds. Qualitative attributes are described by name and a linguistic or numeric scale. Methods for evaluation of attribute weights and methods for final ranking of alternatives are implemented as separate software modules. Other modules contain statistical and graphic tools. The number of methods in the system can grow without limitation. The dBASE III package is used as a data base management system for MDS.

4 Hardware requirements

MDS runs on an IBM–PC, XT, AT or compatibles and requires 512K of RAM and one floppy drive. A color monitor and printer is recommended.

5 Availability of the program

A preliminary version of the program is available from the authors. Please contact the Institute for Applied Cybernetics, Hanulova 5A, 844–16 Bratislava, Czechoslovakia.

IAC–DIDAS–L — Dynamic Interactive Decision Analysis and Support System

T. Rogowski, J. Sobczyk, A. P. Wierzbicki
Institute of Automatic Control, Warsaw University of Technology
Warsaw, Poland

1 Purpose of the program

There are many examples of decision situations that can be modelled and analysed by using a substantive model of multiobjective linear programming type. DIDAS–L is a Dynamic Interactive Decision and Support system for multicriteria analysis of linear and dynamic linear models running on professional microcomputers. This system can help in the analysis of decision situations when a mathematical model of the problem can be formulated in the form of a multiobjective linear programming problem, possibly of dynamic structure. DIDAS–L system can be used, for example, in analyzing various environmental and technical problems, strategic planning, planning energy policies, planning agricultural policies and other areas.

2 Methodological and theoretical backgrounds

DIDAS–L is based on the methodology of reference point optimization and the theory of the achievement function. The interactive analysis of the problem stress the aspects of learning by the user by generating various possible efficient decisions and outcomes. The interaction is organized through system's response to user–specified aspiration levels or reference points for objective outcomes.

3 Description of the implementation

The demonstrative version of DIDAS–L system programmed in Pascal is capable of editing and solving multiobjective linear programming models with 50 columns and 50 rows, from which some may be defined as objective functions. System supports an interactive definition and edition of the substantive model by the user, in an user–friendly format of a spreadsheet. DIDAS–L is designed to work with substantive models of linear–programming type, to perform and graphically represent the results of interactive multiobjective analysis of such models.

4 Hardware requirements

IAC–DIDAS–L runs on IBM–PC, XT, AT and compatibles (with Hercules Graphic Card, Color Graphic Adapter or Enhanced Graphic Adapter and, preferably, with a numeric coprocessor and a hard disk) and requires 512K of RAM.

5 Availability of the program

Please contact IIASA or Institute of Automatic Control, Warsaw University of Technology, ul. Nowowiejska 15/19, 00–665 Warsaw, Poland.

STRUM–COMPA — Problem Structuring Tools

Dimitri P. Solomatin
Institute for System Studies (VNIISI), USSR Academy of Sciences
Moscow, USSR

1 Purpose of the program

Problem structuring interactive tools STRUM and COMPA may help at the early stages of complex problem situations study and/or pre–decision stage, in particular, in identifying the links between the problem's parts or elements. STRUM aids in structurization of problem situation (identification of its elements and their inter–relationships, i.e. construction of directed graph). COMPA helps in identification of comparative significance of the elements using the criteria chosen by experts. These tools were used also for constructing objectives structures and cross–impact graphs for technology assessment.

2 Methodological and theoretical backgrounds

To construct the graph of problem situation the method of pairwise comparisons is used. The expert group must form the list of problem's elements and enter them into computer. Then STRUM suggests a set of questions about the inter–relations (in the meaning of verbal binary relation also entered in the computer). If the relation is supposed to be transitive (in a lot of applications it is so, e.g. *cause–effect*, *precedence in time*, etc.), then the specially designed *algorithm of d–transitive closure* is used to form the graph. The algorithm usage decreases the total number of questions by 50 to 70% compared with the number of all possible pairwise comparisons. The STRUM version for processing multiple–context relations is under development.

In COMPA system the method of pairwise comparisons is used to identify the comparative significance of the elements. The user may choose various linguistic scales — the Saaty's linear 9 point, non–linear 7 point as well as other scales and methods for specifying weights of elements and criteria. The vector of weights is obtained through calculating the eigenvector of the matrix of pairwise comparisons. Multi criteria problems can be analysed through calculating absolute weights, displaying projections of various types of Pareto set etc.

3 Description of the implementation

STRUM allows to work with up to 80 elements, to print the graph or to display it on the virtual screen in RAM and to inspect it through the window on physical PC screen.

COMPA works with up to 40 elements. The computer — user interface is menu based and self explanatory.

4 Hardware requirements

IBM–PC or compatible with 512K RAM, color display, color graphic adapter, MS–DOS 2.x or 3.x.

5 Availability of the program

Please contact the developer, VNIISI, Prospekt 60–Let Oktyabria 9, 117 312 Moscow, USSR.

Software System GENERATOR

Ivan Stanchev, Damian Ivanov
Economic University "Karl Marx"
Bulgaria, Sofia

1 Purpose of the program

Within the context of decision making, certain problems emerge and can be solved only with the support of the information offered by experts who work in the field in which they have to make decisions, as there are no formalized methods which would give an answer to these problems. The program helps to create the individual list of objects with their characteristics and gives the group priority order, the aposteriori competence of the experts, identification of coalitions.

2 Methodological and theoretical backgrounds

The program is based on classical models and methods (rank correlation and concordation).

3 Description of the implementation

The program is capable to work with 99 experts in the same time and 99 objects per expert.

The dialogue is organized in a series of windows and menues with on line help. There are some other features like password protection of the session and the experience, individual color specification, backup possibilities etc.

4 Hardware requirements

GENERATOR runs on an IBM–PC, XT, AT or compatibles, local area network 3COM and requires 512K of RAM and at least one floppy disk.

5 Availability of the program

The program is property of IIASA. Please contact the Laboratory of Systems Analysis and Management, Economic University "Karl Marx", Bu. Georgy Dimitrov 53, Sofia, Bulgaria.

Scientific Management System Based on Object–Oriented Approach

Tamara Uskova
Computing Center of the USSR Academy of Sciences
Moscow, USSR

1 Purpose of the program

The system supports the management of a scientific organization. It is based on a software package SPECTRUM which serves as a toolkit for building applications. It contains the object–oriented data base, dialogue organizer, graphic processor, decision support package and a set of utilities.

2 Methodological and theoretical backgrounds

The system is based on object–oriented approach to information model representation. The object–oriented data base deals with informational objects which may be arranged in complex hierarchical model. Each object is a named data structure with appropriate external view. The object consists of typed data elements; each element being a string of characters, number, text fragment, reference to any other object or arbitrary DOS command. The data are entered and visualized through the customized tables and forms. Numerical data can be viewed as diagrams and graphs. Data exchange with dBASE–III, Lotus 1-2-3 and Framework is possible.

3 Description of the implementation

The system provides uniform access to all kinds of objects. Its behaviour is described by the formally defined dialogue schemata which control the user's access to different model components. Easy selection of the relevant data subsets and its external presentation in the most appropriate forms including text, graphics and tables, support the decision making process. High–level programming language provides object manipulation. The system can be used for creating an environment which can efficiently support the process of group decision making.

4 Hardware requirements

The system runs on an IBM–PC, XT, AT and compatibles with minimum 512K of RAM, color graphic monitor with standard or Enhanced Color Adapter. National alphabet is implemented by PROM character generator or special driver for EGA card. Dot matrix printer (Epson FX–80) or equivalent is recommended. The system runs under MS–DOS 3.3.

5 Availability of the program

The system is distributed by the Computer Center of the USSR Academy of Sciences with the trademark of AcademySoft.

VCU–TASA — Tolerance Approach to Sensitivity Analysis

John M. Weiss, Cu D. Ha and Subhash C. Narula
Virginia Commonwealth University
Richmond, USA

1 Purpose of the program

Consider the linear programming problem:

1. Maximize the objective function
$$Z = cx$$

2. subject to constraints
$$Ax \leq b, \quad x \leq 0$$

The purpose of the program is to determine the maximum amount λ by which the coefficients of the right–hand side b can be independently and simultaneously varied, without changing the optimal basis of the problem. Furthermore, this program allows the user maximum flexibility to interactively change the limits on one or more of the coefficients and observe the effects on λ.

2 Methodological and theoretical backgrounds

Linear programming is among the most important scientific advances of the last few decades. This technique has been successfully applied to a wide variety of problems involving the allocation of limited resources among competing alternatives. *Sensitivity analysis* allows the user to identify the parameters which are more critical in determining the optimal solution, and which ones may vary within a certain range without affecting the validity of analysis. However, in traditional sensitivity analysis, the model parameters are treated one at a time, without allowing interactions among parameters to influence the analysis.

The *tolerance approach to sensitivity analysis* (Wendell, 1985; Ha et al., 1987) allows the user to determine the bounds within which the individual parameters may vary without affecting the optimal basis of the problem, when all parameters are allowed to vary simultaneously. This method greatly enhances the power and flexibility of traditional analysis.

3 Description of the implementation

VCU–TASA is an implementation of the tolerance approach algorithm proposed by Ha and Narula, written in the C programming language. This program includes a basic implementation of the simplex algorithm, traditional sensitivity analysis, and tolerance approach to sensitivity analysis. The current version supports up to 80 constraints and 80 variables. Simplex input may come from a file, or may be entered directly by the user. Sensitivity analysis is performed by repeated modification of lower and upper bounds on the coefficients, thus allowing the user maximal interaction with the analysis process.

4 Hardware requirements

VCU–TASA runs on the IBM–PC, XT, AT or compatibles, and requires at least 256K RAM and one floppy drive. The display may be either monochrome or color.

5 Availability of the program

This program is distributed free of charge to any educational institution. Please include a stamped, self–addressed mailer and a formatted floppy diskette (5.25 inch, 360K) with your order.

Dr. John M. Weiss
Division of Computer Science
Department of Mathematical Sciences
Virginia Commonwealth University
1015 West Main Street
Richmond, VA 23284–2014 USA

References

Ha, C. D., Narula, S. C. and Weiss, J. M. (1987). Interactive postoptimal analysis for linear programming problems, lecture presented at the ORSA/TIMS Conference, St. Louis, MO, October 25–28, 1987.

Wendell, R. E. (1985). The tolerance approach to sensitivity analysis in linear programming. *Management Science*, Vol. 31, pp. 564–578, 1985.

THE INTERNATIONAL INSTITUTE FOR APPLIED SYSTEMS ANALYSIS

is a nongovernmental research institution, bringing together scientists from around the world to work on problems of common concern. Situated in Laxenburg, Austria, IIASA was founded in October 1972 by the academies of science and equivalent organizations of twelve countries. Its founders gave IIASA a unique position outside national, disciplinary, and institutional boundaries so that it might take the broadest possible view in pursuing its objectives:

To promote international cooperation in solving problems from social, economic, technological, and environmental change

To create a network of institutions in the national member organization countries and elsewhere for joint scientific research

To develop and formalize systems analysis and the sciences contributing to it, and promote the use of analytical techniques needed to evaluate and address complex problems

To inform policy advisors and decision makers about the potential application of the Institute's work to such problems

The Institute now has national member organizations in the following countries:

Austria
The Austrian Academy of Sciences

Bulgaria
The National Committee for Applied Systems Analysis and Management

Canada
The Canadian Committee for IIASA

Czechoslovakia
The Committee for IIASA of the Czechoslovak Socialist Republic

Finland
The Finnish Committee for IIASA

France
The French Association for the Development of Systems Analysis

German Democratic Republic
The Academy of Sciences of the German Democratic Republic

Federal Republic of Germany
Association for the Advancement of IIASA

Hungary
The Hungarian Committee for Applied Systems Analysis

Italy
The National Research Council

Japan
The Japan Committee for IIASA

Netherlands
The Foundation IIASA–Netherlands

Poland
The Polish Academy of Sciences

Sweden
The Swedish Council for Planning and Coordination of Research

Union of Soviet Socialist Republics
The Academy of Sciences of the Union of Soviet Socialist Republics

United States of America
The American Academy of Arts and Sciences

Vol. 236: G. Gandolfo, P.C. Padoan, A Disequilibrium Model of Real and Financial Accumulation in an Open Economy. VI, 172 pages. 1984.

Vol. 237: Misspecification Analysis. Proceedings, 1983. Edited by T.K. Dijkstra. V, 129 pages. 1984.

Vol. 238: W. Domschke, A. Drexl, Location and Layout Planning. IV, 134 pages. 1985.

Vol. 239: Microeconomic Models of Housing Markets. Edited by K. Stahl. VII, 197 pages. 1985.

Vol. 240: Contributions to Operations Research. Proceedings, 1984. Edited by K. Neumann and D. Pallaschke. V, 190 pages. 1985.

Vol. 241: U. Wittmann, Das Konzept rationaler Preiserwartungen. XI, 310 Seiten. 1985.

Vol. 242: Decision Making with Multiple Objectives. Proceedings, 1984. Edited by Y.Y. Haimes and V. Chankong. XI, 571 pages. 1985.

Vol. 243: Integer Programming and Related Areas. A Classified Bibliography 1981–1984. Edited by R. von Randow. XX, 386 pages. 1985.

Vol. 244: Advances in Equilibrium Theory. Proceedings, 1984. Edited by C.D. Aliprantis, O. Burkinshaw and N.J. Rothman. II, 235 pages. 1985.

Vol. 245: J.E.M. Wilhelm, Arbitrage Theory. VII, 114 pages. 1985.

Vol. 246: P.W. Otter, Dynamic Feature Space Modelling, Filtering and Self-Tuning Control of Stochastic Systems. XIV, 177 pages. 1985.

Vol. 247: Optimization and Discrete Choice in Urban Systems. Proceedings, 1983. Edited by B.G. Hutchinson, P. Nijkamp and M. Batty. VI, 371 pages. 1985.

Vol. 248: Plural Rationality and Interactive Decision Processes. Proceedings, 1984. Edited by M. Grauer, M. Thompson and A.P. Wierzbicki. VI, 354 pages. 1985.

Vol. 249: Spatial Price Equilibrium: Advances in Theory, Computation and Application. Proceedings, 1984. Edited by P. T. Harker. VII, 277 pages. 1985.

Vol. 250: M. Roubens, Ph. Vincke, Preference Modelling. VIII, 94 pages. 1985.

Vol. 251: Input-Output Modeling. Proceedings, 1984. Edited by A. Smyshlyaev. VI, 261 pages. 1985.

Vol. 252: A. Birolini, On the Use of Stochastic Processes in Modeling Reliability Problems. VI, 105 pages. 1985.

Vol. 253: C. Withagen, Economic Theory and International Trade in Natural Exhaustible Resources. VI, 172 pages. 1985.

Vol. 254: S. Müller, Arbitrage Pricing of Contingent Claims. VIII, 151 pages. 1985.

Vol. 255: Nondifferentiable Optimization: Motivations and Applications. Proceedings, 1984. Edited by V.F. Demyanov and D. Pallaschke. VI, 350 pages. 1985.

Vol. 256: Convexity and Duality in Optimization. Proceedings, 1984. Edited by J. Ponstein. V, 142 pages. 1985.

Vol. 257: Dynamics of Macrosystems. Proceedings, 1984. Edited by J.-P. Aubin, D. Saari and K. Sigmund. VI, 280 pages. 1985.

Vol. 258: H. Funke, Eine allgemeine Theorie der Polypol- und Oligopolpreisbildung. III, 237 pages. 1985.

Vol. 259: Infinite Programming. Proceedings, 1984. Edited by E.J. Anderson and A.B. Philpott. XIV, 244 pages. 1985.

Vol. 260: H.-J. Kruse, Degeneracy Graphs and the Neighbourhood Problem. VIII, 128 pages. 1986.

Vol. 261: Th.R. Gulledge, Jr., N.K. Womer, The Economics of Made-to-Order Production. VI, 134 pages. 1986.

Vol. 262: H.U. Buhl, A Neo-Classical Theory of Distribution and Wealth. V, 146 pages. 1986.

Vol. 263: M. Schäfer, Resource Extraction and Market Structure. XI, 154 pages. 1986.

Vol. 264: Models of Economic Dynamics. Proceedings, 1983. Edited by H.F. Sonnenschein. VII, 212 pages. 1986.

Vol. 265: Dynamic Games and Applications in Economics. Edited by T. Başar. IX, 288 pages. 1986.

Vol. 266: Multi-Stage Production Planning and Inventory Control. Edited by S. Axsäter, Ch. Schneeweiss and E. Silver. V, 264 pages. 1986.

Vol. 267: R. Bemelmans, The Capacity Aspect of Inventories. IX, 165 pages. 1986.

Vol. 268: V. Firchau, Information Evaluation in Capital Markets. VII, 103 pages. 1986.

Vol. 269: A. Borglin, H. Keiding, Optimality in Infinite Horizon Economies. VI, 180 pages. 1986.

Vol. 270: Technological Change, Employment and Spatial Dynamics. Proceedings 1985. Edited by P. Nijkamp. VII, 466 pages. 1986.

Vol. 271: C. Hildreth, The Cowles Commission in Chicago, 1939–1955. V, 176 pages. 1986.

Vol. 272: G. Clemenz, Credit Markets with Asymmetric Information. VIII, 212 pages. 1986.

Vol. 273: Large-Scale Modelling and Interactive Decision Analysis. Proceedings, 1985. Edited by G. Fandel, M. Grauer, A. Kurzhanski and A.P. Wierzbicki. VII, 363 pages. 1986.

Vol. 274: W.K. Klein Haneveld, Duality in Stochastic Linear and Dynamic Programming. VII, 295 pages. 1986.

Vol. 275: Competition, Instability, and Nonlinear Cycles. Proceedings, 1985. Edited by W. Semmler. XII, 340 pages. 1986.

Vol. 276: M.R. Baye, D.A. Black, Consumer Behavior, Cost of Living Measures, and the Income Tax. VII, 119 pages. 1986.

Vol. 277: Studies in Austrian Capital Theory, Investment and Time. Edited by M. Faber. VI, 317 pages. 1986.

Vol. 278: W.E. Diewert, The Measurement of the Economic Benefits of Infrastructure Services. V, 202 pages. 1986.

Vol. 279: H.-J. Büttler, G. Frei and B. Schips, Estimation of Disequilibrium Models. VI, 114 pages. 1986.

Vol. 280: H.T. Lau, Combinatorial Heuristic Algorithms with FORTRAN. VII, 126 pages. 1986.

Vol. 281: Ch.-L. Hwang, M.-J. Lin, Group Decision Making under Multiple Criteria. XI, 400 pages. 1987.

Vol. 282: K. Schittkowski, More Test Examples for Nonlinear Programming Codes. V, 261 pages. 1987.

Vol. 283: G. Gabisch, H.-W. Lorenz, Business Cycle Theory. VII, 229 pages. 1987.

Vol. 284: H. Lütkepohl, Forecasting Aggregated Vector ARMA Processes. X, 323 pages. 1987.

Vol. 285: Toward Interactive and Intelligent Decision Support Systems. Volume 1. Proceedings, 1986. Edited by Y. Sawaragi, K. Inoue and H. Nakayama. XII, 445 pages. 1987.

Vol. 286: Toward Interactive and Intelligent Decision Support Systems. Volume 2. Proceedings, 1986. Edited by Y. Sawaragi, K. Inoue and H. Nakayama. XII, 450 pages. 1987.

Vol. 287: Dynamical Systems. Proceedings, 1985. Edited by A.B. Kurzhanski and K. Sigmund. VI, 215 pages. 1987.

Vol. 288: G.D. Rudebusch, The Estimation of Macroeconomic Disequilibrium Models with Regime Classification Information. VII, 128 pages. 1987.

Vol. 289: B.R. Meijboom, Planning in Decentralized Firms. X, 168 pages. 1987.

Vol. 290: D.A. Carlson, A. Haurie, Infinite Horizon Optimal Control. XI, 254 pages. 1987.

Vol. 291: N. Takahashi, Design of Adaptive Organizations. VI, 140 pages. 1987.

Vol. 292: I. Tchijov, L. Tomaszewicz (Eds.), Input-Output Modeling. Proceedings, 1985. VI, 195 pages. 1987.

Vol. 293: D. Batten, J. Casti, B. Johansson (Eds.), Economic Evolution and Structural Adjustment. Proceedings, 1985. VI, 382 pages. 1987.

Vol. 294: J. Jahn, W. Krabs (Eds.), Recent Advances and Historical Development of Vector Optimization. VII, 405 pages. 1987.

Vol. 295: H. Meister, The Purification Problem for Constrained Games with Incomplete Information. X, 127 pages. 1987.

Vol. 296: A. Börsch-Supan, Econometric Analysis of Discrete Choice. VIII, 211 pages. 1987.

Vol. 297: V. Fedorov, H. Läuter (Eds.), Model-Oriented Data Analysis. Proceedings, 1987. VI, 239 pages. 1988.

Vol. 298: S.H. Chew, Q. Zheng, Integral Global Optimization. VII, 179 pages. 1988.

Vol. 299: K. Marti, Descent Directions and Efficient Solutions in Discretely Distributed Stochastic Programs. XIV, 178 pages. 1988.

Vol. 300: U. Derigs, Programming in Networks and Graphs. XI, 315 pages. 1988.

Vol. 301: J. Kacprzyk, M. Roubens (Eds.), Non-Conventional Preference Relations in Decision Making. VII, 155 pages. 1988.

Vol. 302: H.A. Eiselt, G. Pederzoli (Eds.), Advances in Optimization and Control. Proceedings, 1986. VIII, 372 pages. 1988.

Vol. 303: F.X. Diebold, Empirical Modeling of Exchange Rate Dynamics. VII, 143 pages. 1988.

Vol. 304: A. Kurzhanski, K. Neumann, D. Pallaschke (Eds.), Optimization, Parallel Processing and Applications. Proceedings, 1987. VI, 292 pages. 1988.

Vol. 305: G.-J.C.Th. van Schijndel, Dynamic Firm and Investor Behaviour under Progressive Personal Taxation. X, 215 pages. 1988.

Vol. 306: Ch. Klein, A Static Microeconomic Model of Pure Competition. VIII, 139 pages. 1988.

Vol. 307: T.K. Dijkstra (Ed.), On Model Uncertainty and its Statistical Implications. VII, 138 pages. 1988.

Vol. 308: J.R. Daduna, A. Wren (Eds.), Computer-Aidod Transit Scheduling. VIII, 339 pages. 1988.

Vol. 309: G. Ricci, K. Velupillai (Eds.), Growth Cycles and Multisectoral Economics: the Goodwin Tradition. III, 126 pages. 1988.

Vol. 310: J. Kacprzyk, M. Fedrizzi (Eds.), Combining Fuzzy Imprecision with Probabilistic Uncertainty in Decision Making. IX, 399 pages. 1988.

Vol. 311: R. Färe, Fundamentals of Production Theory. IX, 163 pages. 1988.

Vol. 312: J. Krishnakumar, Estimation of Simultaneous Equation Models with Error Components Structure. X, 357 pages. 1988.

Vol. 313: W. Jammernegg, Sequential Binary Investment Decisions. VI, 156 pages. 1988.

Vol. 314: R. Tietz, W. Albers, R. Selten (Eds.), Bounded Rational Behavior in Experimental Games and Markets. VI, 368 pages. 1988.

Vol. 315: I. Orishimo, G.J.D. Hewings, P. Nijkamp (Eds.), Information Technology: Social and Spatial Perspectives. Proceedings, 1986. VI, 268 pages. 1988.

Vol. 316: R.L. Basmann, D.J. Slottje, K. Hayes, J.D. Johnson, D.J. Molina, The Generalized Fechner-Thurstone Direct Utility Function and Some of its Uses. VIII, 159 pages. 1988.

Vol. 317: L. Bianco, A. La Bella (Eds.), Freight Transport Planning and Logistics. Proceedings, 1987. X, 568 pages. 1988.

Vol. 318: T. Doup, Simplicial Algorithms on the Simplotope. VIII, 262 pages. 1988.

Vol. 319: D.T. Luc, Theory of Vector Optimization. VIII, 173 pages. 1989.

Vol. 320: D. van der Wijst, Financial Structure in Small Business. VII, 181 pages. 1989.

Vol. 321: M. Di Matteo, R.M. Goodwin, A. Vercelli (Eds.), Technological and Social Factors in Long Term Fluctuations. Proceedings. IX, 442 pages. 1989.

Vol. 322: T. Kollintzas (Ed.), The Rational Expectations Equilibrium Inventory Model. XI, 269 pages. 1989.

Vol. 323: M.B.M. de Koster, Capacity Oriented Analysis and Design of Production Systems. XII, 245 pages. 1989.

Vol. 324: I.M. Bomze, B.M. Pötscher, Game Theoretical Foundations of Evolutionary Stability. VI, 145 pages. 1989.

Vol. 325: P. Ferri, E. Greenberg, The Labor Market and Business Cycle Theories. X, 183 pages. 1989.

Vol. 326: Ch. Sauer, Alternative Theories of Output, Unemployment, and Inflation in Germany: 1960–1985. XIII, 206 pages. 1989.

Vol. 327: M. Tawada, Production Structure and International Trade. V, 132 pages. 1989.

Vol. 328: W. Güth, B. Kalkofen, Unique Solutions for Strategic Games. VII, 200 pages. 1989.

Vol. 329: G. Tillmann, Equity, Incentives, and Taxation. VI, 132 pages. 1989.

Vol. 330: P.M. Kort, Optimal Dynamic Investment Policies of a Value Maximizing Firm. VII, 185 pages. 1989.

Vol. 331: A. Lewandowski, A.P. Wierzbicki (Eds.), Aspiration Based Decision Support Systems. X, 400 pages. 1989.

Vol. 332: T.R. Gulledge, Jr., L.A. Litteral (Eds.), Cost Analysis Applications of Economics and Operations Research. Proceedings. VII, 422 pages. 1989.

Vol. 333: N. Dellaert, Production to Order. VII, 158 pages. 1989.

Vol. 334: H.-W. Lorenz, Nonlinear Dynamical Economics and Chaotic Motion. XI, 248 pages. 1989.

Vol. 336: T. Puu, Nonlinear Economic Dynamics. VII, 119 pages. 1989.

Vol. 337: A. Lewandowski, I. Stanchev (Eds.), Methodology and Software for Interactive Decision Support. VIII, 309 pages. 1989.